The

CIVIC

CULTURE

REVISITED

The Little, Brown Series
in Comparative Politics

Under the Editorship of
GABRIEL A. ALMOND
JAMES S. COLEMAN
LUCIAN W. PYE

AN ANALYTIC STUDY

The
CIVIC
CULTURE
REVISITED

General Editors

Gabriel A. Almond

Sidney Verba

Contributors

Alan I. Abramowitz
Gabriel A. Almond
David P. Conradt
Wayne A. Cornelius
Ann L. Craig
Dennis Kavanagh
Arend Lijphart
Carole Pateman
Giacomo Sani
Sidney Verba
Jerzy J. Wiatr

Boston • Toronto

LITTLE, BROWN AND COMPANY

LIBRARY OF CONGRESS CATALOG CARD NO. 79-89764

FIRST PRINTING

Published simultaneously in Canada
by Little, Brown & Company (Canada) Limited

PRINTED IN THE UNITED STATES OF AMERICA

Preface

The Civic Culture: Political Attitudes and Democracy in Five Nations was published in 1963 by Princeton University Press, and in a somewhat abridged form was published as a paperback by Little, Brown and Company in 1965. The book has been widely quoted and its data reported here and abroad in books and journals in the fields of political science, sociology, anthropology, psychology, education, and other social sciences. The data set of the study has been available for secondary analysis by other scholars since 1968, and has been widely used for instructional and research purposes.

The surveys were administered in 1959 and 1960, and hence the data are now almost twenty years old. Much has transpired in the last two decades to suggest that the patterns of political culture in the five countries studied have undergone substantial change. Yet the data and the findings are still frequently cited in the contemporary social science literature. The book has also been sharply criticized on methodological and philosophical grounds. Thus there are important questions as to the validity of the inferences drawn from the findings and the soundness of the conceptions of democracy advanced in the study.

These several considerations led us to the decision to revisit the civic culture, to subject its philosophy, its methodology, its national and comparative findings to searching critiques by appropriate scholars. We thought that an effort of this kind might make a small contribution to our understanding of how the social sciences grow, that it might serve as a case study in the history of the social sciences. We were also concerned with updating its findings insofar as more recent research on British, American, German, Italian, and Mexican political culture was available.

Apparently subscribing to the view that a foundation has some responsibility to help sweep up the messes sometimes created by its grantees, the Carnegie Corporation of New York helped us cover the costs of this critique and updating of *The Civic Culture*. It goes without saying that the Carnegie Corporation bears no responsibility for the content of this critique. Arlee Ellis of the Department of Political Science at Stanford University facilitated our work in many ways, and Lois Renner followed the manuscript through to publication with intelligence and care.

Gabriel A. Almond
Stanford University

Sidney Verba
Harvard University

Contents

The

CIVIC

CULTURE

REVISITED

CHAPTER I

The Intellectual History of the Civic Culture Concept

Gabriel A. Almond
Stanford University

EARLY NOTIONS

Something like a notion of political culture has been around as long as men have spoken and written about politics. The prophets in their oracles, exhortations, and anathemas impute different qualities and propensities to the Amalekites, the Philistines, the Assyrians, and the Babylonians. The Greek and Roman historians, poets, and dramatists comment on the culture and character of the Ionians and Dorians, Spartans, Athenians, and Corinthians; the Rhaetians, Pannonians, Dacians, Parthians, and Caledonians.

The concepts and categories we use in the analysis of political culture—subculture, elite political culture, political socialization, and culture change—are also implied in ancient writings. Jacob on his deathbed foresaw differing fates and roles for his twelve sons, whose offspring were to constitute the tribes of Israel. Reuben would be as "unstable as water" and would not achieve eminence; Simeon was an angry man who would be divided in Israel; Issachar would bow "his shoulder" and would become a "slave at forced labor." As for Judah, "The scepter shall not depart from Judah,/nor the ruler's staff from between his feet, . . ./and to him shall be the obedience of the peoples." [1] And so on. The great families and gentes of Athens and Rome —the Eumolpidae and the Butadae, the Claudii and the Julii— each had its founder-deities, its sacred fires, its traditions, and its civic-political propensities.[2]

In the Israel of kingship at least four elite political cultures were in conflict: the relatively cosmopolitan royal court engaged in war and diplomacy, pitted against the prophets and their supporters affirming and perfecting the Sinaitic revelations and covenant; and the Jerusalem priesthood and temple officialdom pitted against the surviving local cult leaders of the "high places."

The notion of political culture change is one of the most powerful themes of classical literature. Each Greek city-state had its memory of an austere Solonic or Lycurgan past by which to measure the corrupt present. Both the older and the younger Cato were celebrators of the frugal, martial, and civic virtues of the early Roman republic. The Greeks had a cyclical theory of political change, and explained the rise and fall of political constitutions in social psychological terms.[3]

Nowhere do we find a stronger affirmation of the importance of political culture than in Plato's *Republic* when he argues "that governments vary as the dispositions of men vary, and that there must be as many of the one as there are of the other. For we cannot suppose that States are made of 'oak and rock' and not out of the human natures which are in them." He speaks of aristocratic, timocratic, oligarchic, and democratic polities and men, deriving the structural and performance characteristics of the first from the values, attitudes, and social-ization experiences of the second. In ways that surely would intrigue, if not embarrass, our contemporary psychohistorians he explains the qualities of the aristocratic, oligarchic, and democratic polity by the prevailing personal character types, which are in turn explained by typical family constellations with cultivated, glory-seeking, or money-grubbing fathers, dominant, compliant, or complaining mothers, and the like. And just as he stresses the importance of political culture, so does Plato in both *The Republic* and *The Laws* lay enormous weight on political socialization. ". . . [O]f all animals the boy is the most unmanageable, inasmuch as he has the fountain of reason in him not yet regulated; he is the most insidious, sharp witted, and insubordinate of animals. Wherefore he must be bound with many bridles. . . ." [4] Mothers and nurses, fathers, tutors, and political officials all have the obligation to guide and coerce the incorrigible animal into the path of civic virtue. The last book of Aristotle's *Politics,* a fragment to be sure, was devoted to education. Plutarch reports how Lycurgus engineered the Spartan character from the moment of birth, so to speak, counseling the women to bathe their newborn sons in wine, rather in water, in order to temper their bodies. The nurses used "no swaddling bands; the children grew up free and unconstrained in limb and form, and not dainty or fanciful about their food; not afraid in the dark, or of being left alone; and without peevishness, or ill-humour, or crying. . . ." [5]

Aristotle is a more modern and scientific political culturalist than Plato, since he not only imputes importance to political culture variables, but explicitly treats their relationship to social stratification variables on the one hand and to political structural and performance variables on the other. He argues that the best attainable form of government is the mixed form in a society in which the middle classes predominate. Mixed government is one organized on both oligarchic and democratic principles, hence giving some representation in governing to both the rich and the well born as well as to the poor and the base. Such a government is likely to arise and work best when wealth is widely distributed and when there is a large middle class which imparts its character to the state. He points out that the

middle amount of all the good things of fortune is the best amount to possess. For this degree of wealth is the readiest to obey reason. . . . And the middle class are the least inclined to shun office and to covet office, and both of these tendencies are injurious to states. And in addition to these points, those who have an excess of fortune's goods, strength, wealth, friends and the like, are not willing to be governed and do not know how to be (and they have acquired this quality even in their boyhood from their homelife, which was so luxurious that they have not got used to submitting to authority even in schools) while those who are excessively in need of these things are too humble. . . .

A society in which the middle class is small produces a state "consisting of slaves and masters, not of free men, and of one class envious and another contemptuous of their fellows. This condition of affairs is very far removed from friendliness, and from political partnership . . . ," which Aristotle believed to be the cultural basis of the best and most lasting form of government.[6]

Aristotle's conception of mixed government with a predominant middle class is related to what some of us in recent years have characterized as the civic culture in which there is a substantial consensus on the legitimacy of political institutions and the direction and content of public policy, a widespread tolerance of a plurality of interests and belief in their reconcilability, and a widely distributed sense of political competence and mutual trust in the citizenry.

While the political historians and philosophers who observed and wrote in the more than two millennia that elapsed between Aristotle and the sociologists of the nineteenth century dealt with political culture and socialization themes, none of them attained Aristotle's sophistication and rigor. Indeed, a few diagrams with causal arrows would turn Aristotle's theory of constitutional government, and its cultural components, into a model that would meet the contemporary standards of the *American Political Science Review,* though the great philosopher might have thought that the delivery of these ideas as lectures in the Lyceum in Athens was a sufficient honor.

Surely Machiavelli, in his contrast between the vigor and probity of the citizens and leaders of republican Rome, and the corruption, servility, and fickleness of the populace of the empire and of the contemporary Italians, was sharply aware of the importance of political-cultural variables, of moral values, of feelings of identity and commitment for political strength and weakness, for grandeur and decay. In this connection his actual discussion of Roman history in the *Discourses on Livy* begins with the importance of Roman religion and with the role of Numa Pompilius in inculcating it. He points out that "Whoever runs through the vast number of exploits performed by the people of Rome as a whole, or by many of the Romans individually, will see that its citizens were more afraid of breaking an oath than of breaking the law, since they held in higher esteem the power of God than the power of man." [7] But Machiavelli, while emphasizing political culture and socialization themes, tends to treat them anecdotally and illustratively rather than analytically as do Plato and Aristotle.

Two centuries later Montesquieu, reflecting similarly on Roman history as a way of deriving generalizations about politics, attributes the triumphs of republican Rome to the patriotic passion of the Roman citizenry fostered by their religion, by a constant pursuit of military conquest, and by a lively antagonism between the patriciate and the plebs. The corruption of the late republic and empire he attributes to the opening of Roman citizenship to the culturally heterogeneous Italian and non-Italian peoples, and the overwhelming of the simple virtues of the republic by the conquests, spoils, and commerce of far-flung territories and strange cultures and religions.[8] While it is clear in his reflections on the Roman experience, in his treatment of French culture and society in *The Persian Letters,* and particularly in his *Spirit of Laws,* that Montesquieu has recourse to sociological, anthropological, and social psychological variables in explaining national histories and political institutions and processes, his method is essentially aphoristic and illustrative. There is something of a decline in analytic rigor from the classical formulations.[9]

Rousseau's appreciation of the importance of political culture and socialization in the shaping of the public policy and legislation of nations reflects the influence of Montesquieu, and in turn is a prominent influence on Tocqueville. He cites Montesquieu as authority for the view that political systems and systems of legislation vary with the "local situation and the temper of the inhabitants. . . ." [10] The terms Rousseau uses to identify political culture are *morality, custom,* and *opinion.* He treats these as a kind of law more important than law properly speaking, a kind of law that is "engraved on the hearts of the citizens. This forms the real constitution of the State, takes on every day new powers, when other laws decay or die out, . . . keeps a people in the ways it was meant to go and insensibly replaces authority by the force of habit. I am speaking of morality, of custom, above all of public opinion. . . ." [11]

Tocqueville's analysis of American democracy and of the origins of the French Revolution are among the most sophisticated treatments of these themes. In *Democracy in America* he points out:

> . . . the manners of the people may be considered as one of the great general causes to which the maintenance of a democratic republic in the United States is attributable. I here use the word customs with the meaning which the ancients attached to the word *mores;* for I apply it not only to manners properly so called—that is, to what might be termed the *habits of the heart*— but to the various notions and opinions current among men and to the mass of those ideas which constitute their character of mind. I comprise under this term, therefore, the whole moral and intellectual condition of a people.[12]

Tocqueville had a similarly keen sense of political subculture. His analysis of the political attitudes of the French peasantry, bourgeoisie, and aristocracy on the eve of the revolution is a similar masterpiece of political culture analysis.[13] But with Tocqueville we are already into the beginnings of modern political sociology, which we discuss below.

ENLIGHTENMENT AND LIBERAL VIEWS

If the notion of political culture has in some sense always been with us,[14] how do we explain its sudden popularity in the 1960s and the proliferation of research dealing with it in recent decades? We suggest that the failure of enlightenment and liberal expectations as they related to political development and political culture set the explanatory problem to which political culture research was a response, and the development of social theory in the nineteenth and twentieth centuries and of social science methodology after World War II (particularly survey methodology) provided the opportunity for solving this problem. The intellectual challenge plus the theoretical developments and methodological inventions explain the emergence of this field of inquiry.

The enlightenment and liberal theories of political development of the seventeenth to nineteenth centuries were essentially political socialization/political culture theories. Science and the spread of secular knowledge were to lead, on the one hand, to the increase in the wealth of nations and the spread of welfare and, on the other, to the rationalization of government organization and law, and to democratization. Whether in its natural law/natural rights aspect à la Locke–Condorcet, or in its utilitarian aspect à la Helvetius–Bentham, enlightenment political theory was a psychological political theory deriving and justifying political institutions and legislation from man's nature as an inalienable "right-bearing" creature, as a hedonic pain avoider and pleasure seeker, and as a creator, transmitter, and consumer of knowledge.

By the second half of the nineteenth century these beliefs, stimulated by the industrial revolution, strengthened by the success of political and social reforms in Britain and by the American example, and fortified by the development of evolutionary ideas in biology, took on a sense of inevitability.[15] It was this liberal faith in the inevitability of incremental economic and political progress pushed forward by the progress of science and the spread of reason that underlay the discipline of comparative government and politics as it emerged in the late nineteenth century.

Woodrow Wilson wrote with sublime confidence in 1893:

> If Aristocracy seems about to disappear, Democracy seems about universally to prevail. Ever since the rise of popular education in the last century and its vast development since have assured a thinking weight to the masses of the people everywhere, the advance of democratic opinion and the spread of democratic institutions have been most marked and most significant. They have destroyed almost all pure forms of Monarchy and Aristocracy by introducing into them imperative forces of popular thought and the concrete institutions of popular representation; and they promise to reduce politics to a single pure form by excluding all other governing forces and institutions but those of a wide suffrage and a democratic representation—by reducing all forms of government to Democracy.[16]

But this confidence in inevitable incremental progress at this time of Wilson's writing had already been challenged by the Marxist version of enlightenment expectations, and was about to be challenged by the disillusioned elitists of the turn of the century. Marx was surely in the tradition of the enlightenment, save that he arranged the theoretical variables differently and viewed the historical process in dialectic rather than incremental terms. Instead of intellectual improvement pressing forward material and political–moral progress in a benign sequence, material improvement produces three political subcultures: an exploitative and ever concentrating capitalist class; an exploited, propagandized, and coerced working class; and an enlightened organization of revolutionaries. As the processes of material concentration press forward to their logical conclusions, the popular masses shake themselves free of their illusions, the revolutionaries acquire resonance in the working class, and the ruling class is swept aside, making possible the enlightenment culture and society of mass welfare and political rationality.

The "elitist" political theorists—in particular Gaetano Mosca, Vilfredo Pareto, and Roberto Michels—attacked both the liberal and the Marxist versions of inevitable progress in political culture and organization, picturing in their stead a future of permanent elitist exploitation and authoritarian rule based on a different set of psychological and sociological premises.[17]

This European pessimism had its echoes among British and American political theorists. Graham Wallas even before World War I challenged the complacence of the assumption of increasing rationality and spreading democratization, and in the 1920 edition of his book pointed out "[t]hat the assumption that men are automatically guided by 'enlightened self interest' has been discredited by the facts of war and the peace. . . ."[18] In a prophetic chapter entitled "Nonrational Inference in Politics," he affirmed the importance of feelings and habit in political thought and action: "men often act in politics under the immediate stimulus of affection and instinct, and that affection and instinct may be directed toward political entities which are very different from those facts in the world around us which we can discover by deliberate observation and analysis."[19]

Walter Lippmann challenged the easy assumption of growing mass rationality by developing a cognitive political psychology which stressed the discrepancies between the pictures of reality in the minds of men and the reality itself, concluding that popular government could succeed in becoming good government only when professional political scientists advised elites and interested publics on the nature of political reality and their political interests.[20]

Thus the writers on comparative government who followed Woodrow Wilson were less complacent than he, registering the theoretical challenges of both antiliberal writers, and of threatening and disillusioning events. James Bryce, writing on the future of democracy in the immediate aftermath of World War I—some thirty years after Wilson's textbook on comparative government had appeared—found it possible to express merely hope rather than confidence in the future of democracy.[21] William B. Munro writing in the 1920s still could echo Wilson's complacency.[22] Munro claimed: "It is hardly an exaggeration to say, therefore, that the democratization of the entire civilized world, largely through the influence of Anglo-Norman leadership, is the most conspicuous fact in the whole realm of political science." But the principal comparative-government text writers of the 1930s—Herman Finer and Carl J. Friedrich—were deeply troubled as liberal expectations were challenged first by the success of the Bolshevik Revolution in Russia and the triumph of Fascism in Italy, and more fundamentally by the Nazi seizure of power in Germany. Finer concluded his massive work on a note of exhortation to the forces of good—education—to overcome antidemocratic evil;[23] Friedrich concludes the preface of his first edition in a defiant reaffirmation of enlightenment faith: "Within the lifetime of this generation, the present barbarities will be abandoned, and finer, more noble conceptions of life will reassert themselves." [24]

Other students of politics in these decades, as we have suggested, began to go beyond these reaffirmations of enlightenment faith and hope as they confronted overwhelming evidence that the historical forces at work were more complex and ambivalent. If the historical trend was in the direction of democracy, then how explain the Bolshevik Revolution and its outcome, and the triumph and popularity of explicitly antienlightenment ideologies in such countries as Germany and Italy? And these big doubts began to trigger many smaller doubts. Enlightenment expectations didn't even hold fully in such a country as France, notorious for the persistence of clerico-traditionalism, the *incivisme* of its people, and the instability of its cabinets, or as England with its aristocratic institutions and Tory working class, or as the United States, where participation in enlightenment values was denied to people of color.

It was not that the earlier generations of students of comparative politics like Wilson, Bryce, Finer, and Friedrich were unaware of differences in the political propensities of peoples and groups. On the contrary, their stock in trade was the explication of differences in the concentration and dispersion of power among nations, differences in electoral arrangements, party systems, legislative organization and procedure, bureaucratic arrangements, and judicial structure and process. But the differences they discovered could be ordered according to their approximation to or deviation from "emerging-enlightened" political forms—universal suffrage, representative government, political decision through rational deliberative processes, rational and efficient implementation of law, and the protection of rights against arbitrary action. These deviations could be explained by historical experience and by the "character" of nations and groups, which had been shaped primarily by their environments and their histories. Wilson speaks of "nation-marks," Munro refers to the racial genius of the British, Andre Siegfried and Salvador de Madariaga discuss in some detail the national characters of such peoples as the English, the French, the Americans, and the Spanish.[25] But the powerful transformative engine of education and the spread of knowledge was presumed to be moving mankind in the direction of these enlightened norms. The deviations were residuals or pathologies, and while the expected or hoped-for convergence toward enlightenment political norms would never be complete, national character, or the social character of groups, was a distinctly minor explanatory theme.

THE INFLUENCE OF EUROPEAN SOCIOLOGY

As the discipline of sociology developed in the course of the nineteenth century, the importance of subjective variables in the explanation of social and political phenomena was generally recognized. Henri de Saint-Simon attributed more importance to ideological-religious attitudes than economic ones in the maintenance of social stability and the attainment of social progress.[26] Auguste Comte viewed society essentially as a system of common moral ideas.[27] Marx viewed ideology as a significant weapon in the hands of the bourgeoisie in retarding revolutionary processes, and political consciousness in the working class as a necessary condition of proletarian revolution.[28] Emile Durkheim based his conception of social solidarity on the "conscience collective," or the system of values, beliefs, and sentiments shared by the members of societies.[29] And Pareto's concepts of logical and nonlogical action, of "residues" and "derivations," were parts of a substantially psychological theory of sociopolitical structure and social change.[30]

But of all the European sociologists the most influential in the shaping of research on political culture was Max Weber. For Weber sociology had to be an "empathic" science, a *Verstehende Soziologie* in which attitudes, feelings, and values were important explanatory variables. Perhaps Weber was the first truly modern social scientist. His concepts were empirically grounded; he was methodologically quite inventive and sophisticated. He himself had used questionnaires, developed a form of content analysis, and employed systematic field observation. Weber's work on the sociology of religion was a response to Marxian sociological theory, which stressed economic structure— the relations of production—as the basic formative influence on social institutions and ideas. Weber's comparative study of the economic ethos of the great world religions was intended to demonstrate that values and ideas can be the catalytic agents in changes in economic structure and in political institutions.[31]

Weber's types of political authority—traditional, rational-legal, and charismatic—are subjective categories. They were the three ideal-typical reasons why leaders are obeyed by followers, the three ideal-typical bases of political legitimacy. Structural differences among political systems are treated as subordinate categories to these essentially subjective categories. Traditional orders are those in which the rulers are obeyed because they have been selected according to immemorial rules, and act in accordance with such rules. The main form of rational-legal order that Weber treats is *bureaucracy,* in which officialdom is obeyed because it is selected and acts according to written, rational, and enforceable rules. Charismatic authority is the extraordinary and transitional type of political order characterized by a belief in the superhuman or extra-human qualities of a leader.[32]

Weber's typology of political parties again is based on the subjective reasons for membership and support. Class parties are those which recruit supporters on the basis of their appeal to class interest. Patronage parties are those which appeal to supporters on the basis of the promise of power, office, and other material advantages, while Weltanschauung (World-View) parties are based on an appeal to the ideals of political supporters. Finally, Weber's basic categories of types of social action—traditionality, affectuality, instrumental and value rationality—profoundly influenced theories of development and modernization which entered into political culture research.

Weber's principal interpreter in the United States was Talcott Parsons. His early theoretical work elaborated and specified some of the main Weberian categories. Thus, for example, Parsons's categories of orientation to action and his pattern variables [33] are quite clearly elaborations of the Weberian categories of types of social action. Parsons in his concept of orientation to social action speaks of cognitive, affective, and evaluative modes of orientation. Parsons's pattern variables—his pairs of contrasting modes of orientation to action—reflect the influence of both Weber and Durkheim; from the perspective of Weber, specificity, universalism, achievement motivation, and affective neutrality are properties of rational culture and structure, while diffuseness, particularism, ascriptiveness, and affectivity are aspects of traditionality. These Parsonian categories played an important role in studies of political modernization and in the research design of the *Civic Culture* study.

THE INFLUENCE OF SOCIAL PSYCHOLOGY

A third intellectual stream entered into political culture conceptualization and research—that of social psychology. This discipline emerged in the first decades of the twentieth century largely out of efforts among sociologists and psychologists to understand and explain the social and political catastrophes of those years: the bloodshed and destruction of World War I, the Bolshevik Revolution, the Great Depression, the rise of Italian Fascism and German National Socialism, racial antagonisms, and the like. Social psychology represents an effort to understand and explain how and why the attitudes and behavior of individuals are conditioned and influenced by the presence and impact of other individuals and social groupings. The units of analysis which social psychology has employed as building blocks of explanation are *instinct, habit, sentiment,* and *attitude.* Graham Wallas and Walter Lippmann were instinctivists, as were William McDougall, E. L. Thorndike, and John Dewey.[34] Other early social psychologists stressed habit and sentiment as the basic units of analysis, but the mainstream of social psychology adopted attitude as its unit of analysis. The concept of attitude avoided the heredity or environment bias implied in such concepts as instinct and habit, and also avoided the stress on feeling implied in the concept of sentiment. As defined in social psychology, an attitude is a propensity in an individual to perceive, interpret, and act toward a particular object in particular ways. As the discipline became increasingly empirical, experimental, and rigorous in the 1940s and 1950s, it began to explore how particular social and political attitudes were formed and transformed, the effect of group structure and communication upon attitudes, the structure and interrelations of attitudes, and the like.

Two studies of great importance, stemming out of the issues and problems of World War II, were *The Authoritarian Personality* and *The American Soldier. The Authoritarian Personality* research represented a major collaborative and cross-disciplinary effort to explain racial and ethnic prejudice through a research strategy which combined the methods and theories of psychology, sociology, and psychoanalysis.[35] *The American Soldier* research similarly pioneered in the development of social psychological method and theory, applying them to problems of military morale and the effects of communications on soldier attitudes and behavior.[36]

During World War II and the early postwar years, systematic survey research on voting behavior had its beginnings in the work of Paul Lazarsfeld and his associates. Here the effort was to explain voters' choices in terms of demographic characteristics, attitude patterns, and exposure to communication.[37] These and other empirical social-psychological researches in the 1940s and 1950s had important implications for studies in political attitude formation and for the understanding of the demographic correlates and the internal composition, structure, and consistency of political attitudes.[38]

THE INFLUENCE OF PSYCHOANTHROPOLOGY

A fourth intellectual stream entering into political culture conceptualization and research was that of psychoanthropology, stemming from the work of Freud and his disciples and joining with anthropology in the 1930s in what later became known as the psychocultural approach. Freud himself commented on man's political fate but from a psychobiological point of view.[39] Neither he nor his students dealt with the special characteristics of nations and groups. It was the general fate of man limited by his instinctive endowments and psychological mechanisms that provided the themes for Freud and the early psychoanalytic theorists. The merger of pschoanalysis with the social sciences began in the 1920s and 1930s with the work of Bronislaw Malinowski, Ruth Benedict, Margaret Mead, and Harold Lasswell.[40]

Produced primarily by anthropologists and psychiatrists, this psychocultural literature sought to explain political culture propensities by childhood socialization patterns, unconscious motivation, and psychological mechanisms. During and immediately after World War II, efforts were made to characterize and explain the psychological propensities of the major nations at war—Germany, Russia, America, France, and Japan.[41] But this effort to explain the politics and public policy of large and complex nations in the simple terms of libido theory and family authority and with the assumed homogeneity of the small village or tribal society aroused skepticism and gave way to the more sophisticated formulations of Abram Kardiner, Ralph Linton, Alex Inkeles, and Daniel Levinson.[42] Kardiner and Linton extended the scope of socialization beyond the earlier libidinal stages to the full life cycle, including adult experiences as factors influencing cultural propensities. They also introduced quasi-statistical notions such as "basic" or "modal" personality to correct the earlier assumption of culture-personality homogeneity. Linton was the first to deal directly with the heterogeneity of culture in large societies by introducing the concepts of subculture, role, and status culture. Inkeles and Levinson brought the psychocultural approach to a full statistical formulation, arguing that only rigorous sampling techniques with carefully formulated and tested questions could establish differences in the political culture of nations and the subgroups within them.

THE DEVELOPMENT OF SURVEY
RESEARCH METHODOLOGY

But as so often has happened in the history of scientific work, the invention of a new research technology was the catalytic agent in the political culture conceptualization and research that took place in the 1960s. The increasingly evident failure of enlightenment expectations and the incapacity of a comparative politics based on these expectations to explain the variety of political phenomena help us understand the motivation among social scientists contributing to political culture research; and the development of more complex and sophisticated sociological, anthropological, and psychological theory could partially explain the opportunity which was becoming available for a more effective grappling with patterns of politics and their explanations. But the development of survey research methodology was the immediate and more powerful stimulus. It had now become possible to establish whether there were indeed distinctive nation "marks" and national characters; whether and in what respects and degrees nations were divided into distinctive subcultures; whether social classes, functional groups, and specific elites had distinctive orientations toward politics and public policy, and what role was played by what socialization agents in the development of these orientations. The development of statistical analysis made it increasingly possible to establish the patterns of interaction among attitudes, the relations of social-structural and demographic variables to attitude variables, and the relations of attitude variables to social and political behavior.[43]

This revolution in social science research technology had some four components: (1) the development of increasingly precise sampling methods, making it feasible to gather representative data on large populations; (2) the increasing sophistication of interviewing methods to assure greater reliability in the data derived by these methods; (3) the development of scoring and scaling techniques, making it possible to sort out and organize responses in homogeneous dimensions and relate them to theoretical variables; and (4) the increasing sophistication of methods of statistical analysis and inference, moving from simple descriptive statistics to bivariate, multivariate, regression, and causal-path analysis of the relations among contextual, attitudinal, and behavioral variables.

The development of survey research brought to bear on politics a set of precision tools enabling us to move from relatively loose and speculative inferences regarding psychological propensities from the content of communications, from clinical materials, or from behavioral tendencies. To be sure, the data yielded by survey research were created by the instruments and procedures of the researcher, by the questions asked of respondents, by his sampling decisions, and by his techniques of analysis and inference. As experience in voting studies, attitude studies, and market research accumulated, these sources of error came under greater control, although, to be sure, they can never be fully eliminated.

THE CIVIC CULTURE MODEL

The *Civic Culture* study drew on all these intellectual currents. From enlightenment and liberal political theory it drew the "rationality-activist model" of democratic citizenship, the model of a successful democracy that required that all citizens be involved and active in politics, and that their participation be informed, analytic, and rational. *The Civic Culture* argued that this rationality-activist model of democratic citizenship was *one* component of the civic culture, but not the sole one. Indeed, by itself this participant-rationalist model of citizenship could not logically sustain a *stable* democratic government. Only when combined in some sense with its opposites of passivity, trust, and deference to authority and competence was a viable, stable democracy possible.

The *Civic Culture* study was conceived in the aftermath of World War II. The events of the 1920s and the 1930s and the reflections of social theorists on those events informed their political theory. The tragic collapse of Italian and particularly German democracy and their subversion into participant-destructive manias, and the instability of the French Third Republic, were the powerful historical experiences contributing to this more complex theory of the relationship between political culture and democratic stability.

The theory of democratic stability to which *The Civic Culture* contributed is in the most ancient of intellectual traditions. We have already suggested that the *Civic Culture* model is related to the mixed-government model, celebrated in Aristotle, Polybius, and Cicero, and later influential in the development of separation-of-powers theory. Aristotle proposed the mixed constitution as an answer to the problem of instability in the light of the excesses of Athenian democracy. And Aristotle in particular specifies the attitudes most likely to sustain such a mixed polity: moderation, interpersonal trust, and even a certain diffidence regarding political participation. Again in the aftermath of the Third Punic War and in the Rome of Scipio Africanus, the Greek Stoic Polybius draws the lessons of the tragic Greek and particularly Athenian experience for his Roman masters, stressing the virtues of mixed government, which he finds exemplified in the Spartan and Carthaginian constitutions and in the contemporary pre-Gracchan Roman republic. A century later Cicero, in the aftermath of the disorders and civil wars of the Rome of the Gracchi, Marius, and Sulla, and in the period of the struggle among the Triumvirs—in the twilight of the republic in other words—revives the Polybian version of the Roman constitution, presenting it as the mixed-constitutional solution which might still save the republic.[44]

Neither Polybius nor Cicero explicates the psychological aspects of politics and of varieties of political systems in the way that Plato and particularly Aristotle do. Aristotle elaborates the psychological variable in the context of his discussion of the best realistically possible constitution, which is a mixture of oligarchy and democracy in a society in which the middle classes predominate, either in the sense of being more numerous than the rich and the poor, or at least numerous enough to maintain a balance of power. This kind of mixed-government/middle-class-predominant polity is likely to be characterized by the "balanced disparities" of the civic culture—a kind of moderate political participation which accords discretion to political leaders and government officials; a kind of political involvement which is neither fully pragmatic nor simply passionate; and a form of partisanship which is dynamic yet contained within overarching norms of a common civic unity.

Though Polybius and Cicero either witnessed or lived in the

vivid memory of passionate and bloody civil disorders in democratic Athens and democratizing Rome, their treatment of the
mixed constitution tends to be mechanical and structural rather
than psychological. It may be that they assumed that a mixed
constitution would require a Stoic culture to produce it; or
that such a political culture would result from it. In any event
it is an unambiguously clear implication of their treatment of
mixed government that it would be a government in which the
institutional arrangements would encourage moderation, and in
which the moderation of its members would contribute to
preserving the institutional arrangements.

The French Revolution, the American democratic "experiment," and the democratization of Britain in the eighteenth
and nineteenth centuries produced similarly sober reflections
among political theorists. Tocqueville, writing on the condition
of opinion and political culture in France on the eve of the
revolution, spells out the very obverse of the civic culture in
his effort to explain the collapse of the *ancien régime,* the
destructiveness of the revolution, and the instability of the
postrevolutionary regimes: the irresponsibility of the aristocracy,
the intense jealousy among the bourgeoisie of aristocratic privilege, the rancor and wrath of the peasantry over their exploitation, and the self-intoxication of the French intellectuals with
their grand and abstract theories and designs.[45]

Tocqueville, seeking to allay anxiety about the prospects of
democracy in America, in effect repeats the mixed-government/
civic-culture theory of his predecessors. The tyranny of the
majority and the dangers of mass democracy are contained in
America by the institutional separation of powers, but in addition by a "legal aristocracy." He points out that "The aristocracy
of America is on the bench and at the bar. . . ." It has a kind
of corporate quality in common with aristocracies and it is the
"only aristocratic element that can be amalgamated without
violence with the natural elements of democracy and be ad-
vantageously and permanently combined with them. . . . Men
who have made a special study of the laws derive from this
occupation certain habits of order, a taste for formalities, and
a kind of instinctive regard for the regular connection of ideas,
which naturally render them very hostile to the revolutionary
spirit and the unreflecting passions of the multitude."[46]

To this separation of powers, aristocratic admixture as an assurance of stability, Tocqueville adds his characterization of American political culture. He attributes the stability of American democracy to its geography and ecology, to its constitution or laws, but most important of all to its customs, by which he meant "the moral and intellectual characteristics of men in society." He leaves no doubt about the importance he attaches to what we would call political culture today: "If I have hitherto failed in making the reader feel the important influence of the practical experience, the habits, the opinions, in short, of the customs of the Americans upon the maintenance of their institutions, I have failed in the principal object of my work." [47] He then goes on to describe a political culture, at least on the East Coast of America, as marked by habits of "restraint" and "tranquillity," one in which a substantial part of the population pursues "self-interest rightly understood" with "temperance, moderation," and "self-command." [48]

In the process of democratization in Britain in the course of the nineteenth century, John Stuart Mill reacted against the rational democratic simplism of the earlier English radicals, recognizing the dangers of majority tyranny and moral incompetence in a full realization of democracy without regard to competence and responsibility. Leadership by better-qualified citizens may counteract these tendencies. Mill favors a kind of mixed government with the principles of participation and competence somehow reconciled in the major political institutions.[49] A. V. Dicey points out that, while Mill remained a democrat until his dying day, "his belief in democracy was very different in spirit from the confident democratic faith of his father. It was limited by the dread, inspired by Tocqueville, of the tyranny of the majority. . . . The democrat who holds that the majority ought to rule, but that wisdom is to be found mainly in minorities, and that every possible means ought to be adopted to prevent the ignorant majority from abusing its power, has retreated a long way from the clear, the confident and the dogmatic Radicalism of the 1830's." [50]

Walter Bagehot, later in the century, reflecting on the characteristics and conditions of "a polity of discussion" comes very close to the "balanced disparities" of the civic culture. He speaks of the importance of "animated moderation" in the maintenance of "government by popular discussion," a "vigorous moderateness," "a certain combination of energy of mind and balance of mind, hard to attain and harder to keep." [51] And in *The English Constitution* he spells out the attitudinal prerequisites of elective and cabinet government as including mutual trust among the voters, a "calm rational mind," widespread knowledge and analytical capacity, and deference to rank and authority, enabling the government to govern.[52]

The rise of totalitarian movements after World War II produced another wave of theoretical speculation regarding the conditions of democratic stability. Democratic instability and collapse was said to be the consequence of "mass society." Mass society was said to be a by-product of the processes of industrialization, urbanization, and democratization, resulting in the destruction of social ties and organization in which the anomic masses become susceptible to demagogic leadership and authoritarian movements.[53] In those societies in which social and economic organization remained vigorous despite urbanization and industrialization there were defenses against the disintegration and anomic consequences of the forces of modernization. Alexis de Tocqueville had, of course, attributed the success and stability of American democracy in part to the prevalence of voluntary associations, to the cooperative creativity of Americans in contrast to the continental Europeans. In the crisis decades of the 1930s and 1940s the pluralist hypothesis was advanced as a partial explanation for the incidence of democratic instability and collapse. The role of interest groups in articulating the demands and needs of different social groups, the affiliation of individuals with a variety of interest groups as tending to reduce the intensity of interest, and the emergence of skilled-interest-group elites was said to mitigate the consequence of mass society. In its stress on the development of skilled elites and subelites, and in integrating individuals into social structure and mitigating the intensity of alienation and antagonism, pluralist theory had much in common with the mixed-government/civic-culture theory of democratic stability.[54]

Whether the explanation for the success of authoritarian mass movements stressed socioeconomic or psychological conditions, the prescriptions proposed by social and political theorists had much in common with the mixed-constitution/civic-culture tradition that we have just reviewed. Thus Joseph Schumpeter, drawing the implications of the political developments of these decades, proposed five "Conditions for the Success of the Democratic Method." The first of these was a set of politicians, not only of good character and intelligent, but skilled in bargaining, coalition making, electoral campaigning, and the like. In other words, democratic politics requires skilled professional politicians. A second requirement was that the political process should not be overloaded with a multitude of projects and programs, that the scope of government be in some measure limited. A third requirement was a professional bureaucracy to provide continuity and expertise to the legislative and administrative processes, a bureaucratic professionaldom strong and confident enough to "instruct the politicians." "Democratic self control" was Schumpeter's fourth requirement, which brought him into the domain of what we would call political culture. Government and shadow government, parliamentarians on both sides of the aisle, and the electors in the countryside must respect the political division of labor. This meant that "backbenchers" should accord discretion to "frontbenchers"; and while the opposition has the duty to oppose, they "must resist the temptation to upset or embarrass the government each time they could do so." Schumpeter also argues that "The voters outside of parliament must respect the division of labor between themselves and the politicians they elect. They must not withdraw confidence too easily between elections and they must understand that, once they have elected an individual, political action is his business and not theirs." The fifth and final requirement for democratic stability is tolerance of difference of opinion. He points out that "democratic government will work to full advantage only if all the interests that matter are practically unanimous not only in their allegiance to the country but also in their allegiance to the structural principles of the existing society." [55]

It is easy to see from Schumpeter's analysis that he has in mind primarily British, and to a lesser extent American, democracy in spelling out his five requirements, and that his negative models are Germany, France, and Italy. He was asking the question that most if not all political and social scientists were asking in the decades immediately prior to and after World

War II. Why did democracy survive in Britain and the United States, and why did it collapse on the European continent? And his answer falls into the mixed-government/civic-culture tradition which we have traced back to the origins of human speculation about politics.

THE CIVIC CULTURE: RESEARCH DESIGN

The authors of *The Civic Culture* were the heirs of this intellectual tradition and were seeking to test this theory of stable democracy in the dramatic laboratory of recent history. British and American democracy had somehow weathered the crises of the 1920s and 1930s; Germany and Italy had not. Was it possible by empirical research to establish that there was indeed a significantly higher incidence of Aristotle's "political friendliness" and "partnership" and political restraint, "the self interest rightly understood," the "temperance, moderation and self command" of Tocqueville, the "animated moderation" of Bagehot, the "balanced disparities" of Eckstein in the successful democracies than in the ones which had given way to populistic tyranny?

The authors of *The Civic Culture* had available to them the hypotheses and theories of political sociology, social psychology, and psychoanthropology, but most important of all they had available to them the research technology of sample surveys, which led them to a much sharper specification and elaboration of the subjective dimensions of stable democratic politics. The original plan was to include Britain and the United States, with long histories of relatively stable democracy; France and Germany, with historical records of democratic instability; and Sweden, as an example of a stable democracy with a multiparty system. Since France was in the early throes of the Gaullist regime, her party system in disarray and her democratic future in doubt, the decision was made to substitute an Italian for a French study. Sweden at the time had no survey organization with experience in political research, and Mexico was substituted with the thought that a developing, non-European country with mixed democratic-authoritarian features might furnish some interesting contrasts with the European and American cases.

The decision to use a national probability sample of only a

thousand interviews in each country was based on the experimental character of the undertaking and on considerations of cost. The study was a pioneering venture, a kind of pilot investigation. We wanted to have a sample large enough to permit inferences about national populations as a whole, and some demographic subgroups such as the educated and the uneducated, occupational and income groups, men and women, young and old, and the like. This decision, based on considerations of risk and cost, turned out to have been an unfortunate one, since it limited our capacity to deal with the phenomena of subculture. With a sample of a thousand cases, if we tried to control for more than one demographic variable we rapidly ran out of cases. Our American sample yielded only under a hundred black respondents, hardly representative of the black population. Hence we failed to deal with the political attitudes of American blacks. In addition, though we appreciated their importance, we did not include special samples designed to get at the orientations of particular elite groups such as politicians, bureaucrats, interest-group officials, journalists, and local-opinion and political elites. We did provide for the re-interview in depth of one hundred cases in each country, selected to represent significant "types" of respondents in each country. These "political-life-history" interviews were used for illustrative purposes in reporting and interpreting the study's findings.

The intellectual currents discussed here contributed to the form and content of the study. The enlightenment theory of political culture was tested by several sets of questions dealing with level of education, media exposure, and political knowledge and skill. Education and media exposure turned out to be powerfully related to civic competence and participation. The educated in all five countries were more like each other in these respects than they were like the uneducated respondents in their own countries.[56] However, the study brought to light that the political propensities associated with education were primarily cognitive in character; they included information and communication about politics, confidence in understanding politics and in one's ability to be politically effective. Higher education did not as significantly affect attitudes toward civic obligation and other democratic values, nor did it affect attitudes of political trust and partisanship. Here national historical experience tended to create special patterns in which education seemed to have relatively little influence.

But taken all in all, some aspects of enlightenment political-culture theory were substantiated by our study. Later studies have overwhelmingly confirmed the importance of education as an explanatory variable for civic propensities.[57] However, our study showed that education in the formal sense does not necessarily produce the affective and evaluative components of a civic culture, such as civic obligation and trust. These attitudes and values seem to be significantly affected by national and group historical and life experience.

Sociological theory entered into the study in part through stress on the stratification variables of occupation, income, and education. The intercorrelation of these three aspects of stratification (as other studies have shown as well) was found to be strong, but education was found to be the most powerful predictor of civic competence. Nevertheless it was clear that position in the occupational and income hierarchy independent of education was associated with civic competence and activity. The pluralist hypothesis received some test and confirmation in the study. There was in Britain and the United States a higher incidence of organizational affiliation and activity, as well as a more widely distributed sense of cooperative competence, than in Germany, Italy, and Mexico.[58]

The sociological concepts of Weber and Parsons provided the major analytic categories employed in the study. The interview instrument was designed in such a way as to make it possible to separate the cognitive, affective, and evaluative aspects of orientations to political objects, and to ascertain the interrelation among them and their association with demographic variables. The Weberian types of authority and the Parsonian pattern variables entered into our major categorization of types of political culture—parochial, subject, and participant—and hence provided the conceptual bits out of which the civic-culture mix was constructed. It was the persistence of traditional and parochial attitudes and their fusion with participant ones that explained the balanced disparities of the civic culture—the combination of political activity, involvement, and rationality with passivity, traditionality, and commitment to parochial values.[59]

Psychoanthropological hypotheses were tested in the *Civic Culture* study primarily through a series of questions on experiences with authority patterns in family, school, and workplace. The difficulty with this part of the interview was that it asked individuals to recall early family life and the structure of school authority. Recall data of these kinds are known to be unreliable. The longer the time lapse of the recall the less reliable the response. Thus our findings in these areas are open to question. For what they are worth, they suggested that authority structure in the family had only a weak relationship to adult participant propensities, that later experiences in school but particularly in the adult workplace were more closely correlated with political competence and participation.[60] We also noted that membership and activity in organizations could independently produce civic competence.[61] Though we sought to test psychocultural hypotheses in our study, we cannot claim to have tested them in any effective way, not only because of the unreliability of recall data but also because our study focused on system and process political culture, and not on policy propensities.

The impact of social psychological theory on *The Civic Culture* was manifested in those parts of the study which were concerned with the internal structure of political attitudes. Thus we employed Guttman scaling in developing a measure of subjective competence, which showed that the capacity to understand politics was related to a sense of ability to influence politics and to actual experience in attempting to influence it.[62] We also reported relationships between the sense of political competence, political participation, and positive support for the political system, and relationships between general trust in people and cooperativeness in politics.

Other opportunities to examine the interconnection of attitudes and their relation to political behavior were not exploited in the first report of the *Civic Culture* data because of the state of the survey analysis art in the early 1960s. The computer revolution was in its beginnings. There were no computer programs available specially adapted to our material; *The Civic Culture* was perhaps the last major social investigation to be analyzed by a statistical sorter. Thus simple considerations of time and cost limited the indulgence of our imaginations and the richness and rigor of our analysis. Similarly, statistical analysis was moving into its more powerful phase of multi-variate, regression, and path analysis. Leafing through the pages of *The Civic Culture* fifteen years after its publication gives one something of a sense of archaism. The tables, charts, and graphs report or represent raw percentages and simple one-level associations for the most part.

POLITICAL CULTURE AND POLITICAL THEORY

Political culture is not a theory; it refers to a set of variables which may be used in the construction of theories. But insofar as it designates a set of variables and encourages their investigation, it imputes some explanatory power to the psychological or subjective dimension of politics, just as it implies that there are contextual and internal variables which may explain it. The explanatory power of political culture variables is an empirical question, open to hypothesis and testing.

As political culture research has developed in the last two decades, there has been a polemic of sorts organized around three questions: (1) differences of opinion as to definition and specification of the content of political culture; (2) controversy over the analytic separation of political culture from political structure and behavior; and (3) debate over its causal properties.

The various definitions of political culture are in most cases pretheoretic categorizations intended to affirm the importance of these cultural variables in the explanation of political phenomena, or preceding empirical investigations of some specific aspect or aspects of political culture. In an early formulation drawing on the work of Talcott Parsons, I defined political culture as consisting of cognitive, affective, and evaluative orientations to political phenomena, distributed in national populations or in subgroups, and then I proceeded to suggest some cultural hypotheses which might explain the differences in performance among Anglo-American, continental European, totalitarian, and preindustrial political systems.[63] In a formulation published around the same time, Samuel Beer, also drawing on Talcott Parsons, argued that a political culture orients a people toward a polity and its processes, providing it with a system of beliefs (a cognitive map), a way of evaluating its operations, and a set of expressive symbols.[64]

In *The Civic Culture* the definition of the concept was adapted to the analysis of the cultural properties assumed to be associated with democratic stability. Consequently the elaboration of the concept stressed political knowledge and skill, and feelings and value orientations toward political objects and processes— toward the political system as a whole, toward the self as participant, toward political parties and elections, bureaucracy, and the like. Little or no stress was placed on attitudes toward public policy.[65]

In a major collaborative investigation of varieties of political culture, Lucian Pye and Sidney Verba offered more comprehensive elaborations of the concept. Pye, focusing on political-development themes, discussed the variety of ways the concept of political culture can help explain developmental problems and processes.[66] Verba defined the important dimensions of political culture as including the sense of national identity, attitudes toward oneself as participant, attitudes toward one's fellow citizens, attitudes and expectations regarding governmental output and performance, and knowledge about and attitudes toward the political processes of decision making.[67]

Dahl, in his study of political oppositions, discusses in detail several types of political orientation that have a bearing on patterns of political partisanship. The first of these is orientation toward the political system as a whole, which affects the extent and distribution of loyalty in a national society; attitudes toward cooperation and individuality and toward other people in general, which affect the formation of political groups and their interaction; and orientation toward problem solving (e.g., whether it is pragmatic or ideological), which affects the interactions of political parties. He then proceeds to show how these attitudes may affect the policies and tactics of political movements, drawing for illustrative purposes from case histories of the United States and a number of Western European democracies.[68]

In a recent formulation, Almond and Powell elaborate the concept of political culture in three directions: (1) substantive content, (2) varieties of orientation, and (3) the systemic relations among these components. An analysis of a nation's political culture would have to concern itself with all three. From the point of view of substantive content we may speak of "system" culture, "process" culture, and "policy" culture. The system culture of a nation would consist of the distributions of attitudes toward the national community, the regime, and the authorities, to use David Easton's formulation.[69] These would include the sense of national identity, attitudes toward the legitimacy of the regime and its various institutions, and attitudes toward the legitimacy and effectiveness of the incumbents of the various political roles.

The process culture of a nation would include attitudes toward the self in politics (e.g., parochial-subject-participant), and attitudes toward other political actors (e.g., trust, cooperative competence, hostility). The policy culture would consist of the distribution of preferences regarding the outputs and outcomes of politics, the ordering among different groupings in the population of such political values as welfare, security, and liberty.

Orientations toward these system, process and policy objects may be cognitive, consisting of beliefs, information, and analysis; affective, consisting of feelings of attachment, aversion, or indifference; or evaluative, consisting of moral judgments of one kind or another.

A third aspect of a political culture would be the relatedness or systemic character of its components. Philip Converse [70] suggested the concept of "constraint" to characterize situations in which attitudes toward political institutions and policies go together. Thus, in a given population, attitudes toward foreign policy, domestic economic policy, and racial segregation may be parts of a consistent ideology; for most individuals in this group, if one knew how they stood on foreign policy one could predict their views on taxation, on busing, and the like. In other groups these attitudes might be independent. Similarly, information, beliefs, feelings, and moral judgments are interrelated. Generally speaking the political cultures of nations and groups may be distinguished and compared according to their internal constraint or consistency.[71]

The principal criticism of the political culture literature is that it imputes a causal direction to the relation between culture and structure, implying that the culture produces the structure. Brian Barry in a detailed critique argued that the actual causal pattern might be one in which a satisfactory democratic experience produces the civic culture in a rational, learned way.[72] Richard Fagen, in a study of the political culture of Cuba, argues that the very separation of the attitudinal dimension from the behavioral dimension tends to give a conservative bias to political culture research, attributing great power to socialization variables, and tends to overlook the importance of political structure, particularly deliberate and organized efforts to transform political culture as in Cuba and other Communist countries. Robert Tucker argues a similar position also with reference to the culture–structure relation in Communist societies.[73]

The criticism of *The Civic Culture* that it argues that political culture causes political structure is incorrect. Throughout the study the development of specific cultural patterns in particular countries is explained by reference to particular historical experiences, such as the sequence of Reform Acts in Britain, the American heritage of British institutions, the Mexican Revolution, and Nazism and defeat in World War II for Germany. It is quite clear that political culture is treated as both an independent and a dependent variable, as causing structure and as being caused by it.[74]

The position taken in *The Civic Culture* that beliefs, feelings, and values significantly influence political behavior, and that these beliefs, feelings, and values are the product of socialization experiences is one that is sustained by much evidence. But *The Civic Culture* was one of the earliest studies to stress the importance of adult political socialization and experiences and to demonstrate the relative weakness of childhood socialization.[75] These points are made unambiguously and are substantiated by evidence.

This relatively open conception of political culture, viewed as causing behavior and structure, as well as being caused by them, and including adult political learning and a rational cognitive component, is the special target of Ronald Rogowski, who rejects political culture theory as being too loosely and diffusely formulated to be acceptable as explanatory theory. He argues that there are clear-cut rational relationships between socioeconomic, ethnic, and religious interests and political structure, and that a rational individualist explanation of political structure is a more powerful and parsimonious theory than political culture theory.[76]

This polemic about the explanatory significance of political culture as defined in *The Civic Culture* can only be resolved by empirical research, and such research as has been done suggests that Rogowski's position is not sustainable by evidence. Much of human history stands in disproof of the argument that the structure of political institutions and their legitimacy can be explained by simple reference to rational self-interest. Surely the rational self-interest of social class and of ethnic and religious groups is a powerful dynamic illuminating political movements and conflicts, and contributing significantly to historical outcomes. But patriotism, community loyalty, religious values, and simple habit and tradition obviously enter into the explanation of political structure and legitimacy.

Fagen's emphasis on the plasticity of political attitudes and the importance of deliberate efforts to transform them is supported in only quite limited ways by studies of political culture in communist countries. Communist ideology takes a rather extreme position on the malleability of human beings, arguing that attitudinal differences are the simple consequences of social and political structural arrangements. Change the social and political structural arrangements and a new kind of socialist man can be created. From this point of view a comparison of the real political culture in communist societies with the official communist political culture may be a kind of test of the explanatory power of cultural variables. As Archie Brown puts it in a recent comparative study of political culture in communist countries, there has been "a radical break in the continuity of political institutions in Communist societies" and "an unusually overt and conscious attempt to create new political values and to supplant the old. Indeed, the validity of the concept of political culture cannot be said to have been fully tested until it has been used in a comparative study of Communist states, for if the political cultures of societies which have become Communist can be readily moulded into a new shape with old values cast aside, the explanatory value of political culture may reasonably be regarded as marginal." [77]

This recent study of communist political cultures concludes

that there are two party cultures—an aspirational "new socialist man" culture, and a tacit "operational code" consisting of the actual working rules and beliefs of the system. On the central question as to the success or failure of the massive communist effort to transform political attitudes in the seven countries included in the study (USSR, Yugoslavia, Poland, Hungary, Czechoslovakia, China, and Cuba), the scholars who examined the admittedly inadequate data on political attitudes came to the following tentative conclusions.

> The attempt to create a new socialist man has been on the whole a depressing failure. . . . Almost everywhere apathy, privatism, and "economism" are prevalent and tolerated and sometimes even encouraged. . . . Perhaps the most striking implication of our study is the relative failure of Communist processes of socialization and education, in spite of all the institutional powers which a Communist political system bestows.[78]

> It is quite clear that national political cultures have played some part in the political changes which have taken place throughout the Communist world. . . . There has been little sign of much penetration of the national political cultures by the official culture, except in the form of a vague general commitment to Socialism, undefined.[79]

> There is substantial and significant contrast between those countries in which Russian influence puts sharp limits on the possibility of change, and those countries (China, Cuba, and Yugoslavia) which are independent. The degree of divergence in these countries is very great. Cuba may be a case merely of incomplete *convergence,* but in the other two countries free of Russian dominance the Communist system has been wholly remodeled in ways powerfully influenced by national tradition.[80]

> Perhaps the most important conclusion which this book suggests is that in countries where there has in the past been experience of the fruitful play of competing ideas and competing interests, experience of Communist government has not weakened but actually strengthened the conviction among the population that political freedom brings both greater justice and greater efficiency.[81]

This study does indeed lend confirmation to the argument that political-cultural variables, and the socialization processes which create and maintain them, play an important part in the explanation of political structure and process. Among the more interesting findings of political culture research, these conclusions as to the intractability of these "pre-communist" attitudes despite the awesome effort to transform them, stand in the sharpest contrast to the overwhelming evidence that some humane and participant consequences flow from modern education wherever it is introduced.[82] It would thus appear, not that political culture is an intractable variable, but that there are limits to its plasticity, and inherent propensities of a modestly encouraging sort.

NOTES

1. Genesis 49:4, 15, 10 rsv.

2. Fustel de Coulanges, *The Ancient City* (Garden City, N.Y.: Doubleday, 1956), p. 106.

3. The cycle of political change from kingship to tyranny to aristocracy to oligarchy to democracy to mob rule is first formulated in detail in Plato, *The Works of Plato,* trans. Jowett 1 vol. ed. (New York: Dial Press, n.d.), p. 307 *(The Republic)* it is elaborated in Aristotle, *Politics,* trans. H. Rackham (London: Heinemann, 1932), pp. 285ff., and is presented in a somewhat stylized form in Polybius, *The Histories,* Book 6, trans. W. R. Paton (London: Heinemann, 1923), vol. 3, pp. 269ff. This cycle of political change explained in social psychological terms appears and reappears in the history of political theory well into the nineteenth century.

4. Plato, op. cit., p. 445.

5. Plutarch, *The Lives of the Noble Grecians and Romans,* trans. John Dryden, rev. by Arthur Hugh Clough (New York: Random House, Modern Library, n.d.), p. 62.

6. Aristotle, *Politics,* pp. 329–31.

7. Niccolò Machiavelli, *The Discourses,* trans. Leslie Walker (New Haven: Yale Univ. Press, 1950), p. 240.

8. Montesquieu (Charles de Secondat), *Considerations on the Causes of the Greatness of the Romans and Their Decline,* trans. David Lowenthal (New York: The Free Press, 1965), pp. 91ff.

9. Montesquieu, *The Persian Letters* (Indianapolis: Bobbs-Merrill, 1964); and, particularly, *The Spirit of Laws* (New York: Colonial Press, 1899), 1: 292ff.

10. Jean Jacques Rousseau, *The Social Contract* (New York: Carlton House, n.d.), p. 41.

11. Ibid., p. 43.

12. Alexis de Tocqueville, *Democracy in America* (New York: Alfred A. Knopf, 1945), 1: 299.

13. Alexis de Tocqueville, *The Old Regime and the French Revolution* (Garden City, N.Y.: Doubleday, 1955).

14. The term *political culture* seems first to have been used by the German enlightenment philosopher J. G. Herder in the late eighteenth century; see F. M. Barnard, "Culture and Political Development: Herder's Suggestive Insights," *American Political Science Review* (June 1969), p. 392. Carl Friedrich uses the term quite casually in his discussion of constitutionalism as an aspect of the political culture of English-speaking people;

see Carl J. Friedrich, *Constitutional Government and Democracy* (Boston: Ginn & Company, 1950), p. 28. The term was apparently used by Lenin and more recently by Brezhnev; see Stephen White, "USSR: Autocracy and Industrialism," in Archie Brown and Jack Gray, eds., *Political Culture and Political Change in Communist States* (New York: Holmes and Meier, 1977), p. 58. Lewis Namier entitles a lecture "History and Political Culture"; see Fritz Stern, ed., *The Varieties of History* (New York: Meridian Books, 1956), p. 372.

15. A. V. Dicey, *Law and Public Opinion in England During the Nineteenth Century* (London: Macmillan & Co., 1962), lecture 12.

16. Woodrow Wilson, *The State* (Boston: D. C. Heath, 1893).

17. Vilfredo Pareto, *Les Systemes Socialistes*, vol. 5 of Complete Works, 3rd ed. (Geneva: Droz, 1965); Gaetano Mosca, *The Ruling Class* (New York: McGraw-Hill, 1939); Robert Michels, *Political Parties* (New York: The Free Press, 1962).

18. Graham Wallas, *Human Nature in Politics* (New York: Alfred A. Knopf, 1921), pp. 5–6.

19. Ibid., p. 118.

20. Walter Lippmann, *Public Opinion* (New York: Harcourt Brace, 1922), chap. 1 and part 8.

21. James Bryce, *Modern Democracies* (New York: Macmillan, 1921), 2: 606ff.

22. William B. Munro, *The Governments of Europe* (New York: Macmillan, 1925), p. 1.

23. Herman Finer, *Theory and Practice of Modern Government* (New York: Henry Holt and Company, 1932).

24. Carl J. Friedrich, *Constitutional Government and Politics* (New York: Harper & Row, 1937), p. xvi.

25. Andre Siegfried, *France: A Study in Nationality* (New Haven: Yale Univ. Press, 1930); Salvador de Madariaga, *Englishmen, Frenchmen, Spaniards* (London: Oxford Univ. Press, 1928); and *The Americans* (London: Oxford Univ. Press, 1930).

26. Henri de Saint-Simon, *Social Organization* (New York: Harper & Row, 1964).

27. Raymond Aron, *Main Currents in Sociological Thought*, vol. 1 (New York: Basic Books, 1965).

28. Shlomo Avineri, *The Social and Political Thought of Karl Marx* (Cambridge, Eng.: Cambridge Univ. Press, 1968), pp. 220ff.

29. Harry Alpert, *Emile Durkheim and His Sociology* (New York: Russell & Russell, 1961).

30. Vilfredo Pareto, *The Mind and Society*, 4 vols. (New York: Dover Books, 1963). These concepts are developed in vols. 1, 2, and 3.

31. Max Weber, *Gesammelte Aufsatze zur Religionsoziologie* (Tübingen: J. C. B. Mohr, 1920).

32. Max Weber, *Wirtschaft und Gesellschaft* (Tübingen: J. C. B. Mohr, 1925), part 3.

33. Talcott Parsons and E. A. Shils, *Toward a General Theory of Action* (Cambridge, Mass.: Harvard Univ. Press, 1951).

34. Gordon W. Allport, "The Historical Background of Modern Social Psychology," in Lindzey and Aronson, eds., *The Handbook of Social Psychology*, 2nd ed. (Reading, Mass.: Addison-Wesley, 1968), 1: 56ff.

35. T. W. Adorno, Elsa Frenkel-Brunswik, Nevitt Sanford, and Daniel Levinson, *The Authoritarian Personality* (New York: Harper & Row, 1950).

36. Samuel Stouffer et al., *The American Soldier*, vols. 1 and 2 (Princeton,

N.J.: Princeton Univ. Press, 1949); Carl J. Hovland et al., *Experiments in Mass Communication* (Princeton, N.J.: Princeton Univ. Press, 1949).

37. Paul Lazarsfeld et al., *The People's Choice* (New York: John Wiley and Sons, 1960); Bernard Berelson et al., *Voting* (Chicago: Univ. of Chicago Press, 1954).

38. Samuel Stouffer, *Communism, Conformity, and Civil Liberties* (Gloucester, Mass.: Smith, 1955); Kurt Lewin, *Field Theory in Social Science* (London: Tavistock, 1963); Leon Festinger, *A Theory of Cognitive Dissonance* (New York: Harper & Row, 1957); Milton Rokeach, *The Open and Closed Mind* (New York: Basic Books, 1960); M. Brewster Smith, Jerome S. Bruner, R. W. White, *Opinions and Personality* (New York: John Wiley and Sons, 1956).

39. See, for example, his *Civilization and Its Discontents* (1930) in *Complete Works,* vol. 22 (New York: Macmillan, 1962).

40. B. Malinowski, *Sex and Repression in Savage Society* (New York: Harcourt Brace, 1927); Margaret Mead, *Coming of Age in Samoa* (New York: William Morrow, 1928); Ruth Benedict, *Patterns of Culture* (Boston: Houghton Mifflin, 1934); Harold Lasswell, *Psychopathology and Politics* (Chicago: Univ. of Chicago Press, 1930).

41. Examples of this literature are Bertram Schaffner, *Fatherland: A Study of Authoritarianism in the German Family* (New York: Columbia Univ. Press, 1948); Margaret Mead, *Soviet Attitudes Toward Authority* (New York: McGraw-Hill, 1951); Geoffrey Gorer, *Exploring English Character* (New York: Criterion Books, 1955); Rhoda Metraux and Margaret Mead, *Themes in French Culture* (Stanford, Calif.: Stanford Univ. Press, 1954); Ruth Benedict, *The Chrysanthemum and the Sword* (Boston: Houghton Mifflin 1946); Margaret Mead, *And Keep Your Powder Dry* (New York: Morrow, 1950).

42. Abram Kardiner, *The Psychological Frontiers of Society* (New York: Columbia University Press, 1945); Ralph Linton, *The Cultural Background of Personality* (New York: Appleton-Century-Crofts, 1945); Alex Inkeles and Daniel Levinson, "National Character: The Study of Modal Personality and Socio-Cultural Systems," in Lindzey and Aronson, *Handbook,* vol. 4; Alex Inkeles, "National Character and Modern Political Systems" in Franklin L. K. Hsu, ed., *Psychological Anthropology* (Homewood, Ill.: Dorsey Press, 1961).

43. For a general discussion of survey research in the study of politics, see Richard W. Boyd and Herbert Hyman, "Survey Research," in Greenstein and Polsby, eds., *Handbook of Political Science* (Reading, Mass.: Addison-Wesley, 1975), pp. 265ff.

44. Polybius, *The Histories,* trans. W. R. Paton, vol. 3, book 6 (New York: G. P. Putnam's Sons, 1923); M. T. Cicero, *On the Commonwealth,* trans. George H. Sabine and S. B. Smith (Columbus, Ohio: Ohio State Univ. Press, 1929).

45. Alexis de Tocqueville, *The Old Regime and the French Revolution,* Trans. Stuart Gilbert (Garden City, N.Y.: Doubleday Anchor Books, 1955), pp. 204ff.

46. Alexis de Tocqueville, *Democracy in America,* 1: 272ff.

47. Ibid., pp. 319ff.

48. Ibid., pp. 305ff.

49. Dennis F. Thompson, *John Stuart Mill and Representative Government* (Princeton, N.J.: Princeton Univ. Press, 1977), pp. 176ff.

50. A. V. Dicey, *Law and Public Opinion,* p. 427.

51. Walter Bagehot, *Physics and Politics* (New York: Colonial Press, 1899), pp. 122ff.

52. Bagehot, *The English Constitution* (Ithaca, N.Y.: Cornell Univ. Press, 1966), pp. 239ff.

53. See inter al. Emil Lederer, *The State of the Masses* (New York: W. W. Norton, 1940); Hannah Arendt, *The Origins of Totalitarianism* (New York: Meridian Books, 1951); William Kornhauser, *The Politics of Mass Society* (Glencoe, Ill.: The Free Press, 1959); Erich Fromm, *Escape from Freedom* (New York: Holt, 1941).

54. See inter al. David Truman, *The Governmental Process* (New York: Alfred A. Knopf, 1955); Robert E. Lane, *Political Life* (Glencoe, Ill.: The Free Press, 1959); Edward C. Banfield, *The Moral Basis of a Backward Society* (Glencoe, Ill.: The Free Press, 1958).

55. Joseph A. Schumpeter, *Capitalism, Socialism, and Democracy* (New York: Harper & Row, 1942), pp. 289–96.

56. G. A. Almond and Sidney Verba, *The Civic Culture* (Princeton, N.J.: Princeton Univ. Press, 1963), pp. 379ff.

57. Herbert H. Hyman, *The Enduring Effects of Education* (Chicago: Univ. of Chicago Press, 1975).

58. Almond and Verba, *Civic Culture,* Chap. 11.

59. Ibid., chaps. 1 and 15.

60. Ibid., chap. 12.

61. A reanalysis of our data suggested that organizational involvement was the most powerful predictor of all the variables associated with participation. See Norman Nie et al., "Social Structure and Participation," *American Political Science Review,* June and September, 1969.

62. Almond and Verba, *Civic Culture,* pp. 231ff.

63. G. A. Almond, *Political Development* (Boston: Little, Brown, 1970), pp. 35ff.

64. Samuel Beer's most recent formulation, which elaborates his views first formulated in *Patterns of Government* (1958), is to be found in S. Beer and Adam Ulam, eds., *Patterns of Government,* 3rd ed., part 1 (New York: Random House, 1974).

65. Almond and Verba, *Civic Culture,* chap. 1.

66. Lucian Pye and Sidney Verba, *Political Culture and Political Development* (Princeton, N.J.: Princeton Univ. Press, 1966), chap. 1.

67. Ibid., chap. 12.

68. Robert A. Dahl, *Political Oppositions in Western Democracies* (New Haven: Yale Univ. Press, 1966), pp. 352ff.

69. David Easton, *A System Analysis of Political Life* (New York: John Wiley and Sons, 1965).

70. Philip Converse, "The Nature of Mass Belief Systems," in David Apter, ed., *Ideology and Discontent* (New York: The Free Press, 1964).

71. See also Donald Devine, *The Political Culture of the United States* (Boston: Little, Brown, 1972).

72. Brian M. Barry, *Sociologists, Economists and Democracy* (London: Collier-Macmillan, 1970), pp. 48ff.

73. Richard Fagen, *The Transformation of Political Culture in Cuba* (Stanford, Calif.: Stanford Univ. Press, 1969), chap. 1; for Tucker's views, see Robert C. Tucker, "Culture, Political Culture, and Communist Society," *Political Science Quarterly* (June 1973), pp. 173–90.

74. Almond and Verba, *Civic Culture,* chaps. 1 and 15.

75. Ibid., chap. 12.

76. Ronald Rogowski, *A Rational Theory of Legitimacy* (Princeton, N.J.: Princeton Univ. Press, 1976).

77. Archie Brown and Jack Gray, *Political Culture and Political Change in Communist States* (New York: Holmes and Meier, 1977), p.· 12. The various country contributions to this symposium refer to the literature describing political culture patterns in Communist countries, including China and Cuba. Some of this literature is of a theoretical sort, and some reports empirical research on political culture patterns. It is of interest that the concept has been widely accepted in Eastern European countries, where it tends to legitimate national and ethnic autonomy. For references to political culture in Soviet and Eastern European literature, see Jerzy Wiatr's contribution to the present volume, and the extensive bibliographical citations in Brown and Gray, *Political Culture.* Also papers presented at the Roundtable on Political Culture held under the auspices of the International Political Science Association at Krakow, Poland, September 1977, in particular, Stane Juznic, *Typology of Political Culture*; Ioan Ceterchi and Ovidiu Trasnea, *Political Culture and Political Development;* Kazimierz Opalek, *The Concept "Culture" in Legal Theory and in Political Science;* and Marek Sobolewski, *The Postulative Model of the Socialist Political Culture in Poland.*

78. Brown and Gray, *Political Culture,* pp. 270–71.

79. Ibid.

80. Ibid., p. 271.

81. Ibid., p. 272.

82. See Almond and Verba, *Civic Culture,* pp. 379ff.; and Herbert Hyman, *The Enduring Effects of Education* (Chicago: Univ. of Chicago Press, 1975).

/

CHAPTER II

The Structure of Inference

Arend Lijphart
University of California, San Diego

ALTHOUGH THE BULK of *The Civic Culture* deals with the comparative description and analysis of the patterns and dimensions of five political cultures, the larger question that motivates the study and that is discussed extensively in the introductory and concluding chapters concerns the relationship between political culture and political structure. The dependent variable is the stability and effectiveness of democratic government. The identification of the independent variable presents a bit of a problem. In their preface, Gabriel A. Almond and Sidney Verba state their main themes in the following words: "what the Greeks called civic virtue and its consequences for the effectiveness and stability of the democratic polity; and . . . the kind of community life, social organization, and upbringing of children that fosters civic virtue." [1] And the first sentence of the first chapter reads: "This is a study of the political culture of democracy and of the social structures and processes that sustain it." [2] These statements suggest that the argument is structured around three variables or sets of variables: the

I wish to thank the Netherlands Institute for Advanced Study in the Humanities and Social Sciences in Wassenaar, where I was a Fellow during the year 1974–75, for the opportunity it provided me to write this chapter.

A. L.

independent variables (social structures and processes), the intermediate variable (political culture, especially the degree of "civic virtue" or, as it is usually called, civic culture), and the dependent variable (democratic stability). Political culture is then narrowly defined as the pattern of cognitive, evaluative, and affective orientations toward *political* objects.

In their analysis, Almond and Verba approach the social structures and processes that sustain the political culture mainly through the subjective orientations of their respondents: the nonpolitical or not directly political culture. And they find that the political and nonpolitical culture are closely linked: "the political orientations that make up the civic culture are closely related to general social and interpersonal relations." [3] The relationship is so close, in fact, that cooperativeness and social trust are called "a *component* of the civic culture." [4] This suggests a somewhat broader definition of the term *political culture* and the fusion of the independent and intermediate variables into a single set of independent variables.

In my discussion of the structure of inference in *The Civic Culture,* I shall adhere to the narrower and purer definition of political culture, but concentrate on the links between political culture, to be treated as the independent variable, and political structure as the dependent variable, leaving aside the antecedent influence of the social structures and processes. The following methodological aspects of the investigation of this relationship must be examined: the measurement of the two basic variables, the selection of the cases for the comparative analysis, the nature of the relationship and in particular the question whether *The Civic Culture* commits the "individualistic fallacy," the causal direction, and the explanation of the relationship.

THE PROBLEM OF MEASUREMENT

POLITICAL STRUCTURE

Most of the efforts of measurement in *The Civic Culture* go into the measurement of various components of political culture and related aspects of the general culture. The political structure side of the relationship receives much more cursory attention. This can be justified on the ground that the former variable is less well known and therefore deserves a more thorough examination. Brian Barry overstates the relative neglect of the political structure variable when he calls it "an extraordinary fact" that Almond and Verba "do not address themselves to the question how 'democratic' their five countries are." And he argues that what is needed is "either a criterion for the presence of relative amounts of . . . 'democracy,' or a scale . . . on which at least ordinal positions could be established." [5]

Four comments are in order here. A minor first point is that Almond and Verba's concern is with the stability of democracy rather than with democracy as such. A second equally small point is that they do indicate how stable their five democracies are: Great Britain and the United States are regarded as "the two relatively stable and successful democracies." [6] My third comment follows from the previous one but is of greater substantive importance. The ideal way of measuring democratic stability would be to use an interval scale; the next best method is the ordinal scale that Barry recommends; and the least refined method is the dichotomous classification into more and less stable democracies that Almond and Verba use. But although the last method is a rough kind of measurement, there is nothing basically wrong with it. And the cross-tabulation of two dichotomously categorized variables gives a good idea of the strength of the relationship between them. To anticipate slightly, Almond and Verba find that Great Britain and the United States approximate the civic culture and that the other three countries deviate quite considerably from this ideal. If we dichotomize the political culture variable, too, and then cross-tabulate it with democratic stability, we get the results shown in Table II.1.

Fourth, a more sophisticated measurement of democratic stability has a number of drawbacks that the admittedly crude dichotomous classification does not have. Let us assume that we would operationalize democratic stability and arrive at a cardinal scale with values from 100 to 0. Such a scale would be acceptable only if Great Britain and the United States turned out to have values that were very close together and if the other three countries had considerably lower values; enough is known about these countries (with the possible exception of Mexico) for us to rely on intersubjective expert judgment, and there is little doubt that the experts would be close to

TABLE II.1. *Civic Culture and Democratic Stability (2 × 2 Table)*
Civic Culture

		High	Low
	High	Great Britain United States (2)	(0)
Democratic Stability			
	Low	(0)	Germany Italy Mexico (3)

unanimous on this ranking (at least as of 1959–60, when the citizenship surveys were conducted). This also means that the whole procedure of operationalization is not really necessary. Robert A. Dahl ran into this problem when he tried to measure polyarchy as accurately as possible. When he inspected the results of his operationalization, he discovered that France appeared in the same low category as Bolivia, and that therefore "France was badly misplaced." He then disregarded his operational code and simply reassigned France to a higher category.[7] This difficulty indicates both that the measurement of all the other countries of which much less is known than about France should be taken with a grain of salt and that the "careful" measurement of the better-known countries can be dispensed with because it is acceptable only when it is in agreement with intersubjective expert opinion. Moreover, a simple ranking of the five countries would not be much of an improvement over the dichotomous classification because Britain and the United States would have to be given approximately the same rank, and so would Germany and Italy.

Almond and Verba freely admit their reliance on their subjective judgments for the classification of the five countries: "a brief glance at history will tell which of these [nations] are more stable."[8] This, of course, raises the problem: To which period of history do the authors refer? As Barry states, "it would make a big difference whether or not one went back beyond 1945."[9] Almond and Verba do not specify this temporal dimension, but they appear to have especially the post–World War II period in mind. In the German case, this is of crucial importance, and here it is clearly specified that the Bonn Republic is meant, for instance, when its new political structures are contrasted with the persistence of older attitudinal patterns.[10]

POLITICAL CULTURE

The measurement and analysis of the political cultures of the five countries in *The Civic Culture* is based on a wealth of survey data. These data constitute hard and detailed evidence, which Almond and Verba use to measure various aspects of the five political cultures, but they do not provide a composite index to measure the degree of civic culture. The civic culture is described as a "cultural pattern" with "several significant components," but there is no precise specification of either the empirical indicators of these components or the exact weight they contribute to the overall pattern.[11] The most important component appears to be subjective political competence, measured by two questions concerning the respondent's perception of whether he can do something about an unjust or harmful national law or local regulation, and by a Guttman scale based on five questions about local political orientations and activity.[12] A person's belief in his competence is described as "a key political attitude" and the "self-confident citizen" is called "the democratic citizen." [13]

It is a weakness in the argument of *The Civic Culture* that the analytical step from the separate components of political culture to the degrees to which the five political cultures approximate the civic culture requires an impressionistic leap. On the other hand, the subjective judgment that the authors make does seem to be in rough agreement with the detailed empirical data, and it is not very likely that an operational measure of the civic culture would have led to a different ranking of the countries. The eventual classification is the result of three divisions. First, "the closest approximation to the civic culture" is found in Britain and the United States, whereas the other countries deviate from it to an important extent. Second, in the former category Britain is rated slightly higher because its political culture "represents a more effective

Table II.2. *Civic Culture and Democratic Stability (4 × 2 Table)*

Civic Culture

		High	Medium-high	Medium-low	Low
Democratic Stability	High	Great Britain (1)	United States (1)	(0)	(0)
	Low	(0)	(0)	Germany Mexico (2)	Italy (1)

combination of the subject and participant roles." And finally, in the category of weak civic cultures, a further division is made between Germany and Mexico, which "have some of the components of the civic culture," and Italy, which is deficient in most respects.[14] This fourfold classification of political cultures means that Table II.1 must be amended (see Table II.2). The relationship between the variables remains a perfect one.

The time element does not present a problem with regard to the measurement of the political culture variable. It is determined by the periods in which the surveys were conducted (1959 and 1960). The preface to *The Civic Culture* characterizes the study as "a snapshot in a rapidly changing world."[15] Actually, the underlying assumption is that political cultures change only slowly. It requires the most revolutionary and traumatic upheavals as well as deliberate efforts to change the political culture to accelerate the process, as Verba has shown in a later study of Germany.[16] But it is nevertheless the conclusion of *The Civic Culture* that the new democratic institutions of the Bonn Republic "have not taken root in the Germans' feelings toward politics and partisanship; earlier attitude patterns seem to persist among the people."[17]

A final problem concerning the measurement of political culture is what Stein Rokkan has criticized as the "strong nation-orientation of the survey design" and the tendency to present "straight comparisons between total national cross-sections."[18] A more detailed analysis of differences within the five countries might have been interesting for its own sake, but the basic research design that focuses on the link between political cultures and structures requires that the nations rather than subnational groups or individuals be treated as the cases for analysis. It should be noted, however, that Almond and Verba take a significant step below the national level; they argue that the "connections between sets of attitudes and the characteristics of the political system can be made more convincing by internal analysis of the attitudes within the nations." They illustrate this approach with the following example:

> Suppose one finds that a particular attitude toward interpersonal relations exists most frequently in a system where political participation of a particular sort is most frequent; if one also finds that it is precisely those individuals who hold that attitude who are more likely to be the political participants, one can then support the hypothesis that the particular attitude is connected with a particular kind of participatory system.[19]

This kind of indirect evidence adds plausibility to a proposition stated at the systemic level but does not constitute proof. It also raises the danger of the individualistic fallacy, which will be discussed later.

THE SELECTION OF THE NATIONAL CASES

Three criteria for the selection of the cases investigated by Almond and Verba can be gleaned from *The Civic Culture*.[20] First, the countries must be democratic. Second, they must be nations with "a *wide range* of experience with democracy." [21] This means that both countries "representing relatively successful experiments in democratic government" and those representing less successful experiences should be included.[22] Third, there is a special reason for the inclusion of the United States: not only does it represent one extreme on the range of democratic stability—which would have justified its selection according to the second criterion—but it also serves as a bench mark because of all the prior political research performed in the United States. Almond and Verba state: "By far the greatest amount of empirical research on democratic attitudes has been done in the United States. . . . Our five-country study offers us the opportunity to escape from this American parochialism and to discover whether relations found in the American data are also encountered in democratic countries whose historical experiences and political and social structures differ from one another." [23]

These are unexceptionable criteria. The first one is dictated by the principal research question: democratic stability has to be examined in countries with democratic regimes. The second criterion is especially important: because only relatively few cases can be investigated, it is essential that they represent as wide a variation as possible on at least one of the variables in order to give a clear picture of the relationship between the variables. The usually most suitable method is to maximize the variance of the independent variable; the variance of the dependent variable should not be taken into consideration because this would prejudge the empirical question.[24] But the procedure can also be turned around by maximizing the variance of the dependent variable. This is what is done in *The Civic Culture*: the choice of cases is determined by the range they represent on the dependent variable of democratic stability. Finally, the inclusion of the United States as a bench mark contributes to making the research in this field cumulative.

Although the criteria are beyond reproach, the selection of the specific cases is open to legitimate criticism. In particular, Mexico appears to be a weak case, because it is doubtful that this country can be regarded as fully democratic. For instance, Dahl does not include it among the world's polyarchies or even among the near polyarchies. The location of Mexico in Dahl's low category 14 seems correct and differs considerably from the location of the other four countries in categories 3, 4, and 5.[25] A second weakness of the Mexican case is that it turned out to be impossible to draw a national representative sample in this country: only cities over 10,000 in population were surveyed. The authors call attention to this fact in a footnote and argue in an appendix that this discrepancy does not have serious consequences: "A comparison of the Mexican results with those for cities of the same size in the other four nations suggests that this difference in the sample does not distort the results." [26] This effort to compare the five urban samples is laudable and the optimistic suggestion based on it is to some extent reassuring, but it is only a suggestion and the fact remains that the four national samples and the Mexican urban sample are not really comparable. Secondary analyses of the data of *The Civic Culture* have tended to omit the Mexican sample.[27]

It would have been wiser to increase the variation of the democratic stability variable by choosing a case between Britain and the United States on one extreme and Germany and Italy on the other, instead of picking Mexico, which is so extreme that it does not fit the scale at all. According to this criterion, one of the smaller European democracies could have been selected. Almond and Verba themselves indicate in *The Civic Culture* that the Scandinavian countries, the Low Countries, and Switzerland are in an intermediate position, although they base this judgment on their impressions of the political cultures of these democracies rather than their stability.[28] But Almond's earlier theoretical writings reveal that he considers them to be in a middle position on the structural variable, too.[29] Actually, it was the authors' original intention to include Sweden in the sample and a preliminary version of the interview was even tested there, but shortly afterward the decision was made to substitute Mexico.[30] No explanation for this substitution is given, and in retrospect it appears to have been an unfortunate decision [see page 22].

THE INDIVIDUALISTIC FALLACY

The danger of the ecological fallacy has been widely discussed among social scientists in recent years. The reverse of this fallacy, the individualistic fallacy, has not received as much attention. Erwin K. Scheuch defines it as the incorrect inference of the conditions of higher-order systems from observations on lower-level units.[31] Elsewhere he expresses this idea in slightly different words: "The danger of the individualistic fallacy is . . . present when the units of observation or counting are smaller than the units to which inferences are made." [32] This fallacy is a special danger in research based partly or wholly on survey data, such as *The Civic Culture*. Moreover, it is important to consider the individualistic fallacy in this connection because *The Civic Culture* serves as Scheuch's major example of the fallacy.

There are two aspects of *The Civic Culture* that Scheuch criticizes: the first consists of the uses to which specific questions in the survey are put, and the second concerns the overall relationship between civic culture and democratic stability. He points out that the individualistic fallacy arises when "ego's responses are treated as an observation of one's environment" or as "expert judgments." [33] Almond and Verba do use their questions in these ways, as they explicitly concede: "Though we only talk to individuals and do not observe them interacting with others or engaged in political activity, we do ask them about their attitudes toward others, their relations with others, their social activities, their organizational memberships, and their political activities." [34] Two points can be made in defense of this practice. One is that when Almond and Verba ask questions about the individual's environment, they are primarily interested in his subjective view of the environment instead of in its objective condition.[35] Second, to the extent that they do use individuals' responses as indicators of objective realities, this can be justified on the practical grounds that interviews with individual respondents are, as Scheuch himself admits, "vastly more economical" than direct observations of the units involved.[36]

A much more serious charge is Scheuch's allegation that *The Civic Culture* commits the individualistic fallacy with regard to the main theoretical question treated in the book, which concerns the relationship between civic culture and democratic stability. He states that between-nation differences in responses to questions such as what one is proud of in one's country are "used as expressing stability of political institutions." [37] In my opinion, this charge is without foundation. The political stability of the five democracies is observed and measured quite independently of the results of the surveys. Almond and Verba make this point rather weakly when they say that political structures "might better be studied by some means other than a systematic survey." [38] But later on they state clearly that the classification into more and less stable democracy is made "on the basis of data outside of our study," and that the survey findings "are intended, not to replace, but to supplement other materials used for the analysis of political systems." [39] Furthermore, they warn against two dangers with regard to the relationship between political culture and structure. One is the unwarranted assumption of congruence between these two variables.[40] The other is the tendency to circular reasoning. For instance, the stability of British democracy is often explained "in terms of a basic consensus among the British people. But what is the evidence for the consensus? If one looks carefully, it is often the existence of a stable political system." [41] This circularity involves an inference from political structure to political culture. What Scheuch has in mind is the reverse circularity—from culture to structure. Since these two variables are first observed and measured independently and only then related to each other, neither type of circularity occurs.

CAUSE AND EFFECT

The civic culture is generally treated as the independent variable by Almond and Verba, and democratic stability as the dependent variable. The distinction between independent and dependent variables is purely of an analytical nature and does not necessarily imply that the independent variable is the cause and the dependent variable the effect. Critics of *The Civic Culture*, especially Carole Pateman and Brian Barry, have alleged that it does make this assumption and that it neglects the reverse causal relationship: instead of, or in addition to, political culture influencing political structure, the structure may affect the culture.

For instance, Barry asks the following question, which, he implies, Almond and Verba fail either to ask or to answer: "Might one not argue that a 'democratic' political culture— such as the 'civic culture'—is the *effect* of 'democratic' institutions?" And he continues by saying that there is a prima facie case for answering this question affirmatively: "If you ask people whether they expect to get fair treatment from civil servants or whether they think they could do anything about changing an unjust government regulation, it is possible that their replies add up to a fairly realistic assessment of the actual state of affairs, rather than, say, projections onto political life of childhood conclaves about the best place for a picnic." [42] And he recommends that the question of the direction of causality be solved by studying the naturally occurring "crucial experiment" of a change in regime and by observing whether and when a change in political culture occurs. This is a good suggestion, although, as Barry concedes, it runs into the obvious difficulty that "undemocratic régimes may be hostile to surveys which ask people what they think of their rulers." [43] A more practical method would be to repeat the same survey in a democracy that shows either a clear improvement or an evident deterioration in its stability and effectiveness. Instances of the latter type are not difficult to find in the 1960s and 1970s—and they include Britain and the United States! Such an effort to establish the exact cause-and-effect relationship of the variables would be worthwhile in spite of the fact that, as I shall argue presently, Barry is mistaken when he attributes the hypothesis of unidirectional causality to Almond and Verba.

In a review of the literature on political culture and participation in which *The Civic Culture* figures prominently, Carole Pateman criticizes the prevalent "one-sided view of the relationship between political culture and political structure" in which these variables are regarded as cause and effect respectively. The reverse causal relationship is neglected by Almond and Verba, she states, as a result of their narrow definition of political culture in terms of *psychological* orientations.[44] Consequently, it tends to be forgotten that political culture and structure are "mutually interdependent and reinforcing." [45]

This last conclusion is precisely Almond and Verba's view, and to attribute any unidirectional hypothesis or theory to them entails a perplexing misinterpretation of *The Civic Culture*. First of all, Almond and Verba tend to use terms that are purposely neutral on the direction of causality to indicate the link between culture and structure: the civic culture is said to "fit," to be "particularly appropriate" for, and to be "most congruent" with a stable democracy.[46] Second, the fact that political structure can have an impact on political culture is implicit in the cognitive dimension of the concept of political culture. The political culture of a country consists of cognitive, affective, and evaluative orientations toward political objects, and the cognitive orientation consists of "knowledge of and belief about the political system, its roles and the incumbents of these roles, its inputs, and its outputs." [47] Obviously, such knowledge and beliefs cannot fail to be influenced by the objective realities to at least some extent. An earlier definition, which narrowly equates culture with psychological orientation, is indeed rather misleading, but this is corrected by the subsequent inclusion of its cognitive element.[48]

Third, there are several explicit statements about the mutual impact of political culture and structure: for instance, "if one is interested in political orientation . . . one must expect to study attitudes and behavior that are affected by structural characteristics." [49] Or take the following example:

> If the citizens in one country report more frequently than those in another that their government operates in their interest or that it can be trusted, this is a real difference in attitude with real consequences. But because the object of orientation differs (we are not, for instance, comparing, as one does in a single-nation survey, the attitudes of men and women toward the same government), it is more difficult to explain these differences in attitude toward government. To some extent the explanation may lie among the factors usually adduced in surveys to explain attitudes—social group, personality, other attitudes, and so forth. On the other hand, it may simply be that one government is *in fact more beneficial in its operation or more to be trusted* than another. Or it may be both—the two types of explanation do not necessarily contradict each other.[50]

The authors also indicate their conviction that such factors as socialization, political orientation, and political structure and process must be treated as "separate variables in a *complex, multidirectional system of causality*." [51]

A final point that should be noted is that Almond and Verba repeatedly argue that adult experience in politics rather than childhood socialization is crucial in the formation of political attitudes. Their initial hypothesis is that, in contrast to earlier work on political attitudes, their own research will show that "the importance . . . of *experience with the political system* has been seriously underemphasized." [52] The performance of political structures is therefore both a cause and an effect of the political culture.

ELITE POLITICAL CULTURE AND ELITE PERFORMANCE

The final question that must be asked about the relationship between the civic culture and democratic stability concerns the explanation of the empirical link between the two variables. Why are high degrees of democratic stability and of civic culture, which is a judicious mixture of activist and deferential orientations, mutually reinforcing? As far as one of the directions of causality is concerned—the impact of structure on culture—no lengthy explanations are required. A stable and effectively functioning democracy is bound to stimulate a high level of subjective political competence but also a much lower level of actual participation because of the infrequent necessity of becoming involved in politics when the system operates satisfactorily. With regard to the other direction of the causal link, the explanation is more complicated and controversial. Almond and Verba argue that the civic culture is conducive to stable democracy because there has to be a balance between the responsiveness and the power of governmental elites: "elite responsiveness requires that the ordinary citizen act according to the rationality-activist model of citizenship. But . . . if elites are to be powerful and make authoritative decisions, then the involvement, activity, and influence of the ordinary man must be limited." [53]

This means that the "governing behavior" of the elites is an intermediate variable in the causal link from civic culture to democratic stability. This factor is similar to what Almond and Verba call "role culture," especially the culture of those roles specialized in the formulation and execution of government policies.[54] But no attempt is made to measure elite political culture and behavior either by a systematic survey or by an impressionistic ranking or classification of the five national governmental elites. Because of the strong relationship between the civic culture and stable democracy, the implicit assumption is that in the Anglo-American countries in which the civic culture is approximated, the governing elites possess the favorable mixture of responsiveness and effective power. But as Carole Pateman rightly asserts, particularly with regard to the assumption of elite responsiveness, this is a "premise rather than a conclusion." [55] Her criticism on this score is, it seems to me, the substantive crux of her entire critique of *The Civic Culture*: the assumption that there is an optimal level of elite responsiveness in Britain and the United States disregards the possibility that more participation may both require and foster a higher level of responsiveness than this "optimal" one without necessarily having an adverse effect on governmental performance.[56]

Whether or not the balance between power and responsiveness can safely shift to the advantage of the latter component without endangering the overall stability of the system is an empirical question.[57] This question is not answered by Almond and Verba, but neither is it answered by their critics. In my opinion, Almond and Verba's assumption remains a good deal more plausible than the alternative hypothesis, which overlooks that too much participation may result in governmental immobilism and that increases in participation may well entail greater inequality of participation—and therefore increasingly unequal political influence—among individual citizens. The fact that the two countries where people have long enjoyed various forms of direct democracy such as the referendum and the initiative—Switzerland and the United States—are also rather conspicuously among the politically more conservative and socially and economically less equal Western democracies should serve as a warning to unrestrained advocates of participatory democracy.

The objection raised by Pateman concerns the explanation of the causal link between a *high* level of civic culture and a *high* level of democratic stability. There is a similar but, to my mind, more serious problem with regard to the explanation of the connection between *low* levels of both civic culture and democratic stability. Almond and Verba state that "perhaps the most significant deviations from the civic culture occur in the political participation and commitment" in the three relatively unstable countries. Especially in Germany and Italy, participant orientations are not well developed, and passivity and even alienation are pervasive attitudes. If the reasoning applied to the British and American cases is applied here, we would expect that such passive orientations would make the governmental elites powerful and effective but not very responsive. Britain is said to have a balance of active and passive roles but, in contrast to the United States, this balance in Britain "tends somewhat in the direction of the subject, deferential pole." As a result, there are "strong and effective governments" in Britain but "the extent of democracy" may be rather limited.[58] Germany and Italy tilt even more strongly in the direction of passive attitudes, and their governments should therefore be high on effectiveness and low on democratic responsiveness. In other words, this line of reasoning links an inadequate civic culture to the poor quality of democracy instead of to democratic instability. Since it is the latter empirical finding that must be accounted for, this explanation is not satisfactory.

The second explanation that Almond and Verba attempt stresses the elements of cooperativeness and social trust in the civic culture: "In comparison with Great Britain and the United States, Germany, Italy, and Mexico have relatively low levels of social and interpersonal trust." One effect of this deficiency is that it inhibits political participation. But what is more important is that, particularly in Germany and Italy, the "lack of ability to cooperate politically reflects a more general inability to enter political bargains, to collaborate, and to aggregate interests. The society divides up into closed and relatively hostile camps." [59] This argument generalizes from mass to elite attitudes and plausibly explains democratic instability and ineffectiveness in terms of the inability of the leaders of antagonistic political subcultures to reach agreement on public policy. The weakness of the second explanation is that it overlooks the possibility that the leaders of antagonistic subcultures will *not* behave antagonistically toward each other; as the writers belonging to the consociational school have emphasized, stable democracy may be achieved by means of cooperative arrangements at the elite level in spite of the division of the political culture into hostile subcultures at the mass level. It should also be pointed out that a passive and deferential mass political culture is congruent with consociational democracy because it gives the subcultural elites the necessary leeway to reach compromises on potentially explosive issues.[60] The best empirical examples of consociational democracy are Austria, Belgium, and the Netherlands. In a previous section, the omission of the smaller European democracies from *The Civic Culture* was criticized on the basis of Almond and Verba's own criteria. We now have an additional reason to regret that not at least one of the consociational democracies was included in the sample of countries.

FUTURE RESEARCH ON POLITICAL CULTURE
AND DEMOCRATIC STABILITY

What are the lessons to be drawn from *The Civic Culture* for possible replications of this study? With regard to those aspects of *The Civic Culture* that I have defended against its critics, I naturally offer no suggestions for change. My criticisms, of course, do imply that improvements should be made in future research of this kind, but they cannot be translated directly into specific recommendations. For instance, my suggestion to repeat basically the same survey in the same democracy with intervals of a few years when its stability is clearly either improving or deteriorating in order to establish the causal direction of the relationship between the civic culture and democratic stability requires either a knack for predicting political changes or a lucky break. With the advantage of hindsight, it is easy to say that a repetition of the 1959–60 surveys in Britain and the United States in, say, 1965, 1970, and 1975 would have yielded highly valuable data for the question under consideration, but it is far more difficult to have had the foresight to make such plans in 1960.

It is also much easier to indicate the countries that should ideally have been included in the 1959–60 sample of *The Civic Culture,* instead of or in addition to the five that were in fact included, than to decide which of these should be included in future cross-national studies. According to Almond and Verba's own estimate, one of the Scandinavian countries should have been included as a representative of intermediate democratic stability. Now, approximately two decades later, such advice can still be given, although experts would probably agree that the Scandinavian democracies should be rated higher on this dimension, especially in comparison with the Anglo-American countries. It would have been even more interesting to have had one of the consociational democracies in the original study. As a matter of fact, we now know that they reached their high point of consociational development in the late 1950s—exactly at the time that the five countries of *The Civic Culture* were surveyed—and that they have been declining since then.[61] The inclusion of one or more of them in a new survey would still be of considerable value, but the best opportunity has unfortunately been lost. Another suggestion would be to consider the inclusion of Canada and/or Israel, both of which have sufficient consociational characteristics to be regarded as semi-consociational democracies.[62] Finally, an obvious and unequivocal recommendation that can be made is that future surveys of mass political culture be complemented by explicit attempts to measure the intermediate variable of the patterns of elite political culture.

In conclusion, I should like to point out that my methodological critique as well as the few rather general recommendations that I have made here concern only a quite limited aspect of *The Civic Culture*. The main question that motivates and dominates it, and the treatment of which I have looked at from various angles, is the culture/structure relationship. But the answer to this question is not the major significance of the book; for one thing, it is not a totally surprising answer. The more important contribution of *The Civic Culture* is its painstakingly careful description and analysis of the details of five political cultures. Its purpose is not only hypothesis testing at the macro level but also, and more significantly, exploration and discovery of patterns of attitudes at the micro level. I agree with Philip E. Converse's judgment that a major accomplishment of *The Civic Culture* is its "success in objectifying some of the 'flavor' of differences in political culture which, like Mark Twain's weather, everyone has talked vaguely about but nobody has done much about in a systematic way."[63] It strengthens the structure of inference with regard to the key question, and it is also an achievement in its own right.

NOTES

1. Gabriel A. Almond and Sidney Verba, *The Civic Culture: Political Attitudes and Democracy in Five Nations* (Princeton, N.J.: Princeton Univ. Press, 1963), p. vii.

2. Ibid., p. 3.

3. Ibid., p. 493.

4. Ibid., p. 490 (italics added).

5. Brian Barry, *Sociologists, Economists and Democracy* (London: Collier-Macmillan, 1970), p. 50.

6. Almond and Verba, *Civic Culture*, p. 473; see also p. 479.

7. Robert A. Dahl, *Polyarchy: Participation and Opposition* (New Haven: Yale Univ. Press, 1971), p. 243. I apologize to Professor Dahl for bringing up this example once more after already having used it in two earlier papers; see Arend Lijphart, "Toward Empirical Democratic Theory: Re-

search Strategies and Tactics," *Comparative Politics* 4, no. 3 (April 1972): 427–28, and Lijphart, "The Comparable-Cases Strategy in Comparative Research," *Comparative Political Studies* 8, no. 2 (July 1975): 170. My excuse is that it is such a striking example. I should also like to emphasize that I agree with Dahl's decision to follow his own expert opinion instead of the mechanical outcome of the operationalization in this case.

8. Almond and Verba, *Civic Culture,* p. 74.

9. Barry, *Sociologists,* p. 50.

10. Almond and Verba, *Civic Culture,* p. 119.

11. Ibid., p. 440.

12. Ibid., pp. 218, 231.

13. Ibid., p. 257.

14. Ibid., pp. 455, 479, 497.

15. Ibid., p. vii.

16. Sidney Verba, "Germany: The Remaking of Political Culture," in Lucian W. Pye and Sidney Verba, eds., *Political Culture and Political Development* (Princeton, N.J.: Princeton Univ. Press, 1965), pp. 130–70.

17. Almond and Verba, *Civic Culture,* p. 119.

18. Stein Rokkan, review of *The Civic Culture* in *American Political Science Review* 58, no. 3 (September 1964): 677.

19. Almond and Verba, *Civic Culture,* p. 75.

20. It is striking how even quite serious critics miss obvious points in the books that they review. For instance, Barry remarks that "Almond and Verba do not explain the rationale of their choice of countries for study" (p. 52), although early in *The Civic Culture* (p. 12) the authors signal their intention to do so, and then devote no less than five pages to this question (pp. 36–41).

21. Almond and Verba, *Civic Culture,* pp. 9–10 (italics added).

22. Ibid., p. 37.

23. Ibid., p. 12; see also p. 55.

24. See Lijphart, "The Comparable-Cases Strategy," pp. 163–64.

25. Dahl, *Polyarchy,* pp. 232–33, 248.

26. Almond and Verba, *Civic Culture,* pp. 46, 509.

27. See, for instance, Giuseppe Di Palma, *Apathy and Participation: Mass Politics in Western Societies* (New York: The Free Press, 1970).

28. Almond and Verba, *Civic Culture,* p. 8.

29. Gabriel A. Almond, "Comparative Political Systems," *Journal of Politics* 18, no. 3 (August 1956), esp. pp. 392–93, 405.

30. Almond and Verba, *Civic Culture,* p. 48.

31. Erwin K. Scheuch, "Social Context and Individual Behavior," in Mattei Dogan and Stein Rokkan, eds., *Quantitative Ecological Analysis in the Social Sciences* (Cambridge, Mass.: M.I.T. Press, 1969), p. 138.

32. Erwin K. Scheuch, "Cross-National Comparisons Using Aggregate Data: Some Substantive and Methodological Problems," in Richard L. Merritt and Stein Rokkan, eds., *Comparing Nations: The Use of Quantitative Data in Cross-National Research* (New Haven: Yale Univ. Press, 1966), p. 164.

33. Scheuch, "Social Context and Individual Behavior," p. 139.

34. Almond and Verba, *Civic Culture,* p. 73.

35. Ibid., p. 70.

36. Scheuch, "Social Context and Individual Behavior," p. 140.

37. Ibid., p. 141.

38. Almond and Verba, *Civic Culture,* p. 68.

39. Ibid., pp. 74, 75.

40. Ibid., p. 34.

41. Ibid., p. 47; see also p. 50.

42. Barry, *Sociologists*, p. 51.

43. Ibid., p. 52.

44. Carole Pateman, "Political Culture, Political Structure and Political Change," *British Journal of Political Science* 1, no. 3 (July 1971): 292, 293.

45. Ibid., p. 302.

46. Almond and Verba, *Civic Culture*, pp. 473, 493, 498.

47. Ibid., p. 15.

48. Ibid., p. 14.

49. Ibid., p. 68.

50. Ibid., p. 65 (italics added).

51. Ibid., p. 35 (italics added); see also p. 473.

52. Ibid., p. 34; see also pp. 373, 489–99.

53. Ibid., p. 478.

54. Ibid., pp. 29–31.

55. Pateman, "Political Culture," p. 302.

56. High levels of political participation may also be advocated because participation is considered a value in its own right and regardless of its effect on elite power and indirectly on democratic stability, but this question is not at issue here.

57. See Stanley Rothman, "Functionalism and Its Critics: An Analysis of the Writings of Gabriel Almond," *Political Science Reviewer* 1 (Fall 1971): 254–58.

58. Almond and Verba, *Civic Culture*, pp. 493–95.

59. Ibid., p. 494.

60. Arend Lijphart, "Consociational Democracy," *World Politics* 21, no. 2 (January 1969), esp. pp. 221–22. See also the collection of writings on this subject edited by Kenneth D. McRae, *Consociational Democracy: Political Accommodation in Segmented Societies* (Toronto: McClelland and Stewart, 1974), and Hans Daalder's critical review "The Consociational Democracy Theme," *World Politics* 26, no. 4 (July 1974): 604–21.

61. Val R. Lorwin, "Segmented Pluralism: Ideological Cleavages and Political Cohesion in the Smaller European Democracies," *Comparative Politics* 3, no. 2 (January 1971): 163–67.

62. See Kenneth D. McRae, "Consociationalism and the Canadian Political System," in McRae, ed., *Consociational Democracy*, pp. 238–61, and K. Z. Paltiel, "The Israeli Coalition System," *Government and Opposition* 10, no. 4 (Autumn 1975): 397–414.

63. Philip E. Converse, review of *The Civic Culture* in *Political Science Quarterly* 79, no. 4 (December 1964): 593.

CHAPTER III

The Civic Culture:
A Philosophic Critique

Carole Pateman

The University of Sydney

EMPIRICAL DEMOCRATIC THEORY no longer constitutes the orthodoxy for writers on democracy that was the case when *The Civic Culture* was written, but its basic assumptions are still widely accepted. *The Civic Culture* provides one of the best single "case studies" from which to build a general critique of the postwar school of empirical theory through an understanding of the way in which these assumptions shaped conclusions about democratic theory and practice. There are, of course, many specific differences between individual theorists in the school, but these are overshadowed by a common theoretical perspective within which empirical findings are analyzed. Studies of empirical theory are also characterized, as in *The Civic Culture,* by the inclusion of a concluding chapter in which the significance of data on individual political attitudes

The initial work for this essay was completed while I was Visiting Fellow at the Department of Political Science, Research School of Social Sciences, Australian National University, and I am grateful to colleagues there for their hospitality and discussions. I should also like to thank Sandy Stewart, a fellow visitor to the Research School, for help in disentangling a few of the complexities surrounding "political culture," and especially to thank Gabriel Almond for his comments and criticisms of my arguments.   C. P.

and activities for "normative" democratic theory is addressed. The final chapter of *The Civic Culture* reflects the widespread confidence of the late 1950s and early 1960s in the Anglo-American political system, and is typical in its celebration of the role of political apathy and disinterest. Unlike some other examples of the genre, however, *The Civic Culture* contains evidence about the socialization process through which individual attitudes are developed. This evidence is crucial to a critique of empirical theory and to the development of a democratic theory that can move decisively beyond its theoretical inadequacy and political complacency.

Empirical democratic theory has been much criticized, but the critics and the empirical theorists have often tended to talk past each other on some fundamental issues. The critics wish to defend a tradition of "normative" democratic theory that is rejected as old-fashioned and, more importantly, unscientific, by the empirical theorists. The critics have tended to be timid in the face of the claims of "science" and "objectivity"—even though it has been remarked how rarely this scientific approach has produced critical conclusions[1]—and so have tended to neglect the task of tackling the empirical theorists on their own ground. The central claim that must be challenged is that, in the light of the data revealed by empirical investigations, it is indeed unrealistic to cling to traditional conceptions of democratic theory and the democratic citizen. Ironically, as *The Civic Culture* reveals, the interpretation of empirical data is one of the major weaknesses of empirical democratic theory. It is also a weakness that cannot be remedied without abandoning some basic assumptions of the theory. Despite the claims of empirical theorists, they have not produced a convincing account of the relationship between the pattern of attitudes and activity revealed in their findings and the political structure of the liberal democracies.

Empirical theorists have shown little curiosity about their own theoretical antecedents. Both sides of the controversy about democratic theory have been hampered by the widely accepted belief that there is a classical theory of democracy to be accepted, rejected, or, at the very least, drastically modified.[2] It is not difficult to see that the so-called classical theory can refer to either of two very different traditions of argument about the nature and place of popular participation in political life. The first is the classical liberal theory of constitutional, representative government, to which the empirical theory of democracy, following J. A. Schumpeter's conception of the democratic political method,[3] is direct heir. The second is the neglected classical theory of participatory democracy to be found, for example, in the writings of John Stuart Mill and, preeminently, Jean Jacques Rousseau. Because these two traditions have not been distinguished, the empirical theorists have shown little awareness that their arguments are a contemporary reworking of the liberal classical theory, which explains why their arguments received such an enthusiastic reception. It was not so much a new theory [4] as a mid-twentieth-century version of the liberal theory that developed as, and continues to be, the political theory of the Anglo-American system. Another consequence of the myth of one classical theory is that democratic theory has become identified with liberal theory, and the existing liberal democratic system—that is, liberal representative government plus universal suffrage—has become identified with democracy. *The Civic Culture* illustrates this confusion of two different political traditions. It is therefore not surprising that its critics have so often accused the allegedly scientific empirical theory of being essentially ideological and celebrating the status quo. It is true that in the preface Almond and Verba state that "our conclusions ought not to lead the reader to complacency about democracy in . . . Britain and the United States," yet their historical viewpoint, their interpretation of their findings, and the concluding chapter of the study—all invite the very complacency that they warn against.

One of the virtues of Almond and Verba's sociological approach is that,[5] in principle, they treat liberal democracy as a system and aim to elucidate the relationship between the civic culture and the political structure. They are not successful in this aim, however, because their theoretical perspective runs counter to any such endeavor. Liberal theory, on the one hand, focuses on the "institutional arrangements" stressed by Schumpeter, and treats the political culture as a given. The social inequalities of the political culture of the liberal democracies are treated as separate from, and irrelevant to, the formal equality of citizenship. On the other hand, because liberal theory is also essentially individualist, when, as in *The Civic Culture,* attention is directed to political culture, this is treated as a matter of individual attributes and attitudes that can be correlated with levels of political participation in abstraction from the political structure or institutional arrangements. The implicit adherence of empirical theorists of democracy to an individualist, liberal theory means that they are unable to recognize and discuss as *problems* some of the fundamental questions raised by their empirical findings.

The most important illustration of this failure is the persistent neglect of the significance of the relationship between class, or SES (socioeconomic status), sex, and "participatory" political orientations and political activity, which is one of the best-attested findings in political science and confirmed by the evidence in *The Civic Culture.* Almond and Verba do not ask why such a relationship exists, or what relevance it might have for their characterization of the civic culture as "democratic." Their findings are treated as one aspect of political reality that must be accepted, and, although the correlation between class and civic orientations is reported, it is presented only as a matter of individual attitudes and attributes that happen to be patterned in a specific manner. Yet the most striking finding in *The Civic Culture* is that civic culture is systematically divided along lines of class and sex. The relationship between such a culture and the formal equality institutionalized in the political structure is never confronted or seen as a problem. Or, to make this point in another way, the historical development of the civic culture is presented as if it were in fact as liberal ideology tells us that it is, the development of a system in which the political method works to the advantage of, and protects the interests of, all citizens. But *empirical* theorists should at least be able to ask whether the finding that SES is so closely related to civic orientations and participation casts doubt on that particular view of history.

One reason why empirical theorists' interpretation of their own evidence tends to go unchallenged is that the classic democratic theory, which suggests an alternative interpretation, is so neglected. Classic participatory democratic theory is grounded in an appreciation of the mutual interrelationship between political culture and political structure [6] and, because it embodies the traditional and normative view that a democracy is a system in which all citizens participate, it explicitly raises the character of the civic culture as a problem. As I shall show in this essay, however, a critical examination of the argument of *The Civic Culture* also reveals that the problem exists. The first sections of my discussion look at the historical perspective and conception of "political culture" in *The Civic Culture*. I then turn to the central problem of the evidence on political competence, its relation to SES and the rationality of political inactivity, and the three dimensions of political culture. Finally, the question of the democratization of the civic culture and the concept of civic participation are considered.

In the argument that follows I shall concentrate on the evidence in *The Civic Culture* about Britain and the United States of America because the authors take these countries as their model for, and see them as the main carriers of, the civic culture, and they see Britain as fundamentally important for its historical development.[7]

THE HISTORICAL PERSPECTIVE

One of the most striking features of the book is that although the civic culture is described from the opening sentence of chapter 1 as "the political culture of democracy," the meaning of democracy itself is never discussed. One reason for this omission, and for the way in which the civic culture is presented as a *problem,* is the historical perspective within which the civic culture is discussed. This historical perspective is not an unfamiliar one to readers of postwar democratic theory; it emphasizes the collapse of constitutional regimes between the wars and the threats to democratic stability posed by the development of totalitarian systems. Almond and Verba also stress the gradual development of the civic culture over a long period of time in Great Britain out of "a series of encounters between modernization and traditionalism" (page 7).[8] The traditional political orientations of citizens were fused with modern participatory orientations to form the nice balance of the civic culture, although the authors do not make clear when it was that the civic culture could unequivocally be said to have emerged. The problem about the civic culture, as posed by Almond and Verba, does not concern Britain and

America, where the civic culture already exists, and where it is taken for granted that the political culture is "democratic." Rather, the problem is that of the maintenance and strengthening of the civic culture in countries such as Italy, Germany, and Mexico (examined in *The Civic Culture*), where its existence is precarious, and also its future development in countries of the third world, where it does not yet exist.

There are two important consequences of this historical perspective for the arguments of *The Civic Culture*. First, by taking the findings from Great Britain and the United States on individual civic attitudes and social relationships as unproblematic, Almond and Verba are inhibited from asking questions about the implications of their data for the liberal democratic system and possible developments within it. The "participation explosion" (page 4) of the latter half of the twentieth century is relevant to the developing countries, not to Britain or the United States. Second, this particular perspective tells us very little about the historical background of the civic culture. Except for some extremely general remarks about the gradual emergence of the civic culture in Great Britain, there is little to be learned about its development or that of the idea of a "civic culture." The discussion is abstract and ahistorical because of the lack of a perspective placing the present conception of the civic culture in the context of the development of both Western, liberal-capitalist society, and the political theory of that society, namely, liberal theory.[9] Despite the resemblances between Almond and Verba's concern with the worldwide diffusion of the civic culture and the nineteenth-century British concern with the export of British political institutions, there is no appreciation in *The Civic Culture* of the historical continuity in the conception of the role of the citizen in liberal theory from the time of Hobbes and Locke, through nineteenth-century liberal theory, to empirical democratic theory of the second half of the twentieth century.

The main thrust of liberal theory has always been to give a well-defined but minimal role to the citizen. The focus has been on the role of representative government, or what Almond and Verba call, more broadly, the political elites. It also has to be kept in mind that liberal political theory developed as the theory of, indeed as part of, Western capitalist society. In

Schumpeter's words: "democracy in the sense of our theory of competitive leadership presided over the process of political and institutional change by which the bourgeoisie reshaped, and from its own point of view rationalized, the social and political structure that preceded its ascendency." [10] As liberal theory developed, the political role allotted to the citizen was extended from the complete nonparticipation of Hobbes's theory to the participation consequent upon the emergence of competitive elections and universal suffrage.[11] Yet there has been no substantial change in the basic structure of the theory, or in the conception of the citizen, within which this extension of participation has been encompassed. By the nineteenth century James Mill was calling a more popularly elected representative government "the grand discovery of modern times." [12] The argument became firmly established that regular competitive elections, or the sanction of loss of office, would ensure that representatives protected and furthered the interests of all citizens. Liberal theory became liberal democratic when it was recognized that the whole adult community must therefore exercise the sanction, and universal suffrage was admitted. The idea of popular control of political representatives is absolutely central to any theory of democracy (see page 476), but it must be emphasized that popular participation was added to liberal theory primarily as a way of placing a limitation on political representatives, not as something essential and valuable in its own right. Political participation is still seen as a necessary protective device, a cost that must be paid at least occasionally by some citizens, but ideally as seldom as possible; it is not an integral part of the individual citizen's life.

This brief sketch does, I hope, establish the historical antecedents of the arguments of *The Civic Culture*. Like most other postwar writers, Almond and Verba see "democracy" in liberal terms as the "political method" whereby "individuals acquire the power to decide by means of a competitive struggle for the people's vote." [13] Periodic electoral participation is crucial in ensuring that political elites actually are responsive to citizens; interelectoral pressure-group activity and other actions aimed at influencing governments are a supplement to this. The participatory democratic tradition argues that citizens should not merely vote for representatives but take part in actual political decision making. One would expect that revisions of democratic theory that deny the importance of an active role for citizens and stress the contribution of political apathy to the stability of the system would be concerned to take issue with participatory theory. However, the myth that there is only one classical theory of democracy has had the curious result that often, as in *The Civic Culture*, what is really being revised—if anything at all—is liberal democratic theory itself.

Almond and Verba's version of the classical myth is couched in terms of what they call the "rationality-activist" model of the pattern of political attitudes and political activity that would exist according to "the norms of democratic ideology" (page 473). The only specific source they give for this model is an American civics textbook (presumably written for school-children), but the important point is that, as described, the rationality-activist view is in no way incompatible with liberal democratic theory. The citizen has to be "involved and active in politics, informed about politics, and influential" (page 474), but this is involvement and activity *within* the existing liberal democratic system of competitive elections. Strangely enough, Almond and Verba remark that a democratic political system is one where "the ordinary citizen participates in political decisions" (page 178), and they talk of the citizen who is able to participate in nongovernmental areas of social life expecting to "participate in political decisions as well" (page 328). Not surprisingly, they give no indication of how such participation by the civic citizen of liberal democracies takes place, except in terms of the election of decision makers and attempts to influence (not participate in) their decisions. Earlier liberal writers were never very explicit about the standards of political activity and interest to which citizens should, ideally, conform, but it is clear that those standards were concerned with electoral participation. When Almond and Verba and other writers have looked at the results of empirical investigations into citizens' political orientations, they have argued that these show that the "rationality-activist" version of democratic ideology must have set standards that were "unreasonably high" (page 475). Democratic theory, that is, *liberal democratic theory,* should therefore be rewritten. Only minimal levels of activity and interest, and largely apolitical attitudes, are required from most citizens; anything more would threaten the smooth working of the political system.

Thus in *The Civic Culture* we find an account of the proper role of the democratic citizen that is concerned with the way in which the citizen's activity and participatory orientations are "balanced" or "managed" by subject and parochial orientations, so that citizens display the inactivity and deference that enables political elites to govern unhindered. Although the precise content of the balance is not specified,[14] Almond and Verba actually refer to the adherence by citizens to a belief in active citizenship and a belief that elites can be influenced by citizens as a "myth" (pages 183, 481). They add that if the myth is to be effective "it cannot be pure myth. It must be an idealization of real behavioral patterns" (page 485). But it is indeed a myth of participation that empirical democratic theory requires—not citizens' beliefs and actions that are reasonably held and grounded in the facts of political life. The civic culture of the "potentially active citizen" (page 481) must never become more than an unrealized potentiality. Provided enough citizens vote to keep the electoral machinery in operation and political elites alternating in office, the myth, it is claimed, is enough to ensure that elites act as they should in the interests of all the citizenry: "they act responsively, not because citizens are actively making demands, but in order to keep them from becoming active" (page 487).

The place of the civic citizen of the second half of the twentieth century remains, as it has always done in liberal theory, primarily the private sphere of life. Ordinary citizens, unlike political elites, enter political life only on special occasions, such as elections, or when their interests seem unusually and vitally threatened. The separation of the political sphere and popular political participation from other spheres of social life is a central structural feature of liberal theory and it works to obscure the mutual interaction of political culture and political structure on which *The Civic Culture* focuses. The contemporary version of the liberal conception of the citizen is nicely and revealingly stated by Dahl:

Among his [sic] resources for influencing officials, *homo civicus* discovers the ballot. . . . in fact he may doubt its value and rarely if ever employ it, . . . Or he may see the ballot as a useful device for influencing politicians. . . . But the chances are very great that political activity will always seem rather remote from the main focus of his life. . . . as a strategy to achieve his gratifications indirectly, political action will seem considerably less efficient than working at his job, . . . planning a vacation, moving to another neighborhood or city, . . . *Homo civicus* is not, by nature, a political animal.[15]

But this description of *Homo civicus* merely serves to raise the question ignored by the authors of *The Civic Culture*: What exactly is *democratic* about the civic culture? This is a question to which I shall return.

THE CONCEPTION OF "POLITICAL CULTURE"

Almond and Verba's conception of "political culture" is an essentially Parsonian one.[16] In general, they argue, "political culture" refers to individuals' "attitudes toward the political system and its various parts, and attitudes toward the role of the self in the system" (page 13). It is concerned with *"psychological orientation toward social objects* . . . the political system as internalized in the cognitions, feelings, and evaluations" of citizens. The political culture is the pattern formed by the social distribution of these attitudes (page 14). This suggests that the "civic culture" is a description of orientations as they presently exist, and this is also suggested by the overall argument of the study. But what exactly is the status of the "civic culture"? Is it a description? Or is it an abstract model of orientations that we should expect to find in the political culture of a democracy? The latter interpretation is suggested by the argument that certain countries can be more civic than others. As I shall indicate, one of the problems with *The Civic Culture* is that it hovers uneasily between these two possibilities.

Almond and Verba derive the threefold classification of the dimensions of "orientations" or "internalized aspects" of political culture from Parsons and Shils: cognitive orientations refer to "knowledge of and belief about the political system"; affective orientations to "feelings about the political system"; evaluational orientations to judgments and opinions that involve a "combination of value standards . . . with information and feelings" (page 15). If all three dimensions of political culture are kept in mind, some consideration of the mutual, dialectical inter-action of political culture and political structure cannot be avoided. The cognitive dimension, for example, refers to indi-viduals' knowledge and beliefs about the political structure; that is, it contains a built-in reference to the impact of struc-ture on culture. However, as will become clear when Almond and Verba's discussion of citizen competence is considered, they concentrate on psychological or affective orientations.

I argued above that it is the diffusion of the civic culture that is seen as a problem in *The Civic Culture*. It might appear, however, that there is a problem for the United States and Britain after all because, Almond and Verba claim, their investigation is directed toward the question of whether there is "a democratic political culture—a pattern of political atti-tudes that fosters democratic stability, that in some way 'fits' the democratic political system" (page 473). One of the most significant aspects of the problem of political stability is the "relationship between political culture and political structure," and an "assumption of congruence" between the two should be avoided (page 34). This is a very odd position for the authors of *The Civic Culture* to adopt. As Almond and Verba imply in their discussion of the gradual development of the civic culture, the political culture and political structure of the liberal democracies have developed together. Moreover, they take the United States and Great Britain as their model of "stable" democracies, and it is hard to see how this stability could have been maintained if political structure and political culture did not "fit" each other; it is the lack of such nice congruence that poses problems for stability in, say, Italy or Mexico. Almond and Verba seem to see neither how circular their arguments are nor that the problem of fit is hardly a problem at all.

Nor is it at all clear how the typology of political cultures, the parochial, subject and participant, and the "mixed" civic culture, presented in chapter 1, are derived. The authors state that "rather than inferring the properties of democratic culture from political institutions or social conditions, we have at-tempted to specify its content by examining attitudes in a number of operating democratic systems" (page 12). Yet their presentation of the civic culture is as much a logical inference from a conception of democracy as it is a result of empirical investigation. Indeed, it could scarcely be otherwise, since liberal democratic theory is the theory of the political system of the civic culture; it developed along with that system. It would be strange if a stable system did not exhibit a congruence between its political culture and political structure *and* a congruence between the actual pattern of citizens' political attitudes and those that the theory of the system tells us should exist. Thus the conception of a civic political culture appears to be a model that is derived from a specific conception of democracy—a model that would be confirmed in an empirical investigation of a system that is *ex-hypothesis* stable and democratic. Moreover, unless a specific conception of democracy is *already* at hand, how are we, or Almond and Verba, to know that the civic culture is not simply a participatory culture, but a participatory political culture *"plus something else"* (page 31)? In the absence of such a model, puzzlement arises and the notion of a civic culture appears arbitrary; "I am not even sure why we should regard the [civic] values as 'appropriate' or 'congruent' for such systems, other than because we have discovered them there." [17] That the civic culture is a mixed culture is both an assumption or a premise which structures the argument of *The Civic Culture* as a whole and a conclusion. The empirical evidence presented in the body of the study confirms the assumptions about the civic culture with which we begin in chapter 1—and these assumptions are then presented in chapter 15 as conclusions about the proper role of the citizen in a democracy.

In their opening discussion Almond and Verba state that the conception of political culture provides "the connecting link between micro- and macropolitics" (page 33), between individual political attitudes and the operation of the political structure. This seems to me to be a mistaken view of political culture. If, as Almond and Verba intend, one is going to investigate the interaction between culture and structure, it is difficult to see how political culture itself can provide a link when it is one side of the process to be investigated. Something else is needed to provide the link between political culture and structure, and to provide a basis for an explanation of their interaction. It is the notion of political socialization that serves as a "connecting link" between the micro and macro levels. I do not find Almond and Verba's discussion of political culture as a "link" easy to follow, but it seems to assume what they are trying to avoid, namely, the assumption of congruence between political culture and structure. The authors state that they have "defined the political culture as the particular incidence of patterns of political orientation in the population of a political system" (page 33). It is possible to establish "what propensities for political behavior exist in the political system as a whole, and in its various parts, among special orientation groupings (i.e., subcultures), or at key points of initiative or decision in the political structure (i.e., role cultures). . . . we can [locate] . . . attitudinal and behavioral propensities in the political structure of the system" (page 33).

If political culture itself is to provide a link with political structure, it would seem that it must in some sense be both separate from and congruent with, or even identical to, political structure. The latter is the Parsonian approach: Parsons has said that a "fundamental" proposition about "action systems" is that "their structure as treated within the frame of reference of action *consists* in institutionalized patterns of normative culture." [18] As I have already noted, Almond and Verba's use of "orientations" follows Parsons's essentially psychological conception (in fact if not in principle). Orientations (culture) are internalized and hence become institutionalized—or part of structure. Thus no question of lack of congruence arises. Nor does political socialization need to be seen as a link between culture and political structure, because no link is really needed. Or political culture, rather oddly, can serve as such.

On this account, political socialization appears as a neutral mechanism underlying the existing social distribution of orientations. There is no problem about the social pattern of political culture or the content of political orientations. The pattern remains only to be described and the notion of political socialization makes this possible. Two problems arise at this point: the civic culture as a model is required if the democratic culture is to be described. How else do we know what to look for? Second, the assumption has to be made that it is, in principle, open for any individual to be socialized into specific orientations. If there is no congruence between culture and structure, the actual pattern of political culture is a contingent matter. As I shall indicate in the next section, however, the evidence of *The Civic Culture* is that the distribution of individual political orientations is related to SES; it is not random. Therefore, the pattern of the civic culture does actually pose a problem. Why should such a relationship with class exist? But the approach of *The Civic Culture* requires that the civic pattern can only be described and accepted—not explained. No problem will be recognized, or an opening for an explanation emerge, all the time that political socialization is treated as a neutral notion to be applied externally by the political scientist or theorist, rather than the link between political culture and structure. From the system perspective of *The Civic Culture,* political socialization should be seen as a major mechanism in the maintenance of the "stable" distribution of the civic culture, which is so important for the smooth operation of the liberal democratic political method.

THE POLITICALLY COMPETENT CITIZEN

A democratic political culture, *The Civic Culture* states, "should consist of a set of beliefs, attitudes, norms, perceptions, and the like, that support participation" (page 178). I now want to review briefly some of the data of the study concerning the extent to which citizens feel that they ought to participate and feel themselves competent to do so. Almond and Verba argue that "belief in one's competence is a key political attitude," that the "self-confident citizen appears to be the democratic citizen" (page 257), and that beliefs about political competence have significant consequences for the operation of the political system. To the extent to which citizens feel politically competent they believe they can exert influence over political representatives, that is, "the degree to which governmental officials act to benefit [a] group or individual because the officials believe that they will risk some deprivation . . . if they do not so act" (page 180).

One important finding is that citizens who feel subjectively

competent are more likely than those lacking in a sense of
competence to be politically active and actually to try to influence political elites (see Table 3, page 188). It is found that
individuals' level of education and their occupational status
and sex make a difference as to how subjectively competent
they feel (see Fig. 1, page 206; Fig. 3, page 210; Table 7, page
212). At the local political level, the feelings of competence of
similar educational groups in the different countries "resemble
one another at least as much as, and perhaps more than, do
different educational groups within the same nation" (page
208). Almond and Verba comment on the general relationship
between feelings of political competence and higher levels of
education and occupational status that "whether or not one
believes himself [sic] capable of influencing a local or national
regulation depends a lot on who he is within his own country"
(pages 212–13).

When respondents were divided according to their scores on
a scale measuring feelings of subjective competence, it was
found that those who scored highest were the most likely to be
"committed to democratic values." They were, for instance,
more likely to believe that ordinary citizens should play an
active role in the community than those with lower scores. But
even among the highest-scoring respondents, the level of education made a difference; in the United States, for example,
53 percent of those scoring high on the subjective competence
scale with only primary education thought that citizens ought
to be active, compared to 67 percent of high scorers who had a
secondary, or above, level of education (see Table 7, page 256).
A similar pattern emerged among respondents questioned
whether or not they thought "elections were necessary"; those
most likely to agree were those highest in subjective competence
and with higher levels of education (see Table 6, page 254).
Such citizens, in both the United States and Great Britain,
were also the most likely to report a "feeling of satisfaction"
when they voted (see Table 3, page 243).

The Civic Culture also tells us something about the socialization process that tends to produce persons with feelings of subjective political competence. The essential question is "whether
there is a close relationship between the roles that a person

plays in nonpolitical situations and his role in politics" (page 327). Almond and Verba look at socialization within the authority structures of nongovernmental institutions and organizations and its relationship to feelings of political competence. Their argument is that participation inside nongovernmental authority structures can be seen as training for participation in politics and as developing politically relevant skills. Individuals can be expected to "generalize" from experiences outside political life to politics; if they have participated within nonpolitical authority structures they will expect to do so in the political sphere also (pages 327–28).

The authority structures with which Almond and Verba are concerned are those of the family, the school, and the workplace. Many studies of political socialization have concentrated on childhood socialization. It seems more plausible, however, to argue, with Almond and Verba, that, whatever the significance of the earliest years in the general formation of individual personality, later periods are of more importance for political life when, for example, the individual absorbs a multitude of informal exposures to politically relevant material. The young (and the mature) adult's experience and observation of political life itself or, to put it another way, the impact of the operation of the political structure on the individual's attitudes, is also very important. Authority structures especially relevant for political socialization in the later years are those that are "closer in time and in kind to the political system" (page 325). Socialization within authority structures "remote" from that of the political system may provide an "inadequate training for the performance of civic activities" (page 328). Almond and Verba are not, however, concerned with the extent to which, say, the authority structure of the workplace is *in fact* analogous to that of the political sphere, even though they do state that they are interested in how far a democratic political system depends on "democratic substructures in the society" (page 363). As with political competence, what they are investigating is how far individuals believe or feel that they were or are able to participate within nonpolitical authority structures, and how far this belief is "transferred" or "generalized" to the political sphere itself.

In the United States and Great Britain (as in the other three countries investigated), persons who score highest on the subjective competence scale are most likely to remember participating in the family or at school. For example, in Great Britain 70 percent of family participants scored high on the subjective competence scale, whereas only 51 percent of family non-participants did so (see Table 18, page 348; Table 20, page 354). This relationship does not hold, however, for those with education at the secondary level or above. In the case of both family participation and informal school participation, it is less educated respondents who "generalize" from these areas to political participation. Almond and Verba comment that persons with lower educational attainment are also less likely to have learned participatory skills, or the "norm that one ought to participate," and are less likely to interact with others in contexts where political competence is expected of them. For these individuals the family and the school are important areas of socialization because there are no other areas, such as higher education, that can "substitute" (pages 349, 355).

In the workplace, the relationship between participation and the sense of subjective competence is found at all educational levels (page 365), and the relationship is stronger than with the earlier forms of participation (pages 371–72). The authors state that the structure of authority in the workplace is "probably the most significant—and salient—structure of that kind with which the average man finds himself in daily contact" (page 363). Respondents who report that they are consulted about job decisions and feel free to protest about decisions in their workplace are likely to feel highly politically competent. But the kind of job that the individual does makes a difference; in the United States, of workers who report that they are consulted, 70 percent of those in unskilled jobs score high on the political competence scale, whereas 82 percent of those in white collar jobs do so (see Table 24, page 364). The importance of the relationship between workplace participation and the sense of subjective political competence becomes clearer when the data on the cumulative effect of participation are taken into account. Those respondents whose remembered participation in family or school is now reinforced by participation in the workplace are more likely to feel highly competent than those now in a nonparticipatory workplace (see Tables 26, 27, page 367).

It was, however, also found that workplace participation, unlike higher education, could not substitute for participation within the family or school. Where individuals could participate at their place of work, earlier participation still made a difference in levels of competence; on the other hand, for individuals with higher education, participation in the family and at school was largely irrelevant for feelings of political competence. Workplace participation is related to political competence through the "generalization" process, and differs from higher education—which, *The Civic Culture* suggests, is a complex process, involving such things as the learning of politically relevant skills, the "inculcation of participatory norms," and the placing of individuals in contexts where participation is expected. Higher education, Almond and Verba argue, is a "many-sided experience" which can "increase an individual's potentiality to participate" (pages 370–71).

Another area of adult political socialization is voluntary associations—"small political systems" (page 313)—which are also of great importance as mediators between the individual and political elites. Those with higher education in America and Britain, as in the other three countries, are most likely to be organizational members (see Table 4, page 304), and membership of voluntary organizations is associated with a high score on the political competence scale. Members who belong to organizations that they regard as political are more likely to be high scorers, and so are persons in such organizations with education of at least secondary level (see Table 6, page 308). Almond and Verba also investigated differences between active and passive organizational members, for, as they note, some large organizations may appear very remote to their members, and passive members may receive little or no training in participation. It is the most active members who are likely to be highly subjectively competent (and again there is a relationship with levels of education), and membership of more than one organization has a cumulative effect on political competence (see Table 12, page 317; Table 14, page 321). These data lead the authors to comment that "pluralism, even if not explicitly political pluralism, may indeed be one of the most important foundations of political democracy" (page 322).

THE CIVIC CULTURE AND SES

There are two major and related failings in Almond and Verba's discussion of political competence and its significance for democracy. First, no explanation is offered for the striking relationship that emerges between SES and feelings of political competence. The concluding commentary of *The Civic Culture* is conducted as if the nice balance of the civic culture rested on a random distribution of the appropriate orientations among all citizens. Thus the social pattern of the civic culture is regarded as unproblematic. Second, the question of how this pattern interacts with the political structure is never answered. The aim of *The Civic Culture* is to investigate this relationship in a more exact and systematic fashion than earlier discussions of "national character," and Almond and Verba state that much of the existing literature "fails to make the connection between the psychological tendencies of individuals and groups, and political structure and process" (page 33). But, because *The Civic Culture* remains within the liberal theoretical framework, it shares in this failing; in the final chapter the pattern of the civic culture is counterposed against, not related to, the operation of the political structure of liberal democracy.

Almond and Verba regret the fact that *The Civic Culture* contains no index of the SES of respondents' parents, but, they continue, it can be assumed that the individual's level of education is related to the SES of parents (page 334)—and, it might be added, to the individual's own future status. As illustrated above, *The Civic Culture* reveals a consistent relationship between levels of political competence and levels of education, and, where this is considered, occupational status. This relationship might have been expected. Almond and Verba tend not to relate their findings to other studies (except in a general sense for the purpose of casting doubt on the "rationality-activist" model of the citizen) but the connection between SES, or class, and political participation was well established before the publication of *The Civic Culture*.[19] Moreover, ordinary observation of political life in the liberal democracies would suggest such a relationship. Almond and Verba, as noted, remark that whether citizens feel competent depends on "who they are," and they also refer, for example, to "the sharp differences in political attitudes that one observes among respondents from various social backgrounds" (page 337). They even go so far as to state that "the educated classes possess the keys to political participation and involvement" and that citizens of low educational attainment "tend to constitute subject and parochial subcultures" (pages 381, 386), but their discussion of the findings ignores the significance of this. In the aggregation of data, and in the conclusions of *The Civic Culture,* it is assumed that all citizens can be treated equally as "carriers" of the civic political culture.

Throughout *The Civic Culture* it is also assumed that there are no problems in talking about *the* political culture or *the* civic culture of Britain and the United States. The implication is not only that there is a model of the civic culture at hand, but also, that the model is relevant across the whole community. Yet the finding that the orientations of the civic culture are distributed according to SES suggests that, if there are not two political cultures, then the civic culture is, at the least, a systematically *divided* political culture. This is not only a matter of "subcultures," or random groupings sharing the attributes of the civic culture to a different extent, but a broad social differentiation of upper and lower SES groups or classes. The nice balance of the civic culture, set out in the final chapter of the book is, in fact, a balance based on the virtual absence of working-class citizens from political life. The balance rests on the division between the civic orientations of predominantly upper SES citizens (and it should not be forgotten that political elites tend also to be drawn from this same background) and the less civic political culture of the bulk of the citizenry.

That the orientations of the civic culture are found mostly among individuals from higher SES backgrounds, and that it is also these individuals who are likely to belong to voluntary associations and to be politically active, is not a finding that *empirical* theorists of democracy can take for granted. Such findings suggest that political apathy is not, as one writer dismissively claimed, "nobody's fault" [20]—so that no question of an explanation arises—but that it is a socially structured and

maintained phenomenon; what might be called a nonparticipation syndrome exists.[21] It is precisely this syndrome that
needs to be explained; why lower SES—and female sex—
lack of civic orientations, and political inactivity tend to be
associated.

The findings of *The Civic Culture* suggest that an explanation, and hence an account of the "stability" of the division of
the civic culture, should be looked for within the socialization
process inside the authority structures of everyday life. This
explanation depends on the notion of political socialization as
the link between political culture and political structure, and
as an integral part of their mutual interaction.

Citizens from lower SES backgrounds are unlikely to participate in family and school (although within this group the relationship between participation and political competence holds)
and, most importantly of all, in view of the closeness of the
authority structure of the workplace to political life, they tend
to go into the unskilled, blue-collar, and routinized white-collar
jobs where participation is least likely to occur. Thus, at all
stages in the socialization process, their lack of a sense of
competence receives further reinforcement. Nor are these lower
SES citizens likely to go on to receive higher education, which
"substitutes" for participation in family and school. The very
nature of the workplace participation with which Almond and
Verba are concerned (and I shall comment further on this)
makes it a very weak competitor with the many-sided advantages that higher education brings—not the least of which is
that higher education also leads to occupations where workplace participation can be expected. The cumulative effect of
the political socialization process for most lower SES citizens
is that it "fits" them for their place, a not very "civic" place,
in the liberal democratic political culture. It allows them to
occupy the politically inactive side of the balance of the civic
culture.

The difference between SES groups is not the only systematic
division of the civic culture to emerge from the data of *The
Civic Culture*. The balance of the civic culture is also based
on sex. The civic culture is a male culture. The findings show
that women (in all countries) generally rank lower than men
on all the indices of political attitudes and activity associated

with the civic culture (pages 388–97). Why is there such a division between the sexes? This can, in part, be explained by the differing socialization of men and women.[22] In both Britain and America, women are less likely than men to participate in the family and at school, are less likely to go on to higher education and, when they enter the paid labor force, are much less likely to have higher status jobs and experience of workplace participation. Thus women, too, will tend to be on the inactive side of the civic balance. Nevertheless, Almond and Verba state that in the United States and Britain "politically competent, aware, and active women seem to be an essential component of the civic culture" (page 399). Once again, they are switching to the civic culture as a model; compared to women in the three other countries investigated, women in the United States and Britain appear as more active, or civic. Yet, as a description of the Anglo-American political culture, the civic culture remains sexually divided, and it is this fact that poses a problem—even though *some* active women might be needed, just as *some* active men are required if there is to be a balanced culture.

Earlier, I criticized Almond and Verba for circular arguments but, in one sense, their argument is not circular enough. Nowhere in *The Civic Culture* is there an explanation of the circle of the nonparticipation syndrome, or the relationship among low SES, female sex, lack of civic orientations, and low levels of political participation. The implicit assumption is that the correlation is a contingent matter. Nor is the relationship between the social inequalities underlying the pattern of the civic culture and the formal political equality of liberal democracy confronted; it remains a fortunate coincidence, and Britain and America are happy countries, because the democratic civic culture and democratic political institutions are found together.

In view of the fact that the civic culture is a political culture divided on the basis of SES and sex, the question that I posed earlier must be asked again: What is democratic about the civic culture? The answer can only be: very little at all, except that it encompasses universal suffrage. The civic culture is a democratic culture that reverses the central focus of democracy since its orgins in ancient times, although it retains the traditional assumption that democracy can exclude half of humankind. *Democracy* refers to a political system based on an active and central role by the people, the *demos,* in political life and political decision making. The civic culture rests not on the participation of the people, but on their nonparticipation. Its political focus is on the role of the upper SES (male) citizens, as participants and decision makers. The balance of the civic culture is one that allows these elites "to get on with governing" in the absence of a politically active people. The responsiveness of elites, necessary in a democracy, is ensured, it is claimed, because there is a *potential* for activity by citizens, not because they are or need to be active.

Almond and Verba are able to characterize the civic culture as "democratic" because they are implicitly falling back on the identification of liberal and democratic theory, and the model of the civic culture that this identification supplies. Moreover, liberal theory, from Locke's government of property holders, through James Mill's references to the wise and virtuous middle classes, to the "civic" citizens of the present study, has always argued that it is middle- and upper-class males who are best "fitted" for political participation and decision making. *The Civic Culture,* and other empirical theories of democracy, may parade this argument in a scientific costume, but what they are doing is offering us a more sophisticated but very familiar answer to the problem of how liberalism can accommodate universal suffrage, without disturbing social inequalities or the predominant political role of the (male) middle class. The approach of *The Civic Culture* obscures the need to ask important questions concerning not just the stable maintenance of the balance of the civic culture, but whether the implicit liberal model of the civic culture is the only feasible model of civic political life, and the possibility of democratic development of the civic culture.

I shall turn to the latter questions later. To prepare the way it is necessary, first, to say something more about political socialization and the interpretation of the findings of *The Civic Culture.* So far I have followed Almond and Verba's discussion and have looked in only one direction, from culture to political structure, and have emphasized the affective dimension of the civic culture, the subjective feeling of political competence. As their own introductory discussion of political culture argues, however, there is more than one dimension involved, and furthermore, if the relationship of political culture and political structure is our concern, then some attention must be paid to the impact of structure on culture.

THE DIMENSIONS OF POLITICAL CULTURE AND
THE GENERALIZATION ARGUMENT

There are many passing references in *The Civic Culture* to the impact of political structure, but, as with the relationship between SES and civic orientations, its significance for the civic culture is not pursued. Nor are two dimensions of the three-fold classification of the political culture, the evaluative and the cognitive, given more than passing attention.

Almond and Verba state that they do not wish to deny "the importance of the political system itself as a source of individuals' attitudes toward that system" (page 368), but the source is never given due weight. In Britain and America individuals who score high on the political competence scale are most likely to express "a general attachment to the political system" (page 251; also Table 5). They also are likely to "believe that a democratic participatory system is the proper system to have" (pages 254–55; also, Tables 6 and 7). The differences in extent of "normative allegiance" to their political systems among political competents in the five countries, as Almond and Verba point out, reflect the history of each country. Nevertheless, the authors fail to take into account the evaluative dimension of political culture, and the learning of political norms during political socialization, in their discussion. I have argued that the civic culture as a model is implicitly derived from liberal theory, but citizens of the Anglo-American liberal democracies have their own, albeit often not well formulated, models of the proper role of the citizen; they learn about liberal theory, the theory of their own political system, during the socialization process. The abstract nature of much of Almond and Verba's discussion of the civic culture is related to their neglect of the role of liberal theory or ideology in the stability of the interaction of political culture and structure. It is not only academics who identify democracy with liberal democracy. Almond and Verba's presentation of a divided civic culture as one democratic culture gains plausibility because the division is encompassed within a general acceptance of the existing system as "democracy." [23]

Once the evaluative dimension of political culture in Britain and America is considered, the relationship between the sense of political competence and the political structure becomes more complex than is suggested in Almond and Verba's analysis. The question that needs to be asked is whether or not the replies to questions designed to measure feelings of competence might also be reflecting an acceptance of the "norms of democratic ideology," or the evaluative dimension of political culture. Respondents might be replying on the basis of what they have learned of liberal theory during the political socialization process, what they have learned about how the political system ought to work, and what they are held to be able to do if faced, for example, with the prospect of an unjust law.[24] Feelings of competence are likely to develop in a complicated fashion, to be closely linked both to the citizen's understanding of the liberal democratic theory of his or her political role, and to the citizen's own experience of, and observation of, the working of the political system.

The possibility that the evaluative dimension is relevant to replies to questions aiming to elicit information about feelings of competence illuminates certain features of the findings of *The Civic Culture*. Respondents were asked what they thought they could do if their national legislature or local government was considering a law they regarded as harmful or unjust, and whether, if they atttempted to change it, they thought they would succeed or not. The fairly high proportion of citizens who see themselves as politically competent might appear to reflect, as Almond and Verba remark, "a somewhat unrealistic belief in their opportunities to participate" (page 182). If, however, a sense of competence is not the only thing that is being tapped, the proportion is less remarkable. Furthermore, Almond and Verba themselves are not entirely unambiguous in their view of political competence. They make the significant statement that someone who has participated in nongovernmental areas of social life is more likely *"to accept the belief* that he is a competent citizen" (page 369, italics added). It is not that such participants' beliefs that they are politically competent are reasonably held on the basis of their experience of and assessment of the political system. Instead, they are likely to accept the ideological assumption that citizens are able to influence political elites. And that is a rather different matter. It is, though, quite in keeping with Almond and Verba's view of the belief in citizens' political influence as a myth which "whether true or not, . . . is believed" (page 487).

The third, cognitive, dimension of political culture is important for Almond and Verba's argument that political competence is rooted in a process of "generalization" by individuals from their experiences of participation or nonparticipation in family, school, and workplace. This implies that individuals arrive at their political beliefs in disregard of the political system. Their beliefs are based purely on their nonpolitical experiences. This argument, even given the doubts about the rationality of ordinary citizens that have so exercised political scientists and political sociologists, is rather difficult to swallow. There is no doubt that such experiences are important in developing the individual's general self-confidence and abilities for effective action in social life, but this is not to accept the argument that the feeling of political competence is based on no more than "projections of . . . underlying disposition toward all authority." [25] One obvious additional factor is that individuals may believe what they are taught about the liberal democratic political system; another is that they may autonomously come to an assessment of their political system as more or less responsive to any attempt by them to participate and to exercise influence on elites.

Almond and Verba do touch upon the latter factor (e.g., see discussion on page 368) but they do not consider the relationship of this cognitive dimension of political culture to their generalization argument. One interesting question about the civic culture is why the large gap exists between the proportion of respondents who feel politically competent and the proportion who have actually tried to influence political elites. In the United States 67 percent of citizens feel politically competent, and in Great Britain, 57 percent; but only 33 percent and 18 percent, respectively, have actually tried to influence their local elites (see Tables 2, 3, pages 186, 188). Almond and Verba's interpretation of, and explanation for, this gap is that it is a necessary ingredient in the "balance" of the civic culture to "allow governmental elites to act" (page 481). Individuals believe in the myth of citizen influence, or in the "values associated with a democratic system" (page 257). It is argued, as noted earlier, that belief in this myth is sufficient to ensure popular control of political elites. In other words, the underlying assumption of Almond and Verba's argument is that the system actually works as liberal theory tells us that it should, and that citizens believe this to be the case.

This is why Almond and Verba can suggest that it is rational for many of those who feel competent to act not to do so. There is no need for them to act on the basis of the generalization that they make from experiences in nonpolitical areas of social life. To expect to find anything but a large divergence between political competence and political activity is to set our standards of citizenship "unreasonably high." Almond and Verba argue that "standards" and "theories of politics" should be "drawn from the realities of political life" (page 475). This implies that "the realities" are there, self-evidently, to be drawn upon. But before anything conclusive can be said about standards, a convincing interpretation and characterization of reality itself is required, in particular the reality of the close relationship between competence and SES.

Almond and Verba argue that widespread failure to act politically is connected to the costs involved, which usually means that "it may just not be worth it" to participate (page 476). Citizens have many important nonpolitical interests and, given the time and effort required to engage in the complex business of political activity, it is irrational for citizens to pay the cost of doing so (page 475)—especially when the myth of competence works for them. It is true that individuals always have to make a choice about which activities they are to undertake, but it really is remarkable that "reality" happens to be such that "rationality" works so neatly in a class-based (and sex-based) fashion. It is not a random cross section of citizens who find it "rational" not to pay the "costs" of participation, but lower SES citizens. The problem of the "disappearing" competents is much more complicated than Almond and Verba lead us to believe. The balance of the civic culture is between the rationality of the working-class (and female) tendency not to be politically active, and the male and middle-class rational participation. For the latter, political activity may be regarded as a benefit, not a cost. A. O. Hirschman, for example, cites the case of stockholders who prefer to use their stock to try to influence corporations, rather than "exiting" from them.[26] Stockholders, like other recent activists on public goods issues, tend to be drawn from middle-class backgrounds, and thus fit neatly into the balance of the civic culture and divided rationality about political activity.

Why should there be such a division among citizens? The socialization process examined in the last section has thrown some light onto this. The cognitive dimension of political culture suggests another explanation: there may be a differential evaluation of the political system by members of different SES groups. Hence it would be rational for them to act differently. Indeed, replies of respondents from different SES backgrounds to questions designed to measure feelings of political competence and other orientations suggest that this differential evaluation exists. The replies of working-class citizens indicate skepticism that the system actually operates as it is held to.[27] Thus a straightforward explanation of political inactivity is available—providing that the correlation between SES and participation is not forgotten. Working-class citizens believe that participation "may just not be worth it," and moreover, their withdrawal from political life is legitimized by the liberal conception of the "naturally" inactive citizen.

Almond and Verba's argument completely neglects the association between class and participation and implies that social status is irrelevant to which side of the balance a citizen occupies, or to the citizen's view of the rationality of action or inaction. That class-based differences in evaluation of the political system are rational has now received confirmation from *Participation in America,* a large-scale empirical study which shares an author, Sidney Verba, with *The Civic Culture.* The study finds that the responsiveness of political elites, or "concurrence," goes disproportionately to the most politically active citizens, to the upper SES groups. The general conclusion of the study is that *"participation helps those who are already better off."* [28] The position of those who are already socially advantaged is maintained and reinforced through political participation, and the empirical data recorded in *The Civic Culture* reflect this basic fact. It is no surprise that feelings of political competence, political activity, and allegiance to the liberal democratic system and to "democratic norms" are closely correlated with high SES; middle-class citizens have good reason to be full members of the civic culture. The real surprise is that empirical theorists of democracy have exhibited so little curiosity about the social character of the balance of the liberal democratic political culture. Neglect of the evaluative and cognitive dimensions of political culture has led to a simplified view of the individual's orientations, especially those of working-class citizens and women. Although upper SES citizens (especially males) can appear as unambiguously civic citizens, the orientations of other citizens are a contradictory mixture, reflecting both a "rational" evaluation of the operation of the political system and the worth of participation, and an acceptance of the "values associated with a democratic system." In Britain and the United States "the uneducated tend to share with the educated a common affective and normative allegiance to the political system" (page 387), but this is encompassed within a common identification of democracy with the existing system. Citizens from all classes learn something of liberal ideology, and the argument of *The Civic Culture* gives us no help in disentangling the various dimensions of citizens' responses which apparently measure their feelings of competence.

It took nine years from the publication of *The Civic Culture* for a major investigation to appear that was specifically focused on the relationship of social inequality to liberal democracy. Empirical democratic theorists have failed to ask the questions, not difficult or obscure questions, that empirical findings have demanded, and still demand. In the late 1970s it is no longer so easy to ignore the significance of the well-documented connection between SES and political participation, nor is it so easy to ignore the question of the distribution of the "responsiveness" of elites. It was not that inequality, poverty, and discrimination did not exist at the end of the 1950s—writers of that period could have paused and wondered how the political system actually looked to ordinary citizens, what political participation actually meant to them (a few of them did so) —but inequalities were not then forced to the attention of academic writers as they have been since the dramatic events of the mid-1960s. A few riots, lootings, sit-ins, and protests even from *women* concentrate the mind wonderfully. But what is still not clear is whether they sufficiently concentrate the minds of empirical theorists looking at political culture or at aspects of social inequality through the spectacles provided by liberal theory.[29]

Despite the aim of the study, liberal democracy is not treated in *The Civic Culture* as a complex system. Social inequality, or the civic culture, is not systematically related to the operation of the political structure and the maintenance of a stable system. Rather, the myth of citizenship is both presented as a myth and taken as an accurate characterization of liberal democracy, so that the evidence revealing the socially divided nature of the civic culture can be glossed over. Empirical democratic theory, and the argument of *The Civic Culture,* thus mystifies and obscures, rather than clarifies, the significance of its own data, and fails to explain why there is a fit between the balance of the civic culture and the political structure of liberal democracy.

THE DEMOCRATIC DEVELOPMENT
OF THE CIVIC CULTURE

Almond and Verba see the further development of the civic culture primarily as a matter of its diffusion to countries outside the liberal democracies. But there is also an important question to be asked about its future development in Britain and the United States; namely, whether the civic culture can be shared by the whole of the citizenry, or whether a culture divided by SES and sex is the best approximation to a democratic culture that can be achieved. The crucial problem then arises of how a democratization of the civic culture might be achieved.

In their discussion of "the future of the civic culture," Almond and Verba emphasize education as a possible substitute in the new nations for the long development of the civic culture in the liberal democracies. The importance of education, especially higher education, and its relationship to feelings of political competence have already been indicated. Schooling in the liberal democracies, however, does not do a great deal to cut across the class and sex divisions of the civic culture; in fact, it is now one of the major channels for its reinforcement. Although development of the schooling systems of the new nations may provide a shortcut toward a liberal civic culture, in the developed world schooling, in its present form, is unlikely to provide an avenue for the *democratic* development of the civic culture.

Almond and Verba argue that, in the new nations, formal education might be supplemented by developing "other channels of political socialization" (page 502). No more than minor adjustments are required to the civic culture in Britain or the United States; the former could absorb an increase in the participatory orientations, and the latter an increase in the deferential orientations. The crucial point about this suggestion, however, is that it is presented as an adjustment within the orientations of single individuals. Indeed, the final chapter of *The Civic Culture* refers almost exclusively to the "mixture" of orientations of *each individual,* rather than to the social pattern of the "balance" of the civic culture.[30] However, the mixture of orientations is *not* randomly distributed across all individuals; middle-class males are likely to be "participant" citizens, whereas "parochial" and "subject" orientations tend to be characteristic of working-class females. The individualist theoretical perspective of *The Civic Culture* persistently obscures the class division of the civic culture. Yet it is the social (class and sex) balance or mixture of the culture that is basic to its stable fit into the political structure—as the empirical data presented by Almond and Verba clearly reveal. The authors, however, ignore their own findings and, when they briefly turn from the balance of orientations within individuals, their only comment about the social pattern of the civic culture is that "some individuals believe they are competent and some do not; some individuals are active and some are not" (page 485). Hidden behind that "some" are the systematic social divisions of the civic culture.

The argument of *The Civic Culture* cannot encompass democratic development of the political culture of America and Britain. If participant orientations were to be spread across the whole population, the balance of the civic culture would disappear; it "*depends upon the inconsistencies* between political norms and perceptions, . . . and political behavior" (page 482). But, as I have shown, the middle class tend not to be, and have no reason to be, "inconsistent" in their political lives. They feel competent, allegiant, and are likely to be politically active. It is working-class citizens who are most likely to show a discrepancy between their orientations and their behavior. To change the relevant balance across class and sex, to democratize the civic culture, would therefore require some radical changes in the institutional structure of liberal democracy; the divided culture and the structure have developed together as a complex "democratic" system, with its appropriate "channels of socialization." A democratization of the civic culture, a change in the balance, therefore implies a democratization of the authority structures of liberal democracy.

The empirical findings presented in *The Civic Culture* lead to this conclusion. High levels of the feeling of competence are associated with participation in everyday life, but at present low SES citizens and women are unlikely to have opportunities to participate, especially in the workplace. If, as Almond and Verba argue, pluralism is an important foundation of liberal democracy, *democratic pluralism,* or the democratization of everyday life, is equally important for the development of a democratic political culture, and as a basis for participatory democracy.

There is now a considerable body of additional evidence to support the evidence of *The Civic Culture* on the importance of the authority structure of the workplace for more general political attitudes, and the impact of participation within organizations and associations of various kinds on feelings of competence.[31] It is particularly noteworthy that Almond and Verba's workplace "participation" took place within the existing nondemocratic authority structure of capitalist enterprises (although they imply that the workplace can be regarded as a "democratic substructure"). Their respondents were asked whether or not they were "consulted" about decisions concerning their jobs, and whether or not they felt free to protest about such decisions. This is a very weak and minimal sense of participation, at best amounting to no more than pseudo-participation.[32] Almond and Verba, however, are not alone in finding that even pseudoparticipation does have wide-ranging psychological consequences for those involved.[33] For this reason participatory techniques have been used for group therapy purposes, and "participative" management is now well established as an advanced capitalist management technique, a technique that does not require any changes in the overall authority structure of the enterprise. Nevertheless, the relationship between the weakest forms of participation and levels of the sense of political competence shows that the democratization of the workplace is a necessary basis for the diffusion of participatory political orientations throughout the population. It would also provide a training ground, in a familiar context, for participation in democratic political life.

A feeling of political competence is not, however, sufficient for active citizenship. As I have already argued, participation must also be worthwhile, and this raises some complex and important questions about the implications of workplace democracy. Empirical theorists of democracy have recently begun to turn their attention to participation in the workplace, but their discussions illustrate why many radicals are suspicious of, or opposed to, schemes to increase participation. Many recent discussions suggest that workplace participation may merely extend the divided civic culture or consolidate social inequality over a wider area, rather than changing the balance and extending democracy. Robert Dahl, for example, now argues that industrial democracy can form part of polyarchy, or liberal democracy. In *After the Revolution?* he presents workplace democracy as "one solution too obvious to be ignored" to the problems generated by the "corporate leviathans" and the "appropriation of public authority by private rulers." [34] Dahl also argues that if individuals found that participation "contributed to their own sense of competence and helped them to control an important part of their daily lives, then lassitude and indifference toward participation might change into interest and concern." He is pessimistic about the extent to which interest would develop, however, and suggests that it is most likely that "technicians and lower executives" rather than blue-collar workers would participate.[35]

The evidence on participation in the workplace, including evidence from Yugoslavia, supports Dahl's pessimism. The social pattern of participation resembles that in wider political life, with higher-status, better-educated, and skilled males most likely to be active. Before the conclusion is accepted that, after all, lower SES individuals and women are "naturally" apolitical creatures, and the divided civic culture is the best approximation to "democracy" that can be achieved, some further questions must be considered, however.

Dahl is not concerned with the development of a democratic political culture, but with the power of "private rulers." This is a fundamental problem, but it is not self-evident that the problem discussed in this essay is solved if private capitalist rulers are replaced by an elected central managing board, or a workers' council. Of course, this would be a very real change in the capitalist organization of production (especially given the extensive interrelationship between the corporate leviathans and the liberal democratic state apparatus). Nevertheless, to elect a government in each enterprise is to introduce liberal democracy into a new context: and it is precisely the fact that *liberal* democracy and the divided civic culture fit each other that gives rise to the problem of *democracy*. There is no good reason to suppose that the introduction of an elected council in the enterprise will of itself have very different consequences from liberal elected representative government in the state; it will tend to provide another avenue through which the already socially advantaged may participate.

Investigations of the Yugoslav system of workers' self-management tend to bear this out. Sidney Verba (with Goldie Shabad) has recently investigated participation in workers' councils in Yugoslavia and has found that a close relationship between SES and participation exists: "the better-educated and more affluent citizen is more likely to become a member of a workers' council," although more skilled blue-collar workers participate in workers' councils than in other forms of political activity. Verba and Shabad direct attention to two factors that underlie the evidence that "participation in workers' councils, of the . . . kinds of activity [investigated], is the one most biased in favor of the 'haves' in Yugoslav society." [36] First, only workers in the socialist sector are eligible to participate in workers' councils, and they tend to come from higher SES backgrounds; second, the League of Communists is a less important channel for participation in workers' councils than in other areas. (Although league membership, too, is biased in favor of upper SES individuals, it is generally "both a necessary and sufficient condition of regular political activity in Yugoslavia."[37]) Verba and Shabad also argue that participation in workers' councils is seen as a technocratic activity, based on skills and expertise, rather than as a matter of political commitment. This raises wider questions about the reasons for the similarity of the pattern of participation in the civic cultures of Britain and America and in Yugoslavia's self-management system.

The analysis of *The Civic Culture* fails to look beyond the aggregation of individual characteristics; similarly, Verba and Shabad's discussion of Yugoslavia does not relate the association between SES and participation to the wider social structure. In one vital area the liberal democracies and Yugoslavia are alike. Both liberal capitalism and Yugoslav self-management, since the economic reforms of 1965, are based on the market, which suggests that the relationship between Yugoslav political culture and political structure will, in some crucial respects, resemble that of the civic culture and its political structure. Indeed, in another investigation of Yugoslav political life, it is commented that the Yugoslavs "have instituted equality to the extent that citizens enjoy the same formal political rights, and liberty to the degree that people are free to be economically unequal. This compromise between liberty and equality is called liberalism."[38] To the extent that the Yugoslav system is a variant of liberalism, or a system of formal political equality within substantive social inequality, it raises exactly the same problem of the development of democratic participation as the civic culture does.

Yugoslav workers' self-management involves more than the election of a central workers' council; each enterprise is decentralized into work units with their own councils. Significantly enough, the evidence indicates that despite the correlation between SES and participation in workers' councils, many ordinary workers do wish for more participation within their own work units.[39] The general conclusion that can be drawn from the empirical data is that if the civic culture is to be democratized, some very radical changes are required that go far beyond the multiplication of miniature liberal democracies. A vote for a central managing body in the enterprise will have little relevance for many workers if all else remains the same. The daily organization of work itself is especially important, as Braverman has shown; [40] if the sexual and other divisions on which the capitalist organization of production is built are not challenged, the balance of orientations is unlikely to be greatly disturbed.

The development of a democratic political culture demands, in short, a radical restructuring of all aspects of the organizations and associations of everyday life to provide opportunities for worthwhile participation for all citizens. If such a restructuring is to be achieved it also requires that we begin to look at political life, and the concepts that help constitute it, from a democratic rather than a liberal perspective. I have emphasized how the identification of democracy with liberal representative government prevents the recognition of key problems of democratic theory as problems. Another illustration of this is the problem of the status of participation in the workplace. Dahl remarks that it "is an absurdity" to see economic enterprises as "private." [41] Yet to see them as part of the political sphere— as the notion of "democratization" itself suggests—is to step outside the liberal theoretical framework within which empirical theorists are working.[42] Liberal theory draws a sharp separation between the political and other areas of social life, especially the economic (a separation that is breached once participation in the workplace is surveyed along with conventional forms of political activity). The argument that the foundations of a democratic political culture lie in the democratization of everyday life is also an argument that the political needs to be reconceptualized.

If participation in the workplace is seen as a technocratic activity, or a matter for experts, rather than part of the *political* life of citizens, then the apparent "naturalness" and unproblematic character of a socially divided civic culture will be reinforced. Zukin argues that the increasing shift of power in Yugoslavia toward a technocratic elite is one reason for the withdrawal of lower SES citizens from political activity; they are "refusing to be manipulated." [43] Or, like citizens from similar backgrounds in the civic culture, they do not regard it as "rational," or worthwhile, to participate in an activity for which they lack expertise. Nor is it only participation in

Yugoslav workers' councils that is seen as technocratic or a matter for experts; in the liberal democracies elections are held to "place experts in office for a fixed term, subject to the right of the citizen to protest if he dislikes what they do and to replace them at the next election." [44] The liberal conception of political life, as Wolin has emphasized, is that government is part of the social division of labor.[45] As in other areas, it is "economical" to have experts in the procedure or technique of managing the liberal political method elected to office— although it is far from clear in what this expertise consists.

This conception of representation and political elites underlies Almond and Verba's ideological arguments about the "myth" of citizens' political influence and political apathy in *The Civic Culture.* It is rational not to participate, and so save the costs of activity, because experts will look after political life for you, with the myth ensuring their responsiveness. I have already shown how this claim ignores the fact that the division of political labor, like the division of labor in general, is grounded in sex and class, but it should also be stressed that the liberal conception of political elites as experts obscures another basic problem. From a liberal perspective it is finding well-qualified experts and ensuring their efficiency through the electoral sanction that is the problem; the fact of expertise itself is seen as "politically neutral." [46] But a *democratic* theorist, perhaps especially an empirical democratic theorist, cannot regard political expertise as unproblematic. The ancient and radical idea was that in a democracy *all citizens* were experts about their own political life, no matter what their special knowledge and skills in other areas. This idea has now been cast aside. "Democracy" is now held to be a system where citizens alienate their right to decide about their own political lives to nonpolitical experts (usually, today, lawyers and other professionally qualified men). It is hardly surprising that, in view of this conception of the political and citizenship, working-class individuals and women feel it is not worthwhile to be active; their skills and knowledge are not seen as politically relevant, either in the politics of the state or in the workplace.

Changes in the liberal democratic political structure and changes in political consciousness and political concepts are integrally related to each other. No headway will be made in developing *democratic* theory and practice until it is recognized that liberal theory is part of the problem. An understanding of the relationship between the capitalist economy, or Yugoslav self-management, and their respective political structures will not be obtained merely by adding bits and pieces of "partici-pation" to liberal theory, or investigating the correlates of individual participation. The participatory classical theorists offer insights for an alternative approach, and present alterna-tive conceptions of "representation," "government," and the structure of a "political" community. Empirical theorists argue as if only one technocratic conception of political life exists in democratic theory. But Rousseau offers us a systematic critique of this liberal conception, and presents an alternative democratic theory in which citizens retain political authority in their own hands; they act as their own government. Elected representatives are not precluded, but although they may act on behalf of citizens, representatives do not decide for them.[47] They are not experts to whom citizens alienate their political authority: "the holders of the executive power are not the people's masters but its officers." [48]

The conventional argument against taking participatory theory seriously is that it is empirically unrealistic; that, for example, it is to "talk as if people are willing to participate in decisions without any regard for the costs of time: . . . The cost is, plainly, that the time might be used in doing something else—often, in fact, something a great deal more interesting and important than going to a meeting." [49] The reference to "going to a meeting" indicates a failure of imagination. There are other ways to participate if political activity begins to become part of everyday life, not something extra to it. The objections that appeal to the empirical facts and the realities and treat participatory democracy as inherently impossible ignore the basic problem about that reality: why it is that the costs appear to weigh so much more heavily on women and the working class. This is not to deny that people can usually engage in only one thing at a time, but to insist that the divided civic culture is *not* a "natural fact" about our social world, and that there *are* good reasons to look beyond liberal theory and practice. In the abstract it is very difficult to say anything definite about participation within an alternative sociopolitical context, but it is only if, in a participatory system, a certain proportion of (randomly distributed) citizens choose not to participate that theorists would be justified in writing of the "naturally" apolitical individual.

CIVIC PARTICIPATION

The word *civic* appears in the title of the book, yet readers are not told why this particular description of the pattern of political orientations in Britain and America was chosen. Nor does *The Civic Culture* explain why "civic" participation takes a particular form. I shall consider the latter question first.

The "consolidation" of the civic culture, Almond and Verba argue, meant that the "working classes could enter into politics and, in a process of trial and error, find the language in which to couch their demands and the means to make them effective" (page 8). Certainly, the welfare state has brought a great improvement to the lives of working-class people, although in the recession of the late 1970s this improvement does not appear so far-reaching as it did a decade or more earlier. But the "language" that the working class has "found" is the language of liberal, representative politics and its competing interest groups, with all this implies for ideas about democracy and the form of political theory from which individuals make sense of the world. It is a language that maintains that the working class has the means to achieve its demands in a system in which "participation helps those who are already better off." In other words, it is assumed in *The Civic Culture* that the liberal democratic political method provides a successful mechanism within which interests are protected and the demands of ordinary citizens are met. Civic participation is therefore participation associated with the electoral system. There is no room for, or need to ask, substantive political questions about the form that civic or democratic participation might take.

The Civic Culture and other empirical democratic theory of its period gave no hint that a "participation explosion" was imminent within the civic culture itself. Nor have empirical investigators paid attention to "protests and demonstrations." W. R. Schonfeld has pointed out that there has been an "extremely curious" lack of criticism of this omission,[50] a lack that reflects the widespread acceptance by other theorists of the perspective upon participation provided by empirical theory, a perspective that contains no means of assessing "unorthodox" political activity that goes outside conventional electoral and interelectoral activity. The political method of liberal democracy is unrelated to specific political criteria or specific principles of political morality or right; that is precisely why Schumpeter's conception of democracy has proved so congenial to value-free and scientific empirical theory. This means that theorists are caught in a perpetual present, where established forms of electoral participation can be described and called "democratic," but nothing substantive can be said about other activities, or about possible future developments of democratic political action.

Although unorthodox activities take widely differing forms, they are either ignored or dismissed as "undemocratic," [51] or, as in the case of civil (civic?) disobedience—typically engaged in by middle-class "civic" citizens—so defined as to be robbed of all political impact. As Barry has caustically commented of one such account, it reduces political action to the level of the threat of the little girl in the English children's stories: "If you don't do it I'll scream and scream until I make myself sick." [52] If a democratic theory and practice is to be developed as an alternative to existing liberal democracy, it is necessary that political theorists turn their attention to the formulation of criteria that will enable us to distinguish *democratic* forms from the variety of activities that extend over urban guerrillas, factory occupations, squatting, civil disobedience, the setting up of self-help organizations, electoral participation, and acts of individual witness. As part of this task it is also necessary to consider what counts as political activity. In *The Civic Culture,* participation in the workplace is treated as a nonpolitical arena to develop orientations and skills necessary in political life; but, as argued above, the extension of democratic participation to wider areas of social life should be seen as political participation and as integral to active citizenship.

In using the word *civic* to describe electoral participation, Almond and Verba presumably wish to draw upon its association with valuable and valued political ideals. The culture (and the structure that it fits) is one in which all citizens are able freely to act politically and attain their goals in a peaceful and mutually responsible fashion. The characterization of the liberal democratic system as "civic" or "democratic" appropriates these ideals to liberalism, but again, there is no reason why this identification should so easily be accepted. I take it that the civic culture can be seen as standing in the tradition of civic humanism, which J. G. A. Pocock presents as a tradition in which "the development of the individual towards self-fulfillment is possible only when the individual acts as a citizen, that is as a conscious and autonomous participant in an autonomous decision-taking political community. . . ."[53] This account of civic political life is more appropriate to a participatory democratic system than the socially divided civic culture, notwithstanding that critics of the school of theorizing to which *The Civic Culture* belongs are often accused of throwing away the valuable liberal "civic" heritage.

This accusation misunderstands both the arguments of the critics and the historical tradition to which they belong (a tradition which exists alongside liberal theory and emerged as part of the same socioeconomic developments). The misunderstanding is exacerbated because the "realistic" alternatives in political life are often presented, as in the opening of *The Civic Culture,* as two only: either existing liberal democracy or totalitarianism. In addition, criticism of social inequality and its integral connection with the liberal democratic political method is frequently misrepresented as an attack on civil liberty and all liberal values. Critics of empirical theory are not rejecting the entire history and culture of liberalism, but building from it. Their fundamental argument is that liberal theory has held out a promise to *all* citizens that has not been, and cannot be, fulfilled. If the promise is to be realized, democratization of the civic culture, development beyond liberal democracy is necessary. Parekh has stated this position nicely:

> Liberalism . . . is only one of many possible ways of defining liberal values, and it is possible to hold liberal values—that is, to be a liberal with a small "l"—and yet to interpret and justify them differently from the way Liberalism does. . . . Indeed, it is perfectly intelligible for a person not to be a Liberal precisely

because he is a liberal; that is to say, it is precisely because he believes that the modern Liberal society cannot safeguard the traditional liberal values which he cherishes that he might want to overthrow it.[54]

If liberal values are to be interpreted and justified differently, a theoretical alternative to conventional empirical theory must be developed. This does not imply the neglect of empirical research, but rather, that it should throw light onto basic problems of political participation and democracy. At present, empirical theory all too often obscures or denies the existence of problems, and presents evidence of socially structured inequalities as "natural facts" about the world that constitute insurmountable barriers to increased participation by the presently inactive. If empirical research is to help rather than hinder our understanding of the civic culture, it must be interpreted in a new framework; the individualist basis of liberal theory must be left behind. The aggregation of individual correlates of political activity will not illuminate the relationship between political structure because the basic *problem,* the fact that the structure is grounded in class and sex divisions, never appears as such. Rather, systematically structured inequalities appear as individual psychological and personal attributes that happen to be distributed in a particular way.

During the 1970s a welcome change occurred in political theory; important political problems (both "traditional" and new) are being discussed, and the comforting arguments of earlier years are being more widely questioned. Yet although "theoretical self-consciousness"[55] is more widespread, a great deal remains to be done to produce a worthwhile empirical democratic theory. Once that is achieved we shall really have a theory that enables us to understand our own social and political world, and that can "help us decide what to do [politically] and how to go about doing it."[56] Until then, we shall still lack a "democratic" theory that is the theory of civic, participatory practice of the people and for the people.

NOTES

1. On writers who want to be both "value-neutral" and "impeccable champions of conventional pluralist democracy," see C. Bay, "Politics and

Pseudopolitics," in C. A. McCoy and J. Playford, eds., *Apolitical Politics* (New York: T. Y. Crowell, 1967), p. 19.

2. This is discussed in my *Participation and Democratic Theory* (Cambridge, Eng.: Cambridge Univ. Press, 1970), esp. pp. 16–21.

3. J. A. Schumpeter, *Capitalism, Socialism and Democracy* (London: George Allen and Unwin, 1943), chap. 22.

4. This was the label given to empirical theory in one of the best-known critiques: G. Duncan and S. Lukes, "The New Democracy," *Political Studies* 11 (1963): 156–77. It is also known as the "elitist theory," the "contemporary theory," "polyarchy," etc.

5. The description is that of B. M. Barry, *Sociologists, Economists and Democracy* (London: Collier-Macmillan, 1970).

6. For a discussion of some examples of this theory, see Carole Pateman, *Participation,* chap. 11.

7. I do not specifically consider Almond and Verba's notion of "stability." It seems, as Barry notes (*Sociologists,* p. 86), to mean no more than "the infrequency of unconstitutional changes of regime."

8. References in parentheses in the text are to the pages of G. A. Almond and S. Verba, *The Civic Culture: Political Attitudes and Democracy in Five Nations* (Princeton, N.J.: Princeton University Press, 1963).

9. See B. Jessop, *Traditionalism, Conservatism and British Political Culture* (London: George Allen and Unwin, 1974), p. 255.

10. Schumpeter, *Capitalism,* p. 297.

11. And even this was not seen as essential in Schumpeter's account; see Schumpeter, *Capitalism,* pp. 244–45.

12. James Mill, *An Essay on Government* (Cambridge, Eng.: Cambridge Univ. Press, 1937), p. 34.

13. Schumpeter, *Capitalism,* p. 269.

14. For this criticism, see Barry, *Sociologists,* pp. 49–50; Jessop, *Traditionalism,* pp. 53–55; and the comments of D. Kavanagh, *Political Culture* (London: Macmillan & Co., 1927), p. 65.

15. R. A. Dahl, *Who Governs? Democracy and Power in an American City* (New Haven: Yale Univ. Press, 1961), pp. 224–25.

16. The concept of "political culture" is also discussed in Carole Pateman, "Political Culture, Political Structure and Political Change," *British Journal of Political Science* 1 (1973): 291–305.

17. Kavanagh, *Political Culture,* p. 66.

18. T. Parsons et al., *Theories of Society* (New York: The Free Press, 1961), p. 36 (Parsons's italics).

19. For references to earlier investigations, see L. W. Milbrath, *Political Participation: How and Why Do People Get Involved in Politics?* (Chicago: Rand McNally, 1965), pp. 113–14, 116.

20. G. Sartori, *Democratic Theory* (Detroit, Mich.: Wayne State Univ. Press, 1962), p. 88.

21. This concept is developed in chapter 5 of my unpublished doctoral thesis "Participation and Recent Theories of Democracy," Oxford Univ., 1971. '

22. Almond and Verba also argue that cultural norms about "the traditional female status" are getting weaker in all countries (pp. 399–400). Such optimism has hardly been borne out. Moreover, Almond and Verba do not mention the discrimination that exists against women in political (and social and economic) life. The socialization explanation is certainly not the whole story. The other sources cited by Almond and Verba on women's

political attitudes and activity should be treated with extreme caution. Political scientists, especially in the period of *The Civic Culure,* have either usually ignored women or merely repeated myths and stereotypes; see M. Goot and E. Reid, *Women and Voting Studies: Mindless Matrons or Sexist Scientism?* Sage Contemporary Political Sociology Series, vol. 1 (Beverly Hills, Calif.: Sage Publications, 1975); S. C. Bourque and J. Grossholtz, "Politics an Unnatural Practice: Political Science Looks at Female Participation," *Politics and Society,* Winter 1974, pp. 225–66.

23. For an investigation and interpretation of the British political culture in similar terms, using the conceptions of "hegemony" and "dominant" and "peripheral" value systems, see Jessop, *Traditionalism.*

24. This also raises a whole range of complex questions about the interpretation of replies to surveys like that of *The Civic Culture,* and the relationship of respondents to interviewers, which cannot be dealt with in the scope of this essay. For a very different approach to the problem of the citizens' lack of feelings of competence, and their evaluation of the political structure, see R. Sennett and J. Cobb, *The Hidden Injuries of Class* (New York: Alfred A. Knopf, 1972).

25. Barry, *Sociologists,* pp. 93–94.

26. A. O. Hirschman, " 'Exit, Voice and Loyalty': Further Reflections and a Survey of Recent Contributions," *Social Science Information* 13 (1974): 7–26. (I am grateful to Gabriel Almond for bringing this to my attention.) The rational withdrawal of low SES citizens into political inactivity can be seen as an exit from the political system. M. Walzer, *Obligations: Essays on Disobedience, War and Citizenship* (New York: Simon and Schuster, 1971), p. 226, calls attention to the inactive citizen who is involved "in a kind of boycott of the political system."

27. See Pateman, "Political Culture," pp. 299–301. Also, the evidence presented by M. Mann, "The Social Cohesion of Liberal Democracy," *American Sociological Review,* 35 (1970): pp. 423–37.

28. S. Verba and N. H. Nie, *Participation in America: Political Democracy and Social Equality* (New York: Harper & Row, 1972), p. 338. (Italics added).

29. The conclusions and arguments of *Participation in America* suggest not: I have discussed this study in a review essay, "To Them That Hath, Shall Be Given," in *Politics* 9, no. 2 (1974): 139–45.

30. Almond and Verba also argue that the "balance" is between "apparent contradictions" (p. 476). But these so-called contradictions would exist in any democratic system; there is always a need, for example, for citizens both to participate in decision making and to obey decisions. Nor is there any reason to suppose that social trust (pp. 284–88) would be lacking if inequality decreased and the benefits of participation were more equitably distributed.

31. A review of some of this evidence can be found in Pateman, *Participation.* See also P. Blumberg, *Industrial Democracy: The Sociology of Participation* (London: Constable, 1968); M. L. Kohn and C. Schooler, "Class, Occupation and Orientation," *American Sociological Review* 34 (1969): 659–78; L. Lipsitz, "Work Life and Political Attitudes," *American Political Science Review,* 58 (1964): 951–62.

32. On "pseudoparticipation," see Pateman, *Participation.*

33. Blumberg, *Industrial Democracy* (esp. chap. 5), reviews much of the evidence. It is significant that prewar experiments that were extremely influential for "democratic management" were conducted by Lewin with young (male) children.

34. R. D. Dahl, *After the Revolution? Authority in a Good Society* (New Haven: Yale Univ. Press, 1970), pp. 115, 134.

35. Ibid., p. 136. There is now a large literature on industrial democracy to supplement the evidence in my *Participation and Democratic Theory*. See, for example, G. D. Garson, *On Democratic Administration and Socialist Self-Management*, Sage Professional Papers in Administrative and Policy Studies, vol. 2 (Beverly Hills, Calif.: Sage Publications, 1974); the volumes of *Participation and Self-Management* (1972–73), Institute for Social Research, Zagreb, Yugoslavia; G. Hunnius, G. D. Garson, J. Case, eds., *Workers' Control* (New York: Random House Vintage Books, 1973); J. Vanek, ed., *Self-Management* (Middlesex, Eng.: Penguin Books, 1975); M. Poole, *Workers' Participation in Industry*, rev. ed. (London: Routledge & Kegan Paul, 1978).

36. S. Verba and G. Shabad, "Workers' Councils and Political Stratification: The Yugoslav Experience," *American Political Science Review* 72, no. 1 (1978): 85. See also S. Verba and G. Shabad, "Workers' Councils and Political Participation," paper presented to the Annual Meeting of the American Political Science Association, 1975.

37. Verba and Shabad, "Workers Council and Political Stratification," p. 87.

38. S. Zukin, *Beyond Marx and Tito: Theory and Practice in Yugoslav Socialism* (Cambridge, Eng.: Cambridge Univ. Press, 1975), p. 250.

39. Ibid., pp. 189–90.

40. H. Braverman, *Labor and Monopoly Capitalism: The Degradation of Work in the Twentieth Century* (New York: Monthly Review Press, 1974).

41. Dahl, *After the Revolution?*, p. 120.

42. Many writers on industrial democracy insist that it cannot be the same as (political) democracy; for example, E. Rhenman, *Industrial Democracy and Industrial Management* (London: Tavistock, 1968), p. 42.

43. Zukin, *Beyond Marx and Tito*, p. 190; see also p. 178.

44. Dahl, *After the Revolution?*, p. 38.

45. S. Wolin, *Politics and Vision* (London: Allen and Unwin, 1961), p. 304.

46. Dahl, *After the Revolution?*, p. 34.

47. For further comments on "representation," see Carole Pateman, "A Contribution to the Political Theory of Organizational Democracy," *Administration and Society* 7 (1975): 15–18. Aspects of Rousseau's critique of liberal theory are discussed in Pateman, *The Problem of Political Obligation* (Chichester, Eng.: Wiley, 1979), chap. 7.

48. Rousseau, *The Social Contract*, trans. M. Cranston (Middlesex, Eng.: Penguin Books, 1968), p. 146.

49. Dahl, *After the Revolution?*, p. 44.

50. W. R. Schonfeld, "The Meaning of Democratic Participation," *World Politics* 28 (1975): 134–58.

51. The civic culture is called a "culture of moderation" (p. 500), but the narrow view of "democratic" activities, and the inability to discuss the relationship between class and sex and these activities as a problem, hardly encourages a moderate response.

52. B. M. Barry, *The Liberal Theory of Justice: A Critical Examination of the Principal Doctrines of "A Theory of Justice" by John Rawls* (London: Oxford Univ. Press, 1973), p. 153.

53. J. G. A. Pocock, "Civic Humanism and Its Role in Anglo-American Thought," in *Politics, Language and Time* (London: Methuen, 1972), p. 85. Pocock places Rousseau in this tradition, and argues (p. 103) that civic humanism "provided the point of departure for the concept of alienation"— not a concept usually associated with liberal theory.

54. B. Parekh, "Liberalism and Morality," in B. Parekh and R. N. Berki, eds., *The Morality of Politics* (London: Allen and Unwin, 1972), p. 83. See also S. Lukes, *Individualism* (Oxford: Blackwell 1973), part 3.

55. W. E. Connolly, "Theoretical Self-Consciousness," *Polity* 6 (1973): 5–35.

56. J. Plamenatz, "The Use of Political Theory," in A. Quinton, ed., *Political Philosophy* (London: Oxford Univ. Press, 1967), p. 29.

CHAPTER IV

The Civic Culture from a
Marxist-Sociological Perspective

Jerzy J. Wiatr
The University of Warsaw

THERE IS LITTLE, if any, doubt in the academic community about the widespread impact *The Civic Culture* has had on comparative social science research, not only in the United States but internationally as well. It is one of the most widely quoted studies of the 1960s and, what is by far more important, its basic approach has influenced scholars all over the world. Most particularly, the impact of *The Civic Culture* on comparative social science reflects three main characteristics of the study:

1. the fact that it was the first attempt to explore empirically one of the less studied, albeit very important, realms of politics, namely, the role played by the political culture;

2. the relevance of its theoretical framework, which systematically connected the study of psychological bases of politics with that of the political system;

3. the explicitly cross-national, comparative character of the project, which therefore pioneered cross-national comparisons in the study of politics.

In all these aspects *The Civic Culture* remains a pioneer in the field of political research and retains its influence over further research. At the same time, the study reflects both some implicit or explicit ideological assumptions the authors have taken for granted and some characteristics of the ideological climate of preradical social science in the West. The extent to which they both have impaired the results of the study is not negligible and constitutes an important problem for reassessment. In no case, however, should one interpret the criticism expressed below as questioning the value and importance of the study as such. One of the values of the study is that it provokes discussions and disagreements on methodology and theory of cross-national research, influencing, therefore, its further development.

The present paper, intended as a contribution to the discussion on the reevaluation of *The Civic Culture,* approaches the problem from a Marxist-sociological perspective, which includes: (a) the impact of *The Civic Culture* on political research in and on the socialist countries of Eastern Europe; (b) a comparison of the methodology of *The Civic Culture* with that of the largest cross-national study of politics in which two socialist countries of Eastern Europe have participated, namely, the International Study on Values in Politics, conducted in the late 1960s in India, Poland, the United States, and Yugoslavia[1]; and (c) general problems of theory and methodology of *The Civic Culture* from the perspective of what, to this writer's way of thinking, can be described as contemporary Marxist methodology of empirical political research.[2]

THE CIVIC CULTURE AND SOCIAL RESEARCH IN EASTERN EUROPE

Although *The Civic Culture* is not concerned with the political reality of the socialist countries of Eastern Europe,[3] it has provoked wide interest among the social scientists in those countries and also has influenced some of the studies conducted in and on the socialist states. References to *The Civic Culture* and discussion of its methodology can now be found in several scholarly publications in Eastern Europe, most particularly in the USSR,[4] Poland,[5] and Yugoslavia.[6] While it is generally agreed that the study has great importance for contemporary political research, Marxist scholars express their criticism of the limitations and ideological content of *The Civic Culture*. Among the most important points of criticism expressed in the Soviet and East European comments on *The Civic Culture* are the following:

1. The use of Anglo-American concepts of "democracy" as the yardstick for evaluating political systems has introduced a methodological bias and impaired the possibilities of interpreting the data; this point was first made in my review (1965) and was later elaborated by Fedor Burlatskii and Aleksander Galkin.

2. The study does not show the historical roots of the political cultures of the societies under study and it avoids an interpretation in terms of class structure, points also made by Burlatskii and Galkin.

3. The methodology of *The Civic Culture,* because of its emphasis on obtaining equivalence by using identical indicators in various countries, oversimplifies the rather complex problem of measuring similarities and dissimilarities cross-nationally; this weakness has been deepened by a not always sufficiently careful interpretation of statistical data (see Przeworski and Teune, cited in note 1).

It can therefore be said that East European criticism of *The Civic Culture* covered both the ideological differences resulting from divergent political and/or philosophical perspectives and more specific questions of empirical methodology. Although some of the criticisms could probably be refuted, one cannot consider them as nothing but political polemics. Quite to the contrary, *The Civic Culture,* albeit controversial from the Marxist sociologists' point of view, has received serious and in many respects favorable attention. In a sense this shows that the study, regardless of some of its controversial characteristics, has had a particularly broad impact on contemporary social science, extending beyond political and ideological boundaries.

The same conclusion can be reached by observing the way in which the crucial concept of the study—that of "political culture"—has been adopted in the Marxist social science in socialist countries. In 1970 and 1971 two Marxist sociologists—Burlatskii in the Soviet Union[7] and Markiewicz in Poland [8]—

published important contributions on the problems of political culture in the USSR and Poland, respectively, and discussed the concept of political culture as a legitimate element of Marxist social science terminology. Their definitions of "political culture" differ from that used by Almond and Verba, but the differences are not substantial. Burlatskii defines the political culture as "the level of knowledge and perceptions about power and politics held by various strata of the society and by various individuals, as well as the level of their political activity determined by the former." [9] Markiewicz puts more emphasis on values and defines the political culture as "those elements in the global culture of a society which refer to the values recognized and desired by a given group and which concern the system of state power." [10] My own definition, introduced in a book published in 1973, defines the political culture as "the totality of attitudes, values and patterns of behavior existing in a given society [and] relating to the mutual relationships between the [state] power and the citizens," and includes in this category: knowledge of politics, evaluation of political phenomena, emotional aspect of political attitudes, and patterns of political behavior.[11] In all these definitions one can find an influence of *The Civic Culture,* although the definitions quoted above differ to a greater or lesser extent from that used by Almond and Verba. What, however, is particularly important is the impact *The Civic Culture* has had on the elaboration of a concept not used previously in the Marxist political science terminology.

As far as empirical research on political culture in the socialist countries is concerned, there is relatively little to report. Only in some countries of Eastern Europe, notably Poland and Yugoslavia, have empirical studies been conducted and results published on selected aspects of political culture. In the Yugoslav case, some of the empirical data collected by the Yugoslav and American scholars have been published in the United States and are easily available to interested readers.[12] In general they seem to demonstrate the usefulness of the political culture concept to the study of socialist politics, the points emphasized recently by Kenneth Jowitt on the basis of his research on Romania.[13] Polish studies on political culture concentrated mostly on its cognitive aspect, that is, on the level of interest

TABLE IV.1. *Identification of Politicians: Polish Six-City Sample, 1966*

Name	Position held in 1966	% of correct answers
Adam Rapacki	Polish Foreign Minister	57.4
U Thant	UN Secretary-General	56.3
·Czesław Wycech	Polish Speaker of Parliament	39.5
Gamal Nasser	President of the United Arab Republic	35.9
Lucjan Motyka	Polish Minister of Culture	35.3
Haile Selassie	Emperor of Ethiopia	32.7
Robert McNamara	U.S. Secretary of Defense	27.9

in, and knowledge of, politics among Polish citizens. In general they have demonstrated a relatively high level of political information among contemporary Poles. Thus Andrzej Siciński, in his studies of interest in and knowledge about foreign policy and international relations, found Poles somewhat less informed than Norwegians but more informed than the French.[14] In my own study of the level of political knowledge, conducted in 1966 in six medium-sized cities,[15] respondents were asked to identify (by positions held) seven prominent Polish and foreign politicians; the results, as shown in Table IV.1 indicate a rather high level of political information, particularly if one takes into account the fact that only 55 percent of the sample had education above elementary school, and less than 10 percent above secondary school.

In the same study, 74.4 percent of the respondents identified correctly the abbreviation ONZ (Organizacja Narodów Zjednoczonych—United Nations); 56.9 percent, DRW (Demokratyczna Republika Wietnamu—Democratic Republic of Vietnam); 56.0 percent, ZRA (Zjednoczona Republika Arabska—United Arab Republic); 53.8 percent, FJN (Front Jedności Narodu—Front of National Unity); and 47.5 percent, RWPG (Rada Wzajemnej Pomocy Gospodarczej—Council for Mutual Economic Assistance); etc. In general this study—as well as Siciński's studies referred to earlier—indicates a rather high level of political interest and knowledge among Polish citizens. The fact, however, that these studies emphasized very strongly foreign-policy problems makes it difficult to conclude to what extent this reflects involvement in the political system as different from a general feeling that the international situation may make quite a difference; the latter interpretation may reflect Polish historical experiences in the present century.

In addition to survey research, the questions of political culture occupy an increasingly prominent role in the theoretical interpretations of the functioning of the political system. Characteristic in this respect is Jan Szczepański's book *Polish Society,* whose interpretation of the basic problems of Polish politics stems from the assumption that the traditional, "anarchistic" traits of the Poles have to be overcome by proper activity of the political institutions and by educational effort.[16] Other writers, however, put stronger emphasis on the already achieved transformations and claim that the political culture of the policy-oriented theoretical discussions are based on explicit further development of socialist democracy.[17] The fact that policy-oriented theoretical discussions are based on explicit statements about the prevailing type of political culture testifies to the relevance of the concept and, indirectly, to the influence of the theoretical framework of *The Civic Culture.*

VALUES AND THE ACTIVE COMMUNITY:
SIMILARITIES AND DIFFERENCES

As mentioned before, the largest cross-national political science study with East European participation has been the four-nation project on the influence of local leadership on community "activeness" in India, Poland, the United States, and Yugoslavia. The project did not concern itself exclusively with problems of political culture; a very substantial part of it— the study of local leaders' values and their perceptions of the political process—can be considered a contribution to the comparative research on elite political culture. Because of this —and also because it was a cross-national study—comparisons between the *Values* project and *The Civic Culture* seem justified. It may also be of some interest to note that from the very beginning the participants in the *Values* project referred in their methodological discussions to the then recent experiences of the *Civic Culture* study, both as a source of inspiration and as an example of methodological difficulties which we wished to overcome in a better way. The Przeworski–Teune paper on "Equivalence in Cross-National Research" is one of the expressions of this twofold interest; working documents from the *Values* project conferences (Dubrovnik, Yugoslavia, 1965; Philadelphia, Pennsylvania, U.S.A., 1966; Warsaw, Poland, 1966; Kanpoor, India, 1967; and Bellagio-Budva, 1967) provide numerous references to *The Civic Culture*. The two projects constitute successive steps in the development of cross-national research on political culture and should be compared in terms of their objectives, research strategies, and methods of international cooperation. Before undertaking such an analysis I should, however, like to make two points clear. First, as one of the national directors of the *Values* project, I do not consider myself a truly impartial observer. Second, when comparing the two studies I do not automatically assume that the strategies employed by us in the *Values* project have proved superior to those used in the *Civic Culture* study; retrospectively, participants in the *Values* project have already expressed their criticism of some aspects of their research strategy.[18] With this in mind, let me discuss the similarities and dissimilarities between the two projects point by point.

RESEARCH DESIGN

The Civic Culture is concerned with describing and explaining the emergence and functioning of the type of political culture that the authors view as most functional from the perspective of building a successful democratic system; explicitly it attempts to serve as a preliminary source of policy-oriented knowledge for democratic statesmen in the new nations. *Values and the Active Community* purports also to explain theoretically conditions favorable for achieving a certain goal; the goal, however, is defined as soliciting community activeness, or —to put it differently—creating political conditions functional for mobilization of resources and public participation on the local level. Neither of the two studies solves the problem completely and neither claims to have been doing this. Both, however, can—at least to my way of thinking—be considered substantial contributions to understanding the central problems of practical policymaking.

RESEARCH TARGETS

In *The Civic Culture* the research target has been defined clearly as the general public of five nations, studied through representative survey samples. In *Values and the Active Community* the research targets were subnational "communities" (blocs and districts in India, counties in Poland, municipalities in the United States, and communes in Yugoslavia) studied both as collectives—that is, through statistical analysis of aggregate data on economic development and community activeness—and as seats of local leaders, who were sampled within each community on the basis of positions held at the time of the study. It is, therefore, only the survey part of the *Values* project that can be compared with *The Civic Culture*, but one of the important differences between the two studies is that the former is not exclusively a survey research study. The multimethod character of the *Values* study has been a source of both its strength and its weakness. It allowed us to seek answers to questions extending beyond the study of attitudes, and therefore contributed to the theoretical significance of the study. It has, however, created numerous not completely solved problems, such as the validity of interpreting between-community differences in activeness in terms of leaders' characteristics, values, etc., without studying the atttitudes of the general public and without studying leaders' actual behavior. In short, the *Values* project undertook more ambitious methodological tasks, but paid a heavy price for it in terms of unsolved methodological and theoretical problems.

IDEOLOGICAL ORIENTATION

The Civic Culture is based on clear, explicitly stated ideological principles. It is intended as a contribution to the rivalry between "democratic" and "totalitarian" models of government, as an intellectual instrument in "the transfer of the political culture of the Western democratic states to the emerging nations." [19] The *Values* project, based on the collaboration of scholars from four different political systems, never attempted to define its ideological objectives in such a clear-cut way. Instead, it has been justified in terms of a potential contribution to the solution of a generally acceptable, nonideological objective: creating more active local communities. In fact, however, ideological preferences of the participants—most particularly their belief in the value of citizen participation in managing public affairs—have probably influenced our choices of indicators and our interpretation of some of the data. Neither of the two studies is value-free. *The Civic Culture,* however, has all the advantages that result from explicit expression of ideological preferences by an ideologically homogeneous research team. On the other hand, the *Values* project has demonstrated that—contrary to fears expressed by many—substantial differences in prevailing ideologies do not make it impossible to collaborate successfully in cross-national studies.

INTERNATIONAL COLLABORATION

In terms of Stein Rokkan's typology,[20] *The Civic Culture* is an example of research in which "the design is decided, and analysis and interpretation pursued within one centre in one 'leader' nation while the actual data gathering is carried out by some international network of field organizations." In contrast, the *Values* project is an example of a type of research which Rokkan describes as "the peak of internationalization." All stages of research from the selection of research topics, through elaboration of instruments, data gathering and analysis, to the writing and editing of the volume have been done jointly, by collaborating national teams and through compromises in making decisions. It is my firm belief that the *Values* project demonstrated successfully the superiority of collaborative arrangements under which participants cooperate as equal intellectual partners. It is clear to me, however, that this arrangement has also its weak points, the most important of them being the inevitability of some compromises in making decisions. The most important value of the international type of research, in my opinion, is that it allows for multinational and multitheoretical perspectives to be built into the study and, therefore, contributes to avoiding narrow, "ethnocentric" bias.

METHODS OF ANALYSIS

The years that passed between the execution of the two studies resulted in greater emphasis in the *Values* project on more sophisticated methods of statistical analysis, such as factor analysis, etc. It is partly reflected also in the fact that in contrast to *The Civic Culture,* which focused exclusively on the study of isolated individuals,[21] the *Values* project was confronted with the more complex task of inferring community characteristics from the individual characteristics of local leaders. Retrospectively, I am inclined to consider the *Values* study's statistical sophistication as only a partial asset. While it offered us possibilities to investigate some relationships more deeply than would have been possible with the use of the rather simple statistics of *The Civic Culture,* it also produced some artifacts, the most prominent among them being our concept of "activeness," which caused some justified criticism.[22]

CROSS-NATIONAL EQUIVALENCE

One of the early concerns of the principal participants in the *Values* project was how to avoid methodological distortions caused by the use of formally identical measures in nonidentical conditions. Some of the experiences of the *Civic Culture* study served here as a useful warning.[23] Consequently, the *Values* project has developed a novel research method of establishing equivalent measures through the use of nonidentical indicators, described in the Przeworski–Teune paper and in the methodological annexes to the volume. This seems to me an important step forward compared to the methodology of *The Civic Culture.* At the same time, however, there is reasonable doubt whether we have not gone too far in this direction at the expense of introducing too much nation-specific elements in the research methodology. Further empirical studies and more methodological thinking is necessary to avoid here two extremes, of which *The Civic Culture* and *Values and the Active Community* are prima facie examples.

The comparison of the two studies is not intended to demonstrate that one of them is better than the other. The one that came later has been privileged by the possibility of using the rich experiences of the earlier one. Both, however, have their strong and weak sides, and their greatest contribution for international social science is precisely that they offer different experiences for future efforts.

THE CIVIC CULTURE: A METHODOLOGICAL AND
THEORETICAL REASSESSMENT

From the preceding parts of this paper it should already be clear that I consider *The Civic Culture* a very important book and a great contribution to international social science. It is good to emphasize this when moving to the section in which I intend to discuss those aspects of theory and methodology of the study that I find the most controversial.

My main points of criticism concern: (a) the way in which *The Civic Culture* interprets relationships between political culture and political structure, as well as the role analysis of the socioeconomic structure plays—or does not play—in the study; (b) the preradical, that is, status-quo orientation of the study; and (c) the use the study makes of the explicit ideological assumptions of "democratic theory." This type of criticism does not inevitably result from a commitment to Marxist social theory; nevertheless, the fact that I do consider myself a Marxist has probably more than a casual relation to choosing those aspects for a critical evaluation.[24]

Criticism concerning the way in which *The Civic Culture* interprets relationships between culture and structure has been raised by Carole Pateman and plays a very important role in her evaluation of the whole study.[25] While my own criticism differs from hers, I do agree that the way the culture/structure relationship is interpreted in *The Civic Culture* is a weak point in the theoretical aspect of the study.

The cornerstone of the theory underlying *The Civic Culture* is the proposition that political culture and political structure are interdependent. Almond and Verba stress that "any polity may be described and compared with other polities in terms of (1) its structural-functional characteristics, and (2) its cultural, subcultural and role-cultural characteristics. Our analysis of types of political culture is a first effort at treating the phenomena of individual political orientation in such a way as to relate them systematically to the phenomena of political structure."[26] I cannot agree more. Interdependency between political culture and political structure is, in fact, one of the most important aspects of political theory. If we wish to put it in Marxist terminology, it is the proposition that political consciousness reflects political reality and at the same time shapes it. The problem, however, arises when the authors move to the interpretation of their findings.

Except in chapter 12 where it is done in the way of ex-post-facto historical explanations, the study does not investigate the ways in which political structures of the five countries shape their political cultures. With the use of survey data only, it is difficult to do otherwise; but additional—nonsurvey—data could have been introduced to demonstrate the impact political structure has on political culture. As things are presented in the book, the analysis concentrates on one side of the relationship only. I do not say that this is Almond and Verba's theory. Quite to the contrary. I think that their research design departed here from their explicitly stated theory and impoverished their analysis. This weakness of the study makes it look more incompatible with contemporary Marxist methodology of social science than the authors probably intended. For future research one may suggest a comprehensive study showing interrelationship between political cultures and political structures in terms of (a) the impact of past structures on contemporary structures and contemporary cultures, as Almond and Verba did in chapter 12, and (b) the impact of contemporary structure on political culture, particularly through the analysis of the role of political experiences citizens have with the institutional framework of their system on their political attitudes and values. Moreover, I should go one step further in my criticism. In my opinion, *The Civic Culture* does not exhaust the possibilities for analysis of relationship among socioeconomic structure, political culture, and political structure. The authors do interpret their findings from the perspective of individuals' class membership, SES, etc. While some empirical problems connected with measuring SES may call for further discussion—particularly the role of education in the whole SES syndrome—this side of the analysis is very valuable. What is missing, however, is the analysis of the relationship between socioeconomic reality and political institutions, on the one hand, and the impact this relationship has on political culture, on the other.

Citizens play various roles in the society, and for most of them the nonpolitical roles are more important than the political ones. There is, however, an important relationship between socioeconomic structure and the political system: how, for instance, political pluralism in the form of competing political parties and a free political press is related to the economic structure in which wealth is accumulated in relatively few private hands. This is the classic point raised by Marxism in its criticism of "bourgeois democracy." The problem is extremely complex, since various capitalist societies demonstrate both various levels of private concentration of wealth and various extents to which wealth can be used as political instrument. There is, however, a general problem of contradictions between the formal role of citizens as equals in "political society" and their actually unequal roles in "economic society." Indirectly, some inferences can be drawn from the *Civic Culture* data on selected aspects of this problem, as demonstrated by Carole Pateman in relation to the impact citizens' workplace experiences have on their political attitudes. But generally speaking, the problem of adequacy—or lack of it—of political structure to the economic one and of the consequences this has on political culture has not been sufficiently explored.

In part this results in an implicit adoption of a middle-class perspective in evaluating Anglo-American political culture. The authors seem to look at the system from the perspective of those whose interests are well protected within the system and who, therefore, can realistically expect participation within the system and acceptance of its norms to be their best strategy. Nobody denies that this is true in the case of many—those who are more or less well established within the socioeconomic structure. The problem, however, is with the "underdogs"— those who for a variety of reasons feel that their interests are not sufficiently well protected and their voices unheard. My impression is that they have been more prominently shown in the Italian and particularly in the Mexican parts of the study than in the Anglo-American section. Is this only because, relatively and absolutely, this category is larger in the former than in the latter? This is what warrants Burlatskii–Galkin's criticism of the lack of class analysis in *The Civic Culture,* although I should argue that by omission rather than by explicit statements this demonstrates a class perspective in the study: namely, a middle-class orientation.

The last point brings me to my second main criticism of *The Civic Culture,* that is, that the study reflects the pre-radical atmosphere prevailing in American social science in the 1950s and early 1960s. The study adopts—for the most part implicitly, but in chapter 13 also explicitly—a status-quo perspective in studying political cultures and political institutions. This is particularly strongly expressed in the way in which the British and American systems of government are discussed, but also—although less clearly—in the treatment given the West German and Italian systems. It is only when discussing Mexico that the authors acknowledge—ex-post facto —the importance of radical changes introduced by the Mexican revolution.

The status-quo orientation of the study is reflected in:

1. the definition of citizen participation as participation within the established system alone and according to the norms of the system. Thus, when referring to some European countries where, like France, the radical left is politically strong, the authors clearly indicate their feeling that this is a pathological situation from the perspective of democracy. "In many other European countries the failure of the dominant elites to respond to the moderate demands for structural and policy changes put forward by the left in the first half of the nineteenth century led to the development of the structurally alienated, revolutionary socialist, syndicalist, and anarchist left of the second half of the nineteenth century." Contrasted with this gloomy picture is the Anglo-American experience, where "left and right both tend to accept the existing political structure and differ only on the substance of policy and political personnel." [27] Even more explicitly the pro-status-quo orientation is expressed in Almond and Verba's concept of participation and competence where the stability of political systems is very strongly emphasized.[28] Consequently, sense of competence, that is, the feeling that one is able to perform effectively as a citizen within the system, becomes an important element of political culture. What the authors seem to put aside is the fact that some social groups feel—rightly or wrongly—that their chances of performing effectively within the system are minimal or nil; in this case political apathy may be interpreted

in terms of the critical evaluation of the existing system rather than in terms of the psychological characteristics of inactive citizens. Furthermore, one may be interested in exploring the propensity of some groups in engaging in various forms of antisystem participation.[29] It is by no means obvious that radical participation in antisystem political activity is dysfunctional for democracy, albeit it is dysfunctional for the policies of the existing establishment. Here again, more by omission than directly, the authors see the reality in terms consistent with their pro-status-quo orientation.

2. failure to recognize the political importance of interparty or, generally, intergroup cleavages in those situations when social conflicts lead to political polarization. The extent of partisanship seems to be considered as a negative indicator of the state of civic culture; less partisanship is accepted as a measure of more mature and more democratic political culture. This reflects, in my opinion, the tendency to regard radical protest as either a sign of immaturity or a lack of democratic capacities, or both.[30]

3. a tendency to explain discrepancies between normative standards of democracy and political reality in terms of psychological deficiencies rather than structural contradictions within the system. This criticism has been made very strongly and, in my opinion, justly by Carole Pateman, who wrote about the need of reanalyzing *The Civic Culture* in such a way that the contradictions between norms of political democracy and the socioeconomic situation in the workplaces are taken into account.[31] If the phenomenon of political apathy is interpreted from the perspective of the contradiction between formal norms of democracy and the reality of socioeconomic conditions of the capitalist society, it may become less obvious that those who participate behave rationally, while those who do not show some irrationality. There might be more rationalism in not participating in some forms of institutionalized political behavior, particularly for those who are structurally deprived of full opportunities. How things are in reality is an extremely complex question; I am very far from accepting without question all assumptions the radical leftists make about the Western, particularly American, political system. The point here is, however, not whether all their assumptions are correct or not.

The point is whether or not the theoretical perspective present in the radical criticism of the status quo has at all been taken into account in *The Civic Culture*. In my opinion, it has not. This is what I call here the status-quo orientation of the study.

My third major criticism concerns the way in which Almond and Verba treat the American political system and political culture, on the one hand, and other systems and cultures, on the other. *The Civic Culture* is almost unique in the explicitness with which its authors state their value judgments, making further discussion much easier. They accept the Anglo-American concepts of liberty and democracy as their yardstick for evaluating the extent to which any system is democratic and attempt to find out conditions for and obstacles to its imitation by the emerging nations. Taking one's own system as a yardstick of evaluating others is not uncommon in political science, although usually it is done implicitly rather than explicitly. I consider the openness with which the authors expressed their ideological position good for the clarity of their own position and for further discussion. My criticism, however, refers to something else. I believe that the authors have allowed themselves to accept some of their ideological assumptions as semiempirical findings. The fact that the American and British political cultures were found to be the best fits for the democratic political system is not an empirical finding but a consequence of the way in which democracy has been defined. It is particularly so because the authors have identified democracy mostly with a system that gives high priority to the value of liberty. Because of this, France is referred to as a "mixed" political culture,[32] since the French concept of democracy differs from the Anglo-American in that it puts stronger emphasis on the value of equality, and relatively less strongly emphasizes the value of liberty.[33] What the authors seem to ignore is that political theory has more than one model of democracy. Consequently, they overconcentrate on the values of liberty and participation at the expense of the value of equality. It partly reflects the lack of sensitivity to problems of socioeconomic justice and the general antiradical posture adopted in the study. Moreover, it results in adopting a research strategy which by definition leads implicitly to comparing the three non-Anglo-Saxon countries with the Anglo-Saxon model. The results of this comparison are largely as they could have been anticipated, although in many details they bring some important insights into the ways non-Anglo-Saxons differ from the Anglo-American political model, as well as into some differences between the American and the British systems of government. For future research one may wish to recommend a more explicit definition of various models of democracy [34] as well as an extension of the study to countries offering best possibilities for across-systems comparisons. France would be my number-one candidate for inclusion on the Western side; inclusion of countries with radically different types of government and concepts of democracy, particularly the socialist countries—would lead to serious theoretical problems but would also offer fascinating opportunities for comparisons.[35]

In general, *The Civic Culture* can be considered one of the milestones in the recent history of comparative social sciences. With all its limitations, which can be explained in part by the novelty of this intellectual enterprise, it has served as a source of inspiration for other studies and is still one of the most important analyses of political phenomena across national boundaries. Continuation of the study would increase its impact on international social science, particularly if (a) the theory underlying the study is reconsidered in the light of new political developments of the last decade and new theoretical orientations of critical social science; (b) the research approach is adapted to the needs of truly international collaboration between various national teams, without which cross-national studies in social science are increasingly hard to undertake and to complete successfully; (c) the study is extended to countries with different socioeconomic and political orders, to find the degree to which their political cultures differ; and (d) selected subcultures are studied cross-nationally, with elite political culture being probably the strongest candidate for inclusion.

NOTES

1. International Study on Values in Politics, *Values and the Active Community: A Cross-National Study of the Influence of Local Leadership* (New York: The Free Press, 1971). Methodological experience of the *Values* project has influenced quite a few publications, most particularly Adam

Przeworski and Henry Teune, *The Logic of Comparative Social Inquiry* (New York: Wiley-Interscience, 1970).

2. The present paper develops further some points discussed in my earlier writings on the methodology of cross-national research, particularly "Problems of Theory and Methodology in Cross-National Comparative Research," *The Indian Journal of Politics* 5, no. 1 (1971): 1–18; *The Polish Round-Table* 4 (1970–71): 23–36; and "The Role of Theory in the Process of Cross-National Survey Research," in A. Szallai and R. Petrella, eds., *Cross-National Comparative Survey Research* (Elmsford, N.Y.: Pergamon Press, 1977), pp. 347–72.

3. References to communist political systems are few and, in general, more in line with standard political stereotypes than of a more analytical nature; thus, for instance, the authors refer to "two different models of the modern participatory state, the democratic and the totalitarian," in spite of many criticisms raised against this oversimplified dichotomy. See Almond and Verba, *The Civic Culture* (Boston: Little, Brown, 1965), p. 3.

4. Fedor M. Burlatskii and Aleksander A. Galkin, *Socijologija, Politika, Miezhdunarodnyje otnoshenija* (Moscow: Izdatielstvo Miezhdunarodnyje otnoshenija, 1974), pp. 110–12.

5. Jerzy J. Wiatr, review of *The Civic Culture* in *Social Science Information* 4 no. 2 (1965): 220–23; Jerzy J. Wiatr, *Spoleczeństwo*, 5th ed. (Warsaw: PWN, 1973), pp. 367–68; Adam Przeworski and Henry Teune, "Equivalence in Cross-National Research," *The Public Opinion Quarterly* 30 (1966–67): 551–68, simultaneously published in Polish in *Studia Socjologiczne*, no. 4/23 (1966): 163–75; when working on this paper, Przeworski was still associated with the Institute of Philosophy and Sociology, Polish Academy of Sciences.

6. Adolf Bibić and Pavle Novosel, *Politička znanost* (Zagreb: Naprijed, 1971), p. 482.

7. Fedor M. Burlatskii, *Lenin, gosudarstvo, politika* (Moscow: Izdatielstvo Nauka, 1970).

8. Władysław Markiewicz, "Kultura polityczna społeczenstwa," *Odra* (1971), no. 3, later included in his book *Socjologia a służba społeczna* (Poznań: Wydawnictwo Poznańskie, 1972), pp. 320–40. Cf. by the same author, "Kultura polityczna jako przedmiot badan naukowych" (Political Culture as a Subject of Scientific Inquiry), *Kultura: I Spoleczenstwo* 2, no. 4 (1976) where the definition is further elaborated.

9. F. M. Burlatskii, *Lenin*, p. 55.

10. W. Markiewicz, "Kultura polityczna społeczeństwa," p. 321.

11. J. Wiatr, *Spoleczeństwo*, p. 367. I have developed further this position in my book *Socjologia Stosunkow Politycznych* (Sociology of Political Relations) (Warsaw: Scientific Publishers, 1977), including there a discussion of the theoretical and methodological aspects of *The Civic Culture* based on an earlier version of the present paper.

12. See Gary K. Bertsch, *Nation-building in Yugoslavia: A Study of Political Integration and Attitudinal Consensus* (Beverly Hills, Calif.: Sage Publications, 1971); Gary K. Bertsch and M. George Zaninovich, "A Factor-Analytic Method of Identifying Different Political Cultures: The Multinational Yugoslav Case," *Comparative Political Studies*, January 1974, pp. 219–44; Allen H. Barton, Bogdan Denitch, and Charles Kadushin, eds., *Opinion-making Elites in Yugoslavia* (New York: Praeger Publishers, 1973).

13. Kenneth Jowitt, "An Organizational Approach to the Study of Political Culture in Marxist–Leninist Systems," *American Political Science Review* 68, no. 3 (1974): 1171–91.

14. Andrzej Siciński, "Opinie o problemach miedzynarodowych jako ele-

ment współczesnej ideologii społeczeństwa polskiego," *Studia Socjologiczne,*
no. 2/21 (1966): 137–70; Andrzej Sociński, "Peace and War in Polish Public
Opinion," *The Polish Sociological Bulletin,* no. 2 (1967): 25–40; Andrzej
Siciński, *Młodzi o roku 2000: Opinie, wyobrażenia, postawy* (Warsaw:
Instytut Wydawniczy CRZZ, 1975), pp. 115–17.

15. Marek Kesy and Jerzy J. Wiatr, "Wiedza obywatelska mieszkańców
małych miast," in Bogdan Suchodolski, ed., *Upowszechnianie nauki* (Warsaw:
PWN, 1971), pp. 97–120 (with English summary). In 1975 and 1976 a
follow-up study was conducted by Renata Siemienska and myself, using
similar questionnaires on representative national samples of adult populations. The results—not yet published—show a similar pattern in the
respondents' political knowledge. Using a more sophisticated technique of
scaling, we have found better knowledge of politicians (Polish and foreign)
as well as of political organizations than that of the prerogatives of various
agencies of the government. Using the whole battery of 34 items we have
found that 1.99% of respondents were very well informed (at least 30
correct answers), 30.06% well informed (20–29 correct answers), 39.14%
moderately informed (10–19 correct answers), 25.61% ill informed (1–9 correct answers), and 3.06% totally uninformed (no correct answers). We also
found an association between the level of information and the feeling of
civic competence (belief that one can understand politics). Cf. Renata
Siemienska and Jerzy Wiatr, "Wiedza o polityce i percepcja własnej roli"
(Political Knowledge and Perception of Own Role), unpublished research
report, 1976.

16. Szczepański says: "Foreign observers are inclined to underline the
still-existing difference between the *pays légal* and *pays réel* in Poland, and
the most important aim of the ruling group is to overcome this difference.
Thus education for political leadership is, in a sense, more important than
education for constructive citizenship, even in view of the steadily growing
scope of democratization. It is important to overcome the traditional Polish
individualism and anarchical inclinations that proved to be so fatal in the
eighteenth century and still could not be eradicated in the nineteenth. . . .
To teach Poles the democratic discipline of the kind existing in highly
developed Western democracies will require very able and highly skilled
political elites at both the local and national levels. . . . The years of
foreign rule and the years of underground struggle have accustomed Poles
to disregard the law as something foreign and irrelevant. The overcoming
of this attitude is of crucial importance for the new government. But it
also must be noted that revolutionary governments themselves are inclined
to place higher value on efficient action than on the rule of law. Therefore,
the transformation of the Polish society into a well-ordered and law-abiding
nation will require more time and educational effort, a period during which
the actual and substantive functioning of the state administration and
institutions will be of decisive significance." Jan Szczepański, *Polish Society*
(New York: Random House, 1970), p. 50.

17. See particularly Władysław Markiewicz, "Kultura polityczna społeczeństwa," which concludes with a polemic against those who consider Polish
political culture insufficiently mature for the requirements of the modern
democratic state.

18. See particularly, Przeworski and Teune, *The Logic of Comparative
Social Inquiry* (New York: Wiley-Interscience, 1970).

19. G. Almond and S. Verba, *Civic Culture,* p. 3.

20. Stein Rokkan, "Cross-Cultural, Cross-Societal and Cross-National Research," in *Main Trends of Research in the Social and Human Sciences*

(Paris and The Hague: UNESCO/Mouton, 1970), pt. 1, "Social Sciences," pp. 645–89; quotation from p. 649.

21. G. Almond and S. Verba, *Civic Culture*, p. 41.

22. See Hanna Malewska, "Badania porównawcze (Cele i trudności realizacji)," *Studia Socjologiczne*, No. 4/55 (1974): 131–44.

23. Cf. Przeworski and Teune, "Equivalence in Cross-National Research," *Comparative Social Inquiry*.

24. In addition, I should like to mention some points of criticism that are of a more technical nature and do not refer to the main theoretical issues. First, the way in which data have been tabulated results sometimes in misunderstandings. For instance, Table II.9 (*Civic Culture* p. 61) purports to demonstrate low willingness of the Mexicans with little political information to express their political opinions. If, however, data are re-computed as proportion of column 2 to column 1, i.e., percentage of total sample low on information but who answered four or more opinion questions to percentage of total sample low on political information, a completely different picture would emerge: United States, 84.5 percent; Great Britain, 76.1 percent; Germany, 100.0 percent; Italy, 33.3 percent; Mexico, 64.0 percent. In other words, it is the Italians' rather than the Mexicans' unwillingness to express opinions without sufficient information that has to be explained. Second, some explanations are too simple: e.g., the higher frequency of talking politics being interpreted as showing a greater sense of safety (p. 80), when other potential interpretations have not been tested. Clearly, cultural differences may have played a role. Third, the assumption that education is strongly correlated with other SES characteristics (p. 316) has not been tested cross-nationally. Although many American surveys demonstrated this relationship, there is no reason to believe that the same holds true in other countries. Low-income people with high education are not rare in some underdeveloped countries, for instance in India. Fourth, measuring party distance by the hypothetical marriage question (p. 96) disregards culture-specific differences in the extent to which parents believe that maintaining a close relationship with their children calls for interfering in their spouse selection as well as differences in the patterns of relations between in-laws in various cultures. The last point was first raised by Przeworski and Teune, "Equivalence . . . ," p. 556.

25. Carole Pateman, "Political Culture, Political Structure and Political Change," *British Journal of Political Science* 1, no. 3 (1971): 291–305.

26. G. Almond and S. Verba, *Civic Culture*, p. 32.

27. Ibid., p. 28.

28. Ibid., p. 186.

29. More recent writers are more aware of the importance and value of political activity directed against the wrongs of the status quo. Amitai Etzioni, for instance, emphasized both the inevitability (under existing conditions) and the functionality of what he calls "demonstration democracy": "We would like to stress as strongly as possible that we do not mean that increasing the efficacy of the political process can substitute for genuine responsiveness to material needs, appropriation of resources, sharing of privileges, etc. On the contrary, if 'participation' in politics is offered without the sharing of wealth and extension of rights, the final explosion, while its occurrence might be delayed for a while, will be that much larger." A. Etzioni, *Demonstration Democracy* (New York: Gordon & Breach, 1970), p. 56.

30. This point is made even more clearly in Gabriel Almond and G.

Bingham Powell, Jr., *Comparative Politics* (Boston: Little, Brown, 1966). The authors emphasize the importance of the extent and type of partisanship but clearly consider strong partisanship detrimental to the stability of a democratic system. Their evaluation of the French political system is particularly harsh: "France is the classic case of a nation whose political culture, although manifesting a strong national identity in some respects, appears to be so fragmented as to make effective political performance almost impossible except in crisis, or under an authoritarian regime" (p. 64). Among recent authors who take a more sympathetic and more realistic look at this aspect of the French system, see Sidney Tarrow, *Partisanship and Political Exchange in French and Italian Local Politics: A Contribution to the Typology of Party Systems*, Sage Professional Paper in Contemporary Political Sociology, 1, 06–004 (Beverly Hills, Calif.: Sage Publications 1974).

31. C. Pateman, "Political Culture," pp. 301–2.

32. G. Almond and S. Verba, *Civic Culture*, pp. 3, 35.

33. See George H. Sabine, "The Two Democratic Theories," *Philosophical Review* 61 (1952), quoted by Robert D. Putnam, *The Beliefs of Politicians: Ideology, Conflict, and Democracy in Britain and Italy* (New Haven: Yale Univ. Press, 1973), p. 164.

34. Robert Putnam, *Beliefs of Politicians*, p. 182, introduces, for instance, five models of democracy—authoritarian, polyarchal, liberal, classical, and socioeconomic—to find to what degree they are represented in the elite political culture of Britain and Italy. Putnam's approach allows him to explain cross-national differences in the attitudes toward democracy without imposing any particular country's concept of democracy as a yardstick for evaluating other political cultures.

35. After this paper had been written a new book on political culture in the communist countries was published: A. Brown and J. Gray, eds., *Political Culture and Political Change in Communist States* (London: Macmillan & Co., 1977). The editors and authors approach the problem differently from the Almond-Verba tradition in the sense that they rely more on "objective" than on "subjective" data. They try to make use of relevant East European survey research data, mostly Yugoslav, Polish, and Czechoslovak. The book is the first attempt to use the political culture paradigm for a comparative analysis of socialist political systems. What makes it original but at the same time controversial is its heavy emphasis on continuity of historically rooted patterns of political culture.

CHAPTER V

Political Culture in Great Britain: The Decline of the Civic Culture

Dennis Kavanagh
University of Manchester

THE PUBLICATION in 1963 of *The Civic Culture* was a signal contribution to the empirical study of political culture and a pioneer effort in cross-national survey research. It was based on the first nationwide academic sample survey of political attitudes in Great Britain and was also the first to examine them in a comparative context. Contemporary criticism of this pioneering study is almost inevitable because of developments in research methods, changes of mood in the discipline, and subsequent studies of attitudes in the five states.

Britain has of course long been regarded as a model stable democracy, and the qualities of the political culture have often been advanced as a major explanation for the system's stability and effectiveness. Much emphasis has been placed on the pragmatism and moderation of the political elites, the widespread consensus about the political procedures, and the deference to rulers. *The Civic Culture* is an important part of this tradition; it has been regularly cited because it both purveyed these views

I would like to thank Ivor Crewe for his comments on an earlier version of this paper.   D. K.

and also provided empirical evidence to support them. The recent intensification of challenges to many established ideas about the British political system and its political culture, however, makes it appropriate that we should reassess the work at this time.[1]

This chapter, first of all, examines the study's assumptions and survey methods and indicates its impact on research in Britain. Second, it assesses the extent to which the national characterization and relationships identified in the original study have held up over time. Finally, it considers some of the criticisms advanced of the political culture tool and suggests some implications for future research into British political culture.

A CRITIQUE OF THE BRITISH FINDINGS

INTELLECTUAL ORIGINS

Any review of *The Civic Culture* needs to take account of the particular mood in American political science in the late 1950s. Several assumptions colored many Americans' assessment of Britain. These included: (*a*) a particular interpretation of political development in Britain; (*b*) a concern with stable democracy; (*c*) an assumption about "the end of political ideology"; and (*d*) a perspective on democratic theory.

Almond and Verba present Britain as the model of "the Civic Culture." This culture is characterized by a mixture or balance between participant and deferential or acquiescent attitudes; between a consensus on the rules of the game and disagreement on specific issues; between commitment and pragmatism. The mixture emerged from an incremental pattern of state- and nation-building which permitted the blending of the traditional and modern, subject and participatory values. Hence, according to the authors, "the whole story of the emergence of the civic culture is told in British history" (page 8).* The British experience, in this view, was contrasted with the patterns of state and national formation in France, Germany, and Italy, countries in which disruptive encounters between traditional and modernizing forces had not permitted the emergence of this benevolent synthesis of values. Such a constrast also colored the writings of

---

* Page numbers in parentheses refer to Gabriel A. Almond and Sidney Verba, *The Civic Culture: Political Attitudes and Democracy in Five Nations* (Princeton, N.J.: Princeton Univ. Press, 1963).

many other historians and political scientists who analyzed the development of the British political system, drew lessons from it, and contrasted it with the continental pattern.[2]

The authors also reflected a general concern in the discipline to elucidate the conditions of stable democracy. During the 1950s scholarly attention focused on the problems of political development and socioeconomic modernization in the newly independent states. The contribution of Almond and Verba to this literature was to suggest the cultural conditions for stable democracy, based primarily on a study of attitudes in Britain and America.

These years also witnessed the growth of "the end of political ideology" literature, to take account of the apparent waning of class differences and tensions, and the growth of affluence and social mobility. It was a time of political consensus and quiescence, certainly when compared to the interwar years (and late 1960s). Much of the writing was allusive, impressionistic, and applied mainly, though not exclusively, to Anglo-American and Scandinavian states.[3] Almond and Verba, for example, implicitly assumed that some political plateau had been reached and stated that in Anglo-American societies the political consensus of "cultural homogeneity" had now "extended from structural orientations into policy orientations."[4]

Finally and more controversially, the authors set out to test a model of the good "citizen" of democratic theory, one who is informed, interested, and active in politics. They hoped to find out how widespread this type of outlook was, relate their findings to the ways different political systems performed,[5] contribute "to a scientific theory of democracy" (page 9), and promote the diffusion of a democratic culture (page 12).[6] In fact the authors found that the ideal citizens constituted only a small minority. Their concluding revision of democratic theory along more "realistic" and elitist lines, to take account of these findings, fed into a prominent intellectual stream in American political science. One theme was that because the qualities of civility, tolerance, and support for liberal-democratic principles were disproportionately found among people of higher status and further education, *then* political apathy among the lower socioeconomic groups was a useful safeguard for liberal democracy.[7] There was some admiration among these writers for the

British class system and the deference to social and political elites in Britain; as a consequence the rulers were relatively insulated from mass pressures.[8] Harry Eckstein best expressed this mood with his observation in 1962 that the English "expect their rulers to *govern* more than *represent* them."

IMPACT IN BRITAIN

A major reason why *The Civic Culture* received little attention in Britain lay in the research interests and traditions of the academic community. Few of the two hundred or so political scientists in Britain in 1963 were familiar with or sympathetic to quantitative empirical approaches, survey research, or the use of psychocultural concepts and Parsonian pattern variables.[9] The book was of interest, therefore, to a small segment of a small profession.[10] A decade later, when the profession in Britain had expanded to become more receptive — albeit cautiously — to behavioral approaches, *The Civic Culture* faced broad-based criticisms (also leveled in America) rather than the earlier indifference.

American criticism mainly centered on the authors' methods and concepts, particularly on the attempts to operationalize political culture for survey purposes, definitions of citizenship and stable democracy, and inferences from their data. The book soon became a target for the critics of the behavioralist and pluralist persuasion in political science. What had been avantgarde in 1963 was soon overtaken by a new radicalism, and passages from the book, notably on the restatements of democratic theory and the celebrations of an Anglo-American style of politics, were frequently cited in a debunking vein.

The book produced little reaction as a study of Britain largely because it told most British academics little that they did not think they already knew. It did not challenge the conventional textbook emphases on the qualities of consensus, pragmatism, gradualism, tolerance, limited partisanship, and deference, though it provided quantitative evidence for some of these judgments.[11] Indeed, because it was the only major study of the political culture, many of the findings of the 1959 survey were still being cited ten years later as though the situation had hardly changed.

Subsequent survey research in Britain has largely concentrated on various aspects of voting behavior and owes little to *The*

Civic Culture. But it is possible to trace some effects of the book in studies of working-class political culture and children's political socialization. The outstanding treatment of deference and stable democracy in the British context, for example, has been Eric Nordlinger's *The Working Class Tories*,[12] a theoretical case study inspired by Almond and Verba's emphasis on the balance between acquiescent and participant orientations toward political authority. Many of Nordlinger's survey questions were borrowed from the original 1959 schedule, including those on citizen and subject competence, participation in the family, school and workplace, and styles of political partisanship. Even though his interviews were confined to the English working class, Nordlinger's study remains the most self-conscious attempt to build on the hypothesis of *The Civic Culture*.[13] Later socialization surveys, particularly the cross-national efforts of Jack Dennis and his colleagues, have taken the original *Civic Culture* findings as a baseline for measuring continuity and change during the 1960s.[14]

The study has also had to compete with other explanations for the features of consensus, stability, and deference in Britain. Some historians have emphasized a particular "route to modernity," especially the sequential process of state and nation building. Others have accorded primacy to the international economic dominance of England, arising from the fact that she was the first state to industrialize. A left-wing stress has been on the occurrence of working-class militancy in the 1840s, prior to the availability of a Marxist critique of capitalist society; this, it is argued, facilitated a collaboration between the aristocracy and *haute bourgeoisie* in the nineteenth century, which, in turn, deprived the working class of the bourgeois leaders and ideologists necessary to give it a revolutionary, hegemonic consciousness.[15]

A number of sociologists, though not necessarily dissenting from the portrait of the political culture as consensual, are concerned to ask where the values come from and who gains from the political culture in a capitalist society. They are less acquiescent in face of the survey data and prefer to talk of the domination or hegemony of ruling-class values.[16] According to this view, integration or consensus is achieved by means of a "dominant value system"; this is so pervasive that it reconciles a substantial proportion of the working class to the contemporary social and political order and attenuates a radical working-class subculture. "Real" conflicts of interest and inequalities are muffled over by "false consciousness," which is reflected in such features as working-class deference and the acceptance of a selectively defined version of the national interest that is advantageous to the incumbent elite. This literature, by relating the culture to the British class system, provides a radically different and negative appraisal of the civic culture. However, these authors have been unable to collect the satisfactory empirical data to support their interpretation or to demonstrate what kinds of evidence would support it.

THE CIVIC CULTURE EXAMINED

The authors, Almond and Verba, following Talcott Parsons, regard the political culture as a set of psychological orientations to political objects. Orientations are dispositions to act in a certain way and are assumed to influence how people will behave. But the study is open to criticism because there is little in the way of depth interviewing or personality tests to establish that the survey responses are internalized and are dispositions to behavior. We are presented instead, for the most part, with conventional public opinion data on attitudes, opinions, and beliefs. The major drawback to asking people, at little notice, to declare their opinions about subjects remote from their everyday lives and to which they have given little thought is that one will come up with "nonattitudes."

If the idea of the mixed or civic culture was clearly in mind when the questionnaire was designed, it is doubtful that other important aspects of the theory were. The final chapter, on the conditions for stable democracy, contains a long section on the need for a balance between consensus and cleavage, instrumental and diffuse types of support, and participant and passive orientations. But apart from the latter pair, these features are not operationalized in terms of survey questions and the evidence for their presence is only fragmentary. The authors frequently state that Britain has a mixed, participant-subject culture, one thought appropriate for the contradictory demands of democracy (i.e., that the government should have enough initiative and independence to govern effectively and yet also be responsive to its citizens). The nature of the mix, however, is neither consistently nor satisfactorily conceptualized throughout the volume, and the precise nature of the balance between the different outlooks within individuals or throughout society is not specified. At different points in the volume it is argued that the mix or balance emerges from:

1. *the division of labor* between the confident elites and the passive electorate. Unfortunately the distinctions between the elite and the nonelite are not explored in the book;

2. *the inconsistency between norms and behavior.* The survey, for example, finds that whereas two-thirds of the British sample thought that they could do something about an unjust law, only two-fifths would try to do something and only 6 percent had actually tried to influence the national government. And whereas three-quarters claimed they could exert influence at the local level, only 16 percent had ever tried;[17]

3. *the balance within the population between citizens and subjects.* The study merely indicates the percentage of British respondents who have "citizen competence" (56 percent) and those who have "subject competence" (50 percent). It does not indicate the percentage having both kinds of competence, and the percentage having only one of the two types of competence. Hence it provides no measure of this aspect of cultural mix.

4. *the balance within individuals of the different orientations.* This dimension was not explored in the book, but secondary analysis of the survey data shows that there is some independence between the qualities. For instance, a third of the British sample who are noncompetent as citizens remain confident about their ability to influence the administration.[18]

From the text it appears that the authors have the last two types of balance in mind. There is, however, a crucial distinction between (3), which is a coexistence, and (4), which is a fusion of the different values. Moreover, the concepts of subject and citizen competence refer to participatory orientations in two quite different contexts. They certainly do not relate to the balance between participation and passivity, consensus and cleavage, emotionalism and pragmatism discussed in the final chapter. A more satisfactory analysis of the mixed culture therefore requires some further specification of the differing (either complementary or opposing) values, together with an analysis of individuals who "stretch" rather than "fuse" their value systems to encompass inconsistent elements, and the extent to which different types of values are located in various groups.[19]

In view of the low response rate of the British survey,[20] it is unfortunate that the methodological appendices contain so little discussion of the characteristics of the nonrespondents. The representativeness of those actually contacted was assessed by comparing their age, social class, and region with the 1951 census returns.[21] But these background variables were hardly employed in the study and the more relevant controls of education and party are not mentioned in the appendix. Although the total number of British respondents (963) was comparable to that for the other four countries covered in the study, the actual completion rate (56 percent) and sample size raises two important problems about the analysis.

First, if the completed interviews were disproportionately drawn from persons who were more interested and competent in politics — as is usually the case — then the qualities of such respondents will be overrepresented in the results. This need not detract from the validity of the within-nation analyses, although it will affect the cross-nation analyses. The higher completion rate in Germany (74 percent) — and the probable reduction in the proportion of political competents compared to Britain — may undermine the validity of the authors' interpretation of the different degrees of political and administrative competence between the two nations. It may also affect the authors' theory of the civic culture, given their emphasis on the even balance between political and administrative competence in Britain.

The second problem is that the smallness of the samples (all less than 1000) actually handicapped the authors' major goals of analysis and theory building, for the groups within nations were too small to permit confident analysis. The British sample, for example, contains only 24 respondents who had been to university (a critical control in the tables), 58 members of the Labour party, and only 58 from Wales and 94 from Scotland. This has always been a problem with representative British samples; over 80 percent of respondents live in England and three-fifths share the characteristics of being English, white Protestant, and resident in urban areas. In spite of the authors' early references to role cultures and subcultures, the size of the samples meant that these were hardly referred to again for Britain or, indeed, any other nation.[22] There is much force, therefore, in Erwin Scheuch's appeal for a sampling strategy that would be more concerned with *scope* than *representativeness,* and would oversample those key groups which are important for the underlying theory.[23] Such a strategy in turn requires that hypotheses be made more explicit at the outset of the research.

When we turn finally to the analysis and interpretation of the British data, it is interesting that the book throws so little light on the growing criticism of the British political culture and the institutions. One explanation for this lacuna is that the authors were primarily interested in national and educational comparisons among the five nations. Over 60 percent of the published tables presented the national and/or education patterns. Because variations according to region, class, trade union membership, and even political party are so little explored, what emerges is an analysis of the political culture that is rather undifferentiated and homogeneous.

The survey and the text were little interested in the substantive political issues, personalities, and party images of the time. The authors' concern with a narrow range of orientations, for comparative and theory-building purposes, discouraged them from focusing on attitudes to the contemporary issues of each country. One has to acknowledge that attempting such an exercise would certainly have increased the difficulties of developing equivalent survey questions across the five nations. The cost, however, is seen in a study of British political culture for these years that has *no reference at all* to such major figures as Harold Macmillan, Winston Churchill, and Hugh Gaitskell, to the spread of affluence and social change, to Labour's bitter divisions over its political and electoral strategy following Conservative's third successive electoral victory in 1959, and to the apparent decline of the class basis of party politics. Also neglected is any indication of the abrupt transition from the mood of national self-confidence in 1959 to the self-criticism and evident loss of direction by 1962, when there was an important shift of direction to economic planning and joining the European Economic Community (EEC).

The absence of questions on specific political issues had a further disadvantage. Subsequent surveys of attitudes have shown that there is often an inconsistency between a respondent's views on general or abstract questions and his attitudes to more immediate issues. Some assessment of the relationships between general orientations and specific political issues would have enriched the study and added to our understanding of the features the authors were tapping in the survey.

In spite of the authors' unexceptional comments on British history, there was little attention to the possible determinants of the culture. The ad hoc comments on British history, findings on political socialization, and suggestions about the role of education in general do not amount to an exhaustive or systematic treatment of the sources of the British civic culture. Although the political culture is seen as interacting with the political system and other parts of the environment, the neglect of socio-economic, political, and historical factors led critics to charge the authors with regarding the culture as exercising an independent influence on the system. A different emphasis would be that the orientations of most people to the political system are largely formed by their actual experiences with the authorities, even though these attitudes interact in turn with subsequent actions by voters.[24] In other words, we are suggesting that the political culture substantially depends on the performance of the political institutions over time. Insofar as the political culture consists of expectations about how the political authorities *should* and *will* operate, the values assume a subordinate role in any explanation of stable democracy. Although the authors would not repudiate this, their emphasis on the political culture as consisting of a set of perceiver-determined perceptions lays them open to the charge of such reductionism.[25]

Another interesting feature was that the study takes deference for granted in the British (*sic*) culture.[26] Social and political deference has been a much used term in recent years, referring variously to respect for high-status leaders, working-class support for the Conservative party, allegiance to the government and its actions, and loyalty to the regime. The use and misuse of the feature to explain working-class conservatism and, more generally, stable democracy in Britain have been discussed elsewhere.[27] But, insofar as *The Civic Culture* has been cited by many authors as evidence of British deference,[28] it is interesting to note that Almond and Verba never define the term but simply interchange it with other terms, notably the *subject political outlook*.[29] This quality is shared by respondents who are confident of receiving fair treatment and consideration of their views from the police and civil servants. The survey shows that these qualities are widespread in Britain, but they hardly constitute a case for classifying Britain as "A Deferential Civic Culture." [30] Indeed, on many of the authors' tests of participation and civic competence, lower-status British groups actually score higher than equivalent groups in the United States.

Aside from nationality, the amount of formal education proved to be the favored independent control in the tables. The book confirms the frequent cross-national finding that persons with higher education are more likely to be aware of the role of government, more active in politics, and more politically competent. The authors concluded that greater access to higher education was the major facilitator of the civic culture. This emphasis on education is strange to European social scientists who are usually more inclined to analyze their survey data by religion or social class. But what is clear from the tables in *The Civic Culture* is that the amount of formal education, however useful it may be for the other countries, explains little variation in the attitudes of the British sample. Subsequent research has also shown the limited impact of amounts of formal education on partisanship political attitudes in Britain.[31] Table V.1 draws together the findings from the volume on the differences between

TABLE V.1. *Differences in Levels of Competence by Nation and Education*

Differences between percentages of respondents with primary and university education: (a) who say the ordinary man should be active in his local community, (b) who are local competents; and differences between percentages of respondents with primary and secondary education in (c) citizen competence and (d) subject competence.

	(a)	(b)	(c)	(d)
United States	25	35	34	7
United Kingdom	2	14	11	−2
Germany	35	27	29	10
Italy	31	31	17	6
Mexico	36	27	18	5

Source: Adapted from *The Civic Culture,* op. cit., Fig. 1, p. 219; Table 1, p. 226.

the educational groups in levels of political competence. We see that the differences are much lower in the case of Britain. Indeed, on subject competence those who have received only primary education are slightly more confident than those who have received secondary education; the figure of 74 percent of the primary educated who feel competent about local politics is markedly higher than for any other equivalent national group (the nearest is the United States where 60 percent of the primary educated are locally competent). How then might we explain the perceived high levels of political and subject competence among the less educated British voters?

In Britain, there are problems in coding an individual's education experience before the 1944 Education Act came into effect. Before 1918 schooling was compulsory to the age of eleven, before 1946 to fourteen, and thereafter to fifteen. The variation in the minimum school-leaving age for the British respondents between eleven and fifteen (depending on the time at which they were at school) makes the coding categories for the British sample, namely "primary" and "secondary," rather crude. But the British context also makes the amount of education an imperfect predictor of social class.[32] In 1970, for example, nearly two-fifths of the occupational middle class shared with the working class the fact that they had received the state minimum of education. This makes it risky for Almond and Verba to interchange levels of formal education with social class. A likely explanation for the relatively high levels of competence among the less educated British sample, therefore, is that the group includes many of the middle class.[33]

Another explanation of why education and social class will have only a modest impact on political participation lies in the interrelations between social class and the nature of the party system. In Britain such long-established organizations as trade unions, cooperative societies, and the Labour party have made explicit appeals to the working class and mobilized them into comparatively high levels of political activity. The United States, by contrast, has lacked a class-based party system and such other institutions. In class-stratified societies the working-class party may substitute for education as a facilitator of lower-class political participation and feelings of political competence. The design of the study and the interpretation of the data should have taken more account of the party systems and cleavages in the countries.[34]

The entrails of *The Civic Culture* have been thoroughly picked during the past decade and more, and the foregoing paragraphs have followed a well-trodden path. But there is a need for balance in any critical examination of the volume. The study is important as a cross-national survey of attitudes. The authors do find substantial and significant differences across and within nations. They collected data on such hitherto neglected topics as styles of participation, feelings of obligation to participate in politics, and the nature of partisanship. The volume still stands as an important contribution to the fields of political culture and comparative survey research.

CHANGE IN THE BRITISH POLITICAL CULTURE

A nation's political culture is in a constant state of evolution, though the nature and extent of the change are difficult to measure. The difficulty is compounded in the case of *The Civic Culture* because we are dealing with the relatively short period from 1959 to the present. The fact that the label "traditionally modern" is frequently applied to British politics suggests that the culture is a complex mix of values derived from different points in history and that change in the British culture has usually involved the subtle fusion of new and old values. On many values there is, unsurprisingly, much continuity. But the present cultural mix reflects an altered emphasis on such values as deference, limited government, liberty, public participation, Britain's role as a world power, and the symbols of parliament, empire, and national identity.[35]

The political culture is a set of attitudes to political objects. In a study of change the most important dimensions are the affective and evaluative orientations. For purposes of limiting the range of this chapter we shall focus on attitudes to three broad areas, each of which was regarded as salient by Almond and Verba. These are:

1. *The political system and community.*[36] This concerns such questions as how much pride the British take in their system of government. Is it able to generate loyalty apart from its outputs and benefits for citizens? How much attachment is there to a

shared British identification? What is the nature of partisanship and ideology? How much trust is there in the government?

2. *Subjective political competence.* This has two aspects. First, how confident is the individual as a *citizen*? How confident is he that he can influence the political parties and election process? How would he go about trying to exercise influence? Does he view the system as being responsive to his demands? Has there been a decline in deference? To what extent has the sense of political competence been taken over by a mood of protest? Second, how confident is he as a *subject*? This deals with such topics as the individual's assessments of the local and central government officials who enforce the laws and regulations.

3. *Support for the political system.* To what extent have changes in satisfaction with outputs and benefits been translated into different levels of allegiance to the system?

SOURCES OF CHANGE

A number of factors may have stimulated changes in the culture. One basic datum consists in simple changes in the population. Between 1959 and 1971, deaths and comings of age alone changed the composition of the electorate by 16 million people, or nearly a third. During the same years there was an outflow of 2 million emigrants and an influx of 600,000 nonwhites from the new commonwealth countries. Finally, the balance between age groups also altered; an increase in population of 2.7 million was largely concentrated among the under-fourteens and the over-sixty-fives.[37]

A second stimulus is the possibility of a generational change in values. The idea of political generations rests on the assumption that people are so influenced by the conditions prevailing during their politically formative years that they are likely to retain these values throughout adult life; people of approximately the same age who have been exposed to the same experiences will be expected to display broadly similar patterns of behavior and outlook. For the *Civic Culture* survey the median British respondent was born during the 1914–18 war; he spent his formative years during a period of mass unemployment and threats of war, lived under a succession of Conservative governments or Conservative-dominated coalitions, and at a time when Britain was a world power and the center of a far-flung empire.

The median respondent in a survey conducted today was born in 1931; he experienced the first Labour majority government in 1945, the establishment of full employment and the welfare state, the period of affluence and abandonment of the empire in the 1950s, and economic decline and loss of world status.

In the light of such changes in youthful experience, Ronald Inglehart has argued that the interaction of social and economic change with new political values is producing a new style of politics in Western Europe, one based on differences in basic values between generations.[38] He suggests that younger people, exposed to sustained affluence and peace during their formative years, have developed different values from older generations who were not able to take these phenomena for granted. On the assumption that the material needs of the younger generation are largely satisfied, they will be expected to stress the "post-bourgeois" goals of self-actualization and participation over the "acquisitive" or material needs. However, Britain's relatively low rate of postwar economic growth provides markedly less discontinuity between the generations than is the case in the other West European states and it would be expected that the younger generation will be slower to assimilate the "new" issues of participation and equality. In their 1959 study Almond and Verba found some evidence that younger people across the five nations were becoming more participant in their outlooks as a consequence of social and economic modernization, though they did not systematically study age differences in the political culture.[39]

An alternative emphasis on change is that socialization is a continuous process and that change in a person's values stems from alterations in his circumstances at different steps in the life cycle, for example, increasing political conservatism in response to marriage, home ownership, and old age. Such life-cycle value changes in individuals may produce little net change in a society's culture, however.

Finally, we may consider the impact on values of actual changes in society and the economy over this period. There is, first, the sense of relative economic decline. In the early 1960s the spread of affluence, the wider ownership of consumer goods, and increased social mobility challenged the Labour party to rethink its role as a socialist party. In 1956 Anthony Crosland published his influential *The Future of Socialism,* which assumed that prosperity would continue easily and indefinitely. Between 1959 and 1974 the quest for economic growth was paramount in politics. From 1950–60, the gross national product grew at a rate of 2.7 percent per annum. It rose to 3.4 percent from 1960–65, but dropped to 2.0 percent in the following five years, and has further declined in the 1970s. These figures have been significantly lower than those of any other European country and lower, also, than the promises of British politicians.

A second change has been the large-scale defection from the two major parties in general elections. The combined share of the vote gained by Conservative and Labour parties fell from 89.4 percent in 1970 to 75.1 percent in October 1974, recovering somewhat to 80.8 percent in 1979. There has been a gradual decline in the level of turnout in general elections since 1950, in marked contrast to trends in comparable Western states. This fall in support for the parties is all the more striking if we take account of the falling turnout; in 1951 four-fifths of registered electors voted for one of the two main parties, whereas only 60 percent did so by 1979. Voters have also been increasingly volatile in their support of parties, and governments have seen their levels of public support in by-elections, opinion poll soundings, and even general elections plummet to record low levels.[40] The rise of a strong Nationalist party in Scotland and of the Liberals in England provide other indications of a popular disillusion with the established two-party system.

Finally, there have been changes in the working of the system. The former certainties of the stable, class-based, two-party system, one-party majority government, the sovereignty of parliament, the political unity of the kingdom, and the authority of government are all in retreat. Even since 1973 there has been entry to the EEC and the pooling of British sovereignty, a referendum to decide on Britain's continued membership, the commitment to a devolution of decision making to elected assemblies for Scotland and Wales, and experiments with power sharing and proportional representation in Ulster. Each step, taken from weakness, not strength, has been a constitutional innovation.

Not surprisingly, the British political and economic performance has been viewed in an increasingly critical tone. Much of the criticism has been directed to the once praised political institutions and culture. The appearance in 1963 of *The Civic*

Culture coincided with a vigorous onslaught on the country's institutions and leaders. Dissatisfaction with Britain's loss of a world role and its declining position in the "league tables" of economic growth prompted calls for "modernization" and "reform." Both major parties responded and in turn appointed many royal commissions and committees of inquiry, instigated "new looks" at policy, and made some genuine reforms of institutions. This was a reversal of the old confidence that, according to one observer in 1964, reflected the view "that whatever was, is still right, and that whatever is now right, will continue to be correct in the future." The first moves toward joining the EEC were made in 1961. Successive governments tried and failed to boost growth and break out of the cycle of "stop–go" management of the economy. Over a decade later, with Britain in Europe but, on most indicators of economic efficiency and prosperity, even further behind her competitors, a fair epitaph might be "reform without improvement." The change of mood is also reflected in much of the academic literature on British politics.[41]

ATTITUDES TOWARD THE SYSTEM AND COMMUNITY
POLITICAL PRIDE

The Civic Culture was impressed by the high levels of support among the British population for the political system. The legitimacy of the institutions was not based merely on satisfaction with the outputs but rested largely on a diffuse support. The system thereby satisfied the authors' suggestion that a secure regime required citizens to balance instrumental and affective orientations to politics. When asked to indicate the features they were most proud of in their country, nearly half the British sample spontaneously mentioned the system of government and political institutions, a proportion higher than that in any other country except the United States. Much other evidence confirmed A. L. Lowell's assessment that "the typical Englishman believes that his government is incomparably the best in the world."[42]

More recent evidence, however, suggests that there has been growing dissatisfaction with the way the system works and with the policies it produces. The "what's wrong with Britain" literature in the early 1960s dealt mainly with the economy and society; now, however, there is more criticism of the political

institutions, particularly of the two-party system and the centralization of decisions in London. The large-scale *Attitudes Survey,*
conducted for the Royal Commission on the Constitution in
1970, reported "some general feeling of dissatisfaction" with the
"system of running Britain" and also a widespread feeling for
some change.[43] Nearly half (49 percent) favored some change in
the arrangements and only 5 percent thought that things could
not be improved; this dissatisfaction was widespread regardless
of the respondent's political interest, activity, or social background. At the time the commission found the evidence of dissatisfaction difficult to evaluate and thought its task would have
been easier "if public opinion had crystallised a little further." [44]
But political trends and other survey data in succeeding years
have, if anything, only confirmed their interpretation.

Unpublished data from the Essex Survey of the 1974 general
elections reflects the ambivalent views about parties and politicians. A substantial minority (nearly 30 percent) expressed only
negative views (not satisfactory, unhappy, very unhappy), which
was a higher proportion than those expressing only positive
views. Examination of Gallup Poll ratings also shows a decline in
popular satisfaction with party leaders. An index of the leaders'
joint popularity may be constructed by combining the percentages of those thinking that both party leaders are handling their
jobs well. In the early 1960s the index often exceeded 100 percent; it fell to a record low of 61 percent in 1968 and then
hovered around the 75–80 mark until 1974. Comparative surveys
also suggest a lower level of political satisfaction in Britain compared to other Western states.[45] In sum, the survey evidence,
fragmentary though it is, bears out this sense of dissatisfaction.

A strong consensus on procedures for resolving political differences is characteristic of the British. Agreement on the "rules
of the game" was documented by Robert Putnam in the course
of his lengthy, tape-recorded interviews with British MPs (members of Parliament) and Italian *deputati.* He found a high degree of satisfaction with the system among British MPs, with
only a fifth wishing for substantial changes in the system compared to three-quarters of the Italians.[46] There was also agreement on the meaning of democracy as a system resting essentially
on competition between parties. Putnam reasonably concluded
that this procedural consensus and the close fit between the

realities and ideas in Britain legitimated the system, among the elite at least, in contrast to the Italian situation where there was little consensus on the interpretation of democracy. Since 1970, notwithstanding this elite attachment to the system, there have been a number of constitutional innovations (see page 139). There has also been intense debate about the advantages of importing such devices as proportional representation, federalism, and a bill of rights. The innovations may be regarded as further signs of British adaptability, but there is now less agreement on what constitute the rules of the political game.

Many social scientists have stressed the role of the British monarchy in developing a sense of community and allegiance to authority. According to Shils and Young, for example, the monarchy plays "a part in the creation and maintenance of moral consensus." [47] Successive polls have demonstrated that the public reacts positively to the monarchy, though few regard it as playing an important political role. The queen is viewed as playing a figurehead or ceremonial role in society; she is, however, seen as playing it better than leaders of the efficient institutions (see Table V.2). There is some evidence that the monarchy still adds something to the authority and legitimacy of the system. A study of attitudes to monarchy found that promonarchists are

TABLE V.2. *The Importance and Evaluation of Political Roles*

	Importance			Evaluation of role		
	Very			Very		
Role	important %	Important %	T %	well %	Well %	T %
Prime minister	59	32	91	24	38	61 a
Members of						
Parliament	34	56	90	12	54	66
Top civil						
servants	32	48	80	17	52	70
The queen	22	32	54	—	—	88 b

a The question asked for an evaluation of "whoever is Prime Minister," rather than naming the incumbent, Harold Wilson.

b The two positive replies were merged in coding; the percentage refers to all identifying some royal role.

Source: Richard Rose and Dennis Kavanagh, "The Monarchy in Political Culture," *Comparative Politics* 7:552 (1976).

more likely than antimonarchists to support the regime and comply with its basic political laws.[48]

The monarch's role in supporting the regime may occur much earlier in the socialization process. Many young children believe that the queen actually rules as well as reigns and that the prime minister is merely her subordinate; they perceive the queen in markedly favorable terms, in contrast to their detached and cool assessment of the prime minister.[49] The latter is perceived and evaluated in partisan terms and the office has never been garbed with the trappings of royalty.[50] One may speculate that the royalist and benevolent induction to the political system leads children to generalize this positive affect for the monarchy to other parts of the political system and to adopt a nondeferential "take it or leave it" view of the prime minister.

PARTISANSHIP

Almond and Verba were impressed by the positive nature of political partisanship in Britain and particularly by how very few respondents allowed differences over politics to affect personal relationships. Most voters belong to friendship groups containing supporters of a party different from one they support, and a steady majority of voters favor the principle of parties alternating their control of government.[51] Apart from the issue of Irish Home Rule in 1914, the differences between the parties have not strained the fabric of the society of the constitution.

One explanation for this moderate partisanship lies in the kind of image and appeals the parties have put forward in the postwar years. There has been a convergence in the social backgrounds of the Labour and Conservative front benches as both have become more meritocratic and middle class. The decline of the working-class element in the Labour cabinets (half of Attlee's postwar cabinet had been manual workers compared to only one in Wilson's 1970 cabinet) was paralleled by a similar erosion of the aristocracy on the Conservative side. *Embourgeoisement* of parliamentarians has meant that Labour MPs are increasingly being drawn from the ranks of the professions and university graduates. In the interwar years, 72 percent of Labour MPs were drawn from the working class, in 1945 one-half, and in 1974 only 28 percent.

The weakening of the class basis of party representation was reflected in the electorate's view of politics. Butler and Stokes found that only a fifth of the electorate based their choice of party on class concerns, and that the image of party politics as representing opposed class interest was declining among voters who entered the electorate in the 1960s.[52] Indeed, a growing number of voters saw little to choose between the parties. Table V.3 shows the steady decline down to 1970 in the number of voters perceiving important differences between the parties.[53]

When the Conservatives returned to office in 1951 they largely accepted the achievements of the postwar Labour government; they maintained the welfare state, full employment and the mixed economy, and conciliated the trade unions. In the 1960s Labour abandoned explicit class appeals and portrayed itself as the party of managerial efficiency. The Wilson government's adoption of a statutory prices and incomes policy and its abortive attempts to reform trade unions and enter the EEC further diminished differences between the parties. There was, however, a sharper edge to party politics under the Heath government. It came to a head in the dramatic circumstances of the February election in 1974 and continued as the new Labour government set about dismantling the previous Conservative government's policies on Europe, incomes, industrial relations, land, and housing.

Yet the polarization did not prevent the two main parties from suffering sharp losses of electoral support in the 1974 elections. The proportion of voters strongly identifying with the main parties has fallen from 40 percent in 1964 to 24 percent in October 1974, a decline evenly affecting all age groups.[54] The decline in partisanship among voters is associated with a weakening of

TABLE V.3. *Perceived Differences Between the Major Parties, 1951–74*

	1951	1955	1959	1964	1966	1970	1974 Feb.	1974 Oct.
"Major differences"	71	74	66	59	59	50	49	54
"Much of a muchness"	20	20	29	32	37	44	45	41
"Don't know"	9	6	5	9	8	6	5	5

Source: Gallup Polls: "Do you think there are any really important (major) differences between the parties or are they all much of a muchness?"

the class basis of party support and an apparent fall in class consciousness. By October 1974 only one-half the electorate identified with the party of its social class (i.e., manual workers for Labour, and nonmanual for Conservative). Ivor Crewe reports a blurring of class and party in the minds of many voters and also a fall from 1970 in the proportion of voters assigning themselves to a social class without prompting by the interviewer (from 50 percent to 43 percent). The "end of ideology," affluence, and the political consensus combined to soften the political impact of class divisions in the 1950s and 1960s. Paradoxically, the decline in the electoral importance of class has continued, indeed accelerated, in spite of the return by the main parties in the 1970s to ideological and class-related issues. As the main survey study of the 1974 election comments, "the electorate was well aware of the return to the politics of class conflict — and did not like it." [55]

There is some evidence of a greater interest in ideology. Young MPs, for example, are more ideological than their predecessors, in terms of possessing a coherent, comprehensive set of beliefs.[56] On the Labour side this has coincided with a tendency for younger, newer MPs to be drawn from more white-collar occupations, particularly the teaching profession. But there is no evidence that this mood has been followed by the voters. Butler and Stokes found that only one-sixth of the electorate meaningfully use the terms *left* and *right* to describe the parties. A cross-national survey, asking questions on left/right evaluations of the parties, found that Britain was markedly less ideological than West Germany, Austria, the Netherlands, and the United States.[57]

TRUST

We lack good evidence of trust in the British system of government which, on the surface, is a good indicator of diffuse support. It is also particularly difficult to talk with any confidence about the extent or nature of any change in this area. Some of Almond and Verba's unreported data showed a larger degree of cynicism toward British politicians in 1959.[58] A more recent survey confirmed this skepticism about the motives of MPs; 58 percent agreed with the view that "people become MPs for their own gain and to further their own ambitions" while only 20 percent disagreed, and many were particularly likely to doubt claims and promises made by MPs at election time and during party broadcasts.[59] We may usefully think of two dimensions of trust: intrinsic trust, or a belief in the honesty and probity of the political authorities; and pragmatic trust, or the belief that government carries out its promises.[60]

Data collected by Alan Marsh in 1974 on these two measures and reported in Table V.4 show that only a small minority (10–15 percent) are totally cynical about the conduct of government in Britain. But we also see that for none of the four measures does a majority offer a "trusting" response. A plurality think that government is run by a few big interests, which are concerned only for their own benefits, and many feel that a government is able to do what is right and give priority to the needs of all the people for only some of the time. There is also a political basis to feelings of cynicism toward the system. It

TABLE V.4.   *Trust in Government*

Generally speaking, would you say that this country is run by a few big interests concerned only for themselves, or that it is run for the benefit of all the people?	48% Few big interests 37% All the people 15% Don't know
How much do you *trust* the Government in Westminster to do what is right?	7% Just about always 32% Most of the time 47% Only some of the time 10% Almost never 4% Don't know
When people in politics speak on Television, or to the Newspapers, or in Parliament, how much, in your opinion, do they tell the truth?	3% Just about always 22% Most of the time 60% Only some of the time 10% Almost never 4% Don't know
How much do you trust a British Government of either party to place the needs of this country and the people *above* the interests of their own political party?	7% Just about always 28% Most of the time 45% Only some of the time 15% Almost never 5% Don't know

Source: Alan Marsh, *Protest and Political Consciousness* (London: Sage, 1978), page 118.

is highly developed among those who are dissatisfied with the performance of the government and among those who regard the system as unresponsive to their demands. Without trend data we have no way of knowing whether this low level of confidence represents the normal state of affairs or not. It shows, however, a general lack of trust in the country's leadership and coincides with other indicators of dissatisfaction with the way things are going in Britain.

COMMUNITY

Our assumptions about the secure sense of national community and integration in Britain and the agreement on the boundaries of the United Kingdom have been undermined in recent years. The secession of the predominantly Catholic twenty-six counties to form an Irish state in 1921, combined with the failure of Scotland and Wales to develop nationalist parties, eased problems of national loyalty, and simplified British politics along lines of social class. That religion and nationality were not decisive influences in politics was part of the conventional wisdom until very recently. In recent years, however, changing attitudes in the non-English parts have thrown the future of the United Kingdom as we know it into question. The United Kingdom of Great Britain (England, Scotland, Wales) and Northern Ireland is of course a multinational state. The four populations are distinctive in terms of their religious affiliations, national identities, and party loyalties. The sense of belonging to a "British" community is weak outside England. Most Scots and Welsh people identify with their own respective nationalities and most people in Ulster divide their loyalties between Ulster and Ireland.[61] These differences are not new, but hitherto they lacked political significance because they were not expressed in distinctively nationalist political parties and because some five-sixths of the population reside in England. But there has been a recent upsurge of support for nationalist parties. In 1966 such parties collected only 6 percent of the votes outside England and failed to return a single MP. By October 1974 they had captured a third of this vote and twenty-six seats. The Nationalist party in Scotland, appealing to a separate Scottish identity and holding out the prospect of on oil-rich Scotland since the discovery of North Sea oil, saw its share of the Scottish vote leap from 5 percent in 1966 to 30 percent in 1974 and fall to 19 percent in 1979.

The major challenge to the authority of the British government today is found in Northern Ireland. Since the partition of Ireland in 1921 many among the Catholic minority in Ulster have refused to recognize the Protestant-dominated regime. Catholics and Protestants have continued to protest their exclusive loyalties to the Irish Republic and the British Crown respectively, and have remained separate subcultures.[62] In 1968 Catholics began demonstrations for greater civil rights and Protestants responded with counterdemonstrations. British troops were sent in 1969 to keep the peace, but their presence has not stopped the escalation of violence by the sectarian forces of both sides nor prevented the spread of terrorism to the mainland. In the years since the disturbances broke out more than 1800 people have died as a result of violence. The legacy of history and the conflicts of religion and national identity make politics in Ulster distinctive in the United Kingdom, and it stands as a major qualification to all generalizations about the British political culture. In Britain religion is of little political significance, but it dominates political life in Northern Ireland. Violence is not a part of British politics, whereas in Northern Ireland, riots, assassinations, and terrorism are everyday occurrences. The history of the Irish issue before 1922 and the challenge to British rule in Ulster today show that the British are no more successful than other states in dealing with such conflicts.[63]

The arrival of a substantial number of colored immigrants after 1958 introduced a group of citizens who were visibly different from the rest of the British community. In spite of measures to limit the numbers of entrants, several surveys have shown that the great majority feel strongly that there are too many colored immigrants and want to end immigration. Enoch Powell has attracted much support from voters of all parties by articulating fears that the immigrants, notwithstanding their British citizenship, are "alien" in speech and color, and a threat to "the British way of life." [64] His outspoken comments led Mr. Heath to dismiss him from the Conservative Shadow Cabinet in 1968. But his speeches on the issue in the 1970 elections swung many voters and may have been decisive in turning the election for the Conservatives.[65] British experience of colored immigration and the imposition of strict controls on entry showed that Britain possessed no magic formula for coping with the tensions of mixed races; the legislation was designed to ease strains by maintaining a predominantly white population. The events also showed the relevance of a person's color to many citizens' notions of a British community.

INFLUENCING GOVERNMENT

Almond and Verba were impressed with the large number of British voters who felt themselves capable of influencing the local and national governments. Subsequent research into political efficacy or competence has shown how complex this concept is. Questions about an individual's perception of the responsiveness of government and other authorities to "people like me" may actually measure a person's self-confidence rather than his attitudes to the political system. More than two-thirds of Nordlinger's sample of workers, for example, felt that they could do something about an unjust regulation and a similar number were confident of their ability to influence the government; however, only 10 percent claimed to have a "good deal" of influence on the way the country is run. The self-attributed competence may be a potential one, something held in reserve. At the time, Nordlinger found that the great majority were not dissatisfied with this state of affairs.[66] There was general agreement that leaders should act contrary to public opinion where they considered it in the country's best interests and that there was a willingness by most voters to change their policy preferences to bring them into line with those of the party they supported.[67]

The choice of parties and free elections figures prominently in theories of responsive government. Butler and Stokes found that 60 percent of voters showed some understanding that these institutions facilitated popular control. Yet their surveys also showed that there was an increase during the 1960s in those who doubted the ability of these institutions to make the government responsive to public opinion. In 1963, 50 percent of their sample thought that government paid "not much" attention to the people; by 1969 the proportion had risen to 61 percent. Another test of competence by the Royal Commission in 1970 revealed that the majority of people had a low level of confi-

dence in their political capability vis-à-vis *local* government.
The survey also found that respondents who were dissatisfied
with the present system of governing Britain were very likely
to feel that people were powerless in the face of government.
Other surveys invariably find that respondents, when asked to
rank the influence of various groups in government, place
"people like yourself" near the bottom. Marsh's 1974 survey provides the opportunity for direct comparison with the *Civic
Culture* findings on strategies of popular influence. He replicated
two of the 1959 questions, which asked what citizens would do
to try to influence their national and local governments. The
attitudes reported in Table V.5 show a striking stability, though
there is some increase in the proportions who would "do nothing" in the face of local or national regulations that were regarded as "unjust" and there is a small shift to forms of more
direct action.[68]

In this context it is interesting that there has been an upsurge
of more direct forms of protest and self-assertiveness in recent
years. The continued violence and sectarian murders in Ulster,
resistance between 1971 and 1974 by trade unions and local

TABLE V.5.   *What Citizens Would Do to Try to Influence Their Local
and National Governments in 1959 and 1974* a *(in %)*

| What citizens would do b | 1959 (Almond and Verba) | | 1974 Marsh | |
	Local	National	Local	National
Do nothing. Don't know	23	32	36	43
Contact politicians	45	44	40	45
Contact party	1	2	1	1
Vote	4	3	2	2
Form interest groups	3	3	3	3
Contact bureaucrats	3	1	2	—
Get up ad hoc protest group	34	18	32	18
Petition, use media				
March, demonstrate	—	—	3	2
"Just protest"	—	—	3	1
Number	963		1985	

a The question was "Suppose a regulation were being considered by _____
which you considered very unjust or harmful, what do you think you could
do?"

b Total percentages exceed the sum of the individual cells, since some respondents gave more than one answer.

authorities to Acts of Parliament, and, most spectacularly, Mr. Heath's dissolution of parliament in the face of the miners' strike against his incomes policy spring to mind as examples. Have these incidents made obsolete our image of the law-abiding English?

A number of explanations have been advanced for this development. Individuals may still be politically competent in the *Civic Culture* sense of the term but with the difference that there is a more frequent resort to extralegal or unorthodox methods beyond those associated with voting, party activity, writing to the press, and so on. Britain may also be a more generally dissatisfied society, in comparison either with other nations or with the past; hence the greater potential for protest. And, finally, it may be that the protesters are actually concentrated among the most dissatisfied and among those who connect the causes of their dissatisfaction to the political system.

Alan Marsh's survey of support for unorthodox forms of political protest is useful in helping our understanding here. His scale for measuring protest potential was based on the respondent's degree of approval for various forms of protest and the likelihood that he would engage in acts of protest. Nearly four-fifths expressed approval for, and willingness to engage in, legal forms of protest (signing petitions, boycotts, and demonstrations). This finding confirms our image of the law-abiding Englishman. One-fifth were an unorthodox minority, ready to engage in illegal acts (rent strikes, blockades, and other forms of violence). Marsh also asked, "Is it *ever* justified to break the law to protest about something you feel is very unjust or harmful?" More than half (56 percent) said Yes and 36 percent said No (8 percent "don't know"). But this widespread potential for protest was rarely directed against the regime; few of the latent rebels had in mind the overthrow of capitalism or the government. They were more concerned to defend what they regarded as their "normal" rights, such as their civil liberties, protecting their homes against threat of eviction, resisting threats to living standards, and using industrial action to protect free wage bargaining.

We find something interesting about the character of the protest-oriented minority. Willingness to protest is highest among those who share all three of the following characteristics:

(*a*) a high sense of political efficacy, (*b*) cynicism toward the political system, and (*c*) a sophisticated level of ideological and political conceptualization. It is also related to dissatisfaction with perceived government performance and the state of democracy in Britain. Willingness to protest is not therefore a displacement from conventional forms of political participation; rather, it is regarded as an additional means of redress. The protester is like the good citizen in favoring orthodox political behavior. But because he does not trust the government he believes that only protest will be effective. We have here uncovered one important change in the civic culture. Among the politically competent (or those most expected to support the civic culture in the Almond–Verba survey) there appear to be higher levels of ideology and mistrust and where these are combined there is an enhanced potential for protest.[69]

POLITICAL SUPPORT

The question remains: Do these changes in political values, added to such other features as the retreat from the major parties, demands for devolution and separatism, violence, and so on, indicate some crisis of legitimacy for the British political system? It is notoriously difficult to be sure that respondents are distinguishing between attitudes to the *regime* (the set of procedures and institutions), and the *authorities* (the group of leaders who occupy the important positions at a particular time). It is also tempting to conflate statements of desire for change in particular institutions and incumbents into criticism of the system as a whole. In fact, satisfaction with government outputs or leaders may vary independently of attitudes to the system itself.

In a recent reformulation of his notion of political support, David Easton has distinguished between support that is either *diffuse* or *specific*.[70] The former is a general attachment to the system, is largely independent of the varying performance or outputs of the system, and is relatively enduring. Specific support, on the other hand, is contingent on the individual's perception of the system's performance and may vary greatly even over short periods of time. In spite of the difficulties in operationalizing and measuring the motives on which an individual's support is based and the lack of research into the extent to which citizens actually differentiate the regime from the authorities, the distinction will be useful for our purposes.

Much of the dissatisfaction we have traced is *specific,* that is, it is directed at the political parties, their leaders, and the performance of governments. For the members of a political system to offer and withdraw this type of support depends on such criteria as their awareness of the authorities, particularly the party in government; their ability to associate the satisfaction and dissatisfaction of their needs and demands with the perceived behavior of the authorities; and their attribution of responsibility to the authorities, so that perceived performance actually influences levels of support.[71] A good example of this specific support is seen in the correlation in the 1960s between changes in the macroeconomic measures of unemployment and price inflation and the shifts in the popularity of the parties.[72] Voters saw the actions of the government as affecting their prosperity, and changes in their evaluations of the government's economic performance had a major influence on shifts in levels of party support. In view of the attention lavished on the country's economic performance by the mass media and the politicians, it is not surprising that a government's economic output colors the public perceptions of government — although the particular tests of economic success may vary over time. It is possible, however, that disappointment and consequent loss of specific support for the authorities, if maintained for sufficient time, will carry over and lead to general dissatisfaction with the system or at least to the authority roles. Indeed, we think that something like this has probably happened in Britain over the past decade.

Before pursuing this line of argument, a warning is necessary. We lack satisfactory trend data for accurate assessment of a number of important attitudes to the British system, and where such data exist the changes are usually too small to establish a trend or to warrant firm interpretation; for example, the decline between 1963 and 1968 from 25 percent to 18 percent in the proportion of respondents thinking that "people like yourself" had an influence in the country's future.[73] Table V.6 shows that most people have a poor view of politicians but also that this has been so for many years. Perhaps more critical commentators have only recently become aware of what has existed for

TABLE V.6.   *Evaluation of Politicians*

	1944	(June) 1969	(August) 1972
Politicians are out for themselves	35%	43%	38%
Politicians are out for their party	22	29	22
Politicans do what is best for the country	36	29	28
Don't know	7	20	13

Source: Gallup Polls.

a long time. Perceptions of the limitations or failings of the British government, far from reflecting alienation, may simply indicate appropriately modest expectations of what governments and politicians can achieve.[74] A comparative study of British and American university students noted that the British sample appeared to be more "realistic" if less positive in their attitudes to government, and capable of greater differentiation in their evaluation of political objects. The authors expressed doubts about the consequences of "the textbook account inculcated in the United States" and suggested that "a diffuse and unrealistic glorification of the political system may prove to be a weaker basis for legitimacy than a more balanced point of view." [75]

Moreover, such orientations as we have considered may not matter much for regime support. Research into levels of satisfaction with various aspects of life in Britain today found least satisfaction with the quality of democracy. But, compared with such other domains as marriage, family life, and health, most people did not rate the political realm highly in determining the overall quality of life.[76] In spite of the economic depression of the 1970s, life satisfaction has remained high in most West European countries. Survey indicators of life satisfaction show that it has actually increased while the economy declined, largely because satisfaction with face-to-face relationships has more than outweighed dissatisfaction with major institutions like government, business, and unions.[77] The comparative survey evidence shows that more Britons are satisfied with their lot and the way democracy works than are citizens of other West European countries.

There is other evidence of the tenacity of traditional values. Runciman's 1962 survey showed how socioeconomic inequalities had not led to resentment among most of the working class. When making comparisons, less favored groups usually adopted narrow frames of reference in evaluating their rewards and opportunities, that is, they made comparisons with people like themselves or just a little better off.[78] In 1975 research by W. W. Daniel showed that, in spite of an increasingly egalitarian climate of opinion and more powerful unions, the same restricted comparisons were operating and damping dissatisfaction.[79] These modest expectations may explain the general acquiescence in the statutory restraints on wage rises under the first Wilson government, then under the Conservatives between 1972–74, and the actual fall in living standards in 1976–77. Most people have been prepared to scale down expectations in line with slower economic growth.[80]

Some of the problems in this area have been thoroughly if inconclusively discussed in the exchange between Arthur Miller and Jack Citrin concerning the "meaning" of Miller's claim that survey evidence on the declining levels of political trust, efficacy, and the growing approval for political protest among the more cynical in the United States presaged a crisis of legitimacy for the American system.[81] In a critique of Miller's interpretation of these data, Citrin has fairly urged the need for future research into levels of satisfaction and trust in order to distinguish between attitudes toward the political system or regime, the policies of the present government, the outcome of events and policies, and the present political leader(s).[82] In the British case, these distinctions are particularly crucial. The *Attitudes Survey* conducted in 1970 for the Royal Commission on the Constitution reported that respondents had difficulty in distinguishing between criticism of the government of the day and criticism of the system of government; indeed, the minority report placed a very different interpretation on the survey material from that of the commission.[83]

These qualifications warn us to be cautious in our interpretation of the survey data. But such data are only one source of material in assessing attitudes to the system and they have to be related to other sorts of evidence. The data do become plausible when they are linked to such phenomena as the electorate's increasing volatility, declining support for the two major parties and transference of support to other parties, and demands for devolution in Scotland. We know that the strong identifiers with parties are more likely than nonidentifiers to support the parliamentary system and party politics, be more interested and active in politics, and believe in the efficacy of the election process.[84] The decline in strong partisanship and the erosion of both the working-class deferential Tory and the "traditionalist" Labour voter has made support for party and government more instrumental, tying it to actual performance.

One way to summarize the change may be to speak of the decline of deference. For analytical purposes we may distinguish three different, though mutually reinforcing, senses in which the term has been used to describe the British political culture. Each of these aspects has come under strain in recent years. First, there is *political deference,* the respect for the institution and rulers, which is reflected in the compliance with laws, the lack of a revolutionary tradition, the absence of referenda, and the lack of controls on the administrators and political leaders.[85] Second, there is *social deference,* or the identification of political skills with the possession of high social status. This has been reflected in the large working-class vote for the Tory party and the presence in the political elite of many people with an upper-class and public-school background. As Bagehot observed in 1867, deference to gentlemen with diffuse social status led people to believe that men who excelled in these "indispensable respects were superior also in the more tangible qualities of sense and knowledge." [86] Finally, there is the *self-confidence of the leaders,* allied to a popular liking for strong government and firm leadership. This feature is reflected in the hierarchical nature of British politics, the dominance of the cabinet over Parliament and of the parliamentary leaders over the party in the country. The style is captured in the Whitehall model of the constitution, in which the government derives its authority from the Crown and is independent from popular pressures, and by L. S. Amery's description of British democracy as one "by consent, not by delegation, of government of the people for the people, with but not by the people."

Deference was a shorthand term to describe this combination of the confident elites and trusting electorate. Thus *The Civic Culture* approvingly noted: "In Britain, the persisting deferential and subject orientations foster the development of strong and effective government," and, more generally, "The need for elite power requires that the ordinary citizen be relatively passive, uninvolved, and deferential to elites."

Assumptions about the supremacy of Parliament and the strength of the executive have been challenged on several fronts recently. The decision to hold a referendum in June 1975 on Britain's membership of the EEC is one example. In the event, a possible collision between Parliament and people was avoided in 1975 because the electorate decided by a two-thirds majority to vote for continued membership, thereby endorsing Parliament's earlier vote. Mr. Wilson had declared that his party would be bound by the result, whichever way it went (clearly a derogation of Parliament's supremacy). But claims that the outcome preserved intact the authority of Parliament need to be treated with caution. The precedent is there for parties and other groups to call for the electorate to second-guess a vote of Parliament. After all, the impressive pro-Market majorities, of 117 in 1971 and 226 in 1975, were not thought by critics to reflect "the full-hearted consent" of the people. The final resolution of questions affecting devolution for Scotland and Wales in 1979 also required the use of the referendum.

The quality of lower-class deference has been most spectacularly absent in the area of industrial relations. There has traditionally been a contrast between the order and consensus in the political realm and the disorder in the economic realm. Studies of workers' attitudes suggest that deferential or supportive statements are more frequently expressed on abstract general values or about the political system, but that dissent and even alienation are directed to many features of everyday life.[87] Until recently the political realm appeared to be relatively insulated from these negative reactions. But the efforts by governments of both parties to legislate in the "disorderly" area of industrial relations and incomes policy, in the absence of agreement about "fair wages," has led to major collisions between Parliament and the trade unions and rivalry between groups over wage differentials. Decisions formally "legitimated" in parliament were not accepted outside, as Mr. Heath found to his cost in 1974. As John Goldthorpe has warned, to lay down such policies in the absence of a consensus creates "the very real threat of extending economic into political instability." [88]

Deference to a social elite has also declined. McKenzie and Silver showed that the younger working class were voting Tory less on grounds of tradition and deference than for instrumental or secular reasons (e.g., because the Tories were regarded as more competent). But there has also been a change in the character of the Conservative party. Throughout the twentieth century, observers noted that the party has been suffused with the values of upper-crust England, an "Establishment" of wealth, exclusive London clubs, and the major, expensive public schools.[89] In little more than a decade that apparently secure ruling class has almost disappeared. The watershed is the election of Edward Heath as Conservative leader in 1965. He was a grammar-school boy, from a lower-middle-class background. His cabinet colleagues in 1970 numbered few old Etonians and aristocrats. More self-made, professional politicians took over from the traditional "magic circle." Significantly Heath was directly elected by MPs in a competitive ballot in contrast to the previous system of selection by "informal soundings" and then acclamation of the chosen leader.

Despite the more complex tasks facing ministers and civil servants and attempts to develop a more "professional" approach to government, little appears to have changed. The virtues of the generalist amateur administrator were attacked in the Report of the Fulton Commission (1968) on the civil service. The report called for, among other things, the recruitment of civil servants who possessed relevant knowledge of the work of government departments, more policy analysis, and greater attention to long-term problems. More training is now provided by the Civil Service Commission, analytical tools like program budgeting have been introduced, and the Central Policy Review Staff (1970) provides cabinet ministers with broader, more strategic briefing than that made available through the departments.

But politicians and civil servants in British government still tend to possess similar rather than complementary skills. Civil servants are usually "generalists" who possess arts degrees and they lack subject expertise and experience of managing large undertakings.[90] British cabinet ministers are characterized by a comparative lack of specialist knowledge and managerial experience. The emphasis on the generalist qualities is reflected in the frequent reshuffles of ministers between departments; the average ministerial tenure of two years is one of the shortest in the Western world. Ministers continue to be drawn from a narrow base, namely, people with lengthy experience of the House of Commons.

Finally, the much vaunted strength of the government appears to have waned. For various historical and cultural reasons the British are curiously unaware of the state. Neither ministers nor civil servants possess a sense that they embody the state or a national interest which stands above the claims of various pressure groups; they have no theory of the state or a national destiny which is comparable to that of, say, their French counterparts. Much postwar economic planning, for example, has been limited to what the interests themselves will settle for; the government has usually been seen as a coequal partner with no special qualification to speak for a higher national interest. Andrew Shonfield's wide-ranging study of national styles of economic management comments on "the extraordinary tenacity of older attitudes towards the role of public power [in Britain]. Anything which smacked of a restless or overenergetic state, with ideas of guiding the nation on the basis of a long view of its collective economic interest was instinctively the object of suspicion." [91]

Another consequence of this style of pluralism and related belief in limited government is seen in the reluctance to use the law to assert public power. The British have traditionally emphasized a negative view toward liberty, one which left the citizen free to do as he wished, unless the activity was formally proscribed. There are still few positive legislative guarantees of personal liberties and no bill of rights. There is general agreement that the state should intervene to promote such collectivist goals as full employment, maintenance of law and order, and the setting of safety standards. But in many other areas there is growing disagreement between and within parties about where the line should be drawn between state action and private initiative. In the past decade, reform of the law has reflected increased permissiveness toward abortion and homosexuality. At the same time, governments have moved to regulate socioeconomic relationships and promote new codes of conduct by tutelary law (e.g., in race relations, sexual equality, and industrial relations). But the trade unions, for example, while advocating state intervention in many areas, have consistently upheld their freedom from legislation in matters affecting collective bargaining and have resisted attempts by both Labour and Conservative governments to regulate this sphere.

What now strikes the observer is how British governments appear to lack an impetus of their own. It is not only a question of the constraints imposed by scarce economic resources, international commitments, and the sheer force of incrementalism in the policy process. These are neither new nor unique to Britain. Rather, governments so well reflect the value and interests of British society that there is a tendency to immobilism. Critical observers have suggested that the limits imposed on government result in a form of "pluralistic stagnation" in which groups are able to veto governmental initiatives where these are thought to operate to their disadvantage.[92] What is lacking is a sense of the center. Instead, "the state is submerged by the interests; it continues but only as a form of contest. The so-called government is like a king amid the barons' wars." [93]

EXPLAINING CHANGE

Change may come from a number of factors: political socialization, new values among the younger generation, awareness of foreign political models, and actual experience with the political process.

Studies of children have discovered only modest levels of positive support for many features of the British political system. In one cross-national survey, a team of American social scientists found that British children were the least supportive of their political system.[94] Studies of the attitudes of schoolchildren contrast with much of the data and the commentary in the *Civic Culture* study, and the overall pattern of responses is certainly much less positive than that found among children in other countries. But once more, in the absence of trend data it is difficult to offer firm conclusions. Children may be absorbing more detached and reserved attitudes to the political system from adults and the mass media than previous generations. Alternatively, their outlooks may reflect and replicate a realistic assessment of the limits of government and of the limits of popular influence on government.[95]

Discussions of the socialization process in Britain have emphasized the importance of the selection of children at the age of eleven for academic (grammar) and nonacademic (secondary modern) types of education.[96] Some sociologists have argued that this segregation prepared children for "appropriate" elite and subordinate roles in later life and thereby buttressed the elitist political system and the deferential culture. But the available empirical research has failed to uncover the expected differences in political values and aspirations resulting from the selection process. From Ted Tapper's ambitious study of children in a variety of schools, it appears that type of school has less effect than partisanship and family on youthful aspirations or attitudes to government.[97] A comparative study of the political outlooks of pupils at a highly prestigious public school and at a state grammar school revealed broadly similar political attitudes and aspirations among pupils.[98]

There is little evidence of any overall changes in the values between generations. It is true that Alan Marsh's data on protest show a genuine generational difference, one that holds up regardless of class and party. Nearly two-fifths of his sixteen to twenty-nine age group rated highly on his protest potential scale, five times more than the proportion of over-sixty-fives.[99] But Inglehart's survey uncovered only small variations between the British age groups, in marked contrast to the sharper generational differences on the Continent.[100] Other research into levels of satisfaction and relative deprivation found a broad identity between age groups on major political, social, and economic values.[101] A 1973 Gallup Poll, which asked whether or not "people like yourself have enough to say" in the major institutions like the press, government, trade unions, banks, and so on, found an average difference of only 5.5 percent in satisfaction between the eighteen to thirty-four and over-sixty-five age groups. The same survey again found only modest generational differences in satisfaction with a variety of social conditions in Britain. Studies of attitudes to economic and welfare issues also show age differences to be weaker than class and party differences.

It is not surprising that generational differences seem weaker in Britain than in other industrialized societies. Not only has the growth of affluence been too slow to stimulate the post-bourgeois outlook among the young, but the events and personalities of British politics in the 1960s hardly constituted a set of generationally distinctive stimuli, certainly when compared to those in the United States or on the Continent. In addition, although the number of students in British higher education doubled during the 1960s, it still constitutes less than a tenth of the eighteen to twenty-four age group, compared to 40 percent in the United States.

An awareness of foreign experiences has been important, not least among political and economic elites. During the past decade several political and economic changes were inspired by continental practice: economic planning, the Ombudsman, reforms in the civil service and trade unions, and even entry to the EEC. In large part change occurred as a result of politicians' tendencies to draw unflattering comparisons between the rates of economic growth in Britain and Western Europe. Both major parties have promised a broad "modernization" of British society, economy, and culture as a precondition of a better British performance in the various European "league tables." But comparison is not confined to Western Europe. Innovative young professionals continue to look abroad to the United States for standards to emulate.[102]

Finally, we come to the actual performance of the political authorities as these are experienced by individuals or perceived through the mass media and other agencies. We have already commented on the failures of the parties in managing the economy and how this has meant only a modest real growth in provision of public and private goods. These failures have generated academic and popular critiques of many features of the political system, which in turn undoubtedly colored the evaluations of the system.

PROBLEMS AND POINTERS FOR FURTHER RESEARCH

The Civic Culture is only a part of a large and variegated literature on British political culture. The salient features of different studies are sketched in Table V.7.

Although this is not the place to evaluate the literature it is interesting that, in spite of the popularity of the cultural approach, many of the writings are backed by scanty evidence. Indeed, it is chastening to realize how little good data there are at all. At the end we still lack an inventory even of limited-range propositions, of systematic and reliable findings about the frequency and intensity of values according to social background, structural, psychological, and party variables. Across the literature there is a recurring lack of precision in defining key variables and concepts — deference, stable democracy, "dominant" values, "false consciousness" — and an inadequate provision of actual indicators for the concepts.

There has also been little concern to accumulate knowledge across studies. Only Nordlinger has accepted *The Civic Culture*'s empirical treatment of culture as consisting of the affective, evaluative, and cognitive orientation to political objects. Sociologists have talked more of "meaning systems" or values, and focused on class differences, reference groups, and attitudes to inequality. Inglehart's treatment of cultural variables has been inspired more by Abraham Maslow's psychology. The hypothesized nature and strength of relationships between variables have usually been expressed too loosely (e.g., "molds," "affects," "is related to") to be open to falsification.

No writer who has applied a label to the British/English political culture has been concerned to establish a "threshold" for the frequency of particular attitudes. To what extent must there be such qualities as deference, congruence, and civic culture in order for there to be political stability and effectiveness?

These comments touch on the problems of analyzing the survey material. While data collection is usually performed at the microlevel of the individual, culture is a collective phenomenon; as students of the "individualistic" fallacy are aware, inferring the latter from the former is not always valid. Where the political culture is seen as the aggregate of beliefs, emotions, and values in society, the tendency is to overlook the problems of weighting the individual's values according to his amount of political influence. The political culture, we suspect, is hardly the sum of its parts. Some of the imprecision in discussions of political culture results inevitably from the complex requirements of data collection, analysis, and interpretation, and also from the political scientist's lack of a tradition of evaluating plausibility statements. In response to the question "Can plausibility become a rigorous concept?" Lucian Pye has argued:

> . . . political scientists are able to be increasingly rigorous and precise with respect to measurement at the micro-analysis level, but our theories are not sensitive to the importance of quantitative

TABLE V.7. *Models of the British Political Culture*

Cultural model	Empirical definition	Author	Major *explanandum*	Data base
Deference	Pattern variables of Parsons	Lipset [a]	Stable democracy and elitist ascriptive value system	Literature, statistics on education, etc.
Deference	Preference of working class for high-status leaders	Nordlinger [b]	Stable democracy and working-class conservatism	Surveys
Deference	Preference of working class for high-status leaders	McKenzie [c] and Silver	Working-class conservatism	Surveys
Congruence	Similarity in authority relationships in political and other institutions	Eckstein [d] (1966)	Stable democracy	Literature and impressions of system
Mix	Fusion of passive and participant outlooks	Almond and Verba [e] (1963)	Stable democracy and civic culture	Surveys
Overlapping memberships	Fusion of traditional and modern values	Almond [f] (1956)	Stable democracy and homogeneous integrated culture	Impressions of structure and functions

	Dominant values			
Hegemony		Parkin,[g] Anderson,[h] Miliband[i]	Ruling class domination; political, social, and economic inequality; "reformism" of Labour party	Voting behavior, attitude surveys, and social structure
Mixed model of cohesion and conflict	Consensual and conflictual values	Mann[j]	Inconsistencies between dominant and deviant values found within individuals	Secondary analysis of surveys
Postindustrial	Priority attached to materialist or participatory values	Inglehart[k]	Change in value priorities between generations	Attitude surveys and economic growth

a Lipset, *The First New Nation: The United States in Historical and Comparative Perspective.* London: Heinemann, 1964. Part III. b E. Nordlinger, *The Working Class Tories.* c R. McKenzie and A. Silver, *Angels in Marble.* d H. Eckstein, *Division and Cohesion in Democracy: A Study of Norway.* Princeton, N.J.: Princeton Univ. Press, 1966. e G. Almond and S. Verba, *The Civic Culture.* f G. Almond, "Comparative Political Systems." g F. Parkin, "Working Class Conservatism." h P. Anderson, "Origins of the Present Crisis." i R. Miliband, *The State in Capitalist Society.* j M. Mann, "The Social Cohesion of Liberal Democracy." k R. Inglehart, "The Silent Revolution in Europe."

differences in attitudes and sentiments, only to the necessity of "appropriate" attitudes existing among the critical elements; on the other hand, it is at the *macro*-level that the critical hypotheses must be advanced and "tested," but it is at this level that we lack capacity for rigour and precision.[103]

Implied in some of the alternative historical and socioeconomic approaches is an argument that the culture may not be important anyway, because political values are not independent variables but "are at best the last link in the chain of causation before behaviour itself." [104] Such a devaluation of culture, however, rests on a misguided attempt to place the different explanatory factors in competition with each other. We should instead try to explain the interrelations between them. Political values may indeed be conditioned by history, social structure, and the direct experiences of people with the performance of the political system, but the "distal" historical and structural factors still have to be connected with the behavior of groups and individuals. And it is here, even as an intervening variable, that values and attitudes are important and have to be included in any strategy of explanation. In describing the context in which the values first developed, one need not be confined to the economic determinism of, for example, Barrington Moore. Even if the political values are shown to be derivative at one point they may, once established, be important thereafter in affecting political behavior.

If students of British politics have fed off Almond and Verba's descriptive data for too long, this is largely because later writings have been based on so little empirical research. A replicated study would now need to take account of changes in the British system already referred to, the critical assessment of Britain's political and economic performance, and the questions of social class, partisanship, and national identity, which were neglected in the original study. Possible areas for future research include the following:

1. *The study of subcultures.* Almond and Verba were originally more concerned with national rather than subnational cultural patterns. They warned: "Investigation of the phenomenon of political subcultures and of their relation to demographic characteristics requires a research design of its own." [105] In view

of the uncertainty about the continuation of the United Kingdom in its present form, one might usefully examine national attitudes to the kingdom. The political developments in Scotland, including the impact of North Sea oil on the economy, and the emergence of a distinctive party system and the expression of national identity in politics present a major research focus. A shortcoming of representative British surveys is that they collect a small number of Scottish (or non-English) respondents. One way to compensate for this is to focus on Scottish elites. More generally, there is also a need to study the role of political and community activists. A political culture bears the uneven impress of an individual's values; his impact will vary according to his political resources and activity, with activists being more likely to translate their values into political behavior. American studies have shown that the values and opinions of this sector differ from those of the general electorate.

Another area for further research is the difference in values between social classes and their repercussions on political behavior. Sociologists have related the existence of political subcultures to differences in social structure — though usually with little empirical evidence.[106] To date the attitudes of the working class have been studied from the narrow perspectives of social cum political deference and of *embourgeoisement*. Questions such as the political outlooks of the middle class, or the sources of working-class, right-wing radicalism (e.g., support for Enoch Powell), have been neglected. The same is true of the middle-class support for Labour (which supplies much of the party's local and national leadership). And in analyzing social class, it makes sense to be aware of the frequent divergence between a person's occupation and the set of attributes usually associated with the stereotypes of "middle class" and "working class." In the British case only one-seventh of British manual workers and one-third of the middle class actually conform to the sociological stereotypes; individuals may therefore be regarded as "more or less" working class and middle class, with consequences for their political values and behavior.[107]

2. *The boundaries between politics and other spheres.* In the case of Ulster the connections of politics and religion have obvious consequences for the political culture. In the rest of the United Kingdom an important area concerns the "legitimacy"

surrounding government's involvement in the economy. In 1969
John Goldthorpe pointed to the contrast between the anomic,
and occasionally bloody-minded, pattern of working-class attitudes in Britain's industrial relations and the deference exhibited
in the political sphere.[108] He argued that while various historical,
cultural and social-psychological factors have historically limited
the repercussions of lower-class resentment of socioeconomic inequalities in the political sphere, the resentment militates against
a "stable normative regulation in the economic sphere" because
there is no value consensus on the distribution of economic and
other rewards. But successive governments have legislated on
industrial relations and on prices and incomes, and increasingly
moved into (and politicized) this sensitive area in recent years.
A focus on issues affecting the economy, workplace, social
justice, and their relationships to the political realm would tap
one area of dissensus in British politics that crucially affects the
authority of government and was neglected in *The Civic Culture*.

3. *The areas of political dissatisfaction with, and changing
levels of support for, the system.* What have been the consequences for public attitudes of a decade's commentary on the
failures of successive governments? Does the retreat from the
two major parties, the pollsters' findings of discontent with
MPs, and complaints that voters do not have enough say in
running the country indicate a loss of support for the political
system and a decline in attachment to the institutions since the
Civic Culture survey? If government is seen as a vehicle of interests or of a party, then is its authority weakened? One suspects
that explicit party control of British government both promotes
and weakens the legitimacy of the political system and the
government in complex ways. These perceptions of the legitimacy of a party government's actions become more important,
given the more interventionist politics of government in areas
which hitherto have been regarded as private or as part of the
market and on which there may be little consensus. Above all,
we need more focused research on the different specific and
diffuse types of support for political institutions and procedures
and the linkages between them. Does the difference between
them hinge essentially on the type of political object being
perceived and the motives behind the support? How important

are evaluations of politicians and parties for allegiance to the regime anyway? Are negative responses part of an underlying pattern of alienation from party politics, merely generalized and stereotyped answers to abstract questions which have limited consequences for behavior, or are they part of a skeptical and realistic outlook? Other research suggests that allegiance to the political community may be independent of cynicism about politicians and politics.[109]

4. *Finally, there is the question of comparison.* If we are to explain the relationships between the culture and features of a political system, it seems indispensable that research should be conducted in a comparative framework, be it comparison over time within one state or comparison across states. The studies by Almond and Verba, by Inglehart, and by Putnam achieved several gains from the comparative framework. This topic of comparison is very relevant to much of the literature on British politics; many writers have selected Britain as much for purposes of formulating general theories of political stability as for explaining the British case. Nordlinger, for example, is essentially concerned to show that the mix of attitudes to political authority in Britain correlates with stable democracy and then to recommend the culture as a facilitator of this stability. It is clear, however, that the single case study presents peculiar difficulties to the theory builder, particularly where the case appears to confirm a general theory, as with Britain. As Lijphart suggests, "a single case-study can constitute neither the basis for a valid generalisation nor the ground for disproving an established generalisation."[110] The appropriate strategy for theory building must, therefore, involve comparative research.

CONCLUSION

In 1963 Almond and Verba were optimistic about the prospects for the civic culture in Britain. It was then fashionable to believe that the legacy of the British historical experience and the consequences of further socioeconomic modernization, including the spread of the mass media, greater involvement with voluntary organizations, and a more educated and participatory population, would help the spread of the civic culture. The implicit and benign scenario was that further socioeconomic development would be associated with a less ideological, more participatory, secular, and pragmatic style of politics. These expectations have not been confirmed.

Assessment of change is necessarily tentative; a period of less than two decades is a short term in a country's history and a culture changes slowly. It will require the passage of further time for many recent political events and generational trends to have an impact on the political culture. Although discussion of civic culture in the original volume lacked precision we do feel able to talk about a change in the balance of the cultural mix and a decline in the deferential or supportive elements. The evidence suggests that there is no great popular confidence in the political institutions, though there is also no desire for radical changes. Similarly, while there is no survey evidence to show widespread trust in the political authorities, outright cynicism or support for violence outside the law is confined to a small minority. The dissatisfaction remains more pronounced on the dimensions of the "output affect" rather than the "system affect." There is, in other words, more dissatisfaction with the specific performance of government than with the system as a whole. The recent years of slow economic growth have led to greater social tensions, group rivalries, and growing dissatisfaction with the incumbent authorities. Indeed, apart from the "exceptional" problem of Ulster, the major challenges to the authority of government in Britain in recent years have arisen in the economic sphere, when trade unions resisted attempts to alter methods of wage bargaining and industrial relations. What does seem clear is that the traditional bonds of social class, party, and common nationality are waning, and with them the old restraints of hierarchy and deference.

NOTES

1. For a review of the changes, see Dennis Kavanagh and Richard Rose, eds., *New Trends in British Politics* (London: Sage, 1977).

2. For a representative and influential statement of this thinking, see Almond's article "Comparative Political Systems," *Journal of Politics* 18 (1956). There are, of course, other interpretations of the patterns of political development in Western Europe; see particularly the work of Charles Tilly, Hans Daalder, and S. P. Huntington.

3. For example, see Otto Kirchheimer, "The Waning of Opposition in Parliamentary Regimes," *Social Research* 24 (1957); Daniel Bell, *The End of Ideology* (New York: The Free Press, 1960); and Louis Hartz, *The Liberal Tradition in America* (New York: Harcourt, Brace, 1955).

4. Almond and Verba, *The Civic Culture: Political Attitudes and Democracy in Five Nations* (Princeton, N.J.: Princeton Univ. Press, 1963), p. 28.

5. Almond and Verba claimed to find "a pattern of political attitudes that fosters democratic stability, that in some way 'fits' the democratic political system" (*Civic Culture*, p. 473).

6. In fact, this concern for citizenship was found in C. E. Merriam's Civic Training Series, published by Chicago University Press in the 1920s. See John M. Gaus, *Great Britain: A Study of Civil Loyalty* (Chicago: Chicago Univ. Press, 1929).

7. The literature is now well known. The significant authors were Lipset, Eckstein, McCloskey, Shils, and Hyman.

8. For citations see Dennis Kavanagh, "An American Science of British Politics," *Political Studies* 22 (1974): 261.

9. The scarcity of the authors' references to studies of British politics is interesting. In the wide-ranging chapter 1 they refer only to works by Gorer, Brogan, Eckstein, and Beer in their discussion of British culture. R. T. McKenzie was also working along similar lines at the time; see his "Bagehot and the Rule of Mere Numbers," *The Listener*, November 19, 1959.

10. The book was reviewed by an American, Eric Nordlinger, in the major British journal *Political Studies* 12 (1964): 312.

11. Richard Rose's first edition of *Politics in England* (London: Faber & Faber, 1965) contained eleven references to the book, compared to only three references in the second edition (1974).

12. Nordlinger, *The Working Class Tories* (London: McGibbon & Kee, 1967).

13. Compare the concluding chapters of *The Civic Culture* and *The Working Class Tories*.

14. Jack Dennis et al., "Political Socialisation to Democratic Orientations in Four Western Countries," *Comparative Political Studies* 1 (1968), and Jack Dennis et al., "Support for Nation and Government Among English Children," *British Journal of Political Science* 1 (1971).

15. Perry Anderson, "Origins of the Present Crisis," *New Left Review* 23 (1964): 26–53.

16. Ralph Miliband, *The State in Capitalist Society* (London: Widenfeld & Nicolson, 1969), chaps. 7–8; Frank Parkin, "Working Class Conservatism," *British Journal of Sociology* (1967): 280–90; Michael Mann, "The Social Cohesion of Liberal Democracy," *American Sociological Review* 35 (1970).

17. See the table in Almond and Verba, *Civic Culture*, p. 226.

18. See Richard Rose and Harve Mossawir, "Voting and Elections," *Political Studies* 15 (1967).

19. For a different interpretation of this inconsistency, see Michael Mann, "Social Cohesion."

20. The response rates for the other industrialized countries were Germany, 74 percent; Italy, 74 percent; and United States, 83.3 percent.

21. There was a marked shortfall among respondents in the eighteen to twenty-four age group (8.4 percent compared to the census figure of 14.4 percent).

22. The authors can hardly be criticized for the neglect of regional and national subcultures in Britain between 1958 and 1962. Ulster was neglected by most British scholars until the late 1960s.

23. Erwin Scheuch, "Progress in the Cross-Cultural Use of Sample Surveys," in S. Rokkan, ed., *Comparative Research Across Cultures and Nations* (Paris: Mouton, 1968).

24. Brian Barry, *Sociologists, Economists and Democracy* (London: Routledge & Kegan Paul, 1969), pp. 51–52.

25. Cf. the authors' claim that the slight differences in national patterns of socialization hardly explain the different political cultures. They suggest, therefore, that different cultures must be related to "characteristics of the social environment and patterns of social interaction, to specifically political memories, and to differences in experience with political structure and performance" (Almond and Verba, *Civic Culture,* p. 35).

26. Walter Bagehot was the first and most famous deference-monger. But he, of course, was writing about the English in *The English Constitution.*

27. Dennis Kavanagh, "The Deferential English: A Comparative Critique," *Government and Opposition* (1971), and Robert Jessup, "Civility and Traditionalism in English Political Culture," *British Journal of Political Science* 1 (1971).

28. See Kavanagh, "The Deferential English," p. 339.

29. At another point the authors regard Conservative voting among the working class as a sign of deference (Almond and Verba, *Civic Culture,* p. 456).

30. Almond and Verba, *Civic Culture,* p. 435.

31. See Richard Rose, *Politics in England Today* (London: Faber & Faber, 1974), p. 157, and Giuseppe di Palma, *Apathy and Participation* (New York: The Free Press, 1970), chap. 4.

32. See David Butler and Donald Stokes, *Political Change in Britain,* 2nd ed. (London: Macmillan & Co.), p. 102. It is noteworthy that Butler and Stokes defined the education variable as type of school attended (grammar and fee-paying or secondary modern) rather than amount of education.

33. See Richard Rose, "Britain: Simple Abstractions and Complex Realities," in Rose, ed., *Electoral Behaviour: A Comparative Handbook* (New York: The Free Press, 1974), p. 506.

34. For an emphasis on these features in an explanation of the lower levels of working-class political activity in the United States compared to some West European states, see Stein Rokkan and Angus Campbell, "Citizen Participation in Political Life: Norway and the United States," *International Social Science Journal* 12 (1960); Giuseppe di Palma, *Apathy and Participation,* pp. 141–49; and Norman Nei et al., "Social Structure and Political Participation: Developmental Relationships," *American Political Science Review* 63 (1969).

35. For an inventory of values and symbols, see the table in Richard Rose, *Politics in England,* p. 56.

36. See Almond and Verba, *Civic Culture,* p. 101, for a further discussion of these terms.

37. Butler and Stokes, *Political Change in Britain,* 2nd ed., p. 237.

38. Ronald Inglehart, "The Silent Revolution in Europe: Intergenerational Change in Post-Industrial Societies," *American Political Science Review* 65 (1971).

39. See, for example, Mark Abrams and Richard Rose, *Must Labour Lose?* (London: Penguin, 1960), chap. 4, and Philip Abrams and Alan Little, "The Young Voter in British Politics," *British Journal of Sociology* 16 (1965). For the active support of young middle-class radicals for the Campaign for Nuclear Disarmament, see Frank Parkin, *Middle Class Radicalism* (Manchester: Manchester Univ. Press, 1967).

40. For a useful review of these features, see Ivor Crewe, "Do Butler and

Stokes Really Explain Political Change in Britain?" *Journal of European Political Research* 2 (1974).

41. See the contrasting appraisals of Britain by Harry Eckstein and Samuel Beer in the second and third editions, respectively, of Samuel Beer and Adam Ulam, eds., *Patterns of Government* (New York: Random House, 1962 and 1973).

42. Lowell, *The Government of England* (New York: Macmillan, 1908), p. 507.

43. *Report of the Royal Commission on the Constitution,* Research Paper 7, *Devolution and Other Aspects of Government: An Attitudes Survey* (London: HMSO, 1973), p. 10.

44. *Report of the Royal Commission on the Constitution 1969–1973,* vol. 1, p. 100.

45. See the evidence cited in Dusan Sidjanski, "The Swiss and Their Politics," *Government and Opposition,* vol. 6 (1976), p. 316.

46. Robert Putnam, *The Beliefs of Politicians* (New Haven: Yale Univ. Press, 1973), p. 187.

47. Shils and Young, "The Meaning of the Coronation," *Sociological Review* 1 (1953): 77.

48. Rose and Kavanagh, "The Monarchy in Political Culture," *Comparative Politics* 7:552 (1976).

49. See Fred Greenstein et al., "The Child's Conception of the Queen and Prime Minister," *New Society,* October 23, 1970. It is important to note that the official or "dignified" language of British government is difficult for the uninitiated to "code" or interpret accurately. The queen formally appoints the prime minister, opens and dissolves parliament, gives her assent to bills, and refers to "my government." The notion of the Crown is important in the formal working of the British constitution, and it is not surprising that Bagehot's comments on the gullibility of the masses in 1867 are now more applicable to schoolchildren.

50. For an exception to this, see the study of Churchill in Dennis Kavanagh, *Crisis, Charisma and British Political Leadership: Winston Churchill as the Outsider* (London: Sage, 1974).

51. See Nordlinger, *The Working Class Tories,* p. 186, and D. Butler and D. Stokes, *Political Change in Britain,* 2nd ed., pp. 32–36.

52. D. Butler and D. Stokes, *Political Change in Britain,* 2nd ed., pp. 91ff., 117–18

53. See also Monica Charlot, "The Ideological Distance Between the Two Major Parties in Britain," *European Journal of Political Research* 3 (1976): 178–88, and David Robertson, *A Theory of Party Competition* (London: Wiley, 1976).

54. Ivor Crewe et al., "Partisan Realignment in Britain 1964–74," *British Journal of Political Science* 7 (1977): 143.

55. Ibid., p. 172.

56. Putnam, *Beliefs of Politicians.*

57. Max Kaase and Alan Marsh, "Pathways to Political Action," paper presented to International Political Science Association, Edinburgh, 1974.

58. For example, 63 percent agreed that a few strong leaders would do more for this country than all the laws and talk, and 82 percent were doubtful of candidates' promises at election times.

59. Data from specially commissioned survey on *Attitudes to MPs,* Opinion Research Centre, June 1973.

60. See Alan Marsh, *Protest and Political Consciousness* (London: Sage, 1978), p. 118.

61. See Richard Rose, *The United Kingdom as a Multi-National State*, in Rose, ed., *Studies in British Politics*, 3rd ed. (London: Macmillan & Co., 1974).

62. Richard Rose, *Governing Without Consensus* (London: Macmillan & Co., 1971).

63. Rose, *op cit.*, chap. 14.

64. On race, see Ira Katznelson, *Black Men, White Cities* (London: Oxford Univ. Press, 1973), and Donley T. Studler, "Political Culture and Racial Policy in British Politics," *Patterns of Prejudice*, vol. 8 (1974). On Powell, see Studler's "British Public Opinion, Colour Issues and Enoch Powell," *British Journal of Political Science* 4 (1974), and Douglas Schoen, *Enoch Powell and the Powellites* (London: Macmillan & Co., 1977).

65. See Butler and Stokes, *Political Change in Britain*, 2nd ed., chap. 14.

66. Nordlinger, p. 97.

67. Ibid., pp. 84ff. In recent years party supporters have also been willing to alter their policy preferences on the EEC and prices and incomes policies, in response to their parties' change of direction.

68. See Alan Marsh, "Explorations in Unorthodox Political Behaviour," *European Journal of Political Research* 2 (June 1974), and *Protest and Political Consciousness*, pp. 66–68.

69. For the fuller argument that cynicism allied to a sense of political competence creates the predisposition to protest, whereas cynicism combined with the sense of powerlessness creates apathy, see William Gamson, *Power and Discontent* (Homewood, Ill.: Dorsey, 1968).

70. David Easton, "The Concept of Political Support," *British Journal of Political Science* 5 (1975).

71. Ibid., pp. 437–39.

72. See C. A. E. Goodhart and R. J. Bhansali, "Political Economy," *Political Studies* 17 (1970).

73. Jack Dennis et al. regarded such data as evidence of a decline in political efficacy. See "Support for Nation and Government," p. 45.

74. See the forceful statements on this point by A. H. Birch and Dennis Kavanagh in *British Journal of Political Science*, vol. 1, no. 4; and vol. 2, no. 1, respectively.

75. Jack Citrin and David Elkins, *Political Disaffection Among British University Students* (Berkeley, Calif.: Univ. of California Press, 1975), p. 58.

76. See Mark Abrams, "Subjective Social Indicators," *Social Trends*, no. 4 (1973).

77. Richard Rose, "Ordinary People in Extraordinary Economic Circumstances," unpublished paper, 1977.

78. Runciman, *Social Justice and Relative Deprivation* (London: Routledge, 1966).

79. W. W. Daniel, *The PEP Survey on Inflation*, PEP Broadsheet 553 (London: PEP, 1975).

80. For a different interpretation and a more pessimistic conclusion, see Samuel Brittan, "The Economic Contradictions of Democracy," *British Journal of Political Science* 5 (1975).

81. Arthur Miller and Jack Citrin, "Political Issues and Trust in Government, 1964–1970," *American Political Science Review* 68 (1974).

82. Jack Citrin, *ibid.*, p. 987.

83. See *The Report of the Royal Commission on the Constitution*, vol. 2, "Memorandum of Dissent . . ." (HMSO, 1973, Cmnd. 546–1).

84. Ivor Crewe et al., "Partisan Realignment in Britain."

85. This interpretation is more appropriately identified with the Conservative than the Labour party. See Nordlinger, chap. 1.

86. *The English Constitution* (London, Fontana edition, 1963), p. 271. Joseph Schumpeter also regarded the existence of such a political stratum as a condition for the success of democracy. See *Capitalism, Socialism and Democracy* (London: George Allen and Unwin, 1947), p. 291.

87. Michael Mann, "Social Cohesion."

88. John Goldthorpe, "Social Inequality and Social Integration in Modern Britain," *The Advancement of Science* 26 (1969).

89. W. L. Guttsmann, *The British Political Elite* (London: MacGibbon & Kee, 1963), p. 281.

90. See H. Heclo and A. Wildavsky, *The Private Government of Public Money* (London: Macmillan & Co., 1974).

91. Andrew Shonfield, *Modern Capitalism* (London: Oxford Univ. Press, 1965).

92. S. Beer, *Modern British Politics* (London: Faber & Faber, 1969).

93. W. J. M. Mackenzie, "Models of English Politics," in R. Rose, ed., *Studies in British Politics* (London: Macmillan & Co., 1976).

94. Jack Dennis et al., "Support for Nation and Government."

95. Dennis Kavanagh, "Allegiance Among English Children: A Dissent," *British Journal of Political Science* 2 (1972).

96. See Nordlinger, pp. 23–24, and Rose, *Politics in England*, pp. 65–71.

97. Ted Tapper, *Young People and Society* (London: Faber & Faber, 1971).

98. D. McQuail et al., "Elite Education and Political Values," in Richard Rose, ed., *Studies in British Politics*, 2nd ed. (London: Macmillan & Co., 1969).

99. Marsh, "Explorations in Unorthodox Political Behaviour."

100. Inglehart, "Silent Revolution."

101. Mark Abrams, "Value Systems: Is There a Generation Gap?" unpublished paper, May 1974.

102. Erwin Hargrove, *Professional Roles in Society and Government: The English Case*. Professional Papers in Comparative Politics Series (Beverly Hills, Calif.: Sage Publications, 1972).

103. Lucian Pye, "Culture and Political Science: Problems in the Evaluation of the Concept of Political Culture," *Social Science Quarterly* 53 (1973): 295. Compare this statement with the same author's earlier optimism in Lucian Pye and Sidney Verba, eds., *Political Culture and Political Development*, p. 9.

104. Brian Barry, *Sociologists*, p. 96.

105. Almond and Verba, *Civic Culture*, p. 401.

106. For useful discussions, see Parkin, "Working-Class Conservatism"; J. Goldthorpe and D. Lockwood, "Affluence and the British Class Structure," *Sociological Review* 11 (1963); and David Lockwood, "Sources of Variation in Working-Class Images of Society," *Sociological Review* 14 (1966).

107. Richard Rose, "Britain: Simple Abstractions and Complex Realities," pp. 510–11.

108. Goldthorpe, "Social Inequality and Social Integration in Modern Britain." See also Michael Mann, "Social Cohesion."

109. The recent controversy between Arthur Miller and Jack Citrin over

the validity of measures of political trust in the United States is a warning of the need for a rigorous conceptualization of such terms as *alienation* and *legitimacy*. See Arthur Miller, "Political Issues and Trust in Government 1964–1970."

110. Arend Lijphart, "Comparative Politics and the Comparative Method," *American Political Science Review* 65 (1974), p. 687.

CHAPTER VI

The United States: Political Culture under Stress

Alan I. Abramowitz
College of William and Mary

THE UNITED STATES has passed through a period of political and social turmoil in the years since the publication of *The Civic Culture*. There have been dramatic changes in public attitudes toward government and politics during these years. Trust in political leaders has been replaced by cynicism. Confidence in both governmental and nongovernmental institutions has declined. Americans feel that things have been going badly for the country and they do not expect much improvement in the near future. Yet the significance of these changes in public attitudes is far from clear. Indeed, perhaps the most striking feature of the recent political history of the United States is the stability of its basic institutions despite the stress of assassinations, war, racial strife, political scandals, and economic dislocation. Superficially, at least, the American political system appears to have scarcely been affected by the remarkable sequence of crises the country has recently experienced.

The apparent decline in public support for political leaders and political institutions during the past decade raises a number of serious questions for students of political culture. Has the

177

political culture of the United States actually undergone a transformation in this short period of time? Are changing attitudes toward government and politics a temporary reaction to recent events, or do they reflect more fundamental changes in American society and culture that are likely to have long-lasting consequences? Whatever the explanation for changing public attitudes, what are the implications of declining confidence in governmental and nongovernmental institutions for the stability of these institutions? How long can institutions withstand widespread public dissatisfaction with their performance? This essay will describe recent trends in public attitudes toward government and politics in the United States and attempt to answer the questions raised above. Only the passage of time will reveal whether these answers are correct or incorrect, but the questions are too important to be postponed until more evidence is available.

This is an inquiry into the political culture of the United States. I shall use the definition of political culture proposed by Almond and Verba in *The Civic Culture:* "the political culture of a nation is the particular distribution of patterns of orientation toward political objects among the members of the nation." [1] This definition is, of course, very broad. We must specify what kinds of orientations and what sorts of political objects are of particular interest. Three dimensions of political orientation — cognitive, affective, and evaluative — were discussed by Almond and Verba. The cognitive dimension refers to knowledge and information about government and politics; the affective dimension refers to feelings toward political objects; the evaluative dimension refers to judgments about political objects which combine cognitive and affective elements. [2] In this essay I am concerned mainly with the affective and evaluative dimensions of American political culture, since these have undergone the most dramatic change in recent years.

The most important objects of political orientations, according to Almond and Verba, are the political system and the self as a political actor. [3] Attitudes toward the political system can be differentiated, following David Easton, into attitudes toward the political community, the regime, and incumbent authorities. [4] The political community, here, refers to the nation as a political entity; the regime refers to the basic institutional structures and procedures for resolving political conflicts; incumbent authorities are the persons occupying institutional positions of power at a particular time.

The political culture of the United States, according to Almond and Verba, had two main characteristics: it was an allegiant political culture and it was a participatory political culture. Americans, in comparison with citizens of the other four countries included in the study, had the most favorable opinions about their form of government. Thus, in response to an open-ended question asking what things about their country they were most proud of, 85 percent of the American respondents spontaneously mentioned governmental and political institutions. This was substantially higher than the percentage mentioning governmental and political institutions in any of the other countries. Only 46 percent of the British respondents, 30 percent of the Mexicans, 7 percent of the Germans, and 3 percent of the Italians made spontaneous reference to governmental and political institutions as objects of personal pride.[5]

In comparison with respondents in the other four countries, Americans also displayed a strongly activist orientation toward government and politics, with 51 percent expressing the view that the good citizen was one who participated actively in community affairs. Only 39 percent of the British respondents, 26 percent of the Mexicans, 22 percent of the Germans, and 10 percent of the Italians held this opinion. Moreover, Americans were very confident of their ability to influence the conduct of government by their actions. Seventy-seven percent felt that they could do something to change an unjust local regulation and 75 percent felt that they could do something about an unjust national regulation. Although the British respondents were as confident as the Americans about their ability to do something about an unjust local regulation, only 62 percent felt that they could do anything to change an unjust national regulation. Respondents in the remaining countries trailed far behind the Americans and the British in both local and national efficacy.[6]

Thus the political culture of the United States, according to Almond and Verba, was distinguished by a high degree of positive affect toward political institutions, and an activist view of the self in relation to the governing process. On the negative side, however, Americans did not manifest a very strong sense of

what Almond and Verba referred to as "subject competence."
Thirty-seven percent of the American respondents, compared
with 50 percent of the British and 43 percent of the Germans,
expected to receive serious consideration from both a government
agency and the police in bringing a problem to the attention of
these organizations. Only the Mexican and Italian respondents
displayed a lower sense of subject competence than the Americans. The authors attributed this finding to the revolutionary
origins of the American polity, which gave rise to a tendency to
mistrust any authority not directly subject to popular control.[7]
Another possible explanation, however, would be that Americans
simply had less favorable experiences in dealing with government agencies and the police than citizens of either Great Britain
or Germany. Whatever the explanation, Americans, despite their
generally positive view of government, were somewhat skeptical
about the benevolence of public bureaucracies.

Translating the principal findings of Almond and Verba into
Eastonian terms, it appears that the political culture of the
United States, at the time of the five-nation study, was characterized by a high degree of consensus regarding both the political
community and the regime. Political efficacy and participatory
norms, though related to socioeconomic status, were widely
shared in the population. There are two questions that I wish to
address concerning this characterization of American political
culture. First, how accurate is the description for the time period
to which it applies? Although some qualifications of the authors'
conclusions will be suggested, the portrait of American political
attitudes contained in *The Civic Culture* does appear to be
accurate for the time period in which the research was conducted: the late 1950s and early 1960s. A more troubling question, however, concerns the inferences drawn by the authors of
The Civic Culture from their findings. How reasonable was the
authors' explanation of the distinctive pattern of American
political attitudes and their interpretation of the relationship
between that pattern of attitudes and the existence of a stable
democratic regime in the United States?

One major omission from the description of American political culture in *The Civic Culture,* which seems rather glaring in
retrospect, is the absence of any separate treatment of the political culture of America's black minority. This omission was

probably due in part to the cross-national focus of the five-nation study, which led the authors to choose control variables that could be readily applied in all five countries, such as sex, education, and occupational status. Nevertheless, the omission of a control variable as important in the American political context as race was a costly sacrifice for the sake of comparability, as the events of the subsequent decade made clear.

One practical problem involved in analyzing racial differences in political attitudes on the basis of a cross-sectional survey is the relatively small number of black respondents that can be expected to fall into the sample. Out of 970 completed interviews that were obtained in the American study, there were approximately 100 blacks. This number of cases does impose certain limitations on the kinds of analyses which can be undertaken. Certainly, deliberate oversampling of blacks and, possibly, other minority groups likely to exhibit distinctive political characteristics would have enhanced the opportunities for analyzing these subcultures. Future studies of American political culture should, if at all possible, follow this strategy. Nevertheless, the number of blacks in the original American sample is more than sufficient for the purpose of describing zero-order racial differences in political attitudes.

Although no control for race was used in the five-nation study, racial differences in political attitudes were the subject of a secondary analysis of the American data by Dwaine Marvick.[8] His findings help to fill a significant gap in the description of American political culture during the late 1950s and early 1960s that *The Civic Culture* provided.

In order partially to control for the substantial differences in socioeconomic status and other demographic characteristics between white and black respondents, Marvick compared blacks with a subsample of whites having similar characteristics (Table VI.1). He found that blacks were much less sanguine than whites about receiving considerate treatment from a government agency or the police. Black Americans displayed a much lower level of subject competence than white Americans, a finding which helps to explain why Americans, on the average, were lower in subject competence than citizens of Great Britain or Germany. Blacks were also somewhat less optimistic about their ability to influence government decisions than whites, although on this question,

TABLE VI.1. *Expected Treatment by Officialdom:*
Comparisons of Black and White Counterparts

Opinion expressed	National white cross-section %	Matched subsamples	
		Black %	White %
1. Government officials would give equal treatment	87	49	90
2. Police would give equal treatment	88	60	85
3. Officials would listen and take views seriously	50	30	45
4. Police would listen and take views seriously	58	36	48

Source: Dwaine Marvick, "The Political Socialization of the American Negro," in Edward C. Dreyer and Walter A. Rosenbaum, eds., *Political Opinion and Behavior: Essays and Studies* (Belmont, Calif.: Wadsworth Publishing Company, 1970), pp. 161–79.

regional differences were marked. Southern blacks, for obvious reasons, were extremely pessimistic about their chances of changing an unjust local regulation. Northern blacks, in contrast, felt almost as efficacious in this regard as their white counterparts.

In addition to these racial differences in political outlook, other surveys done during the 1950s and early 1960s found that a large proportion of Southern blacks simply did not relate themselves to the political process, except as passive subjects. In 1958, 28 percent of the Southern blacks interviewed in the Michigan Survey Research Center's national election study were classified as "apolitical." [9] The basis of this classification was an absence of a meaningful attitude toward one of the key institutions of electoral democracy — the political parties. Southern blacks were the only subgroup within the population where these apoliticals were found in significant numbers. Of course, for many Southern blacks at that time, being apolitical was a matter of survival rather than choice. The norm of nonparticipation was enforced by intimidation and, when necessary, coercion. [10]

Despite their politically and economically deprived position in American society, however, blacks had quite positive attitudes toward the national government. In fact, opinion surveys con-

ducted during the 1950s and early 1960s found that blacks had
more faith in the federal government than whites. In 1958 and
in 1964, for example, blacks were less likely than whites to feel
that the federal government was wasting a great deal of tax-
payers' money or that many government officials were crooked
(Table VI.2). Moreover, opinion surveys found that only a relatively small minority of American blacks supported the idea of
a separate black nation. According to a 1964 survey of blacks
residing in metropolitan areas of the United States, 17 percent
of blacks living in these areas favored a separate black nation
and 79 percent rejected this idea. The same survey found that
87 percent of metropolitan blacks felt that the United States
was worth fighting for, compared with only 11 percent who felt
the United States was not worth fighting for, if a war were to
break out.[11] Thus an examination of racial differences in political attitudes does not lead to any major qualification of the
conclusion reached by Almond and Verba that Americans,
during the late 1950s and early 1960s, exhibited a strong sense
of national identity and took considerable pride in their form
of government. Many American blacks, however, particularly in
the South, were restricted to the role of passive subjects in the
political process. For these Americans, the civic culture had not
yet arrived.

Race is only one of many potential control variables not used
in the five-nation study, owing to the authors' stress on comparability. As a result, the political culture of the United States
probably appeared more homogeneous than it actually was at
that time. It would have been interesting, for example, to explore

TABLE VI.2. *Attitudes toward the Federal Government in 1958
and 1964 by Race*

Opinion expressed	1958		1964	
	Blacks %	*Whites %*	*Blacks %*	*Whites %*
1. People in the government waste a lot of tax money	38	43	28	48
2. Government run by a few big interests	12	18	27	28
3. Quite a lot of people in government crooked	20	24	21	30

Source: CPS National Election Studies.

possible regional variations in political culture in the United States. The South, especially, has long been noted for its distinctive political patterns.[12] In general we might expect to find the largest concentrations of individuals having parochial or subject orientations to politics in less economically developed regions like the American South. Comparison of relatively developed and undeveloped regions of different countries in terms of their political cultures could shed light on the relationship between economic development and political culture. Certainly the possibility of regional variations in political culture should be explored in future cross-national studies.

One of the most interesting applications of the concept of political culture to the study of American politics has been Daniel Elazar's attempt to characterize the political cultures of the American states in order to explain variations in their political processes and public policies. While his categorization of states as traditionalistic, moralistic, or individualistic is largely impressionistic, it does suggest a useful direction for future research on political culture.[13]

A more fundamental criticism of the analysis of American political culture in the five-nation study concerns the authors' explanation of the distinctive pattern of political orientations found in the United States. According to Almond and Verba, American political attitudes were largely a product of childhood socialization experiences which fostered both self-expression and interpersonal trust. By comparison with citizens of the other four countries, Americans tended to display greater faith in human nature and attached greater importance to outgoing personality traits such as generosity. These beliefs were, in turn, related to the propensity of Americans to engage in cooperative action. According to Almond and Verba, interpersonal trust facilitated cooperation in the political arena.[14] Americans also reported greater participation in decision making in the family and the school during childhood and adolescence than citizens of the other four countries. These experiences with nonpolitical authority figures, according to the authors, shaped adult political orientations. Respondents who reported participation in decision making in the family and the school, and later on the job, tended to display a high degree of self-confidence about their political-influence capabilities.[15]

Almond and Verba were not oblivious to the possible importance of specifically political experiences in shaping political attitudes. In criticizing what they called the "psychocultural approach to the study of political phenomena," they observed that "the importance of specific learning of orientations to politics and of experience with the political system has been seriously underemphasized." [16] Unfortunately, the authors largely neglected this point in their own work. *The Civic Culture* was almost exclusively concerned with nonpolitical sources of political orientations, particularly childhood socialization. Political influences were largely ignored. This criticism is not meant to suggest that nonpolitical influences on political orientations are not important in their own right, or that differences among the national political cultures examined by Almond and Verba were not at least partially owing to differences in childhood socialization patterns. I do mean to suggest, however, that such prepolitical experiences provide only a partial explanation for variations in political culture both within countries and between countries.

One factor which helps to explain the lack of attention to political influences on attitudes toward government and politics in *The Civic Culture* was the authors' decision to focus on orientations toward "political structure and process" rather than orientations toward "the substance of political demands and outputs." This choice, while understandable in terms of the authors' desire to limit the scope of what was already a major research undertaking, eliminated the possibility of analyzing the relationship between attitudes toward government performance and attitudes toward political institutions and processes. Thus the authors' conclusions were shaped by their own choice of explanatory variables. In the case of the United States, for example, one major conclusion of *The Civic Culture* was that early socialization tended to instill positive feelings toward political institutions which carried over into adulthood. Allegiance to the political system therefore appeared to be based on emotional ties formed during childhood rather than rational evaluations of system performance. This "diffuse support" for the political system, Almond and Verba speculated, might serve to dampen demands for change when system performance dropped below satisfactory levels.[17] The problem with this hypothesis, whatever its inherent plausibility, is that the authors could not present any evidence concerning the relationship between satisfaction with government performance and allegiance to the political system. Thus it is impossible to estimate what impact a sudden or gradual decline in system performance might have on public support for political institutions.

This criticism of the explanatory strategy adopted by Almond and Verba is closely connected with another criticism of the five-nation study: its time-boundedness. To a large extent, the conclusions of *The Civic Culture* with regard to American political culture reflected the political mood of the country during the time period in which the research was conducted. The late 1950s and early 1960s was a period of relative tranquillity and political quiescence compared to both earlier and later periods. These were the years when a number of prominent social scientists concluded that the "end of ideology" had arrived in the United States with the emergence of a broad consensus regarding public policies as well as political institutions.[18] In foreign policy the United States was still committed to a cold war with what was generally perceived as a unified Communist bloc bent on global expansion. During the post-McCarthy years, opposition to the policy of containment was muted and doubts about America's role as the policeman of the "free world" were seldom expressed. On the domestic front, despite occasional lapses into recessions, America's economy seemed capable of producing greater and greater affluence. That the benefits of economic growth were very unevenly distributed, with a large segment of the population virtually excluded from participation in the new affluence, was barely noticed. Americans were, by and large, satisfied with their situation and optimistic about the future. Both political parties responded to this mood, nominating presidential candidates who avoided ideological issues and directed their appeals to the moderate majority of the electorate.

This, then, was the context in which the five-nation study was undertaken. It is not surprising, therefore, that the description of American political culture contained in that study has a peculiarly apolitical and ahistorical quality to it. The authors of *The Civic Culture* were not driven to consider the impact of political issues on political culture because ideological and policy disagreements were not prominent at the time. That this situation was assumed by a good many observers of the American political scene to be typical or likely to continue indefinitely was, events soon demonstrated, a mistake.

The final criticism that I shall direct at the five-nation study concerns the theory of stable democracy set forth by Almond and Verba. The authors argued that there was a "fit" between the pattern of political orientations, which they labeled the "civic culture," and the existence of stable, democratic regimes. What is the nature of the relationship between the civic culture and stable democracy? Almond and Verba appear to be deliberately vague about this, although the impression left by *The Civic Culture* is that this pattern of orientations is a necessary condition for the long-run stability of democratic institutions. Thus the civic culture is a cause, and not just an effect, of stable democracy.[19]

The countries whose political cultures most closely approximated the civic culture pattern were the United States and Great Britain. What distinguished the civic culture from other political-cultural patterns was a mixture of parochial, subject, and citizen orientations toward the political system. Members of the public were interested and active in political affairs, but not so interested and active that they made impossible demands on the governing elite. Most of the time, most members of the public were content to leave political decisions in the hands of elected and appointed officials. This political restraint reflected a high level of confidence in political leaders and, ultimately, in political institutions.

The main concern, here, is with limiting the public's interference with political elites. In the authors' own words: "If elites are to be powerful and make authoritative decisions, then the involvement, activity, and influence of the ordinary man must be limited. The ordinary citizen must turn power over to elites and let them rule. The need for elite power requires that the ordinary citizen be relatively passive, uninvolved, and deferential to elites." [20] Although it is desirable that members of the public feel influential, the ordinary citizen cannot be permitted to have much actual influence. The survival of democracy requires that most citizens not put their feelings of influence to the test of action, for once the public actually tries to exert influence, the stability of the system may be threatened. Democracy exists, in *The Civic Culture,* more as a myth than as a reality.

One of the important findings of the *Civic Culture* study was that there existed a substantial gap between the feeling of influence and the reality of influence on the part of ordinary citizens. In some respects this gap was most spectacular in the United States. When we examine measures of actual participation, rather than attitudes toward participation, Americans do not appear to be far ahead of citizens in other capitalist democracies. The vast majority of Americans, according to the survey done for the five-nation study, had never attempted to influence a decision by either the local or the national government.[21] In fact, in the most common form of mass participation, voting in national elections, Americans are far behind citizens of many other countries. Moreover, the absence of mass-membership parties in the United States, and particularly the absence of working-class parties, has resulted in a more marked class bias in political participation in the United States than in most other capitalist democracies.[22] Inequalities of wealth and status are therefore reflected by political inequalities.

Stable democracy, according to Almond and Verba, requires a balance between governmental power and responsiveness. The authors of *The Civic Culture* seem to have placed a higher priority on governmental power than on responsiveness, however, even suggesting that American political culture overemphasized participatory norms and underemphasized deference to elites.[23] Given the low rates of actual political participation in the United States, this conclusion hardly seems warranted. Moreover, recent history suggests that abuses of power by political leaders constituted a greater threat to democracy in the United States during the past decade than an overzealous public. Democracy may be better served by a public that is skeptical, rather than deferential, toward political leaders.

CHANGES IN AMERICAN POLITICAL CULTURE: AFFECTIVE AND EVALUATIVE ORIENTATIONS

Despite the criticisms set forth here, *The Civic Culture* provided a fairly accurate picture of American political culture during the late 1950s and early 1960s. Other surveys of American political attitudes during the same period generally support the major conclusions of Almond and Verba.[24] It would be remarkable if the description of American political culture contained in *The Civic Culture* did not need some modification fifteen or so years later. In this section I shall describe the most dramatic change in American political attitudes during this time period: the sharp decline in public trust and confidence in political leaders and institutions recorded in many public-opinion surveys.

One indicator of this trend is the declining level of trust in government recorded in successive national election surveys conducted by the Survey Research Center at the University of Michigan. Table VI.3 shows the trend on three questions measuring trust in government between 1964 and 1974. Between 1964 and 1972 the percentage of the public responding in the cynical direction to each question increased considerably, but the most dramatic rise in cynicism occurred between 1972 and 1974. Comparing the responses obtained in 1974 with those obtained only a decade earlier, the decline in trust in government is nothing less than spectacular. It appears that only a minority of Americans now hold trusting attitudes toward the national government.

Declining trust in government cannot be dismissed as merely an expression of dissatisfaction with presidential leadership, although this is certainly one factor involved.[25] The decline in trust in government during the past decade was accompanied by a sharp drop in public confidence in a wide range of governmental and nongovernmental institutions. Table VI.4 shows the trend in public confidence in a number of major institutions recorded by pollster Lou Harris between 1966 and 1972. Every one of these institutions suffered a substantial drop in public confidence during this time period.[26]

Harris was by no means the only observer to note a decline

TABLE VI.3. *Trust in Government, 1964–74*

Opinion expressed	Year of survey			
	1964 %	1968 %	1972%	1974 %
1. Trust government only some of the time	22	37	45	61
2. Government run by a few big interests	29	39	48	65
3. Quite a few people in government crooked	28	25	34	45

Source: CPS National Election Studies.

TABLE VI.4. *Public Confidence in Major Institutions*

Institution	Percentage of public expressing a "great deal" of confidence	
	1966	1972
Medicine	72	48
Higher education	61	33
Television news	25	17
The military	62	35
Organized religion	41	30
Supreme Court	51	28
Senate	42	21
House of Representatives	42	21
Press	29	18
Major companies	55	27
Executive branch of federal government	41	27
Organized labor	22	15

Source: Subcommittee on Intergovernmental Relations, U.S. Senate Committee on Government Operations, *Confidence and Concern: Citizens View American Government,* part 1 (Washington, D.C.: U.S. Government Printing Office, 1973), p. 33.

in public confidence in institutions during the late 1960s and early 1970s. According to surveys conducted by the Michigan Survey Research Center, public confidence in two of the key institutions of representative democracy — elections and political parties — showed a marked decline between 1964 and 1972. In 1964, 65 percent of Americans felt that elections made public officials pay attention to the people. In 1972 only 55 percent of the public still held this opinion. In 1964, 41 percent of Americans felt that political parties made public officials pay attention to the people. In 1972 only 30 percent of the public still held this opinion.

Americans, by the beginning of the 1970s, had become disillusioned with the political process. Moreover, this sense of disillusionment seemed to reflect a feeling that the country was in serious trouble and that no easy solutions to America's problems were in sight. Since 1959 a cross section of the American public has been periodically asked to judge the condition of the nation on a scale devised by Hadley Cantril: a ten-step ladder on which the top rung represents the best possible condition and the bottom rung represents the worst possible condition.[27] Respondents are asked to place the country on the ladder according to the current situation, the situation five years ago, and the situation they expect five years in the future. Table VI.5 shows the trend in national ladder ratings between 1959 and 1974. Two significant findings emerge from this table. First, in all three surveys done during the 1970s, the public perceived the national situation as having deterioriated during the preceding five years. This was in sharp contrast to the results obtained in 1959 and 1964, when the public perceived the national situation as having improved during the preceding five years. Moreover, in 1974, for the first time, the American public expected the national situation five years in the future to be worse than the situation five years in the past. Clearly, a mood of pessimism about the nation had replaced the optimism which prevailed only a decade earlier.

What explains the new cynicism and the new pessimism of the American people? I shall argue that these attitudes reflected growing dissatisfaction with the performance of government. During the 1960s Americans' expectations of what government could accomplish were raised by the rhetoric of public officials and then shattered by the harsh realities of war, social unrest, and political corruption. The new cynicism and the new pessimism were, initially, a reaction to the host of new issues and problems that emerged within a very brief span of time during the late 1960s (Table VI.6). Crime in the streets, black militancy, ghetto riots, student protest, and the counterculture — the nexus of concerns that became known as the "social issue" — had multiple origins. What these issues had in common was that they arose almost simultaneously and that they were disturbing and

TABLE VI.5.   *Average National Ladder Ratings, 1959–74*

Year	Past	Present	Future
1959	6.5	6.7	7.4
1964	6.1	6.5	7.7
1971	6.2	5.4	6.2
1972	5.6	5.5	6.2
1974	6.3	4.8	5.8

Source: William Watts and Lloyd A. Free, *State of the Nation* (Washington, D.C.: Potomac Associates, 1974).

TABLE VI.6.   *Public Perceptions of Most Important National Problem in 1964 and 1968*

Problem	1964 %	1968 %
Poverty and social welfare	24.2	11.9
Civil rights	20.0	8.9
Economic and labor management	8.9	7.0
Agriculture and resources	2.6	1.2
General foreign and defense policy	27.9	7.3
General government	3.0	1.7
Protest, disorder, civil liberties	3.7	18.7
Vietnam	9.7	43.3

Source: CPS National Election Studies.

threatening to large segments of American society. Overshadowing all these issues, though, was one that proved more divisive than any other in recent years: Vietnam.

The war in Vietnam emerged as a major issue with the escalation of American involvement during the Johnson administration. The decline in public support for the war during the late 1960s and early 1970s closely paralleled the decline in trust in government noted earlier.[28] We cannot, however, attribute rising political cynicism simply to growing opposition to the war. Political cynicism increased substantially among supporters of the war as well as among its opponents, although members of the public who favored either an immediate withdrawal from Vietnam or a drastic escalation of the war were considerably more cynical in 1964 and in 1970 than supporters of the status quo.[29] Nevertheless, Vietnam contributed to the growth of political cynicism by calling into question the trustworthiness and capability of America's political and military leaders. As the war dragged on, and American casualties soared, pessimism regarding the chances for either a negotiated settlement or a military victory rose. The optimistic statements of top political and military figures were belied by the news Americans received daily from the battlefront, especially after the Tet offensive demonstrated the resilience of the insurgent forces. Americans were unhappy about the situation in Vietnam, even if they could see no alternative preferable to the administration's policies.

The emergence of Vietnam as a political issue was, of course, closely related to the intense, and sometimes violent, political turbulence that shook the United States during the late 1960s, but Vietnam was by no means the sole cause of this unrest. During the same time period, the rising aspirations of America's black minority in the aftermath of the civil rights revolution of the early 1960s collided with the fears of many Northern and Southern whites that too rapid gains by blacks threatened their own hard-won progress toward middle-class respectability.[30] Meanwhile, the children of the middle class were questioning the values their parents had worked so hard for, and experimenting with alternative values and lifestyles.[31] The most significant feature of the new issues of the late 1960s, from the standpoint of public confidence in government, was their divisiveness. Regardless of their views on these issues, many Americans felt that the country was in trouble. In April 1971 a national sample of the American public was asked the following question:

> There has been a lot of talk in the news recently about unrest in our country and ill-feeling between groups. In general, how concerned are you about this unrest and ill-feeling? Do you think it is likely to lead to a real breakdown in this country or do you think it is likely to blow over soon?

Almost half the respondents, 47 percent, said that they expected rising unrest to lead to a "real breakdown"; only 38 percent felt the problem would "blow over soon." [32]

Confidence in both governmental and nongovernmental institutions fell during the late 1960s because of a widespread sense that the country was passing through troubled times. However much they disagreed about how to deal with the problems of war and social unrest, Americans agreed that these were serious problems. During bad times, confidence in societal institutions can be expected to decline. Some Americans, of course, were more dissatisfied with the way the government was handling the country's problems than others. The dissatisfied included those at the right end of the political spectrum as well as those on the left.[33] Blacks, who were more positive in their evaluations of government than whites during the Kennedy and Johnson years, became more cynical than whites during the first two years of the Nixon administration, which was much less sympathetic to the aspirations of black Americans.[34] Despite these variations, however, the outstanding feature of the new cynicism and the new pessimism was the extent to which these attitudes permeated American society. Supporters as well as opponents of government policies were affected by this mood. Declining public trust and confidence in leaders and institutions was a function of the nature of the times.

By 1973 American involvement in Vietnam had ended, unrest on the nation's college campuses was rapidly diminishing, and the black ghettos of the inner cities were quiet. The new values spawned by the counterculture during the 1960s continued to make headway among young people, spreading from college students to noncollege youth, but these values were becoming disconnected from the political activism that marked the youth movement of the late 1960s.[35] With the fading of many of the divisive issues of the late 1960s, some recovery of public confidence in societal institutions might have been expected. Yet, as we have seen, trust in government declined dramatically between 1972 and 1974. The most important reason for this development was Watergate.

Watergate came to symbolize official misconduct in the Nixon administration, including activities having little or no connection with the actual break-in at the headquarters of the Democratic party in the Watergate complex. Among the events that transpired during 1973 and 1974 were the implication of President Richard Nixon in the coverup of the Watergate break-in by his former counsel, John Dean; the revelation of the existence of the White House tapes; the revelations concerning the activities of the White House "plumbers"; the firing of Special Prosecutor Archibald Cox and the subsequent resignations of Attorney General Elliot Richardson and Deputy Attorney General William Ruckelshaus; the resignation of Vice-President Spiro Agnew after pleading nolo contendere to charges of income tax evasion; the revelation of the existence of a mysterious eighteen-and-one-half-minute gap on one of the subpoenaed White House tapes; revelations concerning "dirty tricks" and illegal fund raising in the 1972 Nixon presidential campaign; President Nixon's tax problems; the indictment of several top aides and former cabinet members in the Nixon administration for conspiring to obstruct the Watergate investigation; the release of the edited transcripts of the White House tapes; the impeachment vote by the House Judiciary Committee; President Nixon's resignation and his succession by Gerald Ford; and, finally, President Ford's decision to grant a full and unconditional pardon to Richard Nixon.[36]

Never before in the history of the United States had an administration been so tarnished by scandal. Never before had a president of the United States been directly implicated in illegal activities and forced out of office. It is not surprising that trust in government declined between 1972 and 1974. Yet this is not the full story of the public's reaction to Watergate. Declining trust in government conceals the fact that this reaction was selective. The only major institution that suffered a substantial decline in public confidence between 1972 and 1974 was the executive branch of the federal government (Table VI.7). Public confidence in a variety of other institutions either remained stable or increased slightly. It appears, therefore, that trust in government, as it is measured by the Michigan Survey Research Center, is heavily weighted in the direction of attitudes toward the executive branch of the federal government. Attempts to use these questions to measure general confidence in governmental institutions may produce misleading conclusions, as the divergent trends shown in Table VI.7 indicate. Attitudes toward government are more differentiated than some studies have assumed. A decline in confidence in one institution does not necessarily

TABLE VI.7. *Public Confidence in Major Institutions*

Institution	Percentage of public expressing a "great deal" of confidence or "some" confidence		
	1972	*1974*	*Change*
Executive branch of federal government	76	42	−34
Supreme Court	66	71	+ 5
Congress	72	68	− 4
State government	67	75	+ 8
Local government	64	72	+ 8
Business and industry	60	56	− 4
Labor unions	45	50	+ 5
The mass media	67	68	+ 1

Sources: This table is based on findings presented in William Watts and Lloyd A. Free, *State of the Nation* (New York: Universe Books, 1973); and Watts and Free, *State of the Nation* (New York: Universe Books, 1974).

imply a decline in confidence in other institutions or a decline in support for the regime.

The trend in public confidence in societal institutions between 1972 and 1974 was either level or slightly up, with the important exception of the executive branch of the federal government. Thus this recent period was fundamentally different from the period that preceded it. The Watergate scandal and the public reaction to it obscured this shift in sentiment. As Watergate fades from public consciousness, it seems likely that there will be a gradual recovery of public confidence in the presidency along with other institutions, assuming that no further shocks are forthcoming. It seems unlikely, though, that public confidence in political leaders and institutions will quickly return to the levels of the early 1960s. Even without any new shocks, the events of the past decade have undoubtedly left an imprint on American political attitudes. If the new cynicism and the new pessimism wear off slowly, the aftereffects of the past decade of turmoil may be noticeable in American political attitudes for a long time. Moreover, declining trust and confidence in leaders and institutions was not the only significant change in political orientations during the past decade. Participatory orientations were also affected by the political turmoil of the late 1960s.

PARTICIPATORY ORIENTATIONS

The events of the past decade have affected American attitudes toward political participation as well as evaluations of political leaders and institutions. There has been a decline in public interest and confidence in the electoral process. Americans today appear to have less faith in elections as a mechanism for keeping government responsive to the people than they did in the past. Participation in electoral activities has either remained constant or declined slightly during the past decade. At the same time, however, the salience of politics has increased. Americans have not lost interest in politics. Rather, they have become more interested in nonelectoral modes of participation as their faith in the electoral process has declined.

I have already presented evidence that public confidence in the electoral process declined during the past decade. Between 1964 and 1972 the percentage of Americans holding the opinion that elections make public officials pay "a good deal" of attention to the people fell from 65 to 55, according to the Michigan Survey Research Center's data. Public interest in presidential election campaigns also declined during these years. In 1964, 42 percent of the public said that they were "very interested" in the presidential campaign; in 1968, 39 percent of the public expressed this degree of interest in the campaign, and by 1972 only 31 percent of the public claimed to be "very interested" in the presidential campaign.

Declining public interest in presidential elections has apparently been accompanied by a modest decline in voter turnout. According to the Michigan survey data, 78 percent of those eligible to vote did so in 1964, compared with 76 percent in 1968 and 73 percent in 1972. Actual voter turnout in these elections was considerably lower than these figures indicate, however, since surveys tend to exaggerate voter turnout, owing to sampling biases and misrepresentation by respondents who are embarrassed to admit that they did not vote. According to an independent estimate of voter turnout by the United States Census Bureau, based on the actual number of votes cast and the estimated eligible population, voter participation declined from 61.8 percent in 1964 to 60.9 percent in 1968 and 55.7 percent in 1972.[37] Some of the decline in voter turnout between 1968 and 1972 was almost certainly caused by a change in the composition of the electorate: the lowering of the voting age from twenty-one to eighteen. Nevertheless, even a finding that voter turnout has remained constant is somewhat surprising given the steady rise in educational levels over time and the dramatic increase in voting participation among Southern blacks during this time period. That these changes have not produced any overall increase in voter turnout probably reflects a general decline in public faith in the electoral process.[38]

Voting is only one form of electoral participation. Fortunately, the Michigan election surveys provide time-series data on a variety of electoral activities beyond voting. Once again, these data indicate that the overall level of participation has remained relatively constant over time despite rising educational levels and despite the efforts of parties and candidates to stimulate greater grass-roots participation in the electoral process (Table VI.8).

There is one important exception to the general finding that electoral participation has either remained constant or declined

TABLE VI.8. *Participation in Electoral Activities beyond Voting*

Activity	1964 %	1968 %	1972 %
Trying to persuade someone to vote for a candidate	31	33	32
Displaying a campaign button or sticker	16	15	14
Giving money to a candidate	11	9	10
Attending a political speech or rally	9	9	9
Working for a party or candidate	5	6	5

Source: CPS National Election Studies.

slightly during the past decade. That exception is Southern blacks. Although the level of voting participation among blacks residing in the states of the former Confederacy had been slowly increasing during the 1940s and 1950s, it was not until the enactment and enforcement of strong federal voting-rights legislation, during the 1960s, that black voting participation increased dramatically in the South. During the 1960s, the proportion of Southern blacks registered to vote more than doubled, from 29 percent in 1960 to 60 percent in 1970. Simultaneously there was a dramatic decline in the proportion of Southern blacks who were labeled apolitical by the Michigan Survey Research Center: from 28 percent in 1958 to only 3 percent in 1970. The civil rights movement and legislation of the 1960s succeeded in eliminating the last major vestige of subject political culture in the United States.[39]

I have presented evidence of a decline in public interest and confidence in the electoral process during the past decade. It would be incorrect, however, to read into this trend a general decline in political activism. In fact, there is persuasive evidence that public interest and participation in nonelectoral political activities has risen in recent years. Although interest in presidential campaigns declined during the late 1960s and early 1970s, the salience of politics was increasing among the general public. In 1964, 1968, and 1972 the Michigan surveys included the following question:

> Some people seem to follow what's going on in government and public affairs most of the time, whether there's an election going

on or not. Others aren't that interested. Would you say you follow
what's going on in government and public affairs most of the time,
some of the time, only now and then, or hardly at all?

The proportion of the public claiming to follow public affairs
"most of the time" rose from 30 percent in 1964 to 33 percent
in 1968 and 37 percent in 1972. Apparently people were more
interested in government and politics in 1972 than in 1964, even
though they were less interested in the presidential campaign.
These seemingly contradictory trends reflect a growing awareness
on the part of the American public of nonelectoral strategies for
influencing public officials. Thus in 1964 only 26 percent of the
American public disagreed with the following statement: "Voting
is the only way that people like me can have a say about how
the government runs things." In 1972, 59 percent of the American public disagreed with the same statement. Most Americans no
longer regarded voting as the only effective means of influencing
government officials.

According to a major recent study of political participation
in America, by Verba and Nie, people participate in politics in
several distinct ways. Electoral activities are only one form of
participation, although they have been studied more thoroughly
than other forms.[40] Electoral participation has remained relatively constant during the past decade, but other types of political activity have been increasing. In 1964 only 17 percent of the
respondents in the Michigan national election study claimed to
have ever written a letter to a public official. By 1972 the proportion of respondents claiming to have written a public official
reached 27 percent. It appears that although Americans were not
turning out in greater numbers in elections, they were becoming
more active in expressing their views to public officials between
elections.[41] But the most significant development of the 1960s
in the area of popular participation was the emergence into
prominence of the style of participation known as "protest."

Protest was not new to the American political scene, of course.
Prior to the 1960s, however, the last major outbreak of protest
in the United States had occurred during the Great Depression
of the 1930s. When *The Civic Culture* was written, protest was
almost unknown in the United States. The total number of protest incidents recorded during the decade of the 1950s was less

than the number recorded in every single year between 1960 and 1967.[42] By 1973 a Harris survey found that 11 percent of the adult population had taken part in a street demonstration of some kind and 2 percent had taken part in a demonstration involving violence. These proportions are still considerably lower than for many conventional political activities, but protest activity varied considerably across different segments of the population. The proportion of protesters was much higher among persons between the ages of eighteen and twenty-nine (18 percent) than among persons between the ages of thirty and forty-nine (11 percent) or among persons fifty years of age or older (6 percent). Protest participation was also more common among blacks (20 percent) than among whites (10 percent). What makes these findings especially interesting is that the groups highest in protest participation — young people and blacks — are the same groups that are lowest in most conventional forms of participation. In fact, among the young and among blacks, the level of protest participation was higher than the level of several more conventional political activities. More young people reported protesting (18 percent) than working for a presidential candidate (13 percent). More blacks reported protesting (20 percent) than working for a presidential candidate (7 percent), writing to their congressman (12 percent), or giving money to a political candidate (15 percent). Among young people, and to an even greater extent among blacks, protest became an important form of political participation during the 1960s, and one that was often preferred to more conventional political activities.

Although only a small minority of Americans actually engaged in protest activities during the 1960s, there was a substantial shift in public attitudes toward such activities. Between 1968 and 1972 the proportion of the public expressing at least qualified approval for legal protest marches and demonstrations rose from 43 percent to 59 percent; the proportion expressing at least qualified approval for civil disobedience increased from 35 percent to 55 percent; finally, the proportion expressing at least qualified approval for demonstrations aimed at disrupting government operations — the most drastic action which respondents were questioned about — increased from 23 percent to 41 percent. Thus by 1972 many Americans had come to regard protest as a legitimate form of political participation, even if they had not themselves been involved in any protest activity.

The emergence of protest as a significant form of political participation in the United States during the 1960s leads to the qualification of one of the major conclusions of *The Civic Culture*. According to Almond and Verba, participatory attitudes were related to positive evaluations of the political system in the United States.[43] This may be true of conventional forms of participation, although the evidence on this point is unclear,[44] but it is certainly not true for protest participation. Protest participation is strongly related to negative evaluations of political leaders and institutions.[45] The conclusion of Almond and Verba that participation and positive evaluations of the political system are mutually reinforcing is not supported in the case of protest.

The same events which produced declining trust and confidence in leaders and institutions during the late 1960s also produced the dramatic rise in protest activity. The outcome of this activity was that participatory orientations were altered as citizens observed that elections were not the only, or necessarily the most effective, means of influencing the government. Elections, after all, are a highly inefficient mechanism for expressing policy preferences. During the 1960s, Americans discovered that more direct techniques, including protest, could be effective in communicating policy preferences to political decision makers.[46] The events of the 1960s, therefore, can be said to have produced a more politically sophisticated public.

ISSUES AND PARTISANSHIP

Changing attitudes toward political participation were not the only sign of change in the electorate. The events of the 1960s also contributed to an increase in issue-awareness among the American people. Policy issues became a more prominent feature of political debate at the elite level, with the new issues of Vietnam and social unrest overlaying the older issues of civil rights and economic justice. These new issues have also become more connected with what is probably the most significant political choice made by the public: the vote for president. Simultaneously, traditional party loyalties have diminished as a factor in presidential voting. There has been a gradual decline in the proportion of the public identifying with either major party along with a decline in party loyalty among party identifiers, at least in presidential elections.[47] The new issues of the late 1960s split the dominant Democratic party. The traditional Democratic coalition of blue-collar workers, white ethnics, blacks, and Southerners, forged during Franklin Roosevelt's presidency, was torn apart in 1968 and 1972 by the issues of Vietnam and social unrest.[48] The principal beneficiary of this split in the Democratic coalition was Richard Nixon. His victories did not, however, signal an "emerging Republican majority," but a growing tendency on the part of voters to ignore party labels and cast their ballots on the bases of issue preferences and candidate images. Rather than a party realignment, the events of that period seem to have produced a party "dealignment." [49]

Although the issues responsible for the weakening of party loyalties during the late 1960s and the 1970s have faded in importance, the electorate's new-found independence will probably persist. Young people today are much more independent of the parties than in the past. Moreover, Paul Abramson's recent analysis of cohort differences in party identification through time casts considerable doubt on the earlier notion that party identification increases in strength with age.[50] If today's age-related differences in party identification represent a true generational change, we can expect an increasingly independent electorate in the future as the natural process of replacement proceeds and as the younger generation of independent voters passes its partisan orientations on to its children. It appears likely that one of the legacies of the political turmoil of the 1960s will be an electorate that is not only more politically sophisticated, but also more independent of the two major parties and therefore more susceptible to appeals based on issue-positions and candidate images. The electorate of the future will probably remain more volatile than the electorate of the post-World War II era described in *The American Voter.*

POLITICAL CULTURE AND POLITICAL STABILITY

The evidence presented in this essay indicates that there have been important changes in mass attitudes toward government and politics in the United States since the *Civic Culture* study.

Americans today are more cynical about politicians, less confident in their institutions, and more politically sophisticated than they were only a decade earlier. Yet the basic institutions of American government remain intact. What, then, of the fit between political culture and political institutions, which Almond and Verba regarded as an important condition of political stability? To begin, we recognize that the original hypothesis concerning the existence of a fit between political culture and political institutions is too vague to permit a definitive test. We do not know how changes in political attitudes at the mass level are supposed to affect political institutions. It seems likely that there is a good deal of slack in this relationship. Certainly a change in one of these variables is neither a necessary nor a sufficient condition for change in the other. In the United States there have been dramatic changes in political attitudes in the past decade without any major alterations in the institutional structure. In contrast, some Western European democracies, such as France and Italy, have experienced considerable institutional instability in recent years without any significant changes in the popular political culture. Students of political culture need to specify the conditions under which institutional change is likely to result from changes in mass political culture and vice versa.

One point can be made concerning the relationship between political culture and political institutions that has some bearing on recent developments in the United States. The stability of political institutions should not be threatened if discontent is focused on specific policies or incumbent authorities rather than on the regime or the political community. Although dissasifaction with the performance of political institutions did increase considerably during the late 1960s, the legitimacy of political institutions was not seriously questioned except by elements of the radical left that had little popular support. Discontent was focused mainly on specific policies and the individuals responsible for those policies rather than on the institutions themselves. The public's attachment to the political community and the regime remained strong. In an attempt to measure public support for the regime in 1972, the Michigan Survey Research Center asked a cross section of Americans to choose one of the following statements: "I am proud of many things about our form of government," or "I can't find much about our form of

government to be proud of." Eighty-six percent of the respondents chose the first statement. Even among those who scored
low on a measure of trust in government, three-fourths expressed
pride in their form of government.[51] Thus it appears that
cynicism about political leaders is not inconsistent with strong
support for political institutions and loyalty to the political
community.

Public dissatisfaction with the performance of political leaders
and institutions during the late 1960s and early 1970s did not
lead to a massive erosion of support for the political community
or the regime. With regard to the institutional structure, the
public was willing to accept reforms but not radical alterations.
Another question included in the 1972 Michigan survey asked
Americans whether they felt a "change in our whole form of
government" was desirable, or whether "no real change" was
necessary. Only 15 percent of the public favored a radical change
in the American form of government. Twenty-six percent did
volunteer the opinion that some change was desirable, however.
This percentage would probably have been larger had limited
reform been offered as an alternative. Thus, although regime
support remained high, a large segment of the public did favor
reform. Just what kind of reform was favored cannot, unfortunately, be determined.[52]

The public's reformist sentiment did not escape notice at the
elite level, especially in the aftermath of the Watergate scandal.
Congress has moved to reassert its prerogatives in the field of
foreign policy in the aftermath of the Vietnam war. It seems
likely that recent congressional attempts to expose and correct
abuses of power by government agencies within the United States
and abroad were stimulated, to a large extent, by public outrage
at the conduct of the Nixon administration. Nevertheless, although public opinion was probably more favorable to political
reform during the early 1970s than at any time since the end of
World War II, very little has come of this reformist sentiment.
The most significant change that has occurred — the new assertiveness of the legislative branch — could well prove to be
ephemeral. It appears that the discontent of the 1960s and 1970s
was either suppressed or absorbed by the political system with
few noticeable effects.

Three factors have limited the political impact of public discontent. These are apathy, the reluctance of political elites to mobilize support for structural reforms, and the ability of the two-party system to defuse and channel discontent. In the first place, it is clear that only a small minority of Americans who were dissatisfied with the performance of political leaders and institutions took any action to express their dissatisfaction. Although the volume of political demand making did increase during the 1960s, the "silent majority" was more than a slogan invented by conservative politicians. Not all of those who remained silent were satisfied with the status quo, of course. Nevertheless, most Americans remained preoccupied with their personal affairs, with politics a distinctly secondary concern. In the personal sphere, Americans continued to display an optimistic outlook. Despite growing pessimism about the condition of the country, most Americans were satisfied with their personal lives.[53] At the same time as ratings of the country on Cantril's ladder were falling (see Table VI.5), the ratings that Americans gave their personal situations remained almost unchanged (Table VI.9). Contrary to citizens in many other countries, Americans tend to compartmentalize the personal and political realms.[54] They do not regard political problems as personal problems. This tendency probably cushioned the impact of political discontent during the 1960s and 1970s.

The stability of American political institutions also owed much to the reluctance of political leaders to mobilize public discontent behind a program of structural change. Many studies of public opinion have demonstrated that mass opinion tends to follow elite opinion. In the United States during the late 1960s and early 1970s, political leaders did appeal to the discontented,

TABLE VI.9. *Average Personal Ladder Ratings, 1959–74*

Year	Past	Present	Future
1959	5.9	6.6	7.8
1964	6.0	6.9	7.9
1971	5.8	6.6	7.5
1972	5.5	6.4	7.6
1974	5.5	6.6	7.4

Source: William Watts and Lloyd A. Free, *State of the Nation* (Washington, D.C.: Potomac Associates, 1974), p. 11.

but that appeal was based almost entirely on criticism of particular policies and incumbent office holders, rather than attacks on the regime or the political community. The Republican party, during the Nixon years, appealed to the discontented right, seeking to win over voters who supported George Wallace in 1968. The Democratic party, after its capture by the McGovern forces in 1972, appealed to the discontented left. By the time of the 1972 presidential election, many of the political grievances that had emerged during the late 1960s had been incorporated into the platforms of the two major parties. The parties largely succeeded in channeling discontent into the normal political process.

The restraint shown by political elites in the United States during the late 1960s and early 1970s was undoubtedly due in large part to strategic considerations. Political leaders recognized that a program of radical structural change would have little appeal to the bulk of the electorate. Beyond such self-interested calculations, however, another factor may have operated to restrain criticism of the institutional order: elite political culture. It is well known that support for the norms of constitutional democracy is greater among elites than among the mass public.[55] It seems likely that elite support for the "rules of the game" would inhibit attacks on the institutions of constitutional democracy during periods of stress. Such appears to have been the case during the late 1960s and early 1970s.

CONCLUDING REMARKS

The central argument of this essay has been that changes in American political culture during the late 1960s and early 1970s were produced by short-term issues and events rather than fundamental changes in American society. This is not to deny the existence of longer-term forces shaping American political culture. Increasing geographical mobility, greater availability of leisure time, the growth of higher education, and the development of the mass communications media have contributed to a gradual secularization and homogenization of American culture. This is reflected in changing attitudes toward religion, family life, and careers, as well as politics. These gradual changes in American society and culture cannot, however, account for the rapid shifts in political attitudes during the period under discussion. Americans today are more cynical about politicians, less confident in political institutions, and more politically sophisticated than they were only a few years ago. The issues and events of the 1960s and 1970s — from Vietnam to Watergate — were an important resocialization experience for many Americans. Yet the political culture of the United States has not undergone a complete transformation since the *Civic Culture* study. Dissatisfaction with government policies and incumbent officeholders has not resulted in a massive erosion of public support for the regime or the political community. Attitudes such as political cynicism and confidence in political institutions can be expected to fluctuate, depending upon the nature of the times. The late 1950s and early 1960s was a period of unusually high trust and confidence in political leaders and institutions. The current period may, with the passage of time, appear to be one of unusually low trust and confidence in leaders and institutions. We should not make the mistake of projecting recent trends to predict the future of American political culture. American attitudes toward government and politics at present could best be described as ambivalent. If there are no major shocks to the political system in the near future, a restoration of trust and confidence is quite conceivable. On the other hand, a new crisis, such as a prolonged economic slump or an unpopular war, could result in a gradual erosion of regime support and, eventually, demands for structural change. The future of American political culture depends largely on the future performance of American political institutions in dealing with the problems of economic stagnation and international tension.

NOTES

Unless otherwise indicated, data presented in this chapter are taken from the University of Michigan Survey Research Center's national election studies. These data were made available by the Inter-University Consortium for Political Research.

1. Gabriel Almond and Sidney Verba, *The Civic Culture* (Princeton, N.J.: Princeton Univ. Press, 1963), pp. 14–15.

2. Ibid., p. 15.

3. Ibid. For a somewhat more elaborate scheme for classifying political orientations, see Walter A. Rosenbaum, *Political Culture* (New York: Praeger Publishers, 1975), pp. 5–12.

4. David Easton, *A Systems Analysis of Political Life* (New York: John Wiley & Sons, 1965), chaps. 11–13.

5. Almond and Verba, *Civic Culture*, p. 102.

6. Ibid., p. 185.

7. Ibid., p. 224.

8. Dwaine Marvick, "The Political Socialization of the American Negro," in Edward C. Dreyer and Walter A. Rosenbaum, eds., *Political Opinion and Behavior: Essays and Studies* (Belmont, Calif.: Wadsworth Publishing Company, 1970), pp. 161–79.

9. Philip E. Converse, "Change in the American Electorate," in Angus Campbell and Philip E. Converse, eds., *The Human Meaning of Social Change* (New York: Russell Sage Foundation, 1972), p. 307.

10. For an intensive analysis of black political participation in the South during the early 1960s, see Donald R. Matthews and James W. Prothro, *Negroes and the New Southern Politics* (New York: Harcourt, Brace and World, 1966).

11. Gary Marx, *Protest and Prejudice: A Study of Belief in the Black Community* (New York: Harper Torchbooks, 1969), pp. 28–30.

12. The classic study of Southern politics is V. O. Key, Jr., *Southern Politics in State and Nation* (New York: Vintage Books, 1949). A more recent collection of essays dealing with various aspects of Southern politics is William C. Havard, ed., *The Changing Politics of the South* (Baton Rouge: Louisiana State Univ. Press, 1972).

13. Daniel J. Elazar, *American Federalism: A View from the States* (New York: Thomas Y. Crowell, 1966). See also Ira Sharkansky, "The Utility of Elazar's Political Culture: A Research Note," *Polity* 2 (Fall 1969): 66–83.

14. Almond and Verba, *Civic Culture,* pp. 233–78.

15. Ibid., pp. 330–68.

16. Ibid., p. 34.

17. Ibid., p. 242. For a more extensive treatment of the concept of "diffuse support" in relation to the process of political socialization, see David Easton and Jack Dennis, *Children in the Political System* (New York: McGraw-Hill, 1969).

18. See, for example, Daniel Bell, *The End of Ideology* (New York: The Free Press, 1962), esp. pp. 393–407; Robert E. Lane, "The Politics of Consensus in an Age of Affluence," *American Political Science Review* 59 (December 1965): 874–95; Almond and Verba, *Civic Culture,* p. 29.

19. Almond and Verba, *Civic Culture,* chap. 15.

20. Ibid., p. 478.

21. Less than 28 percent of the American respondents had ever attempted to influence a government decision at the local level. Less than 16 percent had ever attempted to influence a government decision at the national level. These percentages are reported in Sidney Verba and Norman H. Nie, *Participation in America: Political Democracy and Social Equality* (New York: Harper & Row, 1972), p. 27.

22. Using the data gathered in the five-nation study, Nie, Powell, and Prewitt found a stronger relationship between social status and political participation in the United States than in any of the other countries. The zero-order correlation between status and participation was .43 for the United States, .30 for Great Britain, .28 for Italy, .24 for Mexico, and .18 for Germany. See Norman H. Nie, G. Bingham Powell, Jr., and Kenneth Prewitt, "Social Structure and Political Participation: Developmental Relationships, II," *American Political Science Review* 63 (September 1969): 812.

23. Almond and Verba, *Civic Culture,* p. 440.

24. Much of this evidence is summarized in Donald J. Devine, *The Political Culture of the United States* (Boston: Little, Brown, 1972).

25. There is a fairly strong relationship between trust in government and evaluation of the incumbent president. See Jack Citrin, "Comment: The Political Relevance of Trust in Government," *American Political Science Review* 68 (September 1974): 977.

26. This evidence is presented in a report prepared by Harris for the Subcommittee on Intergovernmental Relations of the Senate Committee on Government Operations. See Subcommittee on Intergovernmental Relations, U.S. Senate Committee on Government Operations, *Confidence and Concern: Citizens View American Government,* pt. 1 (Washington, D.C.: U.S. Government Printing Office, 1973), p. 33.

27. For a discussion of this scale, see Hadley Cantril, *The Pattern of Human Concerns* (New Brunswick, N.J.: Rutgers Univ. Press, 1965), pp. 23–26.

28. For a discussion of the relationship between the issue of Vietnam and trust in government, see Arthur H. Miller, "Political Issues and Trust in Government: 1964–1970," *American Political Science Review* 68 (September 1974): 958–60. Miller's argument that opposition to administration policies in Vietnam by both doves and hawks contributed to declining trust is not supported by his own data, however. There was a sharp decline in trust among supporters of administration policies between 1964 and 1970.

29. Ibid., p. 960.

30. See Joel D. Aberbach and Jack L. Walker, "Political Trust and Racial Ideology," *American Political Science Review* 64 (December 1970): 1199–1219.

31. The impact of the counterculture on the values of college students is examined in Daniel Yankelovich, *The Changing Values on Campus* (New York: Washington Square Press, 1972).

32. Albert H. Cantril and Charles W. Roll, Jr., *Hopes and Fears of the American People* (New York: Universe Books, 1971), p. 31.

33. Miller, "Political Issues and Trust in Government," p. 961.

34. Ibid., p. 959. The decline in trust among blacks between 1968 and 1970 was spectacular. The percentage of blacks holding the opinion that the government was run by a few big interests jumped from 29 to 63; the percentage holding the opinion that quite a few government officials were crooked rose from 22 to 49. These dramatic shifts indicate that trust in government can be powerfully affected by short-term events, such as a new administration.

35. See Daniel Yankelovich, *The New Morality: A Profile of American Youth in the 70s* (New York: McGraw-Hill, 1974).

36. For a more detailed chronology of Watergate, see Congressional Quarterly, *Watergate: Chronology of a Crisis,* vols. 1 and 2 (Washington, D.C.: Congressional Quarterly, Inc., 1974) . For an analysis of the impact of Watergate on political attitudes, see Paul M. Sniderman, W. Russell Neuman, Jack Citrin, Herbert McClosky, and J. Merrill Shanks, "Stability of Support for the Political System: The Initial Impact of Watergate," *American Politics Quarterly* 3 (October 1975): 437–57.

37. U.S. Department of Commerce, *Statistical Abstract of the United States 1974* (Washington, D.C.: U.S. Government Printing Office, 1974), p. 437.

38. For a general discussion of trends in electoral behavior since World War II, see Richard W. Boyd, "Electoral Trends in Postwar Politics," in James David Barber, ed., *Choosing the President* (Englewood Cliffs, N.J.: Prentice-Hall, 1974), pp. 175–201.

39. See Converse, "Change in the American Electorate," pp. 303–7, for a

discussion of mobilization of the Southern black population into political participation during the 1960s.

40. Verba and Nie, *Participation in America*, chaps. 3–4.

41. For an analysis of participation between elections, see James N. Rosenau, *Citizenship Between Elections: An Inquiry into the Mobilizeable American* (New York: The Free Press, 1974).

42. Charles Lewis Taylor and Michael C. Hudson, *World Handbook of Political and Social Indicators*, 2nd ed. (New Haven: Yale Univ. Press, 1972), Table 3.1. 1967, the last year for which data are available, was before the major outbreak of antiwar protest. The average number of protest demonstrations recorded in the United States between 1950 and 1959 was 5.9. The average number between 1960 and 1967 was 139.8.

43. Almond and Verba, *Civic Culture*, p. 247.

44. Citrin has presented data indicating almost no relationship between trust in government and political involvement in 1964, 1968, and 1972. See Jack Citrin, "Comment: The Political Relevance of Trust in Government," pp. 983–84.

45. Data gathered by the Survey Research Center at the University of California, Berkeley, indicate a strong relationship between protest activity and negative evaluations of the political system among residents of the San Francisco Bay Area. I am grateful to Professor Paul Sniderman for making these findings available to me.

46. For evidence concerning the effectiveness of protest as a political strategy, see Paul D. Schumaker, "Policy Responsiveness to Protest Group Demands," *Journal of Politics* 37 (May 1975): 488–521.

47. These trends are discussed in Gerald Pomper, *Voters' Choice: Varieties of American Electoral Behavior* (New York: Dodd, Mead and Company, 1975).

48. On the 1968 presidential election, see Richard W. Boyd, "Popular Control of Public Policy: A Normal Vote Analysis of the 1968 Election," *American Political Science Review* 66 (June 1972): 429–49, and Philip E. Converse, Warren E. Miller, Jerrold G. Rusk, and Arthur C. Wolfe, "Continuity and Change in American Politics: Parties and Issues in the 1968 Election," *American Political Science Review* 63 (December 1969): 1083–1105. On the 1972 election, see Arthur Miller, Warren Miller, Alden Raine, and Thad Brown, "A Majority Party in Disarray: Policy Polarization in the 1972 Election," *American Political Science Review*, 70 (Sept. 1976): 753–778.

49. For a discussion of recent trends in party identification and loyalty, see James L. Sundquist, *Dynamics of the Party System: Alignment and Realignment of Political Parties in the United States* (Washington, D.C.: The Brookings Institution, 1973), chaps. 15–16.

50. Paul R. Abramson, *Generational Change in American Politics* (Lexington, Mass.: Lexington Books, 1975), chap. 4.

51. Citrin, "Comment: The Political Relevance of Trust in Government," p. 975.

52. One reform for which public support increased dramatically during the late 1960s and early 1970s was public financing of presidential elections. See the *Gallup Opinion Index*, October 1973.

53. See Ben J. Wattenberg, *The Real America* (Garden City, N.Y.: Doubleday, 1974), chap. 12.

54. Cantril found that the correlation between personal and national ladder ratings in the United States was very low in comparison with the correlation found in other countries investigated. See Hadley Cantril, *The Pattern of*

Human Concerns (New Brunswick, N.J.: Rutgers Univ. Press, 1966), p. 233. The political significance of personal problems has been investigated in Richard A. Brody and Paul M. Sniderman, "Personal Problems and Public Support for the Political System," paper presented to the Conference on Political Alienation, Iowa City, Iowa, January 8–11, 1975.

55. See Herbert McClosky, "Consensus and Ideology in American Politics," *American Political Science Review* 58 (June 1964): 361–82.

CHAPTER VII

Changing German Political Culture

David P. Conradt
University of Florida

SHORTLY AFTER the appearance of *The Civic Culture,* Sidney
Verba, in a related volume, observed that "to a large extent the
psycho-cultural study of politics has its origin in German experience." [1] This German political experience, so well known to
both authors of *The Civic Culture,* has confounded most theorists of democratic political development who have attempted to
relate aggregate socioeconomic data to the presence or absence
of democratic institutions and processes. [2] During the interwar
period German political developments profoundly affected the
conception of democracy held by that generation of political
scientists. Their optimistic faith in the capacity of the common
man to measure up to the requisites of classical democratic
theory was severely shaken by the success of National Socialism;

This chapter could not have been completed without the cooperation of
Professor Elisabeth Noelle-Neumann, Director of the *Institut für Demoskopie,*
who has over the years generously allowed me access to the institute's archive
of survey data. Sole responsibility for the presentation, analysis, and interpretation of these data rests with me. Support for computational work was
provided by the Northeast Regional Data Center at the University of Florida.
This work has also benefited from the comments of Professors Donald
Schoonmaker of Wake Forest University, Taylor Cole and Ronald Rogowski
of Duke University, and Gerhard Lehmbruch, Universität Konstanz. D. P. C.

the emergence of an "elitist" theory of democracy is inextricably connected with German developments.[3]

While *The Civic Culture* marked an important development in the systematic and comparative study of political culture, in the German case it is difficult to consider the work apart from a larger series of studies which sought, through the use of psychological and social variables, to explore the nonpolitical sources of political attitudes and behavior. With *The Civic Culture*, Almond and Verba became part of this tradition associated with the names of Adorno, Pollock, Horkheimer, Lewin, and Fromm, together with numerous postwar students of German political values.[4]

This essay will focus on changes in the German political culture both before and after the 1959 Almond and Verba survey. The commitment of Allied and German policymakers to *change* the culture has produced an unusually large body of empirical data for us to draw upon. Before proceeding, however, to an examination of the nature and character of these changes and their sources, an account of the impact of *The Civic Culture* in Germany and some critical comments on the design and theoretical focus of the work, as it relates to Germany, will be made.

IMPACT IN GERMANY

Prior to the 1959 *Civic Culture* survey, extensive studies of political attitudes and values had been conducted under official and semiofficial auspices by both the Western occupation authorities and the post-1949 German government. The Western allies and especially the United States were committed to an extensive program of reeducation designed to change German political values and attitudes so that the formal democratic institutions established after the war, in contrast to those of the Weimar Republic, would have widespread popular support. Reeducation included the punishment of Nazi war criminals, the elimination of all antidemocratic groups and organizations, major changes in the school system as well as a massive nationwide campaign of political education designed to reach Germans at every age and socioeconomic level. In theory at least, "reeducation entailed the most extensive plan in recorded history to induce rapid cultural change in an entire population."[5] To determine the effects of these reeducation programs, the military government conducted several hundred surveys from 1945 to 1955.[6]

The first West German government constituted under the provisions of the Basic Law was also strongly concerned with the population's knowledge, feelings, and evaluations of democracy. Beginning in 1950 the Adenauer government's Press and Information Office commissioned German polling organizations to conduct monthly surveys that in various ways were designed to examine German political culture.[7]

Both the German- and the American-sponsored studies employed rather elementary measures of support for democratic political institutions, attitudes, and values, for example, political competition, freedom of speech and expression, and representative institutions. Attitudes toward more complex problems such as participation, political conflict, civil liberties, and socioeconomic inequality were not extensively studied. The surveys themselves reflected the defensive posture of the occupation authorities and the new German government toward German mass publics and to some extent reveal the stability and security orientation of German and Western elites during the early years of the republic. Yet, in reviewing these early surveys, one is struck by the similarity of their substantive concerns and those of *The Civic Culture.* An extensive analysis of these data by Almond and Verba, given the absence of comparable materials for the other four countries, would have been beyond the scope of their study. Their availability, however, is testimony to the acute relevance of the *Civic Culture* study to the German case.

Among German political scientists, however, the work received little serious attention. Indeed, political science as an academic discipline was formally represented at only a few universities and most scholars approached the study of politics from a historical, legal, institutional, or philosophical perspective. The type of cross-national empirical research, represented by *The Civic Culture,* and Almond and Verba's emphasis on the nonpolitical sources of political attitudes and behavior were genuinely "foreign" to most of their German counterparts.[8] There were, of course, some exceptions. The political historian Karl-Dietrich Bracher cited the work in several publications, termed it *bedeutend* (significant), applauded its general purposes, but questioned its Anglo-American bias and the relevance of the framework to countries like Italy and Germany whose relationship to stable democracy "can only be *ermittelt* [ascertained] through a detailed historical and sociological analysis of both the requisites and 'handicaps' of democracy in different countries." [9] In short *The Civic Culture*'s approach to the problem of German democratic political development was in Bracher's opinion of less value than more traditional methods. The book has never been formally reviewed in the major German political science journal, *Politische Vierteljahresschrift (PVS)*; the *Political Culture and Political Development* (1965) volume was reviewed in *PVS* by an American scholar.

The only extensive German confrontation with the theory, method, and data of *The Civic Culture* took place among the few political sociologists, mainly at the University of Cologne, who were involved with cross-national empirical research. Chief among these was Erwin K. Scheuch, who in a number of publications used *The Civic Culture* to illustrate the problems of comparative survey research. Also, in 1961, Scheuch together with the political scientist Rudolf Wildenmann undertook the first major German academic study of voting behavior, the *Wahlstudie*. This project consisted of a three-wave national survey, panel studies in four selected constituencies, elite interviews, media content analysis, and a simulation study of the effects of different types of electoral systems upon the distribution of parliamentary mandates. The first major publication of this project was *Zur Soziologie der Wahl* (1965).[10]

The model for this electoral project was the American-voting studies of Lazersfeld and his associates and, to a lesser extent, the Survey Research Center at the University of Michigan. Although the surveys used several questions from the 1959 *Civic Culture* study, there is little indication that the substantive arguments of Almond and Verba had any significant impact upon the contributors to *Zur Soziologie der Wahl*. Only one of the book's eight articles cites the work, Scheuch's "The Visibility of Political Preferences in Everyday Life," in connection with Almond and Verba's interest in political conversations.

Beginning in the late 1960s research projects initiated at Cologne and, later, the University of Mannheim did reflect some influence of the Almond and Verba research. Scholars in Cologne in 1965 began an extensive research program into political radicalism and democratic values. Originally stimulated by the emergence of the radical right, if not neo-Nazi, National Democratic party (NPD), the work of the Cologne group focused on the distribution of antisystem orientations and opinions among mass publics and the structural and attitudinal correlates of support for antisystem parties.[11] At Mannheim the research program of Rudolf Wildenmann and his associates, in addition to electoral behavior, included several elite studies and national surveys of political attitudes and values.[12] The more recent work of the Mannheim group has also been put into a comparative context through extensive collaboration with other European and American research teams.[13]

The critique of *The Civic Culture* by Scheuch was by no means limited to that work, but applied to cross-national survey research generally. Focusing on the problems of equivalence in question meaning and the problem of verbal communication across cultures, the subjects of chapter 2 of *The Civic Culture*, Scheuch, along with many others, pointed out "that since certain words are unique to a language or altogether absent from it, this may signify that the phenomenon to which they refer is unique or absent." [14] Specifically he argued that Almond and Verba's attempt to explore the *affective* (as opposed to instrumental) component of German political culture, resulted in question wording and answer coding of dubious value in the European context. To list, for example, "spiritual and moral betterment" as a possible political problem to be dealt with by government was, he argued, "plain silly." [15] To ask the respondents to describe their feelings when going to the polls and to offer as an answer category "I get a feeling of satisfaction," an alternative which Scheuch termed a "hedonistic" dimension or component to political participation, was "in most European countries unwarranted." [16]

The absence of any systematic examination of contextual effects upon the respondents was another major point in Scheuch's critique of the work and reflected his own interest in "context analysis," the integration of individual (survey) and collective (aggregate) data. In the case of *The Civic Culture*, he was particularly concerned that the authors failed to deal with such elementary contextual matters as the timing of the surveys in the different countries — for example, Great Britain was on the verge of an election campaign, and Germany was between elections — and its possible effect upon responses. Turning to the sample, the 74 percent completion rate was regarded as "exceptionally high" and he criticized the absence of any discussion about the characteristics of those who refused to be interviewed. The underrepresentation of citizens in rural areas and young people was also noted. In addition, Scheuch doubted the validity of the formula given for the computation of standard errors. He found the distributions for Germany "highly skewed" and argued that the formula given might often lead to an underestimation of sampling errors. Finally, since the sample was to be not only representative but also analytical, its scope was too narrow for the study's theoretical concerns. This problem was especially evident with the education variable and the minuscule number of college educated (n = 24) yielded by Almond and Verba's sampling procedure.

These rather limited critical comments of Scheuch represented, nonetheless, the only extensive critique given the work by any German scholar when it first appeared. Later generations of German political scientists, strongly committed to radical or Marxist modes of analysis, found the book's emphasis on stable democracy and its narrow conception of the political of little interest.[17] *The Civic Culture,* together with other empirical work, has usually been dismissed as "bourgeois science" with little substantive importance. Thus, apart from the rather limited methodological comments of Scheuch, *The Civic Culture*'s impact in the Federal Republic was, in the words of one informant, *"äusserst gering"* (extremely limited).[18]

THE CIVIC CULTURE AND GERMANY

The pattern of political culture found by Almond and Verba in Germany had the following key components: (1) High levels of political cognition and output affect. Sizable majorities of German respondents, like their American and British counterparts, perceived government as influencing their lives in a favorable manner and were well informed about political institutions and leaders. (2) Low levels of system affect as measured by questions tapping pride in governmental and political institutions and feelings about voting, elections, campaigns, and parties. On this dimension the German democracy in 1959 parted company with the American and British systems. (3) Low levels of active political communication (talking politics) and "harder" forms of political participation (party membership, organizing political groups). Germans were more likely to feel restricted about discussing politics and revealing their political preferences and opinions to fellow citizens than were the American and British respondents. (4) Alienation and negativism toward political parties and other political aspects (voting, campaigns) of the governmental structure, especially among educated Germans ("wherever political feelings are concerned, the educated Germans show greater alienation and negativism than the less-well educated").[19] (5) A lower frequency of "open partisans" than in the United States or Britain and, conversely, more parochial and intense partisans and a partisan fragmentation which was traced to a "relatively strong tendency toward clerical-traditionalism, particularly among church-going Catholic women." [20] (6) A lack of congruence between citizen (political) and subject (administrative) competence. German respondents felt more competent in dealing with administrative officials than with politicians and parties. Few would form groups for political action. (7) In Germany, in contrast to the United States, Britain and Mexico, the lack of a relationship between the sense of the ability to participate (subject or citizen competence) and system pride except for Germans who had attained some higher educational level.[21] (8) Stability of the political system was more dependent upon system performance than was the case in the other four countries.[22]

The sources or determinants of this German pattern of political culture were found in (1) a weaker propensity to use leisure time for "outgoing" activities as compared to the United States and Britain; (2) low levels of social trust, consideration for others and generosity (the "public virtues"), and "faith in people"; (3) low propensity for cooperative activities; [23] to the Germans (and Italians and Mexicans as well), "politics appears to be a special realm where the norms and attitudes of more general interpersonal relations do not prevail";[24] (4) low levels of active membership in voluntary associations with some political concerns; [25] although Germans were found to be just about as likely as Englishmen or Americans to be members of voluntary associations, they were found to be least likely to be active, and the comparatively low proportion who had ever been officers in any group indicated to Almond and Verba that their membership tended "to be formal in nature involving little direct individual commitment and activity";[26] (5) low levels of participation and discussion in decision making in the family, school, and employment experience, especially among those respondents with only primary education; (6) Germany's "traumatic," "bitter" political history.

Their summary evaluation of Germany's prospects for achieving a stable democracy similar to Almond and Verba's Anglo-American ideal was thus generally negative:

> Though there is relatively widespread satisfaction with political output, this is not matched by more general system affect. Germans tend to be satisfied with the performance of their government, but to lack a more general attachment to the system on the symbolic level. Theirs is a highly pragmatic — probably overpragmatic — orientation to the political system; as if the intense commitment to political movements that characterized Germany under Weimar and the Nazi era is now being balanced by a detached, practical, and almost cynical attitude toward politics. And the attitudes of the German citizen to his fellow political actors are probably also colored by the country's political history. Hostility between the supporters of the two large parties is still relatively high and is not tempered by any general social norms of trust and confidence. And the ability of Germans to cooperate politically also appears to have serious limitations. . . . In Germany the lack of commitment to the political system that is relatively independent of system output suggests that the stability may be in doubt if the level of output becomes less satisfactory. There is little capital of "system affect" to draw upon if governmental performance should weaken. Furthermore, weakness of the participant role in Germany, especially the lack of an informal participatory culture, suggests that too much reliance is placed upon hierarchical leadership. Though the formal political institutions of democracy exist in Germany and though there is a well-developed political infrastructure — a system of political parties and pressure groups — the underlying set of political attitudes that would regulate the operation of these institutions in a democratic direction is missing.[27]

To overcome this lack of "system affect," Almond and Verba prescribed "a symbolic event, or a symbolic, charismatic leader, or some other means of creating commitment and unity at the symbolic level. But also important are expanding educational opportunity, experiences in industrial contexts, and exposure to the media of communication, to political parties, and voluntary associations. Governmental performance, too, has a crucial effect on the growth of a civic culture." [28] As this citation indicates, Almond and Verba said relatively little about how system affect develops beyond a general listing of several possible sources: symbolic events, leaders, "some other means" of creating commitment, educational opportunities, and system performance. What mix of the factors listed are necessary to produce what degree of system affect? What is the relative weight of these sources? Can performance or output itself become a symbol and create system affect?

Developmental questions such as these were not addressed by Almond and Verba. And this is the work's major shortcoming as it relates to Germany: the study is time-bound and neither their data nor their discussion deals systematically with the question of change.

Apart from several important but unfortunately insoluble problems with the 1959 sample — its size, the underrepresentation of university-educated citizens and young people — pointed out by Scheuch and others, and the relative absence of multidimensional controls and more sophisticated multivariate statistical techniques in the analysis, Almond and Verba were true to their data. Significantly, none of the many secondary analyses of their data that this author is familiar with, many of which have employed a variety of high-powered statistical techniques, has ever contradicted their basic portrait of German political culture.

Although an accurate portrayal of German political culture in the late 1950s, it was only a snapshot and could neither trace patterns of development that preceded the 1959 survey nor outline possible future changes in the culture.

From this absence of a focus on change and development follow three other flaws in the work: the distinction between "affective" and "instrumental" support, the use of "history" as an explanatory variable, and the absence of any data or discussion of the relationship between national identity and system affect.

AFFECTIVE VS. DIFFUSE SUPPORT

The theoretical framework of the five-nation study put major emphasis on the "mixed" character of the "civic culture," which combines "some measure of competence, involvement, and activity with passivity and non-involvement." [29] Consistent with the theoretical distinction between instrumental and affective attitudes, the survey instrument contained a number of items which tried to tap the respondents' "feelings" toward politics: pride in the political system, attitudes toward elections and campaigns, and feelings about the act of voting. In their discussion Almond and Verba tended to equate the presence of affective, or "feeling," orientations with "system affect," which a stable political system requires to see it through periods of crises.[30]

This identification of feelings with system affect leads Almond and Verba to be skeptical about the long-run prospects of the German political system, "if the level of output becomes less satisfactory." [31] Since they found such low system affect (operationalized through the feeling questions), they had to reserve judgment about the capability of the system to remain stable in the event of a decline in system output.

Yet by the late 1970s, by all measures, the Federal Republic, in spite of occasional declines in system output (the recessions of 1966–67 and 1974–76), is a model of democratic political stability. Indeed, on some measures that will be discussed, Germany today is closer to the civic culture than Britain or the United States. The question remains whether or not "feelings" of pride and satisfaction are the only valid indicator of system affect or "rain or shine" support. Is it not possible for a system to develop a reserve of "support capital" from an extended period of high-level system performance? Almond and Verba are somewhat unclear on this crucial point. At times they suggest that there is no relationship between "output" and "affective attitudes," [32] and yet elsewhere they postulate a linkage between "performance" and long-range support.[33]

The concept of diffuse support, developed by Easton, is more relevant in the German case than system affect as conceptualized and above all operationalized by Almond and Verba. Like system affect, diffuse support is not directly related to system performance (output) "except in the long-run." [34] Diffuse support is present, according to Easton, if the political system is regarded as legitimate and trusted by its members, or if a strong sense of personal identification (common interests) exists with the political community. Unlike Almond and Verba's system affect, diffuse support can be measured by means other than feeling questions, such as (1) citizen support for key system *values* (a close fit between individual values and official system values), (2) a consensus on the validity of system *structures,* and (3) identification with system *leadership.* Unlike system affect, diffuse support need not take the form of an emotional commitment. In later work Easton attempted to delineate the sources of such diffuse support. Of particular interest for our purposes is his specification of "experience" as a source of diffuse support in addition to the more conventional source of childhood and adult socialization:

> Members do not come to identify with basic political objects only because they have learned to do so through inducements offered by others — a critical aspect of socialization processes. If they did, diffuse support would have entirely the appearance of a non-rational phenomenon. Rather, on the basis of their own experiences, members may also adjudge the worth of supporting these objects for their own sake. Such attachment may be a product of spill-over effects from evaluations of a series of outputs and of performance over a long period of time. *Even though the orientations derive from responses to particular outputs initially, they become in time dissociated from performance. They became transformed into generalized attitudes towards authorities or other political objects. They begin to take on a life of their own.*[35]

Thus a system's high level of performance, its output, can over time "take on a life of its own," that is, become a symbol aiding in identification with the political institutions and processes of the regime. The "economy" and the "net of social welfare and security" have been cited by some German observers as important symbols of the postwar polity as well as sources of legitimacy, which engender in mass publics a "feeling of being cared for," of security.[36] This attitude may not be expressed in the form of undying love or emotional expressions of support for the system, but neither does it leave the political system without a reservoir of goodwill.

Moreover, the concept of a "reserve of goodwill" implies that a system, through performance, can accumulate such capital, which can then be drawn upon in times of crisis or low performance levels. Certainly no political system can draw on such a reserve indefinitely, and, likewise, low performance levels can erode diffuse support. Kavanagh, in his essay for this volume, seems to be making a similar argument for Great Britain where he observes the "decline of the civic culture" including a drop in system affect which is related to system performance (page 124).

The absence of any significant challenge to the legitimacy of the Bonn system since 1949, the concentration of support for the parties committed to the constitution, the ability of the system to introduce major policy innovations, for example, *Ostpolitik,* without disrupting the republican consensus, and the absence of any increase in antisystem or extremist sentiment during the relatively severe 1974–76 recession are all at least surface indicators that support for the system can remain high even in periods of low system performance or change. We suggest that a "reserve of goodwill" has been accumulating during the past three decades of high-level performance, that socialization processes are transmitting this record to new generations, thus further increasing the capital of diffuse support. Yet this support need not necessarily be expressed or measured solely, if at all, through feelings.

Almond and Verba's concept of system affect was perhaps too constrictive — theoretically and empirically — to encompass the German case. By attempting to measure the concept through a limited number of feeling questions they could not adequately discuss the possibility that outputs (system performance) could serve as the basis for the emergence of the "rain or shine" support they found so lacking in 1959.

An example of what is meant by the growth of diffuse support is provided in Table VII.1, which relates the respondent's attitude toward the current performance of parliament to the more general question of whether a parliament is needed at all. We treat the question "Do you have a favorable or unfavorable impression of the parliament's work in Bonn?" as one calling for a fairly specific judgment of the institution's performance. The

TABLE VII.1.   *Attitudes Toward Parliament by Estimation of Parliamentary Performance, 1962–72*

Estimation of Parliamentary Performance

| | 1962 | | 1972 | |
Is Parliament needed?	*Favorable* (%)	*Unfavorable* [a] (%)	*Favorable* (%)	*Unfavorable* [a] (%)
Yes	84	59	89	86
No	7	29	4	6
Undecided, no answer	9	12	7	8
Total	100	100	100	100
(*N* =)	(322)	(148)	(754)	(520)

[a] "Don't knows" on the parliamentary performance question have been excluded.

Source: Institut für Demoskopie, Survey nos. 1069 and 2085. These and all other Demoskopie (Allensbach) opinion polls cited in this essay were obtained from the *Institut* and the Roper Public Opinion Research Center, Williamstown, Massachusetts.

second question, "Looking at it entirely from the practical side, do we really need a parliament in Bonn and all these deputies or could we do without it?" calls for a more general evaluation of the institution. If German political culture is so pragmatic and output-oriented, there should be a negative relationship between a respondent's opinion of the institution's performance and its general necessity, that is, those unhappy with parliamentary output should be most likely to see little need for the institution. If, however, we find that even those Germans who have an unfavorable impression of parliament still regard it as necessary, we contend that one can speak of "diffuse" (non-performance-related) support for the institution. Fortunately we have two surveys covering a ten-year time span (1962–72), in which both questions were asked of national samples. As Table VII.1 shows, the proportion of Germans with an unfavorable opinion of parliament's performance, who nonetheless regard it as necessary, has increased over time. In 1962 there was a strong relationship between attitudes toward the institution's performance and more general evaluations of its necessity. In 1962, 84 percent of those respondents favorably impressed with parliamentary performance regarded the institution as necessary, but only 59 percent of those with an unfavorable impression of the institution's work saw it as necessary. Ten years later, however, it made little difference in judging its necessity whether one had a favorable or unfavorable impression of parliamentary performance. In 1972, 89 percent of those satisfied with current parliamentary output felt that the institution was really needed, and fully 86 percent of those currently dissatisfied with the institution's performance still acknowledged that "we cannot get along without it."

"HISTORY" AS AN EXPLANATORY VARIABLE

At numerous times throughout the study, Almond and Verba, after describing specific characteristics of a country's political culture, attempted to "plug-in" history or "historical development" as an explanatory variable. Yet, in spite of the systematic, empirical orientations of the authors, their use of history was vague and imprecise. After describing German political culture as "detached," more "subject than participant oriented," for example, they refer merely to Germany's "traumatic history" to explain this pattern.[37] But this hypothesized relationship between historical experiences and political values was only asserted and never tested. Specific questions about the respondent's experiences and attitudes toward the past, and specifically the National Socialist and postwar periods, could have been asked in the sample survey and the responses related to the political culture variables. Were those respondents subjected to de-Nazification more cynical than others not so affected? Was there any relationship between sympathy for past regimes (monarchy, the Third Reich) and orientations toward democratic norms and values?

In neglecting to examine directly or systematically the effects of history upon political culture, the authors were unable to deal satisfactorily with the problem of change. If there is a relationship between a country's "traumatic history" and its political culture, what happens to political values over time as the traumatic events become increasingly remote to an increasingly larger segment of the population? Would not those aspects of the culture related to the traumatic past (detachment, cynicism, low affectivity) decrease in aggregate saliency when less traumatic, if not satisfactory, experiences become predominant in the minds of younger generations?

Consider, for example, the data presented in Table VII.2. At the time of the *Civic Culture* survey (1959) a majority of West

TABLE VII.2.   *Attitudes Toward the "Past," 1951–70*

Q.: When in this century do you think Germany has been best off?

	Year			
	1951 %	*1959 %*	*1963 %*	*1970 %*
Federal Republic (present)	2	42	62	81
Prewar Third Reich (1933–39)	42	18	10	5
Weimar Republic	7	4	5	2
Empire (pre–1914)	45	28	16	5
Other	4	8	7	7

Source: Institut für Demoskopie, *Jahrbuch der öffentlichen Meinung,* Vol. V (1968–73), (Allensbach am Bodensee: Verlag für Demoskopie, 1974), p. 223.

Germans still had favorable memories of past regimes or re-garded some past regimes as ones in which Germany was "better off" than during the republic. The 1959 preference level (42 percent), however, represented a sharp increase over that of 1951 (2 percent). In 1951 almost 90 percent of the adult population still thought Germany had been "best off" during either the prewar Third Reich or the pre-1914 empire. Four years after the *Civic Culture* survey, the proportion preferring the Federal Re-public had risen to 62 percent and, by 1970, 81 percent of the adult population thought that Germany in the twentieth century has been best off in the Federal Republic. The age of the respon-dent is an important predictor of responses to this question, with postwar generations taking the lead in identification with the Federal Republic; but by 1970 a majority of age cohorts who had experienced all or part of the Weimar Republic and the prewar Third Reich also preferred the Federal Republic.

A further example illustrating the changing effects of "history" can be found in an analysis of public attitudes toward the res-toration of the monarchy. In 1951 almost a third of the West German adult population supported the return of the Hohen-zollern monarchy. But this support was greatest among the oldest and most parochial segments of the population: women (espe-cially widows) over sixty, with limited education. Respondents over sixty were more than twice as likely to support a restoration (51 percent) than those under thirty (24 percent). And when we controlled for education among the under-thirty group, support for the monarchy dropped to only 12 percent among those with academic training.[38] The passage of time, rising educational levels, and the modernization of German society and politics are factors which by the mid-1960s had all but eliminated popular support for the monarchy.[39]

NATIONAL IDENTITY AND SYSTEM SUPPORT

The Civic Culture's treatment of national identity and pride was also deficient in the German case. As Verba pointed out in a later essay, a basic issue of the German political culture, that of national identity, was in 1959 still unresolved. He suggested "that until a political culture includes a stable and secure sense of national identity all other problems will be subordinated." [40] Yet, although discussing "pride in the political system," *The Civic Culture* did not deal with the problem of the extent of national identity in postwar German political culture. Fortunately there is a wealth of time-series data available dealing with this question and an excellent analysis of the development of national identity is now available.[41]

The boundaries of the nation as perceived by the populace, although not yet as established as in older democracies, have become stabilized in the past quarter century. As Table VII.3 shows, between 1951 and 1976 the proportion of Germans who did not believe that the Federal Republic and East Germany would ever be united increased from 28 to 65 percent. Similarly, the willingness to accept the Oder–Neisse line (the de facto postwar boundary between Poland and East Germany) as the permanent eastern border increased from only 8 percent in 1951

TABLE VII.3. *Attitudes Toward Unification, 1951–76*

Q.: Do you think that the division between the Soviet-occupied part of Germany — I mean the DDR — and the Federal Republic will, in the foreseeable future, be ended and that a unified Germany will again exist?

	1951 %	1958 %	1973 %	1976 %
Yes, Germany will be unified	27	18	9	13
No	28	34	53	65
Uncertain	36	46	32	22
No answer	9	2	6	—
Total	100	100	100	100

Source: EMNID, *Informationen,* No. 26, 1973; for 1976: Institut für Demoskopie, *Jahrbuch der öffentlichen Meinung,* vol. VI (1976), (Allensbach am Bodensee: Verlag für Demoskopie, 1976), p. 83.

TABLE VII.4. *German Unification* vs. *European Unification, 1965–73*

Q.: What do you consider more urgent: the unification of Germany or European unification?

	1965 %	1973 %
German unification	69	23
European unification	24	65
No answer	7	12
Total	100	100

Source: EMNID, *Informationen*, no. 28, 1973.

to 61 percent by 1972.[42] Generally, as Table VII.4 indicates, the relative salience of German unification has declined drastically during the past fifteen years. Responses to these questions are, as expected, related to age; among those under thirty in 1976, almost 75 percent doubted that unification would ever take place, as compared to 54 percent of Germans over sixty.[43] But perhaps more significantly there is a strong relationship between a West German national identity and support for democratic institutions and processes. Those citizens who accept the present borders are more likely to discuss politics, be active in a party, identify with the republican flag, believe that freedom of expression exists in the Federal Republic, and support a competitive party system than citizens who have not yet accepted the permanence of postwar division.[44]

CHANGE IN THE GERMAN POLITICAL CULTURE

Any nation's political culture is in a constant state of evolution; nevertheless, the commitment of postwar Western and German elites to change German political culture and the vacuum created by the demise of past regimes together with the socioeconomic dislocations of the war and the postwar period make Germany an excellent setting for the study of political culture change.

Certain features of the culture found in the 1959 study, however, have remained relatively constant. The levels of political cognition and the rates of participation in formal political activities such as voting remain high.[45] By the mid-1970s, for example, participation in national elections had exceeded 90 percent. In a recent five-nation comparative study Hans-Dieter Klingemann found that only 6 percent of German respondents were *unable* to make any substantive comments (favorable or unfavorable) about their country's party system, as compared to 28 percent of respondents from the Netherlands, 17 percent from Austria and Britain, and 13 percent from the United States.[46] A ten-nation study of school-aged children conducted in the early 1970s found a similar pattern.[47] Nonetheless, these relatively unchanged features of the political culture are the exceptions to the general pattern of change both before and since the 1959 survey.

In this section we shall examine these changes by first bringing the 1959 characterization of German political culture "up to date" and then by presenting additional material, dealing with topics such as national identity and the political past not examined directly by Almond and Verba. After delineating these changes we shall turn to the more difficult task of analyzing the sources or determinants of political-cultural change.

Although an exact replication of the 1959 study has never been conducted in Germany, the large body of survey data available does enable us to find equivalents to the 1959 topics, and in some cases similar or identical questions are available.

Unfortunately we lack abundant data on "affect" that are strictly comparable with the 1959 questions. The German polling organizations, perhaps also aware of Scheuch's caveat that such items are of little value in the European context, have rarely asked such questions. The data available, however, do enable us to relate general attitudes of support or opposition to the system to more specific measures of system performance. If system support is becoming increasingly less related to system performance, that is, more diffuse, we have some basis for contending that the system by the late 1970s is less dependent on output-related support than at the time of the Almond and Verba survey.

SYSTEM AFFECT

One important topic in the 1959 survey, system affect, has been recently reexamined in the Federal Republic. In one of the most oft-cited findings (and frequently reprinted tables) of *The Civic Culture,* the level of pride that Germans had in their political system in 1959 was far below that found in the United States and Great Britain. This low level of system affect, as we have discussed, played a major role in Almond and Verba's relatively pessimistic prognosis for the future of the postwar system.

Table VII.5 reports the changes in the system pride question for Germany over the nineteen-year period 1959–78. The most striking feature of these data is the increase in pride in the political system and institutions of the Federal Republic from only 7 percent in 1959 to 31 percent in 1978.[48] Moreover, among respondents under 30 in 1978, the post-*Civic Culture* cohort, the proportion mentioning the political system as a source of pride was 38 percent.[49] Two other significant changes in Germany are the increase in pride in the Federal Republic's social legislation (pension and welfare plans) and the sharp decrease in the category "characteristics of the people" (frugality, cleanliness, efficiency, hard work) as a source of pride. In the 1959 German sample those who expressed pride in this latter category repre-

TABLE VII.5. *System Pride, 1959–78*

Q.: Generally speaking, what are the things about this country [in 1978: the Federal Republic] that you are most proud of [in 1978: especially proud of]?

| | | 1959 | | 1978 |
	U.S. %	U.K. %	Germany %	Germany %
Respondent is most proud of:				
Governmental, political institutions	85	46	7	31
Social legislation	13	18	6	18
Position in international affairs	5	11	5	9
Economic system	23	10	33	40
Characteristics of people	7	18	36	25
Spiritual virtues and religion	3	1	3	6
Contributions to arts and sciences	4	13	23	23
Physical attributes of country	5	10	17	14
Nothing, don't know	13	21	18	10
Total [a]	158	148	148	176
N	(970)	(963)	(955)	(2,030)

[a] Percentages exceed one hundred because of multiple responses.

Sources: For 1959, *Civic Culture*, p. 102; for 1978, Rudolf Wildenmann, "Das neue Nationalbewusstsein," *Capital*, vol. 17, no. 10 October 1978): 288.

sented the largest proportion of respondents, a pattern which could be interpreted as a residue of the "master race" ideology of the Nazis. In any case, Germans in 1978 were less likely to be proud of the characteristics of the *Volk* and far more likely to be proud of their postwar governmental and political institutions than was the case in 1959. The German level of system pride in 1978, however, was still below the 1959 British level and far below that found in the 1959 American data. While the system pride question has not been repeated, to our knowledge, in these latter two countries, there is considerable evidence, especially for Great Britain, which suggests that the level of pride in political institutions has declined since 1959.[50]

CIVIC COMPETENCE

A key element of the civic culture model was the "sense of civic competence" — the belief that citizens can influence the course of governmental decisions. Almond and Verba also distinguished between "subjective civic competence," the belief that citizens can do something about a local or national law they consider unjust, and "objective civic competence," actual behavior designed to influence government. In all five nations there was, of course, a disparity between these two dimensions of civic competence — a gap or "balance" which Almond and Verba regarded as functional to a democratic political culture.[51] A reserve of subjective competence, they argued, serves as a potential check on the abuse of power and enhances governmental (elite) *responsiveness,* while the "objective weakness of the ordinary man allow governmental elites to act," [52] thus facilitating governmental *effectiveness.*

This formulation of civic competence has been sharply criticized by numerous scholars as elitist, conservative, and incompatible with the tenets of classical democratic theory.[53] But regardless of the elitist or conservative bias in the concept, the German sample in 1959 was further from this balance than either the United States or Britain, especially in the area of national civic competence.

As the data in Table VII.6 show, there have been significant changes in the civic competence dimension of German political culture since 1959. Between 1959 and 1974 the proportion of local competents in Germany increased by eight percent, while

TABLE VII.6.   *Civic Competence, 1959–74* a

| | *Local competents* | | | *National competents* | | |
	1959	*1974*	*Difference* %	*1959*	*1974*	*Difference* %
United States	77	77	0	75	82	+ 7
Great Britain	78	74	− 4	62	66	+ 4
Germany	62	70	+ 8	38	59	+21
Netherlands	b	71	—	b	53	—
Austria	b	48	—	b	41	—

a Percentage who state they can do something about an unjust local or national regulation.

b Not included in 1959 *Civic Culture* survey.

Sources: For 1959, *Civic Culture*, p. 185; for 1974, Kaase and Barnes, *Political Action and Mass Participation,* cited in Martin and Sylvia Greiffenhagen, *Ein schwieriges Vaterland* (Munich: List Verlag, 1979), p. 341.

in the United States and Britain the proportion of citizens stating that they could do something about an unjust law at the local level remained the same or, in the case of Britain, actually decreased during this time period. But the most dramatic change in German civic competence occurred at the national level. While the level of national civic competence in Britain and the United States increased only slightly between 1959 and 1974, the proportion of German respondents who felt competent to influence national legislation they considered unjust rose from 38 percent in 1959 to 59 percent in 1974, a level only slightly below that of Great Britain and above that of the Netherlands in 1974.

In addition, between 1959 and 1974 the proportion of British and American respondents who felt they could do *nothing* to influence a local or national regulation they considered unjust increased by eight percent (from 18 to 26 percent) in Great Britain and by five percent (from 18 to 23 percent) in the United States, while the German level of powerlessness vis-à-vis local or national political institutions declined from 34 percent to 30 percent.[54] Among those German respondents under 30 in 1974 the proportion feeling powerless was only 19 percent, a figure below that of the corresponding British (27 percent) and American (24 percent) age cohort.[55] Thus the post-*Civic Culture* cohort in Germany was *less likely* to state that nothing could be done about an unjust local or national law than the corresponding group in the United States and Great Britain. The rate of change between 1959 and 1974 was greatest among the youngest age cohort in all three countries, with the level of powerlessness among the 18–30-year-old group in Germany dropping by over 10 percent while it increased by 13 and 11 percent for Britain and the United States.[56] If this trend continues, the level of civic competence in the Federal Republic will soon equal or even exceed that found in the "classic" Anglo-American democracies.

SYSTEM SUPPORT

General support for the political system, operationalized through a variety of measures, had by the mid-1970s reached impressive levels. In Table VII.7 the distributions of responses to questions dealing with popular attitudes toward democracy between 1967 and 1976 are presented. In 1967, eight years after the *Civic Culture* survey was conducted, about a fourth of the West German adult population was still dissatisfied, undecided, or unwilling to make an evaluation as to whether or not democracy was the "best form of government" for Germany. Yet this 3 : 1 ratio in favor of democracy was similar for all age groups and supporters of the parties represented in parliament (Social Democrats, Christian Democratic Union, and Free Democrats). Significantly, the only socioeconomic group in 1967 with a relatively low level of support (54 percent) was composed of farmers, a rapidly declining segment of the work force. Yet only 4 percent of this group was opposed to the democratic system; 42 percent withheld their judgment. Only supporters of the radical right National Democratic party (NPD), which received less than 5 percent of the vote at the 1969 election, were clearly dissatisfied with the political system; about half the party's supporters in 1967 wanted some other form of government.[57] Both these groups (farmers and NPD supporters) were marginal in 1967 and were even more so a decade later.

By 1972 fully 90 percent of the adult population was "satisfied" with democracy in the Federal Republic. When the same question was asked again in 1976 this proportion remained unchanged in spite of the relatively severe economic recession of 1974–76, the fall of the Brandt government, and the general disappointment with *Ostpolitik*.

Moreover, by 1976 there was little significant difference be-

TABLE VII.7. *Satisfaction with Democracy, 1967–76*

	1967 %	1972 %	1976 %
Best form of government (satisfied)	74	90	90
Another form would be better (not satisfied)	4	7	6
Undecided, no judgment	22	3	4
Total	100	100	100

1967: Do you believe that democracy is the best form of government for Germany, or can you imagine a better one?

1972 and 1976: What would you generally say about democracy in the Federal Republic of Germany, that is, about our political parties and our entire political system? Are you satisfied, somewhat satisfied, or not satisfied with it?

Sources: 1967: Institut für Demoskopie, *Jahrbuch der öffentlichen Meinung,* vol. V (1968–73), (Allensbach am Bodensee: Verlag für Demoskopie, 1974), p. 223. 1972: *The 1972 German Election Panel Study,* Inter-University Consortium for Political Research, Study 7102. 1976: June 1976 national sample of voters conducted by Infratest. Data kindly made available to the author by Dr. Hans-Dieter Klingemann, Mannheim University.

tween the various socioeconomic (occupation, income, education), demographic (age, sex), and political (party preference) groups in their degree of general satisfaction with political democracy. Ninety-six percent of the supporters of the parties in power in 1976 (Social Democrats and Free Democrats), for example, were satisfied with the democratic order and nearly 90 percent of opposition party adherents shared this judgment.[58] Clearly, by 1976 there was a strong consensus on the basic character and structure of the West German democracy.

A more "affective"-oriented support question was put to a 1975 sample of young people (aged 13 to 24), who were asked: "If, in a public discussion, our form of government and state were sharply criticized what would be your attitude to our present state?" About two-thirds of the total sample replied that their basic attitude toward the present political system was either "very positive" or "somewhat positive"; only 18 percent were "indifferent" and only 8 percent "somewhat" or "very" negative toward the present system. Although the level of positive attitudes toward the political system was lower among the lower age groups and those respondents with minimal formal educational experience, it did not drop below 55 percent among any group.[59]

Finally, according to a 1974 cross-national study on trust in government, presented in Table VII.8 German citizens are now *more* trusting of government than their British counterparts. While almost half the British respondents see their country run by a "few big interests," only about a quarter of the German sample took this position. When asked directly whether they trusted their government "to do what is right," 48 percent of the German sample thought that they could "just about always" or "most of the time"; the corresponding English proportion is 39 percent.

PARTISANSHIP

In both Germany and Italy, Almond and Verba found at least remnants of the traditional *Lagermentalität,* the fragmentation of the political community into isolated camps each with its

TABLE VII.8. *Trust in Government: Britain and Germany, 1974*

Q.: Generally speaking, would you say that this country is run by a few big interests concerned for themselves, or that it is run for the benefit of all the people?

	Great Britain %	Germany %
"Few big interests"	47	27
"All the people"	37	60
Don't know	16	13

Q.: How much do you trust the government in Westminster (Bonn) to do what is right?

Just about always	7	9
Most of the time	32	39
Only some of the time	47	39
Almost never	10	7
Don't know	4	6

Sources: For Britain, Alan Marsh, *The Decline of Deference,* cited in Kavanagh, Table V.5, p. 150; Germany: April 1974, GETAS survey (national random sample), directed by Max Kaase and Hans-Dieter Klingemann, Mannheim University. The author is grateful to Professors Kaase and Klingemann for making these data available.

own sociocultural infrastructure and each suspicious, distrustful, and hostile toward the other camps. Germany had the highest frequency of "intense partisans," those sharply divided from opponents and emotionally involved in electoral contests, and the second highest proportion of "parochial partisans," those citizens, predominantly religious women, who were relatively uninvolved in politics, yet very concerned about interparty marriage.

Numerous scholars have questioned Almond and Verba's measurement of partisanship, especially the interparty marriage item which, they argue, is less a measure of party distance than of social class or religious distance.[60] But apart from the validity of the questions used, there is considerable evidence indicating a decrease in partisan hostility and *Lagermentalität,* especially among supporters of the only three parties continuously represented in parliament since 1949 — the Social Democratic Party (SPD), the Christian Democratic Union (CDU/CSU), and the Free Democratic Party (FDP). On most items measuring support for key system values during the past quarter century, the important party cleavage is not between these three system parties, but between system party identifiers and nonidentifiers or supporters of the various small extremist parties (Communists, Nazis) that have come and gone since 1949.[61] The Grand Coalition (1966–69) between the Christian Democrats and Social Democrats, which brought together the two major contenders for political power since 1949, also reduced interparty hostility.[62]

A further indication of the "moderate" character of partisanship in the Federal Republic comes from a 1976 panel study, which found that the proportion of German voters who regarded *all* major parties as ones they could conceivably support *increased* during the election campaign from 26 percent to 34 percent. At the end of the campaign in 1976 only about a fourth of SPD supporters stated that "under no conditions" could they ever vote for the Christian Democrats, and 35 percent of CDU supporters felt the same way about the Socialists.[63] A solid majority of the supporters of each major party did not exclude the possibility that they may in the future vote for the opposition party. The campaign thus apparently served not to intensify interparty hostility, but made some partisans more willing to consider the "other side" as a possible alternative. Even among strong partisans, the opposing party or parties were not evaluated more negatively, but indeed less so, in the course of the campaign.

Finally, the "parochialism" of Catholic women has clearly eroded since the 1950s. Between 1949 and 1969 Catholic women generally supported the Christian Democrats by about a 3 : 1 ratio over the Socialists. Since 1969, that is, at the elections of 1972 and 1976, the Christian Democrats have received about 60 percent of the Catholic female vote.[64]

Yet the decrease in the frequency of what Almond and Verba termed "apathetic" and "intense" partisanship has taken place within a context of increasing *issue polarization* within the party system. In 1969, for the first time in the history of the Bonn Republic, the electorate turned out the Christian Democrats, the dominant party since 1949, and made the Social Democrats the major governing party. The 1969 election as well as those of 1972 and 1976 were characterized by significant increases in citizen interest and involvement, the greater importance of issues as a determinant of voting behavior, and the sharply competitive character of the interparty electoral struggle.[65]

The combination of experiences during the Third Reich, postwar affluence, and socioeconomic modernization have clearly reduced the *Lager* mentality characteristic of interparty relations during the Weimar Republic. Yet the capacity of Germans to develop both some conceptual overview of their political world and fairly consistent sets of political values has also increased.[66]

POLITICAL PARTICIPATION

In the 1959 survey Almond and Verba found that political participation in Germany was concentrated on formal or passive activities such as voting and mass media exposure, which required little involvement or commitment. And although membership in voluntary associations was high, activity within them was low and the frequency of more informal group formation or political discussions was also comparatively low. Thus a "passive subject orientation" was found to persist, which had yet to be balanced by a "participant orientation," and norms favoring such active political participation were not well developed.

This description of participation in the Federal Republic has changed in several important respects since the 1959 survey.

Participation in formal, low-level activities remains high, but there is increasing evidence that the "participant orientation" found to be lacking in the *Civic Culture* study is emerging. Yet it must first be noted that the absence of *norms* stressing political participation, cited by Almond and Verba, was quite consistent with the intentions of West Germany's political elites after 1945. The founding fathers of the republic had little trust in the German common man. They believed that the great mass of the German people had indeed enthusiastically supported Hitler and the Nazis during the turbulent 1930s and could again respond to demagogic appeals if given the opportunity. Hence those features of the Weimar constitution — the direct election of a strong president, provisions for the initiative and the referendum (which at the time had made Germany the largest political unit ever to experiment with them), and the provisions for proportional representation — which the Nazis had exploited in their efforts to bring down the republic were all either deleted or amended in the Basic Law.[67] Mass political participation beyond voting was simply not encouraged in this document. All other forms of mass political involvement were to be channeled through highly structured political parties and interest groups.

Change in political participation is most apparent in the following areas: political interest, willingness to publicly express party preferences and electoral choices, political conversations, and the formation of grass-roots public-interest groups (citizen-initiative groups).

POLITICAL INTEREST

Most students of political participation assume that it is affected by certain attitudes and dispositions which can stimulate or motivate political activity and in turn be reinforced by it.[68] Thus an "interest" in politics is associated with political behavior which can, through complex feedback mechanisms, intensify the original motivation or "interest." At a very basic level we have a measure of one of these attitudinal antecedents to political participation which can also serve as a general measure of politicization, "political interest" as tapped by the simple question "Generally speaking, are you interested in politics?" The distribution of responses over the twenty-five-year period for which we have data is presented in Table VII.9.

TABLE VII.9. *Political Interest, 1952–77*
Q.: *Generally speaking, are you interested in politics?*

	1952 %	1959 %	1962 %	1965 %	1969 %	1972 %	1973 %	1977 %
Yes	27	29	37	39	45	46	49	50
Not especially	41	36	39	43	42	34	34	41
No	32	35	24	18	13	20	17	9
Total	100	100	100	100	100	100	100	100

Source: Institut für Demoskopie, Survey nos. 0052, 1031, 1069, 2017, 2054, 2085, 2090, and 3038.

The trend over this period is clear. A steadily increasing proportion of West Germans are expressing at least a general interest in politics. Throughout the 1950s this proportion never exceeded 30 percent; in the 1960s the percentage of those interested in politics crossed the 40 percent mark and by 1977 half of the adult population reported they were interested in politics. This question, of course, is quite general and it must not be overinterpreted. At a minimum, however, it does give us some indication of the general level of politicization in West German society.

This increase in political interest may not, however, be functional for democratic stability if the politically active are no more likely, or even are less likely, to support the norms and values of the system than those with little or no interest in politics. If the increases in interest and participation are concentrated among opponents to the present regime, increases in participation could be quite dysfunctional for system stability. Thus we must examine the relationship between political interest and support for key system values and institutions. First, as Table VII.10 shows, there is a substantial relationship between participation and potential *active* opposition to a new Nazi party. In 1972 only 20 percent of those with no (low) interest in politics would do "everything possible" to stop a new Nazi party and 31 percent of those respondents with "some" interest would actively oppose such a party, but 59 percent of the politically interested would actively oppose a neo-Nazi party. Clearly, the politically interested in the Bonn Republic are the most emphatic opponents of a reemergence of the totalitarian past.

TABLE VII.10. *Potential Active Opposition to New Nazi Party by Political Interest, 1959–72*

| | | Year | |
Political interest	1959 %	1962 %	1972 %
High	48	57	59
Medium	27	34	31
Low	19	24	20

Source: Institut für Demoskopie, Survey nos. 1031, 1069, and 2085.

Q.: Assuming that a new Nazi party attempted to come to power, how would you react? ACTIVE OPPOSITION: *"I would do everything in my power to oppose such a party."*

Likewise, support for the key system rule of competition is greatest among the politically interested. By 1972 there was near unanimous agreement (95 percent) among those interested in politics on the importance of political competition for the West German state; only two-thirds of those with no interest in politics supported this rather elementary principle of liberal democracy.[69]

The politically interested are also far more likely to perceive a need for legislative institutions and to be favorably oriented to the constitution than those with little or only moderate interest. Although only 53 percent of those with no interest in politics feel that parliament is necessary, 92 percent of the politically interested are convinced of the need for the institution.[70] As Table VII.11 indicates, this relationship between political interest and attitudes toward parliament has actually become stronger since 1959. Those with low levels of interest in politics in 1972

TABLE VII.11. *Attitudes Toward Parliament by Level of Political Interest, 1959–72*

Political interest	Parliament is necessary [a]			Can get along without it [a]		
	1959 %	1962 %	1972 %	1959 %	1962 %	1972 %
High	88	83	92	8	12	4
Medium	71	71	83	12	13	6
Low	55	49	53	11	16	9

[a] "Don't knows" on the parliament question have not been included.

Source: Institut für Demoskopie, Survey nos. 1031, 1069, and 2085.

were slightly less likely to perceive a need for parliament than thirteen years earlier. The aggregate increase in the perception of a need for parliament from 71 percent in 1959 to 83 percent in 1972 was due largely to changes among those with high or medium levels of interest. The size of these latter two groups, however, also increased during this time period from 65 percent to 80 percent and the proportion of those with no interest in politics had by 1972 dropped to only 20 percent. Although the politically apathetic remain far less likely to perceive the need for a parliament, the proportion of the adult population in this category dropped from 35 percent in 1959 to 20 percent by 1972. This decline in their size greatly diminished their aggregate effect. Thus the increases in political interest over time are related to increasing support for the political system's key values and institutions. Political mobilization, once an indicator of antisystem sentiment, is now largely a system-supportive process.

POLITICAL COMMUNICATIONS

The 1959 survey found that Germans and Italians, in contrast to the Anglo-Americans, did not feel as "free" to discuss political and governmental affairs. In the German case this was interpreted as an "incongruity" between political structures (a liberal republic) and political culture (subject oriented).[71] Specifically, only about one in every three Germans felt they could discuss politics freely with "anyone" or "most people" as compared to about one-half of the English and American respondents. Although we do not have a question with a text identical to the 1959 item, one West German polling organization has repeatedly asked a very similar question:

> Do you have the feeling that today in West Germany one can freely state his political opinion, or is it better to be careful?

As the data in Table VII.12 indicate, the belief that one could freely talk about politics in West Germany was held in 1953 by only 55 percent of the adult population. This proportion increased until 1971 when 84 percent thought that freedom of political expression existed. Much of this increase between 1953 and 1971 came from *opponents* of the "government of the day," whose doubts about the commitment of the government to maintain free speech diminished greatly with the passage of time.[72]

TABLE VII.12. *Attitudes Toward Freedom of Political Expression, 1953–76*

Q.: *Do you have the feeling that today in West Germany one can freely state his political opinion, or is it better to be careful?*

					Year					
	1953 %	1954 %	1955 %	1958 %	1959 %	1962 %	1971 %	1976 (June %)	1976 (December %)
Can speak freely today in West Germany	55	58	71	70	70	71	84	78	73
Are limitations, better be careful	35	35	26	25	24	21	13	18	23
Undecided, other, no answer	10	7	3	5	6	8	3	4	4
Total	100	100	100	100	100	100	100	100	100

Source: Institut für Demoskopie, Survey nos. 0061, 0073, 0083, 1020, 1031, 1069, 2071, 3031, and 3037.

By 1971 this difference between supporters and opponents had disappeared; both the "ins" and the "outs" perceived the Bonn system as one in which political opinions could be freely expressed.[73] Clearly the memories of past regimes which suppressed free political expression had, by the early 1970s, become far less salient than the respondents' experience under the Bonn Republic. This increase in the perception that one can freely express oneself politically is related to the actual increases in mass political participation and especially the more open character of that participation.

When this same question was asked in 1976, however, this trend appeared to be reversed; in the June 1976 survey the proportion of the adult population stating that they could freely express themselves about politics dropped to 78 percent, and when the same question was repeated in a December 1976 survey this proportion dropped still further to 73 percent. In analyzing the June 1976 survey together with the previous studies from 1953–71, it was found that the decline between 1971 and 1976 was not due to doubts among governmental opponents about freedom of expression in the Federal Republic. As in 1971, there was in 1976 little difference between supporters and opponents of the incumbent government.

This decline appears due largely to a sharp shift in the perceptions of younger, better-educated, and politically active Germans toward freedom of expression in the Federal Republic. The aggregate decline between 1971 and June 1976 was 6 percent (84 to 78 percent), but among those respondents under thirty the drop was 15 percent (85 to 70 percent). The eighteen to twenty-nine age group, in contrast to the attitudes of this age cohort between 1953–71, was by June 1976 the lowest in perceiving the Federal Republic as a country where one could freely express political opinions. The same pattern was found among those with above-average education. In 1976 for the first time in twenty-three years, those respondents with more than the basic nine or ten years of schooling were less likely to believe they could freely express themselves about politics than respondents with a lower educational level. When we combine age and education (Table VII.13) we find as expected that younger, educated respondents were in 1976 the least likely to perceive the Federal Republic as a system where they could freely express their politi-

TABLE VII.13. Attitudes Toward Freedom of Expression by Age and Education, 1971-76 (proportion stating that one can freely express political opinions in the Federal Republic)

	Age							
	18-29		30-44		45-59		60-plus	
	Educational level [a]							
Year	Basic	Advanced	Basic	Advanced	Basic	Advanced	Basic	Advanced
1971	88	80	85	90	83	88	77	79
1976	76	63	85	82	81	82	79	78
Difference 1971-76	(−12)	(−17)	(0)	(−8)	(−2)	(−6)	(+2)	(−1)

[a] Basic: only Volksschule and vocational training. Advanced: some academic secondary and/or university.
Source: Institut für Demoskopie, Survey nos. 2076 and 3031.

cal opinions. The drop in perception of freedom of expression was significantly less among other age and educational groups. Moreover, when we add a measure of political involvement or participation — the frequency of "talking" politics — we find that the decline in the perceptions of freedom of expression is still greater (Table VII.14). Among respondents under thirty in 1976 with above average education who report "frequent" political discussions, only 51 percent report that they believe they can freely express their political opinions, in contrast to 84 percent of the national sample in 1971, 78 percent in June 1976, and 83 percent of this group (the politically active) who held such a view in 1959.[74]

That so much of this aggregate decline can be traced to one specific group — younger, educated, and relatively politicized West Germans — suggests that those experiences (events and policies) since 1971 that could have had an inhibitive effect on political expression were largely specific to this group. But what could these policies or events have been? One possible cause for this decline could be the controversy over "radicals in public service," which emerged in 1972. Since that time as a result of a joint administrative decree by the federal chancellor and the chief executives of the various *Länder* (states) in the federal system, all candidates for public employment, including teachers, must undergo an extensive "security check." In some states those candidates who are members of "extremist" parties or organizations (Communist party, National Democratic party, Spartacus League) have been denied employment, and in some cases public employees have been dismissed for their affiliation or sympathy with groups adjudged by state or national governments (but not the courts) to be against the "free, democratic order."

These policies have, of course, had the greatest impact on younger, educated respondents seeking public employment.[75] Fortunately, in the June 1976 survey there are several questions about this issue. Two are of particular interest for our purpose: one asks for the respondent's opinion about the necessity of security investigations for public employees, and the other taps the respondent's personal experiences with these laws in the last five years.[76] As expected, opposition to security investigations is greatest among the under-thirty age group; although only about 15 percent of those over thirty oppose such investigations, over

TABLE VII.14. *Freedom of Political Expression by Age, Education, and Level of Political Discussion, 1976 (proportion stating that one can freely express political opinions in the Federal Republic)*

	Age							
	18-29		30-44		45-59		60-plus	
			Educational Level					
Political discussion level	Basic	Advanced	Basic	Advanced	Basic	Advanced	Basic	Advanced
High [a]	76	51	93	79	86	79	92	85
Moderate [b]	86	65	83	86	83	86	83	75
Low [c]	66	72	84	77	76	80	69	75

[a] "Frequent" political discussions. [b] Occasional political discussions. [c] "Never talk politics."
Source: Institut für Demoskopie, Survey no. 3031.

30 percent of the eighteen to twenty-nine age group feel they are unnecessary. Similarly, 28 percent with above-average educational backgrounds are opposed to the radical decrees as compared to 18 percent with only the basic *Volksschule* training. Also, most of those who stated that their personal freedom was limited by such state regulations were in the under-thirty, above-average education group. Thus when we examined the responses of this group (the under-thirty, better-educated, politically active respondents who oppose the radical decrees), only 18 percent feel there is freedom of expression in the Federal Republic, in comparison to 78 percent of the total sample. This finding is significant especially when one considers that between 1953 and 1971 the younger, educated, and politically active West Germans were most likely to perceive the republic as one where, in contrast to the past, freedom of political expression was present. In 1976 this pattern was reversed; this group is now least likely to perceive a climate of free political expression. This change, moreover, appears closely linked to governmental policy; specifically, the issue of radicals in public service and the resultant wave of security investigations. This change illustrates the effect of governmental policies upon political attitudes at least among the most involved and informed segments of the society. It also suggests that a different approach to this issue by governmental decision makers could change these perceptions of younger, educated West Germans.

In 1959 Almond and Verba, on the basis of the relatively high proportions of Germans (16 percent) and Italians (32 percent) who refused to report their voting decision, found political suspicion "generally distributed in Italian and German society." [77] Scheuch developed a similar argument with data from a 1961 voting study. [78] This reluctance to reveal publicly political preferences has clearly declined. Between 1959 and 1976 the proportion of Germans refusing to report their voting decision dropped from 16 percent to 4 percent; [79] the proportion who "hardly ever" or "never" talked politics with other people dropped from 40 percent in 1952 to 21 percent by 1975. As Table VII.15 shows, the increase in the proportion of citizens with a "high" frequency of political conversations has been especially large since the mid-1960s. It appears from this and other evidence that German democracy reached the "take-off" state at this point. The departure

TABLE VII.15. *Frequency of Talking Politics with Other People: Germany, 1952–75*

| | Frequency | |
| | Low ("hardly ever" or "never") % | High ("sometimes" or "frequently") % |
Year		
1952	40	60
1955	44	56
1956	50	50
1957	45	55
1958	46	54
1959	38	62
1959 (*Civic Culture*)	39	61
1960	38	62
1964	37	63
1972	30	70
1973	22	78
1975	21	79

Sources: Institut für Demoskopie and *Civic Culture* survey. Demoskopie Survey nos. 0050, 0083, 0095, 1010, 1020, 1031, 1044, 1090, 2085, 2090, and 3012.

of Konrad Adenauer, the Grand Coalition, extraparliamentary opposition, the *Machtwechsel* of 1969, the policy innovations of the Brandt governments, the citizen-initiative groups, and public involvement in recent election campaigns are the surface indicators of increased mass interest in politics.

POLITICAL PARTICIPATION IN COMPARATIVE PERSPECTIVE

Recent comparative data on political participation reported in Table VII.16 show that West Germans by the mid-1970s were participating in politics at rates no less than citizens in older democracies like the United States and the Netherlands, and in some areas (party membership, attendance at political meetings) had higher levels of political participation. Also a 1976 survey of the population's attitude toward certain "unconventional modes" of political participation found substantial support, especially among the younger age groups, for participation in rent or tax strikes, boycotts, demonstrations, citizen-initiative groups and petition drives (Table VII.17). There was little support, however, for more extreme forms of political activity.[80]

These changes in attitudes toward participation have coin-

TABLE VII.16.   *German Political Participation, 1974,
in Comparative Perspective*

	Germany %	United States %	Country Nether- lands %	Austria %	Japan %
Regular voters	86	63	77	85	93
Members of party or political organization	15	8	13	28	4
Worked for a party	10	25	10	10	25
Attended a political rally	25–35	19	9	27	50
Active members in a community-action organization	18	32	15	9	11
Worked with a local group on a community problem	14	30	16	3	15
Contacted an official in the community on some social problem	11	5	6	5	11

Sources: United States, Austria, Japan: Norman H. Nie and Sidney Verba, "Political Participation," in Fred I. Greenstein, Nelson W. Polsby, eds., *Handbook of Political Science,* vol. 4, *Non-Governmental Politics* (Reading, Mass.: Addison-Wesley, 1975), pp. 24–25. Germany: Klaus R. Allerbeck, Max Kaase, Hans-Dieter Klingemann, "Selected Items in the German Part of the Eight-National Study," Zentrale für Umfragen, Methoden und Analysen, Mannheim University (1975), pp. 2–3; Günter D. Radtke, "Formen politischer Partizipation in der Bundesrepublik Deutschland," unpublished manuscript, Alfter (1975), p. 47.

cided with the emergence in the late 1960s of, for German conditions, a qualitatively new form of participatory behavior, the citizen-initiative group. By the late 1970s there were about 3000 such groups in the Federal Republic with a total membership of about 2 million.[81] Their purposes range from protesting hikes in streetcar fares to the prohibition of nuclear power plants. Most of these groups have only one issue and operate at the local level. They draw the bulk of their membership from younger, well-educated, middle-class segments of the population. Nonetheless, surveys have found that over a third of the adult population is contemplating membership in some citizen-initiative group.[82] Given the passivity found in the 1959 study, the emergence of

TABLE VII.17. *Approval or Rejection of "Unconventional" Participatory Modes by Age, 1976* [a]

Participation	Total %	Age Group		
		16–25	26–39	40–50
Collecting signatures on a petition				
approval	89	92	90	84
rejection	9	6	8	13
Joining a citizen-initiative group				
approval	88	91	88	84
rejection	9	6	9	3
Taking part in an "approved" political demonstration				
approval	59	70	60	47
rejection	38	27	37	49
Participating in a boycott				
approval	25	29	26	21
rejection	68	61	68	72
Taking part in a rent or tax strike				
approval	14	19	13	11
rejection	80	76	81	83
Blocking traffic with a demonstration				
approval	12	17	12	7
rejection	84	78	84	90
Joining a wild-cat strike				
approval	8	13	8	4
rejection	87	82	88	91
Occupying factories, office buildings				
approval	7	12	5	3
rejection	89	83	91	92
Using force against people				
approval	3	4	2	2
rejection	94	92	95	94
Damaging private property				
approval	1	1	2	1
rejection	96	96	95	96

[a] "Don't know" and no response are not included.

Source: 1976 *Infratest* Survey, cited in *Das Parlament,* no. 42 (October 16, 1976), p. 10.

these groups, even on this scale, underscores the changes that have taken place in political participation during the 1960s and 1970s.

CHANGES IN THE SOURCES OF GERMAN POLITICAL CULTURE

In seeking to explain the pattern of German political culture, Almond and Verba essentially posited the following "independent variables": low levels of social trust and cooperative activities; a subject-oriented socialization process in the family and school; and, as a residual variable, the "bitter" and "traumatic" historical experience. In this section we shall examine changes that have taken place in some of these areas since 1959.

SOCIALIZATION: FAMILY AND SCHOOL

Although giving some credit to the early study of child-rearing practices as a precursor to modern political socialization work, Almond and Verba found in their own data that an authoritarian style of familial governance was more related to the age and social class of the respondent than to nationality.[83] The younger the respondent and the higher his educational level, the greater the likelihood that he participated in familial decision making. Thus, although the Nazi experience may have slowed or arrested the trend toward a less authoritarian family, it did not reverse it.[84] The earlier emphasis on the German family as a source of antidemocratic attitudes and values was thus not supported by the *Civic Culture* data.[85]

Some years later a German-American sociologist, Eugen Lupri, devoted his doctoral dissertation, which used in part the Almond and Verba data, to explore this problem further.[86] He concluded that a democratic or partnership style of familial decision making and nonauthoritarian child rearing comes about through the increased "power" of those married women with outside employment, which in turn increases with socioeconomic modernization. Since National Socialism, contrary to its ideology, in effect pushed modernization even further, the German family became more, not less, "democratic" during the Third Reich. Thus the style of familial governance had little to do with the frequent and sudden changes in political regimes that Germany had experienced in this century.

Yet, regardless of the validity of the study of childhood socialization to explain adult political behavior and ultimately the
fundamental character of political regimes, it should be noted
that public attitudes toward child rearing in the Federal Republic have, over the past quarter century, become more liberal. As
the data presented in Table VII.18 show, the proportion of
adult Germans who regard "independence and freedom of will"
as the most important values that parents should transmit in the
rearing of their children had increased from 28 percent in 1951
to 51 percent by 1976. There were also significant generational
differences in responses to this item. Respondents over fifty in
1976 were much more likely (65 percent) to prefer the "authoritarian" style than those Germans under thirty (40 percent).
Among occupational groups, farmers and manual workers were
the strongest adherents of "love of order" and "obedience." [87]

This trend of less authoritarian child rearing is likely to continue. When a sample of young people between the ages of thirteen and twenty-four was asked in 1975 how they would raise
their children, only 14 percent replied "exactly the same as I was
raised." When a comparable age group twenty-two years earlier
(1953) was asked the same question, 32 percent replied that they
would raise their children in the same manner as they were
raised.[88]

TABLE VII.18. *Attitudes Toward Child Rearing, 1951–76*

Q.: *In the training of children what values should be most stressed: obedience
and deference, love of order and industriousness or independence and free
will?*

Values	1951 %	1957 a	1967 a %	1972 %	1976 a %
			Year		
Independence and free will	28	32	37	45	51
Love of order and industriousness	41	48	48	37	41
Obedience and deference	25	25	25	14	10
Other answers, no response	6	8	5	4	0

a Multiple responses possible in these years.

Source: EMNID, *Informationen,* vol. 28, nos. 6/7, 1976, p. 16.

Turning to the classroom socialization experience, a 1971 ten-nation comparative study found that students (aged ten to fourteen) in Germany were more likely to report that their instructors encourage independent expression in the classroom than their counterparts in such "classic" democracies as the United States, Sweden, and the Netherlands.[89] Judith Torney and her associates also found that "civic education" teachers in the Federal Republic of Germany spend many hours in lesson preparation, emphasize political history, and willingly discuss many issues in class. West German students report that expressions of opinion in class are encouraged.[90] The same study found that German respondents ranked higher in their support for democratic norms than students in the United States, the Netherlands, Finland, or Italy.[91] Thus, although the relationship between childhood socialization in the family and school and adult political behavior, not to mention the functioning of the political system itself, is still unclear, the traditional emphasis upon the "authoritarian" German child-rearing style has become very difficult to support with empirical evidence.

SOCIAL TRUST AND "OUTGOINGNESS"

In *The Civic Culture* both German and Italian political cultures were portrayed as having relatively low levels of general social trust. In the absence of social trust, more suspicion, distrust, isolation, and lower levels of social cooperation prevailed in these countries than in the Anglo-American cases or even Mexico. In the case of Germany, this 1959 finding corresponded to most descriptions of postwar Germany as a privatized, if not anomic society.[92] As the data in Table VII.19 show, however, the low level of trust found in the 1959 study represented an increase from the levels found in 1948 and, moreover, since 1959 Germans have become more, not less trusting of their fellow citizens. Further evidence that Germans by the 1970s perceived their social environment as less hostile than in the early postwar period is also provided in Table VII.19. When asked the general question as to whether "there are more evil-minded (*böswillige*) than good-minded (*gutwillige*) people" almost half of the respondents in 1949 perceived the "evil-minded" as outnumbering the "good-minded." By the mid-1970s, however, the proportion of pessimists had dropped to only 16 percent. Perhaps more

TABLE VII.19. *Attitudes Toward Social Trust, Hostility of "Others,"
and Friendship, 1948–76*

Social Trust
Q.: Can most people be trusted? (percentage "yes")

		Year		
1948	1959	1967	1973	1976
9	19	26	32	39

Sources: 1948: Leo P. Crespi, "The Influence of Military Government Polling Sponsorship in German Opinion Polling," *International Journal of Opinion and Attitude Research* 4, no. 2 (Summer 1950): p. 175. In the survey identified as "German-sponsored," 7 percent felt most people could be trusted; in the "American-sponsored" poll the corresponding figure was 11 percent, hence the 9 percent figure for 1948.

1973: Institut für Demoskopie, *Jahrbuch der öffentlichen Meinung*, vol. V (1968–73), (Allensbach am Bodensee: Verlag für Demoskopie, 1974), p. 138.

1976: Institut für Demoskopie, Study no. 3031, June 1976.

Hostility of "Others"

Q.: Do you think there are more evil-minded than good-minded people?
("Glauben Sie, dass es mehr böswillige als gutwillige Menschen gibt?")

	1949 %	1951 %	1953 %	1971 %	1976 %
More evil-minded	46	43	34	17	16
More good-minded	33	33	40	49	52
Undecided	21	24	26	34	32
Total	100	100	100	100	100

Sources: 1949–53: *Jahrbuch*, vol. I (1956), p. 114.

1971: *Jahrbuch*, vol. V (1974), p. 38.

1976: Institut für Demoskopie, Survey no. 3031, June 1976.

Friendship

Q.: Do you have few or many friends and acquaintances?

	1957 %	1965 %	1967 %	1972 %
Many	42	44	45	57
Some	32	36	37	35
Few	26	20	18	8
Total	100	100	100	100

Source: Jahrbuch, vol. V (1974), p. 143.

significantly, there were no important differences between age or social-class groups in the 1976 responses.[93]

There also appears to be a significant decline in social isolation or privatization. When asked whether they had "few or many" acquaintances, over a fourth (26 percent) of Germans in 1957 reported that they had "few friends." By the early 1970s only 8 percent were in this category. During the same period the proportion indicating that they had many acquaintances increased from 42 percent to 57 percent.

Finally, in 1959, 44 percent of *The Civic Culture*'s German sample reported that they did belong to some voluntary organization as compared to 47 percent of the English sample and 57 percent of the American respondents. By 1967 this German proportion had risen to 50 percent, and in 1975 fully 59 percent of a national sample reported that they were members of at least one organization.[94] But perhaps more significantly, the proportion of respondents who reported that they were *active* in these organizations increased at a *faster rate* than mere membership. In 1959 Almond and Verba found that only 7 percent of German respondents, as compared to 26 percent of the American sample and 13 percent of the British respondents, had been active participants in one of their voluntary organizations. As Table VII.20 shows, this proportion of active members had increased to 10 percent by 1967 and 17 percent by 1975.[95] Clearly, German

TABLE VII.20.   *Organizational Membership and Activity: Germany, 1959–75*

	1959				
	(US) %	(UK) %	%	1967 %	1975 %
Member	(57)	(47)	44	50	59
Active [a]	(26)	(13)	7	10	17
Male			12	15	25
Female			2	6	11

[a] "Activity" was measured in all three surveys by the proportion of respondents reporting that they had at some time been officers (*ehrenamtlich tätig*) in one of their organizations.

Sources: 1959: Almond and Verba, *Civic Culture,* pp. 304, 314, 392.

1967: Institut für Demoskopie, Survey no. 2029.

1975: Institut für Demoskopie, *Jahrbuch der öffentlichen Meinung,* vol. VI (Allensbach am Bodensee: Verlag für Demoskopie, 1976), pp. 20–21.

society by the early 1970s was more "outgoing" and less isolated than in the 1950s.

EXPLAINING CHANGE

The pattern of increased support for the values, processes, and institutions of liberal democracy that has characterized the German political culture both before and after the 1959 *Civic Culture* survey is difficult to explain in the absence of extensive longitudinal panel surveys, which would enable the analyst to isolate the specific variables associated with change. What has been attempted, however, is the analysis of single cross-sectional surveys conducted over a ten- to twenty-five-year period in which the same question texts were used. Thus the same population (German adults) was given the "same" stimulus (question text) at differing time points. A number of scholars have recently used this approach and these surveys to study political change in postwar Germany.[96] Most of these analysts have focused on the following sources of change: (1) postwar socialization, particularly as evidenced through the effects of the age variable; (2) the absence of any credible alternative to liberal democracy; (3) postwar socioeconomic modernization; and (4) system performance. As yet no comprehensive model of change specifying the relative weight and interrelationship of these factors has emerged. Yet all studies are unanimous in finding at least part of the variance related to one or all of these variables.

AGE AND POLITICAL SOCIALIZATION

Given the frequent and sharp discontinuities in the German political experience and the concern of postwar elites to remake the political culture, it is understandable that most analysts have closely examined the effects of age on political attitudes and behavior in the expectation of finding important differences between generations.[97] Most of this research had indeed found that at least part of the change observed over the past quarter century is related to the differential socialization experiences of the various generations. The effects of age have been particularly strong in explaining increased support for values such as political competition, freedom of speech, and democratic representation and symbols such as the republican flag.[98] Those generations socialized since the founding of the Federal Republic are also more likely to assume a critical posture toward nondemocratic regimes, accept Germany's responsibilities for World War II, attribute the foreign distrust and suspicion of the Federal Republic to the effects of National Socialism and the war, and accept the permanency of Germany's postwar division. A West German national identity is also strongest among younger age groups.[99]

Some scholars have sought to explain these findings of generational differences through the application of dissonance theory.[100] Those Germans old enough to remember past political regimes and who had positive memories of at least one of them and yet experienced the policy successes of the postwar republic had to reconcile their "sentimental" attachment to the past with their more "instrumental" experiences after 1949. Dissonance was most likely to be found among these generations and because most people, according to dissonance research, find this difficult to manage or tolerate, attitude change in the direction of both an instrumental and a more diffuse or affective attachment to the republic should be expected. But the rate of change will not be as great as that found among age groups who did not have to unlearn attachments to a past regime.[101] The postwar generations developed a direct instrumental attachment followed by more diffuse ties to the system. We would expect to find, then, that *rates of change* in the direction of support for the republic's values will be greater among those age groups unburdened by the past.

The rates of change have indeed generally been found to be greater among postwar cohorts. Between 1958 and 1972, for example, the growth in support for political competition was 21 percent among the sixteen to twenty-nine cohort in 1958 as compared to 7 percent for the thirty to forty-four cohort, and a minus 1 percent for the forty-five to fifty-nine cohort in 1958.[102] During the same period, the increase in the proportion of respondents who believed that their parliamentary representative would respond to their concerns was 16 percent among the sixteen to twenty-nine cohort, 9 percent for the thirty to forty-four-year-old group, and a minus 10 percent among those aged forty-five to fifty-nine in 1958.[103] Increases in politicization as measured by the political-interest item are also related to age. As Table

TABLE VII.21. *Political Interest by Age Cohort, 1962–72* [a]
                (percentage with "interest" in politics)

1962	Year of birth	1972	% Increase
20–29		20–29	
30%		38%	
	1933–42		
30–39		30–39	
33%		54%	24
	1923–32		
40–49		40–49	
34%		46%	13
	1913–22		
50–59		50–59	
27%		49%	15
	1903–12		
60–69		60–69	
32%		42%	15
	1893–1911		
70+		70–79	
34%		38%	6
Nat. Ave.:			
31%		46%	

[a] 16–19-year-olds were not considered in either sample.
Sources: Institut für Demoskopie Survey nos. 1069 and 2085.

VII.21 shows, between 1962 and 1972 the greatest rate of change was among the twenty to twenty-nine cohort in 1962. By 1972 the proportion of this cohort with an interest in politics had increased to 54 percent, a far greater change than for any other group.

ABSENCE OF A CREDIBLE ALTERNATIVE

This explanation of postwar change, as developed by Boynton and Loewenberg, suggests that

> it is the existence of visible alternatives to an existing regime which causes the withdrawal of public support under conditions which might otherwise be consistent with the maintenance of that support. Because the Fifth Republic stood in the wings while the drama of the Fourth Republic reached its climax, because the Nazi regime existed as a full-blown alternative to the Weimar Republic

between 1930 and 1933, a shift in public support from one regime to another occurred. Because the public perceived no such alternative in Great Britain in 1931 or in the United States in 1933, a weakening of the sources of support for the existing regime did not produce regime change.[104]

The survival of the Bonn system was thus related to the decline of support for its predecessors, especially the empire and the Third Reich. This drop in support for past regimes began in the early 1950s and was largely completed by the mid-1960s. Almost a third of the adult population in 1951 wanted the monarchy restored, with only about 35 percent opposed; but by 1964 only 10 percent favored restoration and over 70 percent were against a restoration.[105] Support for the imperial flag dropped even more rapidly. Between 1951 and 1958 preference for the black-white-red of the Hohenzollerns declined from 37 percent to only 16 percent.[106] In 1953 over a third of the population stated that they would either support or at least be indifferent to an attempt by a new Nazi party to seize power; by 1972 potential support for such a party had dropped to 7 percent and "indifference" to neofascism to 12 percent.[107]

By the mid-1960s any appeal that past regimes had was largely restricted to relatively small, parochial segments of the population: inhabitants of rural areas, older refugees and women, the poorly educated, and supporters of small splinter parties. The most striking common characteristic of these groups is their declining size relative to the rest of the population. With the field steadily cleared of significant support for alternative regimes, the growing proportion of republican supporters became less concerned with the safety of the system, that is, "avoid the errors of Weimar," and more with its future development.

SOCIOECONOMIC MODERNIZATION

The socioeconomic structure of the postwar Federal Republic is more integrated, balanced, mobile, and "modern" than that of the empire, the Weimar Republic, and the Third Reich. There are fewer subcultural cleavages and pockets of parochialism. Groups such as manual workers have emerged from subcultural isolation. Others such as the landed nobility (Junkers) and the military did not survive the Third Reich and postwar division of the country in a condition to reassert their claims to political power.

The persistent urban/rural cleavage of the empire and the Weimar Republic was greatly softened by the loss of the largely agrarian, eastern territories following the war. The influx and successful integration of over 10 million refugees between 1945 and 1961 reduced the importance of regional cleavages.

Additional important changes in postwar social structure have taken place among women and Catholics. The major sociodemographic factor related to the trend of increased interest in politics, discussed earlier in this essay, is sex. In 1952 only 11 percent of female respondents expressed any interest in politics as compared to 46 percent among males. This gap remained relatively constant throughout the 1950s and most of the 1960s. A perceptible convergence, however, began in the late 1960s, and by 1972 the proportion of women with an interest in politics had increased to 38 percent, whereas among males the 1952 level had increased by only 10 percent, to 56 percent. By 1972 education had replaced sex as the most important sociodemographic predictor of political interest.

The traditional female concentration on the apolitical areas neatly encompassed by the classic *Kinder, Kirche, und Küche,* while still predominant, has become less appealing and less necessary to growing numbers of women. In 1961, 57 percent of German women wanted to be "only housewives"; by 1973 only 29 percent were satisfied with this role. The proportion who wanted above all to be occupationally active increased during this same period from 22 percent to 53 percent.[108]

As in other advanced industrial societies, smaller families, labor-saving household devices, the partnership ethic in married life, and participation in the work force gives increasing numbers of women the resources to become "interested in politics." Little wonder that public opinion toward female participation in politics is also changing. Between 1965 and 1976 the proportion of *men* who stated they were "pleased" when women became politically active increased from 27 to 62 percent; the proportion of *women* supporting female political involvement increased from 32 to 66 percent during the same time period. Thus by 1976 about two of every three West Germans had a favorable orientation toward female involvement in politics as compared to only one out of three in 1965 (see Table VII.22). This "eman-

TABLE VII.22. *Attitudes Toward Female Participation in Politics, 1965–76 (by sex)*

Q.: *Are you pleased when a woman becomes active politically, or don't you react so favorably to that?*

| | Men | | | Women | | |
	1965 %	1971 %	1976 %	1965 %	1971 %	1976 %
Pleased	27	56	62	32	68	66
Displeased	52	26	16	37	20	14
Undecided, no answer	21	18	22	31	12	20
Total	100	100	100	100	100	100

Source: Institut für Demoskopie, *Jahrbuch der öffentlichen Meinung*, vol. VI (Allensbach am Bodensee: Verlag für Demoskopie, 1976), p. 160.

cipation" process is quite consistent with the modernization theory and relates to political culture change.

The loss of the largely Protestant east (Prussia, Pomerania, Silesia) meant that Catholics in postwar West Germany were no longer in a minority position, but had roughly the same numerical strength as Protestants. The subcultural character of German Catholicism so evident in the Catholic political party (Zentrum) and interest groups during the Weimar Republic was far less evident in postwar Germany, as most Catholics found a new political home in the biconfessional CDU/CSU or even the SPD. The underrepresentation of Catholics among elite groups also declined.[109] Among mass publics there is also considerable evidence that the Catholic population, traditionally overrepresented among lower-status occupations and educational levels, is better integrated into postwar West German society. From 1950 to 1975, for example, the proportion of Catholics with some educational experience above the basic or general level increased from 19 percent to 34 percent. Moreover, the differences in upper-educational background between Catholics and Protestants narrowed from about 9 percent in 1950 to only 2 percent by 1975. By the mid-1970s Catholic underrepresentation among the better educated had all but disappeared. In 1950 Catholics constituted about 44 percent of the population but made up only 29 percent of the higher-educated; by 1975, however, their share (45 percent) was exactly proportional to their share of the total population.

Ironically, some authors have attributed many of these changes to the National Socialists.[110] By intensifying industrialization, contrary to their ideology, the Nazis favored urban interests over those of the rural sector, and reduced class barriers as a broad new middle class of managers and technicians emerged at the numerical and political expense of the old middle class, proletariat, and aristocracy. Nazi efforts at totalitarian mobilization also affected German family structure as children were "released" from parental control at a relatively early age and the numerous party-controlled groups outside the family increased in importance. The necessities of wartime production also took many women from the home into the workforce. The "social revolution" of the National Socialists thus "prepared a soil conducive to stable democracy in postwar Germany," although, of course, this was hardly the intention of the Nazis in 1933.[111]

SYSTEM PERFORMANCE

The first German republic, in addition to legitimacy problems at birth, was plagued with ineffectual cabinet governments unable, for the most part, to meet citizen demands in key policy areas. Parliamentary democracy, already identified with national disgrace, became further linked with instability, inflation, and economic depression. Thus, in explaining the success of the Bonn Republic, numerous analysts have placed major emphasis on the successful performance of the postwar system.[112] The early years of the Bonn system (1949–57) saw an especially wide variety of domestic and foreign political successes: the Economic Miracle, membership in NATO, the Common Market, the return of the Saar by France, restoration of full sovereignty, expanded educational opportunities, welfare services, and industrial tranquility. The unprecedented electoral triumphs of the Christian Democratic Union in 1953 and 1957 reflected the electorate's identification of strong, effective "chancellor democracy" as practiced by Adenauer with successful postwar reconstruction.

Generally most analysts have found a positive relationship between support for governmental policies and positive attitudes toward the values of liberal democracy.[113] Yet the influence of performance as a predictor of support for the civic culture has probably decreased since the late 1950s. Increases in support for key system values and institutions have come disproportionately from respondents who exhibit little approval of short-run system performance, that is, those who do not think their deputy will respond to their problems, opponents of the "present" government's policies, respondents with unfavorable impressions of the parliament, and lower socioeconomic status groups. Support for key values such as political competition, freedom of political expression, participation, democratic representation, and civil liberties continued to increase throughout the 1960s and 1970s in spite of the frequent and sometimes sharp fluctuations in public evaluation of system performance. The decline in support for the "government of the day" during the recessions of 1966–67 and especially 1974–76, for example, had little discernible effect on the trend of increased support for liberal democracy. The important assumption, of course, is that this dissatisfaction with performance is short run and that there is considerable turnover in the ranks of those dissatisfied with system performance.

CONCLUSION: THE REMADE POLITICAL CULTURE

Throughout most of the postwar period, analysts of German political culture have probed the question of how committed Germans were to the liberal democratic system instituted at the command of Western occupiers in 1949. Verba put this question very well:

> If there is uncertainty about the future of German democracy, it is not so much uncertainty about the constitutional structure of the Bonn Republic as about the political attitudes that lie behind the Constitution. The government institutions of a stable democracy exist as do the nongovernment political institutions. But have German political ways of thinking been reshaped to provide a basis for a democratic political system? [114]

This question is far less relevant in the late 1970s than the problem of whether the institutions and processes of liberal democracy are adequate to the participatory needs and policy demands of a population no longer in its democratic infancy.[115] The question is now not whether there is a consensus and strong support for political democracy, but *what kind* of democracy Germany will have. The emphasis has shifted, as Verba speculated that it perhaps would, from a concern with the security and stability of the democracy to the quality and extent of democracy.[116] But this latter problem is by no means a uniquely German issue. Indeed, it is one common to all advanced industrialized democracies. When German political philosophers such as Habermas speak of the "legitimacy crisis" of "late capitalist societies," they are assuming, quite correctly, that the liberal parliamentary order in Germany is as stable or unstable as it is in Britain, France, the United States, or elsewhere in the Western capitalist world.[117]

The major challenge to the present consensus on liberal, "bourgeois" democracy comes not from the right of the German political spectrum, but from its new left. Like their counterparts elsewhere, they interpret the growing politicization of West Germans and the "contradiction" between citizen attitudes and values and the present structure of political institutions as a sign of impending system change in the direction of greater economic and social equality and, eventually, community or state control of the means of production.[118]

An examination of this development is beyond the scope of this essay. Indeed, our data end at this point. We have, as other authors in this book have pointed out, precious little data to examine the major issues in the "elitist-radical" debate in modern democratic theory. Future cross-national research on political culture certainly should explore popular conceptions of democracy, the capacity of mass publics to "measure up" to the requisites of classical democratic theory, and the effects of different modes of participation on political beliefs and values as well as system output. Finally the German case should alert us to the importance of the study of change and the absolute necessity, if we are to study it effectively, of longitudinal panel studies.

The Civic Culture's treatment of Germany is indeed dated. Almond and Verba in 1959 took a snapshot of a political culture being remade. Apart from the problem of how affective support is measured, their portrait of the German political culture has changed in every important respect. Developments since 1959 underscore the extent of cultural change in Germany. By the mid-1970s Germans had greater feelings of trust in government and were more supportive of their political system than mass publics in Britain.[119] Within this consensus there has been an increase in popular involvement in the political process and policy conflict. While some see increased involvement and conflict as a sign of impending system crises (a return to Weimar or the beginning of the "revolution"), they are, we suggest, more related to a growth in system identification and legitimacy, and hence signs of the health and vitality of the postwar democratic order.

Yet it is ironic that West Germany has become a "model stable democracy" almost exactly at the time when this model both in Germany and elsewhere in the West has come under increasing challenge from both scholars and political activists. But the Bonn Republic, unlike its predecessor, has built up a reserve of cultural support which should enable it to deal with these future issues of the quality and extent of democracy at least as effectively as other "late capitalist," Western democracies.

NOTES

1. Sidney Verba, "Germany: The Remaking of Political Culture," in Lucian W. Pye and Sidney Verba, eds., *Political Culture and Political Development* (Princeton, N.J.: Princeton Univ. Press, 1965), p. 131.

2. See Donald J. McCrone and Charles F. Cnudde, "Towards a Communications Theory of Democratic Political Development," *American Political Science Review* 61, no. 1 (March 1967): 72–79, and D. Neubauer, "Some Conditions of Democracy," *American Political Science Review* 61, no. 4 (December 1967): 1002–09.

3. Peter Bachrach, *The Theory of Democratic Elitism* (Boston: Little, Brown, 1967); Dennis F. Thompson, *The Democratic Citizen* (Cambridge, Eng.: Cambridge Univ. Press, 1970); and Sidney Verba and Norman H. Nie, *Participation in America* (New York: Harper & Row, 1972), pp. 299–344. Since German elites during the Weimar Republic were also hardly bulwarks of support for the democratic order, the relevance of the German case for the "elitist" versus "classical" democratic-theory debate may be questionable. See Karl Dietrich Bracher, *The German Dictatorship* (New York: Praeger Publishers, 1970).

4. For a recent account of the early empirical work of Adorno, Horkheimer, and their associates, see Martin Jay, *The Dialectical Imagination* (Boston: Little, Brown, 1973), pp. 113–72. See also Ralf Dahrendorf, *Society and Democracy in Germany* (Garden City, N.Y.: Doubleday, 1967), and Fritz Stern, *The Failure of Illiberalism: Essays on the Political Culture of Modern Germany* (Chicago: Univ. of Chicago Press, 1975).

5. Richard L. Merritt, "Digesting the Past, Views of National Socialism in Semi-Sovereign Germany," in R. L. Merritt and A. Merritt, *Public Opinion in Semi-Sovereign Germany* (Urbana, Ill.: Univ. of Illinois Press, forthcoming), chap. 1, p. 2.

6. For a summary and analysis of the polls taken between 1945 and 1949, see Anna J. Merritt and Richard L. Merritt, *Public Opinion in Occupied Germany* (Urbana, Ill.: Univ. of Illinois Press, 1970).

7. Gerhard Schmidtchen and Elisabeth Noelle-Neumann, "Die Bedeutung Repräsentativer Bevölkerungsumfragen für die offene Gesellschaft," *Politische Vierteljahresschrift* 4, no. 2 (June 1963): 168–69. The parliamentary council, which drafted the Basic Law, also commissioned surveys in 1948 of public opinion toward specific constitutional issues such as the death penalty, the currency reform, and the borders of the Federal Republic's constituent states.

8. See Ronald D. Pfotenhauer, "Conceptions of Political Science in West Germany and the United States," *Journal of Politics* 34, no. 2 (May 1972): 555–91; David P. Conradt, "The Development of Empirical Political Science Research in West Germany," *Comparative Political Studies* 6, no. 3 (October 1973): 380–91; and Peter H. Merkl, "Trends in German Political Science," *American Political Science Review* 71, no. 3 (September 1977): 1097–1103, for accounts of postwar political science research in Germany.

9. Karl Dietrich Bracher, "Staatsbegriff und Demokratie in Deutschland," *Politische Vierteljahresschrift* 9, no. 1 (March 1968): 2.

10. Sonderheft No. 9, *Kölner Zeitschrift für Soziologie und Sozialpsychologie* (Köln und Opladen: Westdeutscher Verlag, 1965). This book is dedicated to Gerhard Baumert who, as an associate of the DIVO Institute, directed the German field work for the Almond and Verba project. Baumert, who passed away in 1963, was a codirector of the *Wahlstudie*.

11. Erwin K. Scheuch and Hans D. Klingemann, "Theorie des Rechtsradikalismus in westlichen Industriegesellschaften," in H. D. Ortleib and B. Molitor, eds., *Hamburger Jahrbuch für Wirtschafts und Gesellschaftspolitik* (Tübingen: Mohr Verlag, 1967). See also Hans D. Klingemann and Franz U. Pappi, *Politischer Radikalismus* (Munich–Vienna: Verlag R. Oldenbourg, 1972).

12. Max Kaase, "Demokratische Einstellungen in der Bundesrepublik Deutschland," in Rudolf Wildenmann, ed., *Sozialwissenschaftliches Jahrbuch für Politik* 2 (Munich: Olzog Verlag, 1971): 119–326.

13. Max Kaase, "Bedingungen unkonventionellen politischen Verhaltens," in Peter Graf Kielmansegg, ed., *Legitimationsprobleme Politischer Systeme*, Sonderheft no. 7, *Politische Vierteljahresschrift* (1976): 179–216.

14. Erwin K. Scheuch, "The Cross-Cultural Use of Sample Surveys: Problems of Comparability," in Stein Rokkan, ed., *Comparative Research Across Cultures and Nations* (Paris and The Hague: Mouton, 1968), pp. 176–209. See also his "Social Context and Individual Behavior," in Stein Rokkan and Mattei Dogan, eds., *Quantitative Ecological Analysis in the Social Sciences* (Cambridge, Mass.: M.I.T. Press, 1969), pp. 133–55, and "Society as Context in Cross-Cultural Comparisons," *Social Science Information* 6 (October 1967): 7–23.

15. Scheuch, "Cross-Cultural Use of Surveys," p. 181.

16. Ibid., p. 194.

17. Claus Offe, *Strukturprobleme des kapitalistischen Staates* (Frankfurt: Suhrkamp Verlag, 1972), pp. 121–22.

18. Franz-Urban Pappi (Mannheim University), personal communication to the author, July 1976.

19. Almond and Verba, *The Civic Culture* (Princeton, N.J.: Princeton Univ. Press, 1963), p. 153.

20. Ibid., p. 160.

21. Ibid., p. 250.

22. Ibid., p. 251.

23. Ibid., p. 296.

24. Ibid.

25. Ibid., p. 314.

26. Ibid., p. 315.

27. Ibid., p. 429, 496.

28. Ibid., pp. 503–504.

29. Ibid., p. 407.

30. Ibid., p. 488.

31. Ibid., p. 496.

32. Ibid.

33. Ibid., pp. 249, 504.

34. David Easton, *A Systems Analysis of Political Life* (New York: John Wiley & Sons, 1965), p. 273.

35. David Easton, "A Reassessment of Political Support," *British Journal of Political Science* 5, no. 4 (October 1975): 446 (italics added).

36. See Kurt Sontheimer, *The Government and Politics of West Germany* (New York: Praeger Publishers, 1973), p. 40, and Franz-Urban Pappi, *Wahlverhalten und politische Kultur* (Meisenheim am Glan: Anton Hain Verlag, 1970).

37. Almond and Verba, *Civic Culture*, p. 429. In some of the life-history interviews this connection was examined, but these data were not integrated with those from the much larger sample survey.

38. Institut für Demoskopie, Survey no. 0045, March 1951.

39. G. Robert Boynton and Gerhard Loewenberg, "The Decay of Support for Monarchy and the Hitler Regime in the Federal Republic of Germany," *British Journal of Political Science* 4, no. 4 (October 1974): 465.

40. Verba, "Germany: The Remaking of Political Culture," p. 170.

41. Gebhard Ludwig Schweigler, *National Consciousness in Divided Germany* (Beverly Hills, Calif.: Sage Publications, 1975).

42. Institut für Demoskopie, *Jahrbuch der öffentlichen Meinung*, vol. V (1968–73), (Allensbach am Bodensee: Verlag für Demoskopie, 1974), p. 525.

43. *Jahrbuch*, vol. VI (1976), (Munich and Vienna: Molden Verlag, 1976), p. 88.

44. Schweigler, *National Consciousness*, pp. 232–71.

45. There are data, however, which indicate that the high rates of political cognition found in the 1959 survey represented a considerable growth in political knowledge since 1949. Certainly the knowledge levels of West Germans in the late 1940s and early 1950s were anything but high. As late as 1955, 51 percent of adult West Germans stated that they did not know enough about the Basic Law or constitution to make a general judgment as to whether it was "useful" (Institut für Demoskopie, *Jahrbuch der öffentlichen Meinung*, vol. I [1947–55], [Allensbach am Bodensee: Verlag für Demoskopie, 1956], p. 157). In 1951 about two-thirds of the adult population did not know whether they were represented in parliament by a deputy elected from their district, or not (*Jahrbuch*, vol. I, p. 161). Over three-fourths of the same sample did not know the name of their deputy, his or her party, place of residence, or "anything else" about him or her; 88 percent stated that they had heard nothing about their deputy's activity and about 80 percent could not accurately estimate the number of deputies in the parliament (*Jahrbuch*, vol. I, p. 162).

46. Hans-Dieter Klingemann, "Dimensions of Ideological Cognition and Ideological Orientation," Mannheim Univ., Zentrale für Umfragen, Methoden und Analysen, 1976, p. 7.

47. Judith V. Torney, A. N. Oppenheim, Russell F. Farnen, *Civic Edu-*

cation in Ten Countries (New York: John Wiley & Sons, 1975). In a later work one of the coauthors of the civic education study, after a further analysis of the German data, concluded that "political socialization in the Federal Republic of Germany today is, in part, highly successful in achieving its objectives. These social processes, of which the school is but one component, are producing young people with an outstandingly democratic, tolerant, and critical ideology, allied to a reasonable amount of factual knowledge, and undergoing an exceptionally rapid transition from the 'sheltered' to a more realistic or conflictual view of society and of social institutions" (A. N. Oppenheim, *Civic Education and Participation in Democracy: The German Case* [Beverly Hills and London: Sage Publications, 1977], p. 22).

48. Rudolf Wildenmann, "Das neue Nationalbewusstsein," *Capital*, 17, no. 10, pp. 284ff. The text of the two questions differs somewhat. Almond and Verba used the expression "this country" (*dieses Land*) while Wildenmann referred specifically to the "Federal Republic." The latter phrase has a more distinct political connotation which may have inflated the proportion mentioning "governmental, political institutions" as a source of system pride. Also, the Almond and Verba text contained the expression "most proud of" (*am meisten stolz*) as compared to the Wildenmann formulation "especially proud of" (*besonders stolz*). The latter expression in survey questions usually yields more multiple responses. I am grateful to Renate Koecher of the Institut für Demoskopie for bringing this to my attention.

49. Wildenmann, "Das neue Nationalbewusstsein," p. 288.

50. See the Kavanagh chapter in this volume and Alan Marsh, *Protest and Political Consciousness* (Beverly Hills, Calif.: Sage Publications, 1977); for the United States: James D. Wright, *The Dissent of the Governed* (New York: Academic Press, 1976). For additional comparative data see Max Kaase and Samuel Barnes, eds., *Political Action and Mass Participation in Five Western Democracies* (Beverly Hills, Calif.: Sage Publications, 1979).

51. Almond and Verba, *Civic Culture*, p. 476ff.

52. Ibid., p. 481.

53. See Wright, *The Dissent of the Governed*; and Vivien Hart, *Distrust and Democracy* (Cambridge and New York: Cambridge Univ. Press, 1978).

54. Kaase and Barnes, *Political Action and Mass Participation*, cited in Martin and Sylvia Greiffenhagen, *Ein schwieriges Vaterland* (Munich: List Verlag, 1979), p. 341.

55. Ibid., p. 342.

56. Ibid., p. 343.

57. *Jahrbuch*, vol. 5, p. 223.

58. Institut für Wahlanalysen und Gesellschaftsbeobachtung, "Wahlstudie 1976, 1. Welle," Mannheim Univ., 1976, p. 168 (mimeo).

59. Walter Jaide, "Jugend und Politik heute. Soziale und politische Einstellungen und Verhaltensweisen im Spiegel neuerer Untersuchungen in der Bundesrepublik Deutschland," *Aus Politik und Zeitgeschichte*, no. 39 (September 25, 1976), pp. 39–40.

60. Scheuch, "Cross Cultural Use of Sample Surveys," p. 198, and Monica Charlot, "The Ideological Distance Between the Two Major Parties in Britain," *European Journal of Political Research* 3 (1976): 177–88.

61. David P. Conradt, "West Germany: A Remade Political Culture?" *Comparative Political Studies* 7, no. 2 (July 1974): pp. 230–36.

62. Hans-Dieter Klingemann and Franz-Urban Pappi, "Die Wählerbewegungen bei der Bundestagswahl am 28. September 1969," *Politische Vierteljahresschrift* 11, no. 1 (1970): 111–38. See also Frederick C. Engelmann,

"Perceptions of the Great Coalition in West Germany, 1966–1969," *Canadian Journal of Political Science* 5, no. 1 (March 1972): 28–54.

63. Forschungsgruppe Wahlen, "Bundestagswahl 1976, Eine Analyse der Wahl zum 8. Deutschen Bundestag am 3. Oktober 1976," Mannheim Univ., October 1976, pp. 85–86 (mimeo).

64. David P. Conradt and Dwight Lambert, "Party System, Social Structure and Competitive Politics in West Germany," *Comparative Politics* 7, no. 1 (October 1974): 61–62, and Max Kaase, "Die Bundestagswahl 1972: Problem und Analysen," *Politische Vierteljahresschrift* 14 (1973): 157–58.

65. For data on the increasing significance of issues and ideology in German voting behavior, see Hans-Dieter Klingemann, "Issue-Kompetenz und Wahlentscheidung," *Politische Vierteljahresschrift* 14 (1973): 227–56, and his "Dimensions of Ideological Cognition and Ideological Orientation." This seeming paradox of a decline in the intensity of partisan hostility, but an increase in interparty issue and ideological conflicts is nonetheless consistent with recent comparative elite research. Putnam, for example, found in his studies of British and Italian elites that an "ideological style," i.e., one strongly oriented to complex conceptualizations of political problems, and partisan hostility were not related. See Robert D. Putnam, "Studying Elite Political Culture: The Case of Ideology," *American Political Science Review* 65 (September 1971): 672.

66. Klingemann, "Dimensions of Ideological Cognition and Ideological Orientation."

67. Peter H. Merkl, *The Origin of the Federal Republic of Germany* (New York: Oxford Univ. Press, 1963), pp. 20–54, 162–82.

68. Lester Milbrath, *Political Participation* (Chicago: Rand McNally, 1965).

69. Institut für Demoskopie, Survey no. 2085.

70. Ibid.

71. Almond and Verba, *Civic Culture,* p. 119.

72. Conradt, "West Germany: A Remade Political Culture?" pp. 234–35.

73. Institut für Demoskopie, Survey nos. 0052 and 3003.

74. Ibid., Survey no. 1031.

75. For an account of the "radical decrees" controversy, see David P. Conradt, *The German Polity* (New York and London: Longman, 1978), pp. 76–85.

76. The question texts: Members of extremist parties, for example, Communists or NPD supporters, and people who work for the goals of these parties have been summarily barred from becoming civil servants in the Federal Republic. Here are two opinions about these so-called *Berufsverbote* (prohibitions of employment). Which of these opinions would you be inclined to support?

1. I think it's right that Communists and National Democrats are investigated and that any one of them who wants to become a civil servant has to be examined to determine whether he basically supports our state and legal system. Only then should such people be able to become civil servants.

2. I am against such investigations and *Berufsverbote*. I do not think that our free, democratic order will be endangered by a few left- or right-wing radicals in government jobs.

3. Undecided, no judgment.

And what about you personally, do you believe that your personal or professional freedom has been limited in the past five years by state action or laws, or would you say that is not the case?

(1) have been limited   (2) no, not the case   (3) no answer

77. Almond and Verba, *Civic Culture*, p. 118.

78. Erwin K. Scheuch, "Die Sichtbarkeit politischer Einstellungen im alltäglichen Verhalten," *Kölner Zeitschrift für Soziologie und Sozialpsychologie*, Sonderheft no. 9 (1965): 169–214.

79. Figures reported in voting surveys for 1961, 1965, 1969, 1972, and 1976; 1961: *Wahlstudie, 1. Welle*, Zentralarchiv für empirische Sozialforschung, Cologne; 1965: *The October 1965 West German Election Study* (Inter-University Consortium for Political Research [ICPR], 1974); 1969: *The 1969 German Pre and Post Election Study* (ICPR, 1974); 1972: *The 1972 German Election Panel Study* (ICPR, 1974); 1976: Institut für Wahlanalysen und Gesellschaftsbeobachtung, *Wahlstudie 1976 1. Welle*.

80. A recent study based on a very limited, "purposive" sample designed to maximize the number of regime opponents nonetheless found only about 1 percent of the sample (a total of 23 university students) who had actually engaged in "aggressive political behavior" (fighting the police at demonstrations, etc.) and only 11 percent (all but 25 of whom were again university students) who scored high on a civil disobedience scale. Thus a deliberately skewed sample, by no means representative of the adult population of the Federal Republic, revealed little evidence of aggressive, "antiregime" behavior (Edward N. Muller and Thomas O. Jukam, "On the Meaning of Political Support," *American Political Science Review* 71, no. 4 [December 1977]: 1561–95). This research also found only moderate relationships between diffuse (regime) and specific (incumbent) support.

81. Thomas Ellwein, Ekkehard Lippert, Ralf Zoll, *Politische Beteiligung in der Bundesrepublik Deutschland* (Göttingen: Verlag Otto Schwartz, 1975), pp. 136–79.

82. Ibid., p. 139.

83. Almond and Verba, *Civic Culture*, pp. 339–40.

84. Ibid., p. 340.

85. Bertram Schaffner, *Fatherland: A Study of Authoritarianism in the German Family* (New York, Columbia Univ. Press, 1949). Almond and Verba, of course, did not have longitudinal data, which would be more suitable to test propositions about the relationship between childhood socialization and adult political attitudes and behavior. Like many other scholars in the field, they had to rely on recall questions, a sometimes risky procedure. See Richard Niemi, *How Families See Each Other* (New Haven: Yale Univ. Press, 1974).

86. Eugen Lupri, "*The West German Family Today and Yesterday: A Study in Changing Family Authority Patterns*," Ph.D. dissertation, University of Wisconsin, Madison, 1967, pp. 240–55.

87. EMNID, *Informationen*, vol. 28, nos. 6/7, 1976, pp. 16, 22, 23.

88. EMNID, *Jugend zwischen 13 und 24, Vergleich ueber 20 Jahre*, vol. 3, 1975, p. 36.

89. Torney et al., *Civic Education in Ten Countries*, p. 79.

90. Ibid., p. 110.

91. Ibid., p. 221.

92. See Friedrich H. Tenbruck, "Alltagsnormen und Lebensgefuehle in der Bundesrepublik," in Richard Loewenthal and Hans-Peter Schwarz, eds., *Die Zweite Republik* (Stuttgart: Seewald Verlag, 1974), pp. 289–310, and Ralf Dahrendorf, *Gesellschaft und Freiheit, Zur soziologischen Analyse der Gegenwart* (Munich: Piper Verlag, 1961), pp. 303–4.

93. *Jahrbuch*, vol. V, p. 138.

94. *Jahrbuch*, vol. VI, p. 21.

95. Ibid., p. 20.

96. See G. Robert Boynton and Gerhard Loewenberg, "The Development of Public Support for Parliament in Germany, 1951–1959," *British Journal of Political Science* 3, no. 2 (April 1973): 169–89, and their "The Decay of Support for Monarchy and the Hitler Regime in the Federal Republic of Germany." David P. Conradt, "West Germany: A Remade Political Culture?" Bradley Richardson, "Democratic Attitudes in the Federal Republic of Germany," unpublished manuscript, Ohio State University, 1973; Kendall L. Baker, Russell J. Dalton, Kai Hildebrandt, "The Residue of History: Politicization in Post-War Germany," Center for Political Studies, University of Michigan, Ann Arbor, 1975. Klaus R. Allerbeck, *Demokratisierung und sozialer Wandel in der BRD. Sekundäranalyse von Umfragen 1953–1974* (Opladen: Westdeutscher Verlag, 1976), and Peter Kmieciak, *Wertstrukturen und Wertwandel in der Bundesrepublik Deutschland* (Göttingen: Verlag Otto Schwartz, 1976).

97. Baker et al., "The Residue of History," pp. 5–10.

98. Conradt, "Remade Political Culture?" p. 229, and Boynton and Loewenberg, "Decay of Support," p. 465.

99. Schweigler, *National Consciousness,* pp. 235–37.

100. Ibid., pp. 61–71, and Daniel Katz, Herbert Kelman, and Vasso Vassiliou, "A Comparative Approach to the Study of Nationalism," in Peace Research Society, *Papers* 14 (1969): 1–13.

101. Among older generations the recognition and resolution of this dissonance will be most likely to occur among those citizens with the earliest and most intensive experience with the system's output performance, that is, successful upper-status and class groups who clearly benefited the most from the early years of high performance. These groups can serve as opinion leaders "diffusing" supportive attitudes to those below them in the socio-economic hierarchy, who then became attached to the system through a compliance process. See Schweigler, *National Consciousness,* p. 71.

102. Institut für Demoskopie, Survey nos. 1020 and 2085.

103. Ibid., nos. 1069 and 2085.

104. Boynton and Loewenberg, "The Decay of Support," pp. 454–55.

105. Ibid., p. 457.

106. *Jahrbuch,* vol. V, p. 209.

107. Ibid., p. 231.

108. Ibid., p. 91.

109. Rudolf Wildenmann, "Eliten in der Bundesrepublik," unpublished manuscript, Mannheim University, 1968.

110. See Ralf Dahrendorf, *Society and Democracy in Germany,* pp. 381–96, and Charles E. Frye, "The Third Reich and the Second Republic: National Socialism's Impact Upon German Democracy," *Western Political Quarterly* 21, no. 4 (December 1968).

111. Frye, "The Third Reich," p. 670.

112. Sontheimer, *The Government and Politics of West Germany;* Richardson, "Democratic Attitudes."

113. Boynton and Loewenberg, "Support for Parliament" and "The Decay of Support"; Richardson, "Democratic Attitudes"; Conradt, "A Remade Political Culture?"

114. Verba, "Germany: The Remaking of Political Culture," p. 131.

115. Significantly, in a 1971 study of schoolchildren in ten countries, the German respondents ranked highest in support for democratic *values,* but were among the lowest national group in expressing positive attitudes toward

political *institutions.* Specifically they were less likely than their counterparts in countries such as Sweden, Holland, and the United States to feel that their political institutions encouraged participation or were "equitable" (see n. 47, Oppenheim, *Civic Education and Participation in Democracy,* pp. 28–29). A 1977 study of adults found a similar pattern: high support for democratic values, but considerable (71%) dissatisfaction with the amount of influence that citizens have on government (Institut für Demoskopie, Survey no. 3038, January 1977).

116. Verba, "The Remaking of Political Culture," p. 104.

117. Jürgen Habermas, *Legitimationsprobleme im Spätkapitalismus* (Frankfurt: Suhrkamp Verlag, 1974).

118. The German-language literature on this point is voluminous. For a representative example, see Urs Jaeggi, *Kapital und Arbeit in der Bundesrepublik* (Frankfurt: Fischer Verlag, 1973).

119. See Kavanagh's chapter in this volume; for similar findings from a nine-nation European sample, see Ronald Inglehart, *The Silent Revolution* (Princeton, N.J.: Princeton Univ. Press, 1977), pp. 169–70.

CHAPTER VIII

The Political Culture of Italy: Continuity and Change

Giacomo Sani
Ohio State University

THERE IS a curious contrast between the first reception and the subsequent fate of *The Civic Culture* in the United States and in Italy. In the United States, and especially among scholars specializing in comparative politics, the work earned a deserved reputation as an early and well-executed effort to carry out systematic cross-national comparisons. The book has been widely studied, evaluated, and cited by scholars, and it has been standard reading for several generations of graduate and undergraduate students.[1] Moreover, the data made available by the principal investigators have been extensively utilized both for additional scholarly undertakings and for pedagogical purposes.[2] In many ways American students have become acquainted with the politics of the four foreign countries included in the study through

Research for the analysis presented in this chapter was made possible, in part, by a Research Fellowship from the Earhart Foundation. I am grateful to my colleagues Samuel Barnes, Giovanni Sartori, and Alberto Marradi for sharing with me data from their studies of the Italian electorate in 1968 and 1975. Loren Waldman provided useful advice for the preparation of the manuscript. I wish to acknowledge the assistance of the Polimetrics Laboratory of the Ohio State University. G. S.

the findings and interpretations advanced by the authors of *The Civic Culture,* or through their own analysis of the data. Finally, country specialists have used the results reported by Almond and Verba in their own monographs, or in the preparation of textbooks.[3] In short, there seems to be little doubt about the impact of the five-nation study among American political scientists.

On the other hand, the reception of *The Civic Culture* in Italy was less than enthusiastic, as one can see from the few and short reviews of the book in scholarly journals.[4] Certainly there was no controversy comparable with that elicited, for example, by the works of Hadley Cantril, Edward Banfield, or Sidney Tarrow.[5] And unlike other major contributions by American social scientists, such as Parsons, Merton, Lazarsfeld, Lipset, Simon, Easton, Dahl, etc., there was no Italian translation of this work, and only a few pages were included in a "reader." [6] To be sure, one does find references to *The Civic Culture* in the work of Italian social scientists, but they appear to be more gestures of a scholarly ritual than occasions for a serious confrontation of ideas. One has the impression that the study was never fully accepted and incorporated into the mainstream of knowledge about Italian society, nor explicitly criticized and rejected. Finally, in spite of their availability, the data do not appear to have been extensively used by the academic community for research or training purposes.[7] In sum, it seems fair to assert that the impact of *The Civic Culture* on Italian social science has been relatively modest.

To some extent this contrast can be explained by external factors, such as the language barrier, the different characteristics of the two academic traditions, and the relative underdevelopment of the disciplines of sociology and political science in Italy in the early 1960s. But one must also consider the possibility that the relative neglect of the study was due in part to intrinsic reasons, that is, to factors pertaining to the conceptualization, methodology, and interpretation of the data. Could it be that the lukewarm reception of the volume had something to do with the form and the substance of the profile of Italian political culture drawn by the two American authors?

This question provides the point of departure for this essay. In the first part of my analysis I suggest a number of tentative reasons for the limited impact of *The Civic Culture* in the

Italian academic community. In the second section I examine the possibility that the portrait of Italian political culture sketched by Almond and Verba might have been blurred or distorted, at least to some extent, by the techniques of data gathering and analysis that they employed. The third section is an attempt to integrate the findings of *The Civic Culture* with other data and to identify the enduring characteristics of mass orientations in Italy during the postwar period. Finally, the last section of the essay is devoted to an examination of changes in political attitudes that have appeared in Italy in recent years.

THE IMPACT

As an ambitious attempt to break new ground, the five-nation study made a multifaceted contribution to the literature of comparative politics. It introduced an elaborate conceptual framework, it provided a description of mass orientations toward political objects in five nations, it attempted to identify patterns of covariation in these phenomena and, finally, it linked these several elements together to give a broad interpretation of the functioning of democratic political systems. To discern the reasons for the limited impact of *The Civic Culture* on Italian social science it is useful to consider each of these aspects in turn.

First, *The Civic Culture* was the source of a large amount of descriptive information about mass attitudes. Although this might not have been regarded by the authors as an important contribution of their study, one can argue that at least with respect to some of the five countries studied, even the simple description of patterns of political cognition existing among the mass public certainly represented a major advance. This is clearly the case for Italy. Prior to the publication of *The Civic Culture*, very little information had been available in English on the attitudes of the Italian electorate. The two slim textbooks that had appeared in the early 1960s dealt mostly with the institutional aspects of the political system, and the limited treatment of topics related to public opinion and mass political behavior was based on impressionistic evidence.[8] Among monographs such studies as the *Appeals of Communism* by Almond and *The Politics of Despair* by Cantril did concern themselves with mass-level phenomena but they were focused on a narrow segment of the electorate, and thus they were too limited to serve as the basis for description and interpretation of the political orientations of the population at large.[9] Similarly, the few data concerning Italy published in Lipset's work, although useful, were hardly sufficient to satisfy the readers' quest for more information.[10] Given this background, it is easy to see why the publication of *The Civic Culture* came to fill for American scholars and students a large information gap. For the first time the readers were presented with detailed data and comments on exposure to political stimuli, levels of cognition and affect, intensity of partisanship, sense of efficacy, and a variety of other topics that had been previously treated on the basis of subjective speculations and guesswork. Furthermore, the availability of the data set soon made it possible for other scholars to go beyond the analysis of the original investigators in order to explore additional topics, or to test ideas which had been advanced in the literature but which had not been subjected to systematic confrontation with data. In brief, even as a simple repository of descriptive information, the five-nation study represented for American students a great step forward.

On the other hand, the situation was different for Italian scholars. They too could find interesting and novel information in the data presented and commented upon by Almond and Verba. But the impact of the volume was by necessity less significant because much of the ground covered by the American authors had already been described seven years earlier by Luzzatto Fegiz.[11] To the reader familiar with this massive compilation of results of public-opinion polls taken during the first ten years of the postwar period, much of the information presented in *The Civic Culture* did not represent a novelty and served, to a large extent, to confirm what was already known. To be sure, the overlap was only partial and *Il volto sconosciuto dell' Italia* was a far less analytical work. But as a source of information on how much people knew about politics, on how they viewed political affairs, on how they stood on many different issues, and the like, this summary of polls taken by the Doxa Institute over a ten-year span was clearly unrivaled.[12] And when the second volume appeared in 1966, the Italian reader had a comprehensive tool that stretched over twenty years of Italian political life and thus made possible comparisons across time denied to the user of a survey covering a single point in time.[13]

Obviously, the reason for contrasting these two works is not to show that the Italian compilation was superior to the American study, but simply to make the point that a great deal of the information that the English-speaking student found for the first time in *The Civic Culture* had already been available to his Italian counterpart. By necessity, then, the latter was likely to find the study by Almond and Verba a less significant contribution, as a source of information, than those scholars who had access only to sources in English.

Second, *The Civic Culture* was more than a source of information on political attitudes at the mass level. The authors not only charted people's orientations toward political objects but also related these variables to each other and attempted to identify patterns. From this point of view there was much in *The Civic Culture* that could be of interest to an Italian reader. However, even in this second respect I would argue that the discussion by Almond and Verba was likely to be more useful to an American student than to an Italian observer. The reasons for this are to be found largely in the cross-national nature of the authors' undertaking, which led them to seek explanations likely to hold across countries and to ignore others, however meaningful they might have been in the context of a specific society. Appropriate as it was for a cross-national investigation, this choice meant the inevitable loss of a wealth of detail. This information, although superfluous for the purposes of a large-scale investigation, might have provided precious elements for understanding the distribution of orientations in a particular society.

Once again, the contrast with another study seems illuminating. In the same year of publication of *The Civic Culture,* Alberto Spreafico and Joseph La Palombara edited a collection of essays dealing with different aspects of the Italian parliamentary elections of 1958.[14] In this volume, which in many ways marks the rebirth of empirical political science in Italy, the reader found a number of contributions addressing topics not dissimilar from those investigated by Almond and Verba and relying, in some cases, on the same techniques of data gathering and analysis.[15] Since the authors of these studies were concerned only with searching for explanation of phenomena in the Italian setting, their discussions were generally very detailed and highly informative. In many cases the analysis and the conclusions presented, intrinsically no more satisfactory than those advanced by the authors of *The Civic Culture,* seemed to be closer to the realities of the country, and hence were more meaningful to the student of Italian politics. Clearly, the work of Mattei Dogan on the partisan preference of women, of La Palombara on youth, of Paolo Amassari on political information, and of Spreafico on party identification furthered our understanding of mass attitudes and political behavior more than the comparable materials presented by Almond and Verba. This is not to detract from the contribution of *The Civic Culture,* but to point out that while this work remained useful for Italian scholars, it was likely to be of less interest for the reader already acquainted with the content of *Elezioni e comportamento politico in Italia.*

A third aspect of the contribution made by *The Civic Culture* was at the level of conceptualization. The authors presented an articulate conceptual scheme for organizing observations on the relationship between individuals and the political system. The analytical distinction between different aspects of the system and different types of orientations provided the two major dimensions for classifying people's attitudes and, on the basis of the modal distribution of these, for characterizing the political culture of a society. Clearly, such a scheme was ideally suited for the study of the set of phenomena that go under the general label of political participation. And because of this, it is somewhat surprising to find that apparently little use was made of this conceptual framework in the massive study of political participation in Italy conducted between 1963 and 1968 by a large team of researchers under the auspices of the Istituto Carlo Cattaneo of Bologna.[16] Inspection of the four volumes, which present in detailed fashion the findings, show that these students were conversant with the international literature and had obviously seen the analysis by Almond and Verba. Yet in the work of these Italian scholars there is very little trace of the conceptualization presented in *The Civic Culture,* and hardly any reference to pivotal terms such as "parochial," "subjective competence," "self as object," and so on. It is obviously difficult to ascertain why the scheme advanced by the two American authors did not receive more attention and was not utilized for at least part of this large study. One can speculate that in choosing the conceptual tools for their analysis, the Italian scholars found alternative frames of reference intellectually more appealing or more suitable for their research purposes. The study of party activists, directed by Francesco Alberoni, for example, was grounded on a conceptualization that blended the ideas of European sociologists such as Tönnies and Smalembach with the modern theories of collective behavior advanced by Blumer, Turner, and Smelser.[17] It is also possible that the scheme presented in *The Civic Culture* was found to be too narrow and inadequate for capturing the variety of forms of political participation existing outside the Anglo-Saxon experience. This might explain why the Istituto Cattane study and other research projects have stressed other approaches, for example, the typology developed by Alessandro Pizzorno containing a distinction between participation in "systems of solidarity" and in "systems of interest." [18] In any event, it appears that the conceptualization underpinning the five-nation study was not absorbed by Italian social scientists and left little mark in their studies of political attitudes and political behavior.

Somewhat similar conclusions emerge with respect to another aspect of the contribution made by *The Civic Culture*. At the core of this study was a concern for the viability and stability of democratic regimes. In the authors' view it was important to study popular orientations to political objects because different modal configurations of these orientations were of significance for the working and survival of the political system. More specifically, they argued that a particular mix of orientations that they called the "civic culture" was appropriate "for maintaining a stable and effective democratic political process." [19] Their findings as to the modal pattern of orientations obtaining in Italy led them to conclude that this society deviated in important respects from the civic model and that these deviations created a "political culture incongruent with an effective and stable democratic political system." [20] From the point of view of a general interpretation of Italian politics, this was obviously an important observation. And we might ask whether this incongruence between political structure and political culture stressed by Almond and Verba has been extensively used and incorporated into the interpretations of the political system advanced by Italian scholars. It is clearly difficult to answer the question with confidence, but if we limit our attention to some of the major contending interpretations of Italian politics, the conclusion appears to be negative. Neither Giovanni Sartori's "polarized pluralism" nor Giorgio Galli's "imperfect bipolarity" seem to have adopted the view of Italian politics advanced in *The Civic Culture.*[21] In fact, both approaches appear to be a reaction against "cultural determinism." [22] Sartori, Galli, and other scholars would agree that the system has not been working in an effective manner, but they identify the causes of the malfunctioning in a variety of structural characteristics, such as the presence of antisystem parties, the byzantine nature of the party system, the lack of rotation of political forces in power, the influence of constraints from the international environment, and the like.[23]

In these and other analyses of Italian politics the focus is not on mass political actors but, rather, on political elites, and the reasons for the malfunctioning of the system are sought far more often in the behavior (or, better, misbehavior) of the latter than in the attitudes of the former. While this might not be the most satisfactory way of analyzing a regime and gauging its viability, it shows that in the most frequently debated interpretations of Italian politics, cultural factors operating at the mass level do not occupy a central position but are relegated to the background. This might explain the paucity of references to *The Civic Culture* in the contributions to a recent debate on the future of the Italian political system.[24]

There is one final observation that might shed some light on the reasons for the modest impact of *The Civic Culture* in Italian circles. This additional factor might be called the "misalignment" between the image of Italy presented in the volume and the self-image of Italian society held by scholars and commentators. To summarize their findings and interpretations of political orientations in Italy, Almond and Verba wrote:

> The picture of Italian political culture that has emerged from our data is one of relative unrelieved political alienation and of social isolation and distrust. The Italians are particularly low in national pride, in moderate and open partisanship, in the acknowledgment of the obligation to take an active part in local community affairs, in the sense of competence to join with others in situations of political stress, in their choice of social forms of leisure activities, and in their confidence in the social environment. . . . It is paradoxical that the majority of politically involved and informed

Italians are opposed to the contemporary constitution and democratic regime.[25]

It seems quite plausible to think that faced with this dismal
portrait the intellectual elites failed to recognize Italian society
as *they* saw it, or could not bring themselves to admit that the
picture was really so dark. It is obviously difficult to determine
whether and to what extent this has occurred, but I would argue
that it is not an entirely unlikely possibility. It is fair to say that
in spite of marked ideological divergences, opinion makers and
the articulate segments of the population have shared, during
the postwar period, a common democratic ethos. This core of
ideas and beliefs has included a rejection of the fascist experience, pride in the resistance movement, allegiance to the principles of the 1948 constitution, and a general belief in the moral
superiority of the democratic process. It is interesting to note
that the criticisms leveled at the political system by politicians,
observers, and commentators have been grounded on this ethos
and have stressed occasional deviations of political practice from
the spirit of the constitution, and more in general from democratic ideals. This, I would argue, means that during the postwar
period articulate Italians have believed that they were living in
a representative democracy, in a system that could be perfected
but which was essentially democratic. To prove it, they would
point out the transition between the monarchy and the republican regime had been reasonably smooth; that parliamentary
institutions had been working according to the rules of the game;
that several elections had regularly taken place at the scheduled
time and without fraud; that generations of political leaders had
learned to perform their functions in pluralistic arenas at the
national and local level; that the fundamental freedoms by and
large had been guaranteed; that a measure of social and economic progress had been achieved; and finally, that at least
until the late 1960s, political violence had been kept at a reasonably low level. In brief, the defenders of the thesis that Italy
was indeed a democracy could argue that the system had been
viable, that it had overcome strong initial handicaps, and that
it had demonstrated its capacity to function if not perfectly at
least reasonably well.[26] From this it is but a short step to come
to believe that democratic attitudes are widespread in the population at large.[27]

Faced with the problem of reconciling this reasonably optimistic picture with the conclusions presented in *The Civic Culture,* one could take a variety of postures toward the negative assessment contained in this work. First, it might be tempting to dismiss the dark portrait painted by the two American scholars as inaccurate or excessively pessimistic. Second, one could argue that even assuming the correctness of the findings, they were not so damaging after all, since what was really important for the continued viability of the democratic regime was a strong commitment to the rules of the game by political elites, subelites, and the articulate sectors of the population. Finally, one could take the position that, in any case, no good would come from pointing to the lack of a civic culture in Italian society, that is, to stress the noninvolvement, incompetence, and alienation of large segments of the electorate would contribute to undermine the democratic regime rather than to help its consolidation. To an outside observer these reactions might appear as a flight from reality and a demonstration of irresponsible optimism. Perhaps they were. But this does not weaken the supposition that the misalignment between the image of Italy projected by *The Civic Culture* and the self-image embedded in the democratic ethos contributed to minimize rather than to heighten the impact of the work by Almond and Verba in Italy.

THE RETICENT CULTURE

In the immediate postwar period, the pioneers of survey research in Italy quickly came to the realization that it was "difficult to ask a stranger about his party preference." [28] Perhaps the problem was more one of answers than of questions. But the fact that even field-workers felt uneasy or embarrassed about asking political questions is quite revealing. As many other investigators found out in later years, Italians have been, and are, reluctant to reveal their political orientations in a standard interview situation.[29] Although in recent times respondents have become somewhat more willing to answer questions dealing with political matters, it is not unusual to find even in the protocols of recent surveys a fair number of defensive and indignant replies to queries about partisanship.[30]

Not surprisingly, the survey organization employed by Almond and Verba in 1959 encountered similar difficulties. In one of the early chapters of *The Civic Culture,* the authors document the unwillingness of many Italian respondents to talk about politics and rightly point out that this in itself is a significant trait of the political culture of that country.[31] But this observation leads to an intriguing question: Can a "reticent" culture be adequately studied by using the standard survey techniques? Is it not conceivable that the respondents' reluctance to speak openly might affect the findings? In short, could the portrait of the Italian citizenry sketched by Almond and Verba have been blurred or distorted, at least to some extent, by the uneasiness of the population toward political surveys? For obvious reasons these questions cannot be fully answered without comparative methodological inquiries, but inspection of the Italian data provides some interesting clues.[32]

First, the Italian survey is characterized by a high percentage of respondents whose partisan preference is unknown. Only 52 percent of the people interviewed chose to report the party for which they had voted the year before. Other questions aimed at eliciting information on partisanship were even less successful. Only 18 percent of the sample admitted "leaning" toward a party, and the figure for "supporters" was 5.4 percent. It does not seem credible that the phenomenon can be due to a lack of genuine partisanship in large segments of the population. Two-thirds of the respondents whose orientations remain unknown actually refused to disclose their leanings. Another 12 percent claimed they "did not know" for what party they had voted. It does not seem unreasonable to suppose that the answer was an alternative way of eluding disclosure of partisan preference. Finally, a third subset claimed that they had not voted. In some cases this might very well have been the truth, but one remains suspicious in view of the high turnout rates obtaining in Italy. In 1958 a full 94 percent of the electorate went to the polls, and 98 percent of these people cast a valid ballot.[33] It seems likely that part of the "did not vote" answers were a more polite way of denying the information than a straightforward refusal.

Second, the distribution of partisan preferences in the subsample of avowed partisans is markedly different from the pattern obtaining in the electorate in the late 1950s. As Table VIII.1 shows, Christian Democratic voters (DC) are considerably overrepresented and the electors for the smaller parties of the

TABLE VIII.1. Distribution of Party Preference in the 1959 Sample and in the Electorate, in percent

Respondents' Report of Their 1958 Vote

	PCI [a] %	PSI %	PSDI %	PRI %	DC %	PLI %	MON %	MSI %	Not ascertained %	Total %	Number of cases %
A. Entire sample	4.4	5.5	2.0	0.5	35.5	1.3	0.9	1.8	48.1	100	(995)
B. Subsample of respondents indicating partisan preference	8.5	10.6	3.9	1.0	68.3	2.5	1.7	3.5	—	100	(517)

Percentage of the Popular Vote Received by the Parties in the 1958 Election

PCI	PSI	PSDI	PRI	DC	PLI	MON	MSI	Others
22.7	14.2	4.5	1.4	42.4	3.5	4.8	4.8	1.7

[a] Abbreviations used in this table and in the text represent the following parties:

PCI: Partito Comunista Italiano – Italian Communist Party

PDUP: Partito Democratico di Unità Proletaria – Democratic Party of Proletarian Unity

PSI: Partito Socialista Italiano – Italian Socialist Party

PSDI: Partito Socialista Democratico Italiano – Socialdemocratic Party

PRI: Partito Repubblicano Italiano – Republican Party

DC: Democrazia Cristiana – Christian Democratic Party

PLI: Partito Liberale Italiano – Liberal Party

MSI: Movimento Sociale Italiano – Italian Social Movement (Neo-Fascist)

MON: Monarchist Party

center — PSDI (Social Democratic), PRI (Republican), PLI (Liberal) — are somewhat overrepresented. The distortion concerning parties of the right and of the left is more pronounced. The contingent of right-wing voters is about half the size of what it should have been (7.7 percent instead of 13.1 percent), and the two parties of the left are underrepresented to a similar degree (19.1 percent *vs.* 36.9 percent). Moreover, within the left, Communist respondents, Communist Party (PCI) are markedly underrepresented vis-à-vis the Socialists (PSI, Socialist Party).

Third, a perusal of the data for the five-nation study shows that in the Italian survey there is an unusually high frequency of inconclusive responses, such as "does not know," "not ascertained," "other." I call these inconclusive answers because, in the case of several variables, these codes are not directly interpretable and their meaning depends largely on the assumptions the analyst is willing to make. Examination of the distribution of these answers for a sample of questions shows that queries more directly related to partisanship tended to elicit a higher proportion of inconclusive answers than the less politically sensitive queries. Furthermore, respondents who hid their partisan preference were also much more inclined to give evasive answers to other politically sensitive questions.[34]

These appear to be three facets of the same phenomenon: reluctance to make one's ideas known, and hence reticence. The phenomenon is not unique to the five-nation study but has occurred in other Italian surveys as well.[35] According to many observers the key factor appears to be the respondents' anxiety over the possible use of information on party preference. This fear of being exposed can operate in three ways: people might choose not to make themselves available for the interview; or they might refuse to disclose their political leanings; or they might even disguise their true preferences.[36]

The predicament for the analyst is clear. The possibility that many answers are affected by reticence increases the uncertainty as to their meaning and one is forced to rely on assumptions even more than is ordinarily the case. In the presence of alternative assumptions that are equally tenable, or at least defensible, the choice is problematical and can have definite implications on the substantive level. That the choices made by Almond and

Verba did have at least some consequences for their interpretation can be demonstrated by the following illustrations.

Many of the authors' conclusions about the nature of Italian political culture are based on the distribution of answers in the sample taken as a whole. The assumption is that within the limits of sampling error the picture provides a fairly accurate portrait of the Italian electorate. But we know that in terms of partisan preference the half of the sample for which we have information underrepresents severely certain segments of the electorate. We have no way of knowing what the distribution of political leanings is in the other half. We could assume that the two halves balance each other, but it would be equally tenable to assume that the second half is subjected to the same kind of distortion.[37] Following this line of reasoning, one could argue in favor of a technique of analysis that would eliminate this imbalance, that is, weighting the sample to reproduce more accurately the distribution of partisan preference existing in the country at that time. Comparison of the distribution of some attitudes in the original sample and in the weighted sample shows that, indeed, the choice of assumptions and associated techniques of analysis is not without consequences. As we can see from Table VIII.2, the unweighted sample tends to underestimate the degree of involvement of the Italian citizenry in political affairs. The weighted sample has a higher percentage of individuals who feel free to talk politics, are knowledgeable, competent, willing to participate, etc. In short, the second portrait is that of a somewhat "more civic" culture.[38] The fact that the differences are not very large indicates that there is only a moderate departure from the findings of Almond and Verba. The fact that the differences are consistently in the same direction indicates the the bias implicit in the two alternative techniques is systematic. Without extensive investigations, which are beyond the scope of this essay, it is impossible to tell whether similar findings would hold for other variables as well. But certainly the illustration should alert the reader to the possibility that some of the distribution of attitudes reported in *The Civic Culture* might not adequately reflect the actual orientations of the Italian electorate in the late 1950s.

The second illustration concerns the treatment of what I have called inconclusive answers. The meaning of a "does not know,"

TABLE VIII.2.   *Comparison of Orientations Toward Politics in the Original Sample and in the Sample Weighted for Partisan Preference (in percentages)*

	Original sample	Weighted sample
Follow governmental affairs in the newspapers "nearly everyday"	12.9	18.5
Talk politics at least "from time to time"	31.1	41.4
Feel free to talk politics to anyone	21.7	27.3
Understand national issues "well" or "very well"	26.5	36.4
Certain people or groups have influence on the government	30.2	40.6
Church and big business are influential groups	14.5	23.2
Optimistic about outcome of their efforts to change unjust regulation	18.6	26.0
Have feelings of satisfaction in going to the polls	25.5	34.4
Believe campaigns are necessary	38.8	47.1
"The vote decides how things are run in this country"	61.5	76.9

and the decision as to what to do with this category of answers in the course of the analysis, depends on the researchers' assumptions. A "no answer" to a question attempting to measure political cognitions can be legitimately interpreted as genuine ignorance; but it could also reflect the person's unwillingness to talk about political matters.[39] In a reticent political culture a negative answer to a question on the role of citizens in politics is not easy to interpret. The attitude tapped might be fear of appearing involved in politics, as much as the genuine inability of conceptualizing oneself in a participant role. Even greater ambiguity surrounds the interpretation of answers to questions requiring an evaluation or a judgment. The general strategy adopted by Almond and Verba was to include all the answers in the base on which percentages were computed. An alternative strategy would have been to consider uninterpretable answers as missing data and to exclude them from the analysis. Here again, the two methodological strategies have substantive implications. Because in the Italian data set inconclusive answers are rather frequent, their inclusion or exclusion from the analysis makes a great deal of difference (Table VIII.3). Naturally, the exclusion of the missing data codes from the computation of the percentages affects all remaining categories. The procedure magnifies both the "positive" and the "negative" traits of a culture.

As might be expected, cross-national comparisons are affected too by the use of this alternative technique. Since inconclusive answers are less frequent in the other four data sets, there is usually no great change in the percentages for the other four nations, as is the case for Italy. The consequence is that at least in the case of some variables, the differences between Italian respondents and the other nationals are not nearly so pronounced as it appears from the tables of *The Civic Culture*. In the first chapter of the volume, for example, the authors report that Americans are much more aware of the impact of government on their lives than are Italians. Some 85 percent of the United States respondents attributed at least some effect to the

Table VIII.3. *Comparisons of Percentages Computed Including and Excluding Missing Data Codes*

	Missing Data	
	Included	Excluded
Percentage mentioning some activities the ordinary man should perform in his community	46.8 (995)	80.2 (581)
Percentage mentioning at least one effective method to influence the government	58.2 (995)	91.3 (634)
Percentage stating that children should take part in the running of schools	43.0 (995)	62.9 (682)
Percentage agreeing that "all candidates sound good in their speeches but you can never tell what they will do after they are elected"	73.3 (995)	89.6 (814)
Percentage agreeing that "no one is going to care much about what happens to you when you get right down to it"	60.7 (995)	70.7 (852)
Percentage agreeing that "people like me don't have any say about what the government does"	69.2 (995)	83.9 (821)

impact of their national government; the figure for Italy was 54 percent. On the basis of this and similar evidence, the authors concluded that whereas in the United States the bulk of the population was allegiant in the output sense, in Italy there was a high incidence of alienated subjects and parochials.[40] When the missing data codes are excluded from the analysis, however, the two percentages become 88.5 and 74.0 respectively for the United States and Italy. To be sure, it still remains true that the Italian sample had a higher proportion of parochials than the American sample, but the difference is no longer so pronounced as it was in the original distribution. Similarly, in their discussion of social trust, and specifically in their discussion of answers to a question concerning whether or not human nature was fundamentally cooperative, Almond and Verba remark that "the German and Italian percentages are substantially lower than the American, British and Mexican." [41] When the missing data are excluded from the analysis, the differences are considerably reduced. And it seems no longer appropriate to speak of substantially lower percentages (Table VIII.4). In other cases it turns out that the adoption of a different procedure affects the results more drastically. Respondents interviewed for the study were asked whether they agreed with the statement "The way people vote is the main thing that decides how things are run in this country." The two alternative percentage distributions reported in Table VIII.4 show that the decision to include or exclude the inconclusive answers is crucial. If we use all the answers, Americans are more likely to agree with the statement than are Italians. If we remove the missing data codes, the opposite obtains.

The third illustration deals with another problem stemming from the low rates of response, namely, the reduction in the number of cases available for analysis. In the sample there are only forty-four Communists, eighteen Neo-Fascists, twenty Social Democrats, and thirteen Liberals. Since not all of them answered all questions, the data base shrinks even further. This obviously constrains the analyst and casts doubts on the confidence we can place on some of the findings.[42] Even the grouping of respondents by broad political tendencies, such as left and right, does not allow one to push the analysis very far. There are less than twenty leftist respondents from the South and less than twenty

TABLE VIII.4. *Differences Between Cross-National Comparisons Using Percentages Computed With and Without Missing Data*

A. Percentage agreeing with the statement "The way people vote is the main thing that decides how things are run in this country."

	United States	United Kingdom	Germany	Italy
Missing data included	71.4	83.8	82.4	61.5
	(970)	(963)	(955)	(995)
Missing data excluded	74.0	86.7	92.8	82.3
	(936)	(931)	(848)	(744)

B. Percentage agreeing with the statement "Human nature is fundamentally cooperative."

	United States	United Kingdom	Germany	Italy
Missing data included	79.9	84.0	57.7	54.4
	(970)	(963)	(955)	(995)
Missing data excluded	85.5	87.3	78.4	78.1
	(906)	(927)	(703)	(693)

right-wing voters from the North. This is a serious limitation in terms of the mapping of subcultural patterns of orientations. The fact that the analysis focuses on the culture of the larger society does not mean that it is irrelevant to determine whether the overall cultural mix is evenly distributed among the population, or whether it is the result of "adding" two or more non-homogeneous subcultures. For a country like Italy where a Catholic and a Socialist tradition have existed side by side and where regional differences are important, the limitation is a serious one. In short, the reduction of the data base makes it impossible to shed light on important topics such as the controversial "cultural dualism" hypothesis.[43]

The validity of the overall interpretation advanced by Almond and Verba is not seriously undermined by the observations presented in this discussion. For one thing, the alternatives for data analysis suggested here are themselves based on assumptions that can be legitimately criticized. For another, their interpretation fits with the conclusions reached by other scholars. But the points examined do raise some questions as to the accuracy and the depth of the portrait of the Italian citizenry painted in *The Civic Culture*. More generally, they testify to the difficulty of reaching firm conclusions about the attitudes prevailing in a society in which reticence is rather common.

THE ENDURING TRAITS

The Italian Republican regime is now thirty years old. By some standards this is not a long time. But it is sufficiently long to pose the following question: Have there been enduring attributes and salient, dominant traits that have characterized mass attitudes throughout the postwar period? If so, what are they? In this section of the chapter, I shall briefly discuss four aspects of political orientations at the mass level that seem to me to be of considerable significance for understanding Italian politics. In the next section I shall consider those other dimensions along which changes have emerged in recent years.

THE LEFT/RIGHT CONTINUUM

There is little doubt that the left/right dimension has been a fundamental component of political discourse in Italy during the last thirty years. Few concepts are more frequently employed by observers and politicians alike to describe, interpret, and evaluate Italian politics than "left" and "right." [44] Parties are commonly viewed as being distributed on a continuum, their tactical and policy stands are interpreted as "moves" to the right or to the left, and even their internal factional alignments are conceptualized in spatial terms. Similarly, governmental coalitions are immediately labeled, in fact even before they come to life, in left/right terms, and their chances of survival are assessed with reference to a spatial logic. I have suggested elsewhere that

The left-right dimension can be usefully seen as . . . a socially shared mental construct that is used to pattern and give meaning to that particular aspect of reality which is ordinarily called political. The significance of this perspective becomes more clear if we consider some of its traits. (1) The left-right terminology is widely used in the political language of both the specialized actors of the political system and, to a lesser extent, of the general population. (2) It is culturally inherited, i.e. transmitted across generation lines through a variety of socialization mechanisms. (3) It has important cognitive functions, i.e. it helps in identifying or

locating social objects, groups, actors, ideas, policies. . . . (4) It
has evaluative functions as well. Left and right are not for most
people neutral terms; on the contrary they tend to be charged
with positive or negative connotations, eliciting approval or dis-
approval, attraction or repulsion. (5) As a cognitive and evaluative
tool the dimension tends to be general rather than specific, flexible
rather than rigid. This allows it to function as a simplifying device
for reducing the complexity of the world to manageable proportions. (6) As the terminology associated with it acquires wide circu-
lation, the construct is taken for granted and not subjected to
continuous scrutiny; its ability to reflect and interpret reality is
a given and not something problematical. (7) Finally, in so far as
it is internalized by the actors of the political system, the dimension
becomes a constraining force: reality is perceived in left-right
terms and alternative modes of actions or patterns of behavior are
shaped by it.[45]

There is abundant evidence on the diffusion of this left/right
construct in Italian society. First, there is widespread agreement
among observers that parties are distributed along a continuum
and that issues, conflict, and policies can be meaningfully understood in these terms. In general, commentators also agree on
the ordering of political forces in this space, and that order
largely coincides with the views of political elites, as Barnes has
demonstrated.[46] The second and more important fact is that this
conceptualization is not limited to the discourse of the specialized actors of the system but is to be found also in a substantial portion of the electorate.[47] Estimates of the percentage
of voters able (and willing) to locate themselves on the left/right
continuum vary somewhat. On the basis of 1972 data, I have
suggested that the phenomenon might apply to as many as two-
thirds of the voters; according to a later investigation by Inglehart and Klingemann, the figure might actually be higher.[48] It
has also been shown not only that electors can locate themselves
on the left/right continuum but that they are also able to assign
a position to the different political parties. And this ordering of
political forces actually coincides with that of political observers
and elites. To be sure, in the aggregate view of the electorate,
parties occupy segments rather than points, but the amount of
general agreement is considerable.[49] As the distributions of Fig.
VIII.1 show, in 1972 the different groups of Italian partisans had
slightly different views of the location of parties, but the ordering

Positions Assigned to the Parties

Partisan Preference of Respondents

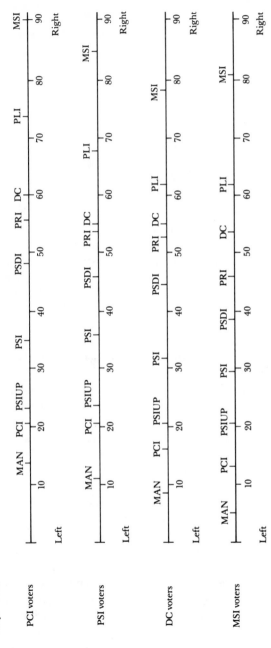

Source: Giacomo Sani, "L'imagine dei partiti nello elettorato," in Mario Caciagli and Alberto Spreafico (eds.), *Un sistema politico alla prova* (Bologna: Il Mulino, 1975), p. 105.

FIG. VIII.1. Positions Assigned to Italian Parties on the Left/Right Continuum by Four Groups of Partisans (1972)

of the different political forces was the same, and the differences in the mean locations assigned to the parties were rather
small.

Third, the voters' self-location in terms of left/right dimension
is closely related to partisan preference.[50] On another occasion
I have suggested that this might be the result of simultaneous
learning of left/right identification and the acquisition of partisan preference. This would mean that the orientation toward
specific political objects is firmly imbedded in a view of the
political world organized, among other things, by the left/right
continuum.[51] Last, spatial location and partisan preference are
excellent predictors of a large number of orientations. This
might not come as a surprise, but it means that in the rather
sketchy and uninformed maps of political reality held by the
average voter, "left" and "right" emerge as fundamental cognitive and evaluative devices. Patterns of hostility toward the different political forces and other politically relevant groups such
as the clergy, unions, demonstrators, etc., appear to be meaningfully organized by the use of a spatial dimension.[52] Similarly,
preferences for given cabinet coalitions, expectations as to the
outcome of elections, feelings of sympathy toward other nations,
as well as positions on many different issues are clearly related
to partisanship.[53]

The self-locations of different groups of partisans on the left/
right continuum have remained substantially unchanged since
the late 1960s, as the figures of Table VIII.5 indicate. Many of
the differences apparent in the data are very small fluctuations
devoid of substantive import. The only significant changes appear to be the more marked isolation of MSI (Italian Socialist
Party) supporters toward the right wing of the spectrum and the
slight convergence of PCI (Italian Communist Party) voters toward the center. But even these changes are not pronounced.
Thus, the evidence suggests that this dimension remains an important key for understanding how people make sense of contemporary reality and evaluate prospects for the future. One can
say that it still represents a manifest and general dimension of
cognition, affect, and evaluation. It is manifest in the sense that
it is socially shared and markedly evident in the actors' awareness. It is general because of its pervasiveness and flexibility,
which allows its application to a variety of changing contexts

TABLE VIII.5. *Mean Self-Location of Different Groups of Partisans on the Left/Right Continuum* [a]

	Party Preference						
	PCI	PSI	PSDI	PRI	DC	PLI	MSI
Barnes study, 1968	12	33		51	55	72	78
Barnes and Sani study, 1972	20	33	45	52	56	65	83
Inglehart and Klingemann study, 1973	18	32	42	48	56	66	87
Sartori and Marradi study, 1975	25	37	47	48	59	67	87

[a] The scale ranged from 0 (left) to 100 (right) in the case of the first two studies. In the 1973 study the respondents were asked to locate themselves in one of ten boxes.

Source: The figures for 1973 can be found in "Party Identification, Ideological Preferences and the Left-Right Dimension Among Western Publics" by Ronald Inglehart and Hans Klingemann in Ian Budge et al., *Party Identification and Beyond* (New York: Wiley, 1976), pp. 226–242.

and situations. Given its centrality it seems likely that the left/right dimension will remain a central feature of Italian political culture for some time to come.

RELIGION AND POLITICS

A second important dimension to be considered has to do with the antagonism between secular and clerical forces, the cleavage between church and state, or what Sartori has called the "laical-confessional" dimension.[54] This cleavage, which is inextricably associated with the important role played by the Catholic church in Italian politics, has been stressed by many scholars and it is indeed hard to overemphasize its importance.[55] The unification of the country was delayed, at least in part, by the presence of the Holy See in the middle of the peninsula. When the emergence of the new nation finally occurred, it brought about a major confrontation between church and state that had long-lasting consequences: it kept Catholics away from the mainstream of political life for a long time; it prevented the merger of the proclerical elites with the already established secular forces; it encouraged the creation of a vast network of Catholic organizations; it favored the consolidation of a Catholic subculture with deep roots at the mass level.

There is plenty of evidence that the division of the population along clerical/secular lines has been one of the central characteristics of mass orientations in Italy for most if not all of the postwar years. Data from the very early surveys as well as from recent investigations indicate the existence of a strong relationship between partisan preference and a number of indicators of the "religious factor." Religious practice, "clericalism," feelings of religiosity, membership in Catholic organizations, sympathy for the clergy, and similar variables have been shown to be powerful predictors of partisan preference in general, and of the vote for the Christian Democratic party in particular.[56] Similarly, the distribution of positions on a wide range of issues, such as education, divorce, abortion, role of the church in social and political affairs, foreign policy stands, etc., can be shown to parallel to a large extent the division between the clerical and the secular segments of the population.[57]

Recent events, and particularly the outcome of the 1974 referendum on the divorce issue, might suggest to the observer the supposition that the religious factor is gradually becoming less important in Italian politics. Although this possibility cannot be entirely ruled out, a little reflection will show that the clerical/secular cleavage is still important in the mid-1970s, and does not seem likely to fade away in the short run. In the first place, the outcome of the referendum, pleasing as it was for the secular forces, indicated only that the other camp no longer had the support of the majority of the electorate. But the division of the vote — roughly 6 to 4 in favor of keeping the divorce law — was hardly indicative of a passing away of this cleavage. A society split in this proportion over an issue that provoked a very heated debate is still far from consensus. Second, among the crucial issues awaiting resolution at the beginning of 1976, the regulation of abortion and the revision of the 1929 Concordat between church and state seemed to be the thorniest. And the efforts made by some political forces to avoid another confrontation indicate that political elites are well aware of the danger of deepening the gulf between the laical and the confessional camps. It is possible that some of the alternative coalition realignments now being discussed, particularly the so-called historic compromise, might bring about a softening of postures on issues that belong to the clerical/secular dimension.

This stance has clearly characterized the strategy of the Communist party in recent years. But the unabated anticlericalism of other forces within the left and the adamantly traditional posture of some groups within the Catholic camp seem to indicate that the demise of the clerical/secular cleavage is not imminent.[58] The fact that there is a decline of the Catholic tradition, as I shall try to show later on, does not necessarily mean a lower likelihood of conflict along laical-confessional lines. The clerical forces might have already lost their position of dominant majority, but this does not imply that the linkage between religion and politics has become a less significant characteristic of mass attitudes.

THE NATURE OF PARTISANSHIP

In his discussion of political culture, Joseph La Palombara characterized Italian society as one in which "jobs are awarded and denied, business with the government expedited or impeded, passports and emigration permits issued or refused, and other values distributed or subtracted in part on the basis of one's political affiliation." [59] Few contemporary observers would disagree with the statement, and the often cited aberrations linked to the practice of *sottogoverno* constitute evidence that confirms the assessment. Partisanship might originate from the drive to secure material interests, as in the case of patronage, or it might be grounded in ideological fervor, or it might simply be a psychological attachment to a party. But the implication is the same; what one is, and is perceived to be, politically makes a difference; partisan affiliation is of consequence. In connection with this phenomenon, several points need to be made.

First, for most of the postwar period there has been a great deal of stability in partisanship, as the analysis of voting records has repeatedly demonstrated.[60] There is also evidence from individual-level data that an overwhelming majority of voters have confirmed their partisan choice election after election.[61] I have suggested elsewhere that even in the regional elections of 1975 the phenomenon of shifts in partisan preference, although more marked than in the past, was probably less pronounced than many observers were led to believe.[62] Perhaps electoral stability will no longer be a feature of Italian politics in future years, but as of now it must still be counted as one of the enduring traits of the system. Second, there is evidence indicating that partisanship has been rooted in primary groups. In the 1959 survey by Almond and Verba, approximately 50 percent of the partisans reported that most or all of their friends and acquaintances supported the same party they did.[63] Evidence of considerable political homogeneity of family groups emerged from a 1972 study. This and other investigations have also shown a high degree of continuity in partisan preference across generations.[64] In short, it appears that partisanship has taken root and that the political homogeneity prevailing in primary groups contributes to reinforce existing patterns.

Third, partisanship is also reinforced by nonoverlapping organizational affiliations. More than ten years ago La Palombara observed:

> The point is that whenever one is speaking of agricultural organizations, professional associations, athletic clubs, youth groups, women's federations, university student movements . . . one is likely to find them fragmented into at least Communist, Socialist, Catholic and Fascist factions. Thus to some extent each of the parties tends to create its own exclusive infrastructure of functional and auxiliary organizations which serve both to inculcate and also to reinforce the kind of attitudes toward politics just discussed.[65]

There are indications that in this respect things have changed somewhat in the last ten years; for example, the union movement in the mid 1970s is considerably less fragmented than it was at the time when La Palombara made his observations. Still, there is evidence showing that at least until the early 1970s organizational affiliations and partisan preference were closely related.[66] Fourth, partisanship has been reinforced by selection of and exposure to political stimuli congruent with one's preferences. According to data collected in 1972, 83 percent of the left-wing newspapers reached individuals who supported the PCI and the PSI; 71 percent of the Catholic-inspired papers were read by DC electors, and 70 percent of the right-wing publications were bought by voters belonging to the center-right part of the political spectrum.[67] Last, many observers have noted the intense character of partisanship. Almond and Verba showed that Italians had rather strong and negative feelings toward marriages across party lines.[68] Another indicator is provided by evidence pertaining to what might be called "negative party preference." Both in 1968 and in 1972 a sizable percentage of the electorate gave an affirmative answer to the question "Are there parties for which you would never vote?" [69]

An important aspect of partisanship has to do with what Sartori has called the "antisystem" dimension. [70] His map of political cleavages in Italy contained, among others, a distinction of political groups on the basis of their acceptance, semiacceptance, or rejection of the political system. The polemic on the antisystem nature of certain forces has centered mostly on the Communist party. [71] As I shall try to show later on, there is evidence indicating that the PCI is gradually becoming more legitimate in the eyes of the non-Communist voters. But this does not mean that the antisystem dimension is no longer of significance in the Italian polity. One must consider, first of all, the fact that the stigma of being antisystem is still attached to the Neo-Fascist party, which in 1972 was the fourth largest political group in the country. Furthermore, a number of self-styled extraparliamentary groups have sprung up in recent times. Although small in size, these have a considerable impact. Their members are very active, they frequently engage in unorthodox forms of political participation, and they have contributed to the climate of political violence which has plagued the country in the last few years. The groups involved might have changed but the prosystem/antisystem dimension is still a meaningful one in contemporary Italian politics.

The consolidation of partisanship, especially of the intense variety, has a number of consequences. Perhaps the most important one is that it crystallizes reciprocal feelings of hostility among political groups, which impedes dispassionate political discourse and heavily influences the evaluation of political objects. In other words, when groups are highly polarized, the proposals, ideas, and policies brought forth by one of the groups are immediately evaluated in negative terms, or at least viewed with suspicion, irrespective of their content. This partisan bias is much more evident at the level of "visible" politics, of exchanges among parties that take place in full view of public opinion. Conversely, there is much less rigidity in elite pronouncements and behavior in less publicized arenas. In brief, intense partisanship in a fragmented and polarized polity constrains bargaining and other forms of political exchange and tends to confine them to the realm of "invisible" politics.[72] Similarly, it seems plausible to argue that intense partisanship tends to slow down the processes of coalition realignment, for these imply the toning down of polemics among formerly antagonistic forces, and persuading the partisan of the legitimacy of pursuing open exchanges in the political arena.[73]

THE PATTERN OF ANTAGONISM

Over the thirty years of the postwar period, the relationships among parties have not remained static. The positions of parties have gradually changed and new coalition alignments have come about, not without intense polemics and bitter feuds. In the early 1960s the centrist coalition formula gave way to the center-left, and the Socialists were brought into the governmental camp. In the mid-1970s the center-left appears to be no longer viable. A new alignment is in the making, one in which the Communist party is likely to play a significant role.

Changes in the perspectives and strategies of political elites have been accompanied by some changes in attitudes at the mass level too, as we shall see later on. But when we analyze the public's view of political actors and its evaluation of the competing forces, we still find that in the mid-1970s there is a great deal of continuity with the past. Reciprocal feelings of sympathy or hostility among partisans, positive and negative orientations toward parties and other significant groups appear to be imbedded in a fairly static view of the political world. In brief, it seems that the fundamental elements of what might be called the pattern of political antagonism have remained rather stable.

What are the components of this enduring pattern? A survey of the Italian electorate conducted in late 1975 contains information useful for exploring this question. A sample of respondents were asked to express their feelings toward the parties and other politically significant objects using a hostility-sympathy scale ranging from 0 to 100. The figures displayed in Table VIII.6 are the mean scores summarizing the feelings of different groups of party supporters toward the various "objects."

Inspection of the data suggests that the pattern of antagonism incorporates the major cleavage dimensions just examined. First of all, it is clear that the feelings are related to the location of

TABLE VIII.6. *Partisan Preference and Feelings Toward Politically Significant Objects* [a]

Politically significant objects	Partisan Preference								Not ascertained
	PDUP	PCI	PSI	PSDI	PRI	DC	PLI	MSI	
Revolutionary groups	78	33	24	14	16	14	8	17	
Protest movement	79	55	46	38	41	34	27	33	
Women's liberation	74	55	53	44	50	41	37	38	
Communist party	70	83	59	41	41	31	25	24	
Unions	66	69	63	49	54	49	37	33	
Socialist party	59	55	76	55	54	44	38	28	
Small business	38	53	62	67	68	63	69	63	
Social Democrats	17	31	46	64	43	46	43	30	
Christian Democrats	12	25	40	49	40	73	46	34	
Police	19	51	58	68	65	72	67	71	
Industrialists	24	48	53	63	57	65	69	63	
Neo-Fascists	2	10	13	17	17	26	35	77	
Clergy	14	26	40	46	41	65	44	41	

[a] Figures are mean sympathy scores. The scale ranged from 100 to 0.
Source: Sartori and Marradi study (1975).

the different groups of partisans on the left/right dimension. In many cases the mean scores increase or decrease regularly as one moves from one group of partisans to another. Second, it is apparent from the score summarizing the feelings toward the clergy that hostility toward this object is not a monopoly of the left but is to be found also on the right and center portions of the spectrum. In fact, only Christian Democratic (DC) voters seem to have positive orientations toward the clergy. Clearly, the pattern of antagonism becomes more meaningful when one adds to the left/right dimension the presence of a secular/clerical cleavage that cuts across, to some extent, the divisions generated by the first. And since DC supporters represent slightly less than 40 percent of the electorate, the significance of this second dimension need not be stressed. Third, the data indicate that political objects identified with the extreme poles of the political spectrum ("revolutionary groups" and "Neo-Fascists") elicit strong negative feelings from very large segments of the electorate, including the traditional left and the traditional moderate sectors. It is apparent that Communist voters have little sympathy for the groups of the ultra-left and have a lukewarm attitude at best toward nontraditional leftist groups such as the "protest movement" and the "feminist movement." Similarly, general if less intense feelings of hostility toward the Neo-Fascists are apparent in the answers given by Partito Liberale Italiano and DC voters. This suggests the existence of yet another cleavage intersecting the first two, a dimension that differentiates between the legitimate and the antisystem forces, and which makes certain objects the targets of hostility of practically all groups of partisans. Last, there appears to be a considerable amount of symmetry in the reciprocal views of partisans toward the parties with which they identified. This point cannot be fully analyzed because only some of the parties were included in the list of object-stimuli presented to the respondents. But if we look at the pairs for which information is available, we find considerable congruence. The hostility of Christian Democrats toward the Partito Comunista Italiano, appears to be reciprocated (the scores are 31 and 25, respectively). For the PCI–PSI pair the values are 55 and 59, thus indicating the existence of reciprocal, if not very intense, sympathy. The pertinent values for other pairs appear to fit this symmetrical pattern.

Differences in the feelings reflected in the data become more sharply defined when we compare in a systematic fashion the scores of two subsets of partisans at a time. It is evident that while some groups tend to give very similar evaluations of the objects considered, the feelings of other subsets of partisans are sharply juxtaposed. For example, centrist voters supporting the PSDI and the PRI tend to agree with respect to most of the objects being evaluated. On the other hand, the mean scores of radical leftist respondents (PDUP) and MSI voters are inversely related. The objects that rank high for the former are almost invariably the target of the hostility of the latter and vice versa. If it were not for the fact that both groups dislike the DC and the clergy, the inverse correlation would be perfect. Comparison of the mean scores summarizing the feelings of the supporters of

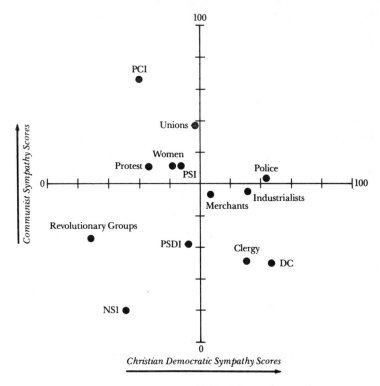

FIG. VIII.2. Evaluations of Different Groups by Christian Democratic and Communist Supporters

the two major parties is of greater significance, since these two segments of the electorate account for over 73 percent of the votes cast in the parliamentary elections of 1976. Examination of the pertinent figures leaves little doubt as to the persistence of sharp differences between these two groups of partisans, not only with respect to the parties with which they identify but also with regard to many of the other objects considered. The plot of the mean scores for the groups of DC supporters (X axis) and PCI supporters (Y axis), is displayed in Fig. VIII.2. The configuration of points that obtains represents, in a way, the joint affective map of a portion of the political world as perceived by a very large segment of the Italian electorate.[74] The location of the various objects in this space provides us with a simplified picture of the pattern of antagonism discussed above. In spite of changes that have occurred in recent times, the persistence of cleavage dimensions dating from an earlier period is unmistakable.

THE NOVEL ELEMENTS

For the first twenty years of the postwar period, few significant changes took place on the Italian political scene. Even the "opening to the left" with the consequent access to power by the Socialist party, momentous as it might have appeared at the time, did not substantially alter the main characteristics of Italian political life. By the early 1970s, however, it became apparent that a number of new developments were in progress and their impact was slowly being felt. Among the most significant events and trends of the late 1960s and the 1970s are the following:

1. The protest movement known as *contestazione,* which started in 1968 among university students but rapidly spread in the following years to other areas of society
2. The massive strikes of workers in the tense confrontation of the "hot fall" of 1969 and the labor unrest of the following years
3. The eruption of political violence involving frequent bombing of public buildings, railroads, utilities, political kidnapings, and an uninterrupted string of almost daily confrontations between the police and activists of different political persuasions
4. The emergence, on both sides of the political spectrum, of extraparliamentary groups operating outside, and consciously against, the rules of the democratic political process
5. A lessening of the ties between some voluntary associations and the political parties, especially the unions and some of the Catholic organizations flanking the Christian Democrats
6. The emergence of highly active, visible, spontaneous, and semiautonomous groups, escaping to a large extent the control of more traditional institutions and organizations
7. The growth of a civil rights movement associated with the revival of a radical party, women's liberation groups, and other minorities
8. Phenomena of dissent within the Catholic world culminat-

ing in the election of a few well-known Catholic intellectuals on the Communist ticket in the parliamentary election of 1976

9. The surfacing of a radical-left party (Manifesto group, later merged into the Partito Democratico di Unità Proletaria) as a response to the more moderate line adopted by the Communists

10. Disaffection toward the democratic system of groups associated with segments of the military with evidence of plots against the regime

11. Eruption of an unprecedented series of scandals involving governmental officials, which have been highly publicized

12. Creation of new and politically significant institutions at the regional level, and within schools and neighborhoods

13. Passage of a law regulating the referendum that made possible the 1974 referendum on the divorce issue and opened the way for the use of this procedure to resolve other issues

14. Extension of the right to vote for the Lower House to people of eighteen years of age

15. Significant gains by parties of the left, and especially by the Communists, in the elections of 1975 and 1976, which have rendered nonviable some of the coalition alignments of the past

16. Polemics and debates over the role that the Communist party should play in the political system, and widely publicized discussions on alternative proposals for new coalitions

Perhaps because of the contrast with the stagnation of an earlier period, commentators have been inclined to hail some of these developments as striking departures from the pattern of the past, and they have generally been interpreted as symptoms that the whole society has been rapidly changing. More cautious students might observe that significant events and changes visible at the elite level cannot be assumed a priori to be an adequate representation of the processes affecting the entire population. Hence we might ask: Is the turmoil that has characterized Italy since 1968 a surface-level phenomenon affecting primarily the more articulate segments of society, or did it reach down, so to speak, to the mass level? And, second, what are the novel elements of Italian political culture? In the pages that follow I shall attempt to show that although the orientations of the broad segments of the population lag somewhat behind, a number of significant changes have taken place among the mass public.

POLITICAL COGNITIONS AND AWARENESS

Several scholars, including Almond and Verba, have stressed the low level of political information and involvement of the average Italian voter.[75] Although there is evidence that the Italian citizenry deviates considerably from the model of the competent and informed electorate, it is possible that the findings of *The Civic Culture* might have painted an excessively dark picture of Italian society. We know from other data that in 1956, 86 percent of the voters knew who the president of the republic was, and 43 percent identified correctly the West German chancellor. In 1958 about half of the electorate reported that they had heard about the French constitutional referendum. A year later 41 percent of the people interviewed knew of the recently established constitutional court. In 1960 half of the sample polled reported having some information on an important speech made by the president of the senate. In 1964, 63 percent of the electorate knew who the Italian premier was and had a fairly good idea of which parties were in power.[76]

Exposure to political affairs and involvement appear to have increased over the years. In 1961 the television program *Tribuna polica* was followed assiduously by 50 percent of the viewers; by 1972 almost two-thirds of the voters reported that they had followed the campaign through a similar program (*Tribuna elettorale*).[77] Similarly, the percentage of people saying that they never talked politics dropped from 66 in 1959 to 53 in 1964.[78] According to another source, there has been an increase in the level of attention paid to political affairs (24.5 percent in 1968 *vs.* 35.5 percent in 1974).[79] And, as one would expect, greater exposure leads to greater awareness of significant social and political phenomena; for example, awareness of the Mafia rose from 69 percent in 1963 to 91 percent in 1975.[80]

These trends can be interpreted as the result of three converging factors: a greater saliency of political phenomena in the people's minds, an increase in the overall level of education of the population, and greater diffusion of mass media. Although changes in the first variable are based mostly on impressionistic evidence (but demonstrations, graffiti, and sit-ins have made politics more directly visible to the common man), changes in the other two can be readily documented with statistical evidence. Since the time of the *Civic Culture* study, the educational system has been greatly reformed and expanded. Between 1962 and 1972 the number of students in secondary (postelementary) schools has increased from 2.5 to 4.4 million and the number of people enrolled in universities has had a threefold increase. Similarly, the number of subscribers to television service jumped from 4.2 million to 10.9 million.[81]

On the basis of 1972 data I have suggested elsewhere that the Italian electorate could be divided in terms of exposure to political information into three groups of approximately equal size, and that only the last one would be a group almost entirely cut off from political information diffused by the media.[82] The trends discussed earlier suggest that as the new and better-educated generations gradually replace the older cohorts of voters, the stratum of politically uninformed citizens will gradually shrink in the future.

SATISFACTION, EXPECTATIONS, AND SYSTEM EVALUATION

At the time of the *Civic Culture* study, Italy was in the midst of an unprecedented period of economic growth. Although in later years the process of expansion has slowed down and even suffered occasional reversals, there is no doubt that over the postwar period the general social and economic conditions of the country have improved considerably. Considering the prospects for the future of the Italian polity, Almond and Verba wrote: "The striking economic improvements in recent years in Italy hold out some prospect of changes in social structure and political culture. Rapid industrial development will certainly weaken traditionalism and rising standards of living, assuming equitable distribution, may increase social trust and confidence in the political system. But the present pattern is of a predominantly alienated political culture." [83]

We should now ask: Has there been any change in the levels of satisfaction? Have Italians become more confident in their government and less alienated?

Analysis of data from the last ten years suggests that one should consider separately the two questions of personal satisfaction and system evaluation, since the answers are very different. In terms of satisfaction with their lives, the evidence suggests that Italians believe that their lot has improved, or at least has become more tolerable; but their evaluations of the political system seem to have become more negative. According to data released by DOXA, a higher percentage of people were happy with their jobs in 1975 than in 1953 or in 1956.[84] More detailed analysis of data from 1968 and 1972 shows some increase in satisfaction with regard to job, housing, and income. In 1972, 40 percent of the people polled said that they were better off than five years before.[85]

When we look at trends in the assessment of the political system, however, we find that negative evaluations have become more pronounced. In May 1971, 17.5 percent of a national sample agreed with the statement that "there is something basically wrong with the social and political system." The percentage increased to 23.1 in June 1972 and reached 34.6 in November 1974.[86] The distribution of answers by partisan preference shows that although left-wing and right-wing voters were somewhat more pessimistic than the rest of the sample, there was considerable dissatisfaction even among moderate electors as well (see Table VIII.7). Even clearer evidence is provided by the comparison of findings from two surveys conducted in 1967 and 1974. Asked to evaluate the "functioning of the state," the "honesty of people in government," and "their competence," many fewer respondents had a positive assessment in 1974 than in 1967.[87] Other investigations provide corroboration of these findings. Perceptions of dishonesty among governmental officials, of waste-

TABLE VIII.7. *Evaluation of the Social and Political System (1974) by Party Preference*

	Party Preference					
The Italian system is:	*PCI*	*PSI*	*PSDI-PRI-PLI*	*DC*	*MSI*	*All*
Fine as it is	6.8	15.8	13.2	37.5	6.8	20.6
In need of immediate, major reforms	42.2	46.8	56.0	38.0	30.5	43.2
Radically wrong, everything must change	49.5	36.3	29.7	22.8	61.0	34.6
Don't know, other	1.5	1.1	1.1	1.7	1.7	1.6

Source: Ricerche Demoscopiche 1, no. 2 (1975): 35. Number of cases not given in the source.

ful use of public monies, of indifference of the government toward the citizens, of limited subjective competence combined to produce a more negative evaluation of public authorities in 1972 than in 1968.[88] For observers who have listened to conversations in public places and read letters to the editors of newspapers and magazines, these findings are hardly surprising and confirm the widespread unhappiness with the political conditions of the country in the last few years.

What accounts for these divergent trends in levels of personal satisfaction and evaluation of the situation of the society at large? To understand these phenomena, one should take into account several factors. In the first place, the economic growth of the 1950s and 1960s was geared more to the satisfaction of private wants than of public needs. Although this provided many people with a greater amount of goods and services, the allocation of resources for public services (hospitals, schools, urban transportation, etc.) has lagged behind. The deterioration of services so evident even to a casual observer is the natural consequence of the policies pursued in an earlier period.

Second, one could argue that the citizens' evaluation of the government simply reflects an objectively negative state of affairs: the ineptness of many incumbents, the fact that many policy decisions benefit specific clienteles rather than the community, the corruption which has come to the attention of public opinion in recent years. In brief, the citizenry is not paranoiac or unduly pessimistic. The political discourse *is* byzantine and almost incomprehensible to the uninitiated; the burden of taxation *is* poorly distributed; the bureaucracy *is* inefficient; the squandering of public monies *has* occurred, and so on. Third, it might very well be that one of the reasons why the electorate has become markedly more pessimistic is that its level of political awareness and information is much higher in the mid-1970s than it was before. To put it simply: the citizens like the system less because they know more about it.

Perhaps the key for understanding the phenomenon is the wide gap between popular expectations as to the role of the government and perceived policy outcomes. Evidence of this discrepancy is provided by the figures of Table VIII.8. In 1975 a sample of Italian voters was queried about governmental responsibility in a number of policy areas and was asked to ex-

TABLE VIII.8.   *Perceived Governmental Responsibility and Evaluation of Governmental Action (1975)*

Policy area	Percentage assigning great responsibility to government	Percentage evaluating governmental action positively
Care for the elderly	67.4	32.0
Jobs for all	77.7	17.9
Education	64.9	48.7
Health assistance	77.6	37.0
Housing	67.7	19.0
Crime prevention	82.6	12.9
Inflation	81.1	7.1

Source: Sartori and Marradi study, 1975.

press a judgment on the adequacy of governmental action. As one can easily see, the data reveal a clear imbalance between expectations and perceived performance. For practically all of the problems listed a large majority of respondents assigned considerable responsibility to the government but only a much lower percentage expressed satisfaction with governmental action. Not surprisingly, inflation, crime prevention, housing, and unemployment were the issues with respect to which the evaluation of governmental performance was lowest. As one learns from the same survey, these are precisely the problems to which an overwhelming majority of respondents attributed great importance.

If this interpretation is correct, it means that socioeconomic development has acted as a destabilizing force. It has raised expectations and made people more aware of the significance of governmental action, with the inevitable result of increasing the demands made upon the political system. The unwillingness and/or inability of policymakers to meet these demands could not but fuel popular dissatisfaction.

POLITICAL PARTICIPATION

Perhaps the most noticeable change in Italian political life in the last decade concerns the phenomenon of participation. New forms of participation have emerged and have expanded the traditional repertoire of mass political behavior (voting, membership in political parties and associated activities, campaign work, etc.). The newer forms include demonstrations; sit-ins; wildcat strikes; unauthorized marches; occupation of plants, offices, and public buildings; blocking of railroads and highways; spray painting of slogans on walls; etc. To be sure, none of these activities represents an absolute novelty. What is new is the high frequency of these behaviors, which in the past were rare, isolated instances. Even more startling is the increase of political violence, a phenomenon which must be regarded as a form of participation, if a pathological one. Episodes of bombing, assaults, kidnaping, burning of cars, destruction of property, and physical confrontations involving the use of clubs, bars, or chains have been frequently reported by the media in the last few years.[89] Indeed, political violence, responsibility for it, and how to cope with the phenomenon have been among the major topics of political debates in the 1970s.

Although there is no sharp break between the older and the newer forms of participation, the two differ in a number of characteristics. First, the newer forms are more socially visible; they occur in public places, indeed they need a public arena in order to be meaningful. If it is to make a point (to protest, show solidarity, pressure decision makers), a demonstration needs some form of public display. Second, the newer forms of participation appear to be often more spontaneous, less controlled by organizations and institutions. This reflects in part the proliferation of small, autonomous political groups that has occurred since the late 1960s and, in part, the decentralization to the grass roots of the decision to act. This explains why some of these participatory activities often flare up suddenly, are poorly coordinated, and are much more likely to be erratic in their development. In this respect the contrast between a mass rally tightly organized and supervised by a party and the spontaneous demonstrations staged by students or workers is striking. Third, the newer style of participation often takes the form of a confrontation between opposing groups, generally ultra-leftists and right-wing extremists, which become involved in a seemingly unending chain of attacks and reprisals. The last and perhaps most important difference is the *direct* nature of the newer forms of participation. By acting, the participants are no longer delegating to others the resolution of an issue; they are doing something about it. Occupying a plant, blocking traffic, refusing to pay utility bills —

all are direct means for attracting the attention of the authorities, demanding a decision or the implementation of a policy. This is a direct form of input considerably different from the older practices of obtaining satisfaction through channels.

As one might expect, these newer forms of participation involve as active participants small segments of the population. But because of the high social visibility of these activities, their impact extends beyond the immediate circle of participants and affects larger segments. Measures of involvement in, and attitudes toward, the newer forms of participation are reported in Table VIII.9. The data indicate that while there is a universal condemnation of violent methods, other and somewhat unorthodox forms of participation have the approval of small but not insignificant segments of the electorate. It would appear that although the new style of participation has not acquired legitimacy in the eyes of most electors, there are groups in the population who justify the recourse to these new means of action.

These findings are in line with what has emerged from our discussion of popular expectations and system evaluation. It seems plausible to argue that high expectations, coupled with frustration resulting from the lack of responsiveness of the traditional input channels, are likely to lead to the utilization of alternative means. The fact that the newer forms of participation

TABLE VIII.9. *Attitudes Toward Different Forms of Participation (1975)*

Activity	Percentage approving	Percentage reporting "they would do it"	Percentage reporting "they had done it"
Peaceful demonstration	75.4	35.9	16.9
Signing a petition	49.4	27.3	9.8
Occupation of a building, sit-in	33.3	15.8	4.2
Refusal to pay bills	23.1	12.7	1.4
Blocking traffic	13.9	6.0	2.2
Wildcat strikes	6.5	3.1	1.1
Painting slogans on buildings	6.1	1.9	1.9
Damaging property	1.1	0.4	0.5
Personal violence	1.5	0.4	0.3

Source: Sartori and Marradi study.

have also a high expressive value makes it even more likely that they will be adopted.

THE EROSION OF THE CATHOLIC TRADITION

We have seen before that the clerical/secular dimension is still one of the important cleavages of the Italian polity. But the persistence of this cleavage dimension does not mean that the balance of clerical and secular forces has remained unchanged. In recent years secularization has made considerable inroads, as the outcome of the 1974 referendum on the divorce issue indicates.

The influence of the church among large masses of voters was based on the important role this institution played in the process of socialization and social control. I have argued elsewhere that

> . . . the effectiveness of the Church in channelling the votes toward the DC depended on the existence of three main conditions. The first condition was the will to do so, that is a strategic choice on the part of the Church of the Christian Democratic party as the force that could represent in the political arena the interest of the Catholic institution and, perhaps more important, prevent "anti-Christian forces" from acquiring political power. The second condition was the availability of an efficient and responsive tool that could be used to supplement the party's efforts and in many cases do the job that the inadequate party organization could not do. The third, and in a sense more critical factor, was the existence of an audience, a large segment of the population for whom the church was a fundamental point of reference, a guiding light even in political matters. In brief, the Church could deliver the Catholic vote, if it chose to do so, because there was a tradition to be tapped and an organizational weapon that could translate attachments to a religious institution into partisan preferences.[90]

In the last few years a number of developments seem to have somewhat impaired the ability of the church to exercise as much influence as it used to be able to in the past.

First of all, the church itself has been divided over the issue of the role it should play in social and political matters. There have been many symptoms of dissent within the hierarchy and of tensions between the lay and ecclesiastical segments of the Catholic world. The church level of support for the Christian

Democrats appears to have declined in recent years. Toward the end of 1975 segments of the hierarchy staged a return to the rigid posture of an earlier period, but it is not clear whether these orientations are widely shared by the clergy or whether they represent the position of a conservative minority. In any event, it cannot be taken for granted that even renewed efforts by the church will be effective. In fact, there is some evidence indicating that the influence of the clergy among the population during the 1974 referendum campaign was limited. As the figures of Table VIII.10 show, in terms of attempts to influence the mass public the clergy appears to have played a relatively minor role as compared to families, friends, party activists, and union members. Perhaps these data underemphasize the true amount of influence still wielded by the clergy; perhaps they reflect low commitment rather than a lower capacity to influence. But the suspicion that the church might no longer be a significant reference group for wide segments of the population is not entirely unjustified.

Second, it is well known that over the last ten years there has been a gradual decay of the organizational network inspired and sponsored by the church. The organizational weapon that was so successful in the political battles of the first part of the postwar period is no longer an effective and pliable instrument. Catholic associations have suffered from loss of members,

TABLE VIII.10   *Sources of Influence in the 1974 Referendum Campaign* [a]

Source of contact	Entire sample	DC voters	Very religious response
Members of the family	38.1	39.5	37.8
Friends, workmates, colleagues	35.6	31.7	27.5
Politicians, party activists	12.0	11.4	10.3
Clergy	9.1	14.7	16.4
Union members, activists	5.2	2.6	3.2

[a] Figures are percentages of answers, not respondents, containing references to the different sources of contacts. Reelaboration of data published in *Ricerche Demoscopiche* 6, no. 2 (May–June 1974).

inadequate recruitment of new cadres, and internal divisions within the leadership. Although there are symptoms of a renewal of enthusiasm among Catholic youth, for example, the emergence of the new movement Comunione e Liberazione, it cannot be taken for granted that the organizational machinery will respond as effectively and enthusiastically in the 1970s as it did in the late 1940s and 1950s.

Third, there are indications that the pool of Catholics loyal to the church and ready to comply with its directives even in political matters is gradually shrinking. Over the last twenty years there has been a gradual but continuous decline in religious practice.[91] In 1972 some 30 percent of the people interviewed reported attending church less frequently than they used to five years before. The decline was more pronounced among the young, the better educated, and the residents of large urban centers.[92] Data collected in 1975 lead to the conclusion that, if anything, the phenomenon has become even more pronounced in recent years. There is also evidence that sympathy for the clergy is declining, as is the willingness of the population to accept the intervention of the church in political affairs. Correspondingly, there has been an increase of secular stances on issues such as divorce and abortion.[93] The fact that the younger cohorts are markedly less "clerical" reflects probably both life-cycle effects as well as genuine generational differences. But it is safe to conclude that the influence of the church and its related organizations is gradually being eroded.

THE LEGITIMATION OF THE COMMUNIST PARTY

In the last few years, and especially since 1973, the focus of political debate in Italy has been on the *questione comunista,* that is, on the role that this party should play in the political system. For most of the postwar period the case against the Communist party (PCI) built by anti-Communist forces, and primarily by the Christian Democrats, rested on three propositions: *(a)* that it was an anticlerical, antireligious force; *(b)* that it was not a democratic force, that is, it had no commitment to the maintenance of the rules of representative democracy; and *(c)* that the party had strong ties with the international Communist movement and particularly with the Soviet Union. These arguments articulated by the elites in their polemical exchanges

TABLE VIII.11.   *Compatibility Between Catholicism, Socialism, and Communism*

Percentage agreeing that one can be a good Communist or Socialist and a good Catholic at the same time	1953	1961	1963	1968	1970	1972
Good Socialist	37	47	58	66	78	—
Good Communist	21	19	28	36	44	55

Sources: Data for 1953 to 1970 are from *Bollettino della DOXA* 24, nos. 7–8 (April 1970). Data for 1972 from the Barnes-Sani study.

with the PCI were reflected quite well in mass orientations existing in the early 1970s. In recent years, however, the positions of segments of the moderate electorate toward the Communist party appear to have changed. While it is clear that the objections toward the PCI are still shared by a considerable portion of the electorate, the anti-Communist barrier is no longer as solid as it once was.[94]

One of the obstacles faced by the PCI for many years was the incompatibility between Communism and Catholicism in the minds of many people. From the 1940s to the mid 1960s this objection to the PCI was widespread. In fact, for a number of years the objection held even against the Socialist party. But as the time series reported in Table VIII.11 indicate, in the 1970s the picture has changed considerably. Some change has also occurred with respect to popular perceptions of the PCI as a nondemocratic force. In the relatively short period of four years the objection to the PCI as a "serious danger to freedom" has become considerably less popular.[95] There is no recent evidence on the third proposition, ties of the party with the Soviet Union, but the highly publicized recent statement by the party's secretary at the 25th Congress of the Soviet Communist party, as well as his proclamations of the Italian way to socialism, have probably affected mass orientations. It is hard to say whether this softening of opposition to the PCI is likely to continue and at what rate. But the evidence reviewed certainly supports the notion that the party is gradually coming to be viewed as a more legitimate political force than was the case in the past.

As to the factors underlying this evolution of the electorate, one can advance several suppositions. It seems to me likely that the changing views of the population are the results of a number of converging factors: the moderate stance of the PCI on many issues; its explicit acceptance of democratic institutions; the toning down of its anticlerical stance; a more favorable disposition toward the PCI by traditionally anti-Communist social and political elites; and a more favorable image of the party projected by segments of the mass media.[96] Whatever other factors might be involved, it is clear that the prospect of the PCI entering a coalition government, which was simply unthinkable for most of the postwar period, is gradually becoming more acceptable.

CONCLUSIONS

In the preceding two sections of the chapter I have briefly reviewed what seemed to me to be the key, enduring traits and the novel elements of contemporary Italian culture. The blend of old and new is typical of a culture in transition that reflects the considerable socioeconomic change undergone by the society, as well as the important political developments of the last decade.

The coexistence of the political beliefs of an older era with the new orientations is explainable, in part, by generational change, the passing away of older cohorts of voters and the entry on the political scene of new generations of political actors. We should keep in mind that approximately half of the 1976 electors have come into political life since the time of the *Civic Culture* study. Perhaps even more significant is the fact that one-fifth of the contemporary voters have become part of the electorate in 1972 or later.

These new generations have been socialized under rather different political circumstances from those of their elders. They have generally enjoyed a higher standard of living, they are better educated, and they have higher expectations. They are politically more aware and more inclined to get involved in political action. They are also much less clerical than older voters and their sympathies go more often to the parties of the left.

Whether the political culture of the new generations can be taken as an indication of the modal set of orientations that will prevail in the future is uncertain. The differences between age groups now apparent might reflect life-cycle phenomena as much as truly generational differences. But in view of the far-reaching transformation of Italian society, a return to the political culture of the first part of the postwar period appears to be highly unlikely.

NOTES

1. The popularity of *The Civic Culture* can be gauged by the relatively high number of citations of this work in the social science literature. See *Social Sciences Citation Index*, 1973, 1974, and 1975 editions (Philadelphia: Institute for Scientific Information).

2. Among the more interesting works based entirely on a reanalysis of the five-nation study data is Giuseppe di Palma, *Apathy and Participation: Mass Politics in Western Societies* (New York: The Free Press, 1970).

3. See, for example, Joseph La Palombara, "Italy: Fragmentation, Isolation, and Alienation," in Lucian W. Pye and Sidney Verba, eds., *Political Culture and Political Development* (Princeton, N.J.: Princeton Univ. Press, 1965), pp. 282–329; Sidney Tarrow, *Peasant Communism in Southern Italy* (New Haven: Yale Univ. Press, 1967); Raphael Zariski, *Italy: The Politics of Uneven Development* (Hinsdale, Ill.: The Dryden Press, 1972), esp. chap. 3.

4. The longest review of which I am aware is from Guido Martinotti, in *Quaderni di Sociologia* 15 (July–December 1966): 440–43.

5. See Gianfranco Poggi's review of Hadley Cantril's *The Politics of Despair*, in *Rassegna Italiana di Sociologia*, I (1961), p. 119. Edward Banfield, *The Moral Basis of a Backward Society* (Glencoe, Ill.: The Free Press, 1958), and the reply by Alessandro Pizzorno, "Familismo amorale e marginalita' storica, ovvero perche' non c'e' niente da fare a Montegrano," in *Quaderni di Sociologia*, July–September 1967. Sidney Tarrow, *Peasant Communism*, and the observations by Giovanni Sartori in *Quaderni di Sociologia* 17 (July 1968), and Tarrow's preface to the Italian translation of his volume *Partito comunista e contadini nel mezzogiorno* (Torino: Einaudi, 1972), p. ix.

6. As far as I know the only excerpts from *The Civic Culture* translated into Italian appear in my section, "Cultura politica e comportamento politico," in Giovanni Sartori, ed., *Antologia di scienza politica* (Bologna: Il Mulino, 1969).

7. One of the few examples of secondary analysis of the Italian data set is Massimo Paci, "Mobilita sociale e partecipazione politica," in *Quaderni di Sociologia* 15 (July–December 1966): 387–410.

8. John Clarke Adams and Paolo Barile, *The Government of Republican Italy*, 1st ed. (Boston: Houghton Mifflin, 1961); Norman Kogan, *The Government of Italy* (New York: Thomas Y. Crowell, 1962).

9. Gabriel A. Almond, *The Appeals of Communism* (Princeton, N.J.: Princeton Univ. Press, 1954); Hadley Cantril, *The Politics of Despair* (New York: Basic Books, 1958).

10. Seymour Martin Lipset, *Political Man* (Garden City, N.Y.: Doubleday, 1960).

11. Pierpaolo Luzzatto Fegiz, *Il volto sconosciuto dell' Italia, dieci anni di sondaggi DOXA* (Milan: Giuffre', 1956).

12. The 1300 pages of *Il volto sconosciuto* contain information about a

wide variety of topics. Part 1 deals with "daily life." Part 2 contains the results of polls on the family, marriage, and divorce. Parts 3 and 4 cover political subjects ranging from the constitution, parties, incumbents in office, to the great powers, etc. Part 5 deals with education, information, and religion. Parts 6 and 7 are devoted to economic problems. It should be pointed out that although this work is basically descriptive, the data presented are broken down by sex, age, social class, partisan preference, region, etc.; thus the reader is given a great deal of information on the distribution of opinions in different social groups.

13. Pierpaolo Luzzatto Fegiz, *Il volto sconosciuto dell' Italia*, 2nd series, 1956–65 (Milan: Giuffre', 1966).

14. Alberto Spreafico and Joseph La Palombara, eds., *Elezioni e comportamento politico in Italia* (Milan: Comunita', 1963).

15. The twenty-two contributions to the volume are based on a variety of data. Among the essays drawing primarily or largely on survey data are Joseph La Palombara, "L'orientamento politico della gioventu,'" pp. 495–516; Alberto Spreafico, "Orientamento politico e identificazione partitica," pp. 689–732; Paolo Ammassari, "Opinione politica e scelta elettorale," pp. 733–84; Mattei Dogan, "Le donne italiane tra il cattolicesimo ed il marxismo," pp. 475–94.

16. The results of the study were reported in the following four volumes: Giorgio Galli, ed., *Il comportamento elettorale in Italia* (Bologna: Il Mulino, 1968); Gianfranco Poggi, ed., *L'organizzazione partitica del PCI e della DC* (Bologna: Il Mulino, 1968); Francesco Alberoni, ed., *L'attivista di partito* (Bologna: Il Mulino, 1967); Agoupik Manoukian, ed., *La presenza sociale del PCI e della DC* (Bologna: Il Mulino, 1968). For a synthesis of the findings in English, see Giorgio Galli and Alfonso Prandi, *Patterns of Political Participation in Italy* (New Haven: Yale Univ. Press, 1970).

17. Francesco Alberoni, Introduction, *L'attivista di partito*.

18. Alessandro Pizzorno, "Introduzione allo studio della partecipazione politica," in *Quaderni di Sociologia* 15 (July–December, 1966): 235–87. See in the same issue a number of empirical studies by Guido Martinotti, Giordano Sivini, Massimo Paci, and Laura Balbo.

19. Almond and Verba, *The Civic Culture* (Princeton, N.J.: Princeton Univ. Press, 1963), p. 493.

20. Ibid., p. 496.

21. Giovanni Sartori, "European Political Parties: The Case of Polarized Pluralism," in Joseph La Palombara and Myron Weiner, eds., *Political Parties and Political Development* (Princeton, N.J.: Princeton Univ. Press, 1966), pp. 137–76; Sartori, "Modelli spaziali di competizione tra partiti," *Rassegna Italiana di Sociologia* (January–March 1965), pp. 7–29; Sartori, "Rivisitando il pluralismo polarizzato," in Fabio Luca Cavazza and Stephen R. Graubard, eds., *Il caso italiano* (Milan: Garzanti, 1974), pp. 196–223; Giorgio Galli, *Il bipartitismo imperfetto* (Bologna: Il Mulino, 1966); Calli, *Il difficile governo* (Bologna: Il Mulino, 1972).

22. Sartori, "European Political Parties," p. 152, n. 25; also pp. 165–66; Galli, *Il difficile governo*, p. 7.

23. The importance of international constraints is rightly emphasized by Gianfranco Pasquino, "Pesi internazionali e contrappesi nazionali," *Il caso italiano*, pp. 163–82.

24. Cavazza and Graubard, eds., *Il caso italiano*.

25. Almond and Verba, *Civic Culture*, pp. 402–4.

26. This conclusion is shared by scholars who have not spared criticism

of the functioning of the political system. See, for example, Giorgio Galli and Alfonso Prandi, *Patterns of Political Participation in Italy*, p. 307; also, Sidney Tarrow, "Italy: Political Integration in a Fragmented Political System," paper delivered at the 1975 meeting of the American Political Science Association, San Francisco, September 1975.

27. That observers and political commentators have generally overestimated the degree of information and involvement of the citizenry is apparent from a perusal of the press. I have discussed this point in my essay "L'immagine dei partiti nell'elettorato," in Mario Caciagli and Alberto Spreafico, eds., *Un sistema politico alla prova* (Bologna: Il Mulino, 1976), pp. 85–126.

28. From a comment made by Luzzatto Fegiz (founder of *DOXA*, the oldest survey organization in Italy), with reference to a survey conducted in September 1947. See Pierpaolo Luzzatto Fegiz, *Il volto sconosciuto dell' Italia* (Milan: Giuffre', 1956), p. 446.

29. Evidence of the phenomenon of concealed partisanship is abundant. See, for example, the following: Alberto Spreafico, "Orientamento politico e identificazione partitica" and Joseph La Palombara, "L'atteggiamento politico della gioventu'," in Alberto Spreafico and Joseph La Palombara, eds., *Elezioni e comportamento politico in Italia* (Milan: Comunita', 1963), pp. 707–9, 510–12; Gianfranco Poggi, *Le preferenze politiche degli Italiani* (Bologna: Il Mulino, 1968), p. 21; Samuel H. Barnes, "Italy: Religion and Class in Electoral Behavior," in Richard Rose, ed., *Electoral Behavior: A Comparative Handbook* (New York: The Free Press, 1974), p. 189; Carlo Tullio Altan, *I valori difficili* (Milan: Bompiani, 1974), p. 50 and Table 83, p. 216; Pierpaolo Benedetti, *I giovani e la politica* (Milan: Angeli, 1974), pp. 60–71.

30. Some examples of these expressions of protest recorded in the protocols of a survey conducted by the author in the fall of 1975 are the following: "The vote is secret," "My vote is my business," "One does not say these things."

31. Almond and Verba, *Civic Culture*, pp. 116–22.

32. For my reanalysis of the *Civic Culture* study I have used the data set made available by the Inter-University Consortium of Political Research. *Codebook* and documentation are to be found in *The Five Nation Study*, rev. ICPR ed., 1968.

33. The turnout rate figures are from Instituto Centrale di Statistica, *Compendio Statistico Italiano* (Rome, 1975), p. 111.

34. The frequency of "don't know" responses given by hidden partisans ranged from 45 to 60 percent for questions involving specific references to political parties. It was much lower (5 to 15 percent) for questions nonpolitical in nature. Moreover, hidden partisans had a less positive attitude toward the interview and were less likely to report their income. There is ground for suspecting that they deliberately presented to the interviewers a somewhat distorted image of themselves, one which emphasized noninvolvement, passivity, and ignorance of political matters.

35. A comparison of rates of underrepresentation in five major Italian surveys is presented in my essay "Mass Level Response to Party Strategy: The Italian Electorate and the Communist Party," in Donald L. Blackmer and Sidney Tarrow, eds., *Communism in Italy and France* (Princeton, N.J.: Princeton Univ. Press, 1975), Table 4, p. 467.

36. It is worthwhile to point out that the respondents' anxiety, although perhaps exaggerated, is not without foundation. In early 1976 a number of

Fiat executives and former police officers were scheduled to be tried on the charge of having assembled in the 1950s large files containing information (including political leanings) about workers and job applicants. According to reports in the press there were over 350,000 such files. See *Corriere della Sera*, January 18, 1976.

37. Some indirect clues on the partisan preference of the hidden partisans emerge from the analysis of responses to questions on church attendance, interparty marriage, etc. Although no firm conclusions can be reached, it seems that the Christian Democrats and moderate voters are overrepresented even among hidden partisans.

38. Naturally this finding does not demonstrate that the second portrait is more accurate than the first. It simply shows that some significant changes result from the adjustment of the sample to fit the pattern of party preference existing at the time. Whether we should accept this second portrait as more accurate depends on the acceptance of a crucial assumption: namely, that the avowed partisans adequately represent party supporters in the electorate. But as Barnes has pointed out, this assumption too can be subjected to crticism. (Samuel Barnes, "Italy: Religion and Class," p. 189.)

39. It is doubtful that the distinction between cognition and evaluation makes much sense to mass political actors. To a respondent who is basically suspicious, even questions that plainly deal with knowledge about politics might appear to be surreptitious ways of ascertaining where he or she stands in terms of partisanship.

40. Almond and Verba, *Civic Culture*, p. 82.

41. Ibid., p. 268.

42. An example of the problems involved in reaching conclusions on the basis of a limited number of cases is Almond and Verba's discussion of different types of partisans. After presenting the pertinent figures for Italy, they conclude that "Italy presents us with a curious anomaly of a political system in which the formal democratic constitution is supported in large part by traditional clerical elements who are not democratic at all. . . . Opposed to the constitution is a left wing which . . . manifests a form of open partisanship that is consistent with a democratic system" (p. 160). As the attentive reader will notice, this rather sweeping conclusion is based on the response of thirty-one Communist voters. It is true that more open partisans were to be found among the thirty-nine Socialist respondents. But in 1959 the Socialists could hardly be classified as part of an anticonstitutional opposition. By the time *The Civic Culture* appeared, the PSI was part of a center-left governmental coalition. In any event it is doubtful that the thirty-one or even seventy leftist respondents were typical of the mass of PCI and PSI voters. Di Palma has correctly observed that "Only a few Italian respondents acknowledged a sympathy for the left; . . . (they may be a special group having an overt commitment to their party and personal strength and articulateness that render them politically more effective and more outspoken," *Apathy and Participation*, p. 102).

43. Sidney G. Tarrow, "Political Dualism and Italian Communism," *American Political Science Review* 61, no. 1 (March 1967); Norman Kogan, "Review of Sidney G. Tarrow 'Peasant Communism in Southern Italy,'" *American Political Science Review* 62, no. 4 (December 1968): 1282–83.

44. As a matter of fact, Italian observers and commentators tend to apply the left/right conceptualization of politics to situations and events occurring in political arenas where this dimension is not so deeply rooted, or is altogether not meaningful. Insofar as this signals their inability to interpret

political realities without the left/right filters, this practice is quite revealing and gives us an indication of the pervasiveness of the construct.

45. Giacomo Sani, "A Test of the Least Distance Model of Voting Choice in Italy, 1972," in *Comparative Political Studies* 7, no. 2 (July 1974): 206–7.

46. Samuel H. Barnes, "Left, Right and the Italian Voter," *Comparative Political Studies*, 4 (July 1971): 157–75; also, "Modelli spaziali e l'identificazione partitica dell' elettore italiano," in *Rivista Italiana di Scienza Politica* 1 (1971): 123–43.

47. Barnes, "Left, Right"; Sani, "A Test of the Least Distance."

48. Sani, "A Test of the Least Distance," p. 205; Ronald Inglehart and Hans D. Klingemann, "Party Identification, Ideological Preference, and the Left–Right Dimension Among Western Publics," in Ian Budge et al., *Party Identification and Beyond* (New York: Wiley, 1976), pp. 226–242. According to this latter source, in 1973 some 83 percent of the sample placed themselves on a ten-point left/right scale.

49. For a distribution of the positions assigned to the four major parties, see my "L'immagine dei partiti nell'elettorato," in Caciagli and Spreafico, eds., *Un sistema politico alla prova*, Fig. 1, p. 103.

50. Inglehart and Klingemann, "Party Identification"; Barnes, "Left, Right and the Italian Voter"; Giacomo Sani, "Determinants of Party Preference in Italy: Toward the Integration of Complementary Models," *American Journal of Political Science* 18 (1974): 315–29.

51. In "A Test of the Least Distance Model," I have argued: "If the learning of orientations to specific political objects occurs contemporarily with the induction in the prevailing terminology of the political culture, position on the left-right continuum and choice of party become inextricably linked. The acquisition of partisan preference and of a left-right identification go hand in hand because of the connections established between specific parties and the positions prevailing in the relevant cultural milieu. In this light, it is little wonder that many respondents assign to themselves exactly the same position they had assigned to the party of their choice" (p. 207).

52. See the data presented in my essay "Mass Level Response to Party Strategy: The Italian Electorate and the Communist Party," in Donald L. Blackmer and Sidney Tarrow, eds., *Communism in Italy and France,* pp. 456–503.

53. Giacomo Sani, "Mass Constraints on Political Realignments: Perceptions of Anti-System Parties in Italy," *British Journal of Political Science* 6, no. 1 (January 1976).

54. Sartori, "Polarized Pluralism," p. 149.

55. For a review of this literature, see Douglas Wertman, "The Electorate of Religiously Based Parties," Ph.D. dissertation, Ohio State University, August 1974.

56. For the evidence, see Gianfranco Poggi, *Le preferenze politiche degli italiani* (Bologna: Il Mulino, 1968); Laurence E. Hazelrigg, "Religious and Class Bases of Political Conflict in Italy," *American Journal of Sociology* 75, no. 4 (January 1970): 496–511; Samuel Barnes, "Italy: Religion and Class in Electoral Behavior"; Sani, "Determinants of Party Preference."

57. The relationship is apparent in a great many of the tables presented by Luzzatto Fegiz in *Il volto sconosciuto dell'Italia;* evidence from other data in Giacomo Sani, "Ricambio elettorale e identificazioni partitiche: verso una egemonia delle sinistre?" *Rivista Italiana di Scienza Politica* 3 (1975): 515–44.

58. The evolution of the Communist party in the 1960s and in the early

1970s is discussed in several essays of the volume edited by Blackmer and Tarrow, *Communism in Italy and France*. Within parties of the left the Radicals, Socialists, and PDUP have been more outspoken in their anticlerical posture.

59. La Palombara, "Italy: Alienation, Fragmentation, Isolation," p. 290.

60. Galli et al., *Il comportamento elettorale in Italia;* Alberto Spreafico, "Risultati elettorali ed evoluzione del sistema partitico," in *Un sistema politico alla prova*.

61. Giacomo Sani and Samuel Barnes, "Partisan Change and the Italian Voters: Some Clues from the 1972 Election," 1973 (mimeo).

62. Sani, "Ricambio elettorale e identificazioni partitiche."

63. Five-Nation Study, ICPR *Codebook*, p. 53.

64. Sani, "Political Traditions as Contextual Variables"; Italia Maria Orlandini, "L'atteggiamento politico delle casalinghe," thesis University of Florence, 1965–66.

65. La Palombara, "Italy: Alienation, Fragmentation, Isolation," pp. 292–93.

66. Barnes, "Italy: Religion and Class in Electoral Behavior"; Sani, "Mass Level Response to Party Strategy."

67. Sani, "Canali di comunicazione politica e orientamenti dell'elettorato," *Rivista Italiana di Scienza Politica* 4, no. 2 (1974): 371–86.

68. Almond and Verba, *Civic Culture*, p. 137.

69. Sani, "Mass Level Response to Party Strategy."

70. Sartori, "European Political Parties."

71. See the discussion in *Il caso italiano*, especially Sartori, "Rivisitando il pluralismo polarizzato," and Juan Linz, "La democrazia italiana di fronte al futuro," pp. 124–62.

72. Franco Cazzola, "Consenso ed opposizione nel parlamento italiano," *Rivista Italiana di Scienza Politica* 1 (1972), and recently Giuseppe di Palma, *Surviving Without Governing: The Italian Parties in Parliament* (Berkeley, Calif.: Univ. of California Press, 1977).

73. Sani, "Mass Constraints on Coalition Realignments."

74. The coordinates of the points representing the different political objects in Fig. VIII.2 correspond to the values of the second and sixth column of Table VIII.6.

75. Almond and Verba, *Civic Culture*, chap. 3; La Palombara, "Italy: Alienation, Isolation, Fragmentation"; Sani, "L'immagine dei partiti nello elettorato."

76. All the figures are from Luzzatto Fegiz, *Il volto sconosciuto della Italia*, 2: 552, 555, 560, 535, 476, 488.

77. Figures for 1961 from *Il volto sconosciuto,* for 1972 from the Barnes–Sani study.

78. Figures for 1959 in Almond and Verba, *Civic Culture*, p. 116; for 1964, in *Il volto sconosciuto*, p. 508.

79. *Ricerche Demoscopiche* 1, no. 2 (1975): 29.

80. *Bollettino della DOXA* 30, no. 4 (February 16, 1976).

81. Figures on levels of education and availability of television are from *Compendio statistico italiano*, 1965 and 1975.

82. Sani, "L'immagine dei partiti nell'elettorato," p. 91.

83. Almond and Verba, *Civic Culture*, p. 403.

84. *Bollettino della DOXA* 30, nos. 21–22 (December 23, 1975).

85. Barnes–Sani 1972 election study.

86. Data for 1971 and 1974 from *Ricerche Demoscopiche* 1, no. 2 (1975): 35; for 1972, from the Barnes–Sani study.

87. *Bollettino DOXA* 30, nos. 9–10 (June 24, 1975).

88. For example, perception of dishonesty increased from 21 to 34 percent and perception of tax revenues wasted from 25 to 37 percent.

89. In January 1977 the Italian prime minister, Giulio Andreotti, reported to parliament that 1200 cases of political violence had occurred in the preceding year.

90. Sani, "Secular Trends and Party Re-alignments."

91. The percentage of respondents going to church weekly has dropped from a high point of 70 percent in 1956 to approximately 30 percent in the mid-1970s.

92. Sani, "Secular Trends and Party Re-Alignments."

93. *Ricerche Demoscopiche* 2 (1974); *Bollettino DOXA,* 39, nos. 7–8(1975).

94. Recent changes in the image of the Communist party are documented in my essay, "La nuova immagine del PCI e l'ellettorato italiano," in Donald L. Blackmer and Sidney Tarrow, eds., *Il Comunismo in Italia e in Francia* (Milan: Etas/Libri, 1976).

95. *Ricerche Demoscopiche* 7 (1975).

96. This argument is developed in my essay, "The PCI on the Threshold," *Problems of Communism* (November–December 1976), pp. 27–51.

CHAPTER IX

Political Culture in Mexico: Continuities and Revisionist Interpretations

Ann L. Craig and Wayne A. Cornelius
University of California, San Diego

GABRIEL ALMOND AND Sidney Verba's eleventh-hour decision to substitute Mexico for Sweden in their cross-national survey resulted in the first large-scale empirical study of political culture in Mexico. Until then, the discussion about politics and political culture in Mexico revolved around eloquent, reflective essays based on subjective interpretations of Mexican history or very limited psychoanalytic data from clinical experiences. Almond and Verba's work shifted the discussion to empirical studies based on research explicitly designed to explore Mexican attitudes and cognitions which might influence political participation. Nearly all survey studies of political attitudes and behavior conducted in Mexico since 1959 have attempted to replicate (though usually in modified form) some portions of the *Civic Culture* survey. And even among Mexicanists whose own work has not been influenced by the study, it has generated considerable debate about the theoretical utility and normative assumptions of the study of political culture. In reviewing this debate in the Mexican context, we must begin by acknowledging that the possibility of the debate depends largely upon having studies like *The Civic Culture* as specific points of reference.

This volume is designed as a critique of *The Civic Culture* and a summary of subsequent research on political culture in each of the five countries included in the original study. In fulfilling this dual task, we have devoted the first section of this chapter on Mexico to a discussion of the principal methodological and substantive weaknesses of Almond and Verba's treatment of the Mexican case. In the second section, we turn our attention to three general themes — authoritarian politics, subjective political competence (political efficacy), and political cynicism — in recent empirical research on political attitudes and behavior in Mexico. These themes also provide useful points of comparison with the *Civic Culture* analysis. In the concluding section, we outline some of the central issues which might be pursued in further research on political culture in Mexico.

MEXICO IN *THE CIVIC CULTURE*: A CRITIQUE

We have carefully reviewed the original volume with attention to the major methodological and interpretive problems. Some of the methodological problems emphasized here became apparent as researchers have become sensitized through experience with sample surveys conducted in Mexico since 1959. Some of our criticisms address weaknesses which are an outgrowth of the complexity and technical demands of cross-national survey research. We focus on three major areas of methodological difficulties: the sample, translation ambiguities or errors, and problems of validity or equivalence. These problems are covered in some detail because they involve the accuracy or generalizability of some interpretations in the Almond and Verba study. The first half of this section is devoted to these methodological problems. In the second half, we turn to substantive criticisms of the Mexican analysis.

METHODOLOGICAL PROBLEMS

The Sample. In Appendix A,[1] we are informed that the Mexican sample for *The Civic Culture* was drawn in 27 cities with populations of 10,000 or more, dispersed throughout the nation.[2] We assume that the sample was limited to this urban population because of the cost and relative difficulty of sampling and interviewing rural dwellers. Nonetheless, the exclusion of rural dwellers (which constituted 63 percent of the Mexican population in 1960), produces a major gap in the data and requires serious qualification of many interpretations, even in cross-national comparisons. In a footnote on Italian–Mexican differences in political cognition and communication, we are told that the Mexican sample was compared with that part of the Italian sample living in towns of 10,000 and larger. "The results differed only by a small number of percentage points and confirmed the conclusion discussed here." [3] This statistical double check assures us that on the point of political cognition the comparisons between the Mexican and Italian samples are valid. Similar checks are not reported elsewhere in the study, despite the possibility that other comparisons involving the Mexican results may have been affected by the exclusion of rural dwellers from the sample.

In the absence of extensive empirical research on political culture in rural Mexico, we can only suggest some possible consequences of the urban bias of the sample. In Mexico there are great advantages accruing to urban residence, in terms of access to basic services, education, and opportunities for economic improvement.[4] As González Casanova has written: "There is a kind of integral marginality. The population which is marginal in terms of one factor is highly likely to be marginal in terms of all the others. Thus there is an immense number of Mexicans who have nothing of nothing." [5] Access to political information and personal contact with political and governmental officials, especially outside the arena of electoral politics, are also strongly associated with urban residence. Opportunities for involvement in most types of politically relevant organizations — parties, labor unions, community action groups, etc. — are also relatively more numerous in urban areas. In short, the average urban dweller is likely to be much better endowed with the opportunities and resources which translate into political involvement than is his rural counterpart. His sense of political efficacy and more generally his image and evaluations of the government may therefore differ significantly. Owing to the much greater visibility of political and governmental activities in urban areas, the urban dweller may be better able to distinguish among political parties, government agencies, and incumbents of certain political roles. The rural population is more strongly influenced by the Catholic Church and its enduring adversary relationship with the civil authorities. In general, then, much of the diversity in Mexican political culture may have been obscured by the urban bias of the sample. In addition, by excluding the rural population, the *Civic Culture* sample also introduced an ethnic bias, since the vast majority of Mexico's Indian population is heavily concentrated in small rural communities.

Furthermore, although the Mexican sample is described as a representative sample of the national *urban* population, a careful reading of the description of the sampling procedure raises questions about the representativeness of the urban sample. We are told that "the assignment of interviews in each city . . . was made through the use of the latest block maps available." [6] Our experience has demonstrated that available block maps are invariably several years out of date and, most significantly, exclude major, low-income zones of the urban periphery which are usually the most recently settled areas, often without urban services, street layouts, or discrete blocks of housing.[7] It is possible, therefore, that not only rural dwellers but also a significant portion of the urban low-income population were excluded from the *Civic Culture* sample.

Another source of bias in Almond and Verba's Mexican sample is the high rate of sample mortality. The rate at which interviews were completed with originally selected elements of the Mexican sample — only 60 percent — compares unfavorably with the rate achieved in three other countries included in the study (74 percent in Germany and Italy, 83 percent in the United States), and with other recent survey studies of political attitudes and behavior in Mexico.[8]

The Translation. Our examination of the English and Spanish versions of the questionnaire used by Almond and Verba revealed several apparent English-to-Spanish translation errors, which may have affected the responses obtained in Mexico. The most significant Spanish deviations from the English equivalent are presented in Table IX.1. In the case of item 7, the second statement presented to the Spanish speaker is much more strongly worded than the English original ("Others say that one should distrust the majority of people" *vs.* "Others say you can't be too careful in your dealings with people"). In items 31a through 32b the English version asks about government "activities," whereas the Mexican respondent is referred to government "laws and regulations." In a country where laws and regulations are relatively unfamiliar compared with government projects and policies (a more likely connotation of "activities"), the differences in terminology may have affected response patterns. The most significant translation error occurs in item 36b. In Spanish, the respondent was asked whether the ideals and goals of the Mexican Revolution had been realized, whether "it is *still necessary to work* in order to realize them," or whether they have been forgotten. The English version of the second alternative asks whether "the people holding [the ideals and goals of the Revolution — presumably government officials] *are still working* to realize them." In this instance, the Spanish version probably inflated the proportion of respondents selecting the second alternative. Sixty-one percent of the respondents chose this alternative. Almond and Verba's interpretation of the responses, stressing the relationship between this question and other expressions of symbolic identification with the Mexican Revolution,[9] suggests that they were unaware of the translation error.

Validity and Conceptual Equivalence. Several questions included in the *Civic Culture* questionnaire may have different meanings or experiential referents in Mexico compared with the other four countries included in the study. A number of these items seem to be inappropriate to the sociopolitical context, or subject to a variety of interpretations by respondents.

Two of the most important items of questionable appropriateness form part of the political competence scale, which plays an important role in the *Civic Culture* analysis. Questions 25 through 29 asked the respondent to consider what he might do if the local and national governments were considering a law or regulation that the respondent considered unjust or harmful, the likelihood that he/she would actually attempt to secure a change in the law or regulation, the probability that this attempt would succeed, and whether the respondent had ever attempted

TABLE IX.1. *Comparison of Spanish and English Version of Selected Items from the* Civic Culture *Questionnaire*

Item no.	Spanish version [a]	Item no.	English version [b]
7	Algunas personas dicen que uno puede confiar en la mayoría de la gente. Otros dicen que uno debe desconfiar de la mayoría de la gente. Qué opina usted al respecto?	7	Some people say that most people can be trusted. Others say you can't be too careful in your dealings with people. How do you feel about it?
31a	Pensando en el gobierno federal de la Ciudad de México, qué tanto afectan la vida diaria de usted las leyes y decretos establecidos—le afectan mucho, regular, nada?	31a	Thinking now about the national government in (London, Bonn . . . etc.) about how much effect do you think its activities, the laws passed and so on, have on your day-to-day life? Do they have a great effect, some effect or none?
31b	Considerando todo, tienden a mejorar la vida de usted estas leyes y decretos del gobierno federal de México, o estaría usted mejor sin ellas?	31b	On the whole, do the activities of the national government tend to improve conditions in this country or would we be better off without them?
32a	Pensando en el gobierno (de la ciudad de . . .) (de Uruchurtu) qué tanto afectan la vida diaria de usted las leyes y reglamentos establecidos por el gobierno (de la ciudad de. . .) (de Uruchurtu) le afectan mucho, regular, o nada?	32a	Now take the local government, about how much effect do you think its activities have on your day-to-day life? Do they have a great effect, some effect, or none?

| 32b | Considerando todo, tienden a mejorar la vida de usted estas leyes y reglamentos del gobierno (de la ciudad de. .) (de Uruchurtu), o estaría usted mejor sin ellas? | 32b | On the whole, do the activities of the local government tend to improve conditions in this area, or would we be better off without them? |
| 36b | (Re principal ideals and goals of the Mexican Revolution mentioned in 36a) (SI MENCIONA ALGO) Diría usted que se han realizado estos ideales y fines, que todavía tiene que trabajarse para realizarlos, o que se les ha olvidado? | 36b | (Re principal ideals and goals of the Mexican Revolution mentioned in 36a) Do you think these ideals and purposes have been realized – Do you think that the people holding them are still working to realize them – Or do you think that these ideals have been forgotten? [c] |

[a] Item number and text refer to the Spanish version of the cross-section interview schedule used in Mexico.
[b] Item number and text refer to the English version of the cross-section interview schedule reproduced in Gabriel Almond and Sidney Verba, *The Civic Culture* (Princeton, N.J.: Princeton Univ. Press, 1963).
[c] Translation from Inter-University Consortium for Political Research, *Codebook for the Five Nation Study: Principal Investigators, Gabriel Almond and Sidney Verba* (Ann Arbor, Mich.: Univ. of Michigan, 1968), p. 46.

such influence. In Mexico 52 percent of the respondents believed that they could do something about a local regulation and 38 percent believed they could do something about a national regulation.[10] These figures are surprisingly high when one considers the way in which such regulations are actually established or modified in Mexico. The highly centralized, presidentially initiated pattern of decision making in Mexico and the general absence of publicity about policy deliberations have the effect of shifting citizen influence on government decision making from the "rule making" to the "rule application" (distributive, implementation) stage. Approaching public officials to seek particularistic (personal or local community-specific) benefits to obtain particularistic "exemptions" from public policies or regulations is both permitted and encouraged by government officials; but demanding major changes in public policies ("laws and regulations") is viewed as threatening and illegitimate activity. The average citizen seems quite aware of the kinds of political action which are likely to be rewarded by the authorities and the kinds which are likely to be ignored or violently repressed. He therefore attempts to influence the government decision-making process only on the output (policy implementation) side.[11] In view of this, we question the utility in the Mexican context of a measure of political competence which ostensibly focuses on citizen influence on policymaking to the exclusion of perceived influence on allocative decisions.

Almond and Verba's interpretation of Mexican political culture as containing "a large aspirational component" [12] depends in part on data demonstrating that Mexicans are willing to express political opinions but have little information on which to base them. This analysis relies on the responses to questions whose appropriateness for measuring political information levels in the Mexican context is doubtful. It would seem most useful to measure political information as that knowledge which respondents would require for the most common or essential forms of political involvement; that is, basic and useful information. If this standard were applied, how appropriate is it, for example, to limit measures of political information in Mexico to the ability to name party leaders or cabinet ministries ("*secretarias o puestos del gabinete*")? The first is a rather esoteric piece of information, since the president of Mexico is also the de facto head of the official party (Partido Revolucionario Institucional — PRI), and the strength and visibility of opposition parties are more regional than national. Such questions could be answered with greater facility in countries where there are numerous prominent party leaders with nationwide constituencies, so that the respondent's level of information need not be limited by the ability to recall a very limited range of alternatives. Furthermore, occupants of most ministerial posts are not key political personages for most Mexicans, but even some of the reasonably well-informed respondents may have been confused by the uncommon word usage ("*gabinete*").

We do not have any estimates of the functional literacy rate for the Almond and Verba sample. According to the official Mexican census in 1960, about 75 percent of the national urban population was "literate," but it is widely acknowledged that the official census statistics include huge numbers of people who are actually functional illiterates.[13] Our concern here is whether functional illiteracy may have reduced the *ability* of numerous interviewees to respond to a substantial number of items included in the *Civic Culture* questionnaire. The survey instrument contains fourteen different questions which asked respondents to read a list of alternatives from a card provided by the interviewer and to select among them. They include items asking about the most effective technique of influencing government decisions (30a), the characteristics of political party supporters (50), patterns of decision making within the family (54a, 54b, 55a, 55b, 55c), the most important problems facing the country (9a), and other topics (6a, 11, 17, 43, 65, 86). In all of the more recent surveys of political attitudes and behavior in Mexico of which we are aware, interviewers were required to read and, if necessary, reread to respondents the alternatives for closed, multiple-choice items. No assumption of literacy was made.

Also problematic in the Mexican context are two additional items used by Almond and Verba as measures of political awareness: questions asking the respondent to assess the impact of government outputs on his daily life (see items 31a and 32a in Table IX.1). The authors report that two-thirds of the Mexican respondents felt that rules and regulations of the national and local governments had no impact on their daily life. In the other four countries, the respondents who perceived no effect of government on their daily lives ranged from 10 to 23 percent.[14] In their interpretation of the data, Almond and Verba suggest that a respondent who believes that the local and/or national government's activities have no effect on his day-to-day life is uninformed or rejects the significance of government outputs.[15] In fact, when one considers that the Spanish translation of these items asks about *laws and regulations* rather than government projects or activities, it is not surprising that relatively few Mexican respondents perceived any relationship between government and their daily lives. Even if the question were understood to refer to government programs and activities, given the extremely unequal distribution of government benefits and services in Mexico, the responses obtained may reflect a highly accurate perception of actual government impact, rather than a lack of "awareness." This is particularly true with regard to local government outputs, which outside of Mexico City, Guadalajara, and one or two other large cities, are of minimal importance.

It is perhaps inevitable that the country specialist will prefer more contextually sensitive measures of certain concepts than the cross-national researcher is able to supply. The measurement problems discussed above were selected, however, with a view toward highlighting the weaknesses these problems introduce into cross-national comparisons based on the resulting data. We do not seek to minimize the importance of the Mexican responses to some of the questionnaire items we have singled out for criticism here. A strong possibility remains, however, that in the Mexican context these questions may have tapped rather different dimensions from those Almond and Verba intended to measure, or that they provide only very partial measures of key attitudes and cognitions.

SUBSTANTIVE CRITICISMS: PATHS NOT TAKEN

In this section we shall consider what we regard as two major substantive deficiencies in Almond and Verba's treatment of the Mexican case: (1) a lack of attention to important within-nation variations, especially in terms of social class and region; and (2) an excessively truncated examination of the process of political socialization. Both of these analytical paths, had they been followed by Almond and Verba, might have led the authors to interpret their data with greater fidelity to the dynamics of political life in contemporary Mexico.

Within-Nation Variations. Students of politics in all five of the nations included in *The Civic Culture* have been critical of its failure sufficiently to examine internal or subnational differences. Such criticisms must be tempered with the acknowledgment that inclusion of the analysis critics find lacking would have resulted in a multivolume work. We believe, however, that a thorough examination of the diversities within each country would have portrayed more accurately the complexity of the national political culture (or cultures), thus satisfying important theoretical concerns and perhaps even amending Almond and Verba's conclusions about democratic participation and stability and the political culture which supports them. *The Civic Culture* does contain some examination of internal differences based on education, party support, competence levels and types, sex, age, and levels of participation in school and family decision making. However, this analysis of subnational differences seems inadequate, particularly for the Mexican case, in two respects: the limited analysis by social class, and the failure to examine regional variations.

First, Almond and Verba's presentation of the data fails to emphasize, as subsequent research in Mexico has demonstrated, that there is an intimate relationship between social class, education, and sex, on the one hand, and political cognitions, attitudes, and behavior, on the other. We consider the absence of extensive class analysis a particularly serious omission based on our reading of subsequent research, although not necessarily because behavior or attitude differences may inhere in class status itself. More important is the *interaction* of sex, income, education, occupational status, and family position, which combine in Mexico to determine one's resources for political participation as well as the terms of individual contact with politics and government.[16] The result, as described by Fagen and Tuohy, is "sharply cumulative patterns of opportunities, resources, and [political] activity," [17] which persist over time because of the absence of corrective mechanisms. We shall elaborate subsequently on the effects of the social status variables as demonstrated in recent research on authoritarianism, political efficacy, and cynicism.

In some respects, Almond and Verba's extensive use of education as an independent and control variable might be taken as quasi-class analysis, were it not that their discussion of the results implies that it is education itself that produces the differences in attitudes and behaviors which they observe. The interrelationships among education and other social status variables alluded to above suggest that the attitudinal and behavioral differences observed may be the result of more complex social processes than Almond and Verba's analysis would indicate. Evidence from recent surveys tends to support such a conclusion. Coleman reports a .65 correlation between education and family income in his sample of Mexico City residents.[18] Fagen and Tuohy found, in their Jalapa sample, a correlation of .61 between education and a class index based on the respondent's income and the interviewer's estimate of socioeconomic status. The same authors report a correlation of .54 between occupation and education. The research in Jalapa also reports marked differences in educational achievement by sex: 55 percent of the upper-class women, compared with 85 percent of the upper-class men, had more than primary education; the figures for the middle class are 18 percent (among women) and 36 percent (among men), and for the lower class, 7 percent and 17 percent, respectively.[19] Fromm and Maccoby report a .55 correlation between family socioeconomic status and sons' schooling, and a .34 correlation between daughters' schooling and the same class measure.[20]

There is, therefore, some suggestive evidence that being male, of middle- or upper-class background, and residing in an urban area contribute powerfully to educational advantage in Mexico. This advantage has repercussions on political culture, most immediately on information and interest in politics. "*Consumers* of politically relevant information constitute a very small proportion of the total Mexican people. These consumers, . . . the 'concerned public,' are principally urban, literate, Spanish-speaking mestizos." [21] Coleman presents evidence that, even in Mexico City, the ability and the desire to acquire information about politics increases significantly with education and family-income level. He was particularly concerned with knowledge related to elections or elective office in Mexico, testing his respondents on questions about the terms of elected officials, the party affiliation of political personalities, and the sectors of the PRI. Of his two samples, the upper-class sample was far better informed than the random sample, with differences of 20 to 30 percentage points in the percent of correctly answered questions.[22]

This evidence on Mexican adults is paralleled by the results of a recent study of the politicization of Mexican schoolchildren. Rafael Segovia's analysis of data from six states relies heavily on comparisons between groups of schoolchildren defined by father's occupational status. Segovia demonstrates that as the father's occupational status increases, children increasingly report discussing politics, a fact which he attributes to greater interest and information in higher-status homes. Similarly, higher-status children could more frequently name state governors and could correctly answer other informational questions.[23] Segovia discusses predictably similar findings in his comparisons of children attending public and private schools, showing that attendance in a private school is associated with much higher frequencies of discussing politics at home, with parents, and with peers, and with higher levels of information, particularly in primary grades where it might be expected that factors outside the schoolroom are particularly influential.[24] These results, and those summarized in the second half of this chapter, suggest that simple cross-tabulations of education with individual item responses as used in *The Civic Culture* do not adequately convey the cumulative impact of educational and class differences on political cognitions and attitudes in Mexico.

Another shortcoming of the subnational analysis provided in *The Civic Culture* is its lack of attention to regional differences. Mexicans and students of Mexico are very aware of the pronounced differences among regions in that country in terms of economic development, land-tenure patterns, occupational structure, ethnicity, religiosity, political participation, relationships with the federal government, and other dimensions.[25] There is also some evidence of important intraregional variations in patterns of community participation, interest-group formation, and competitiveness of politics, associated primarily with intraregional differences in resource base, economic development, and government contact.[26] There is every reason to believe that there may be an interregional parallel for these findings.

So far, however, systematic regional comparisons of political culture rarely have been undertaken, owing to the lack of comparable data from different regions. Segovia's data, which do permit such comparisons, demonstrate that the severe inequalities in regional and rural/urban development in Mexico are reflected in the amount and accuracy of the political information that children possess.[27] Almond and Verba provide only a hint of regional differences:

> There is some difference within nations on the regional distribution of scores on the subjective competence scale, but these differences parallel other differences between regions in levels of national competence, political activity, and the like. Thus it is probable that regional differences in attitudes toward local government are a function, not so much of differences in attitudes toward the local governments, but of differences in general attitudes toward government and politics.[28]

Analysis of regional variations in the *Civic Culture* data for Mexico may have been limited somewhat by the heavy concentration of respondents in the central and northern regions of the country (36.6 percent and 26.1 percent, respectively), but the analytic possibilities remain largely unexplored.

Political Socialization and Participation. At several points in their analysis, Almond and Verba refer to the importance of adult experiences as being equally or potentially more significant than childhood socialization in understanding political culture. Although they do consider childhood (family and school-related) experiences, they suggest that the recency of adult experiences and their more direct relationship to politics and citizen-government relations make adulthood a fertile field for socialization research. Their recognition of the importance of adult learning experiences represented a significant advancement over "national character" and personality studies, which tended to discount the importance of learning after childhood.

In dealing with political socialization during adulthood, however, Almond and Verba limited themselves primarily to work-related experiences. We would argue that, at least in the Mexican case, the study of adult political socialization could very usefully be extended beyond the workplace, to encompass the influence of the local community or neighborhood, peer groups, and individual or collective experiences in dealing with political and governmental agencies. The importance of the local community as an agent of adult political socialization has been demonstrated in research conducted in both urban and rural areas of Mexico.[29] There is also considerable evidence suggesting that personal experience with government structures and the official party contributes not only to the development of cognitions but also to affective and evaluative elements of political culture in Mexico. Attitudes such as political efficacy (or subjective political competence), political cynicism, trust in government, affect for national political institutions, and evaluations of government output performance often seem to have an important experiential basis.[30]

Fuller consideration of the process of adult socialization would also have revealed the importance of various nonelectoral forms of political participation in Mexico. In the Mexican context, for example, voting is relatively unimportant as a political learning experience compared with individual and group petitioning for government benefits, involvement in patron-client relationships, and participation in officially sponsored group gatherings to demonstrate support for the regime.[31] Unfortunately, these modes of political participation receive virtually no attention in *The Civic Culture*. Almond and Verba did include in their survey several items intended to measure "attentiveness to political input," which they regard as a degree of involvement in the political input structure of government.[32] Their measures of political involvement are therefore limited to questions about frequency and perceived freedom of discussing politics, attentiveness to and feelings about political campaigns, perceptions of citizens' responsibilities for community involvement, and an assortment of questions about partisanship. In short, they are questions which essentially tap *cognitive* involvement in politics and public affairs.

Finally, at no point do Almond and Verba examine the various forms of "deviant" political behavior — involvement in protest demonstrations or antisystem political movements, participation in urban or rural land invasions, politically motivated violence, and other behaviors which place the individual in direct confrontation with the regime. Although still relatively rare in Mexico (except for participation in land invasions), such acts are quite significant when they do occur; and the characteristics and motivations of those who engage in them have not received adequate attention in empirical research.[33]

The multidimensionality of political participation and the impact of various participation experiences on attitudes such as perceived political efficacy and cynicism are discussed at greater length in the following section of this chapter. At this point we wish only to underscore the fact that the narrow range of participatory behaviors and socialization experiences considered in *The Civic Culture* excludes many of the experiences of citizen interaction with government which have helped to produce or reinforce citizenship attitudes that Almond and Verba attribute to more individualistic phenomena.

MEXICAN POLITICAL CULTURE: A PROFILE FROM RECENT RESEARCH

In comparing Almond and Verba's conclusions about political culture in Mexico with the findings of subsequent research, we must be specific about our working definition of political culture. We shall consider the political culture of a group to be the set of cognitions, perceptions, evaluations, attitudes, and behavioral predispositions through which member individuals and/or subgroups order and interpret political institutions and processes, and their own relationships with such institutions and processes. It should be noted that this definition encompasses cognitive and behavioral components of political culture as well as the more frequently studied value and attitudinal dimensions.

General studies of political culture have been infrequent and usually unpopular among Latin Americans and Latin Americanists. Many Latin Americanists deliberately chose to avoid broad national studies of political culture, generally for one of two reasons: (1) that internal diversities based on class, ethnicity, region, rural-urban differences, or differences of participation opportunities militated against the possibilities of arriving at meaningful, national generalizations about political culture; and (2) that the basic terms defining the context and outcomes of political activity were determined more by political structures and economic relations than by values or attitudinal orientations, and that, therefore, the significant research questions lay outside the realm of political culture. Although Mexico has been studied by more social scientists than perhaps any other Latin American nation, the Mexican literature is far richer in ethnographic materials than in research relating to political culture. Most of the ethnographic studies make only passing reference to politics and political values. Among the survey studies we shall cite in this section with reference to selected aspects of political culture in Mexico, *The Civic Culture* and Rafael Segovia's study of the politicization of Mexican children [34] are the only studies based on samples not confined to a particular region or locality. Another group of studies to which we shall refer has focused on public policies, political change, or institutional processes at the national level, using data from subnational studies of Mexican political culture to help explain these phenomena.

Early political culture studies on Mexico (roughly prior to 1968) were based largely on field observations, clinical data, newspaper reportage, and elite interviews, conducted primarily in Mexico City. Statements about political culture tended to parallel the national character literature, stressing certain psychological variables or personality characteristics as obstacles to development or modernization. These studies were concerned mainly with questions of national and ethnic identity, integration, and nationalism. Their explanations of Mexican politics and society tended to stress psychological, racial/cultural (miscegenation), religious, and historical factors.[35]

More recent scholarship largely bypasses this earlier tradition of political culture analysis, regarding it as impressionistic, unable to deal with questions of change, and inattentive to key structural variables. This second wave of research generally avoids explanations which rely on personality, turning instead to attitudes and behaviors for which fundamental explanations are most often sought in structural or systemic features. It tends to be both more micro- and more macro-analytic in approach: microanalytic because it is based on surveys or in-depth interviewing of individuals clustered in a limited number of communities or regions; macroanalytic because it attempts to explain how the political system operates. Among the contributors to this literature are a number of researchers who have conducted studies of "community power" or local community politics.[36] The principal survey studies conducted in Mexico since 1959 which have any appreciable political content are listed in Table IX.2.

Since surveys are, by virtue of their scope and design, the most appropriate research instruments for making statements about the distribution of attitudes, cognitions, values, and behaviors within the populations from which their samples are drawn, most of the data to be discussed in this section will be drawn from survey studies. It is important to be aware of several features of the surveys conducted in Mexico, however. Of the studies included in Table IX.2, seven were done in urban areas (all but three exclusively in the Mexico City metropolitan area). All of them include respondents from two or more social classes, but four of the samples are predominantly low-income. Seven include both males and females. All but one are studies of exclusively adult populations. Of the seven studies which include a rural or provincial town sample, all were conducted in relatively accessible localities which could not be considered isolated or primarily Indian.

Although these surveys were conducted over a period of eighteen years, they do not provide a basis for precise statements about changes in Mexican political culture over time, owing to differences in sampling sites, sampling procedures, and sample composition. Comparative analysis of the survey results is also limited by significant differences in question wording, response alternatives, and coding categories. With these caveats in mind, we turn now to discussion of three broad themes emerging from this body of research which are important to an understanding of the basis of political involvement in Mexico: authoritarian politics, subjective political competence (or efficacy), and political cynicism.

AUTHORITARIAN POLITICS

Almond and Verba selected Mexico as "one 'non-Atlantic community' democracy," a country in which the democratic political system was relatively new, but in which the people's hopes and aspirations for democratization and modernization were high.[37] Given Almond and Verba's theoretical concerns with democratic political participation and the stability of democratic systems, as well as the prevailing academic image of the Mexican system at the time they were writing, it is not sur-

TABLE IX.2. *Sample Surveys of Political Attitudes and Behavior in Mexico, 1959-76*

Author	Year of administration	Sampling sites(s)	Sample size	Sample composition
Almond and Verba	1959	27 Mexican cities in all five regions of the Republic	1008 1295 (weighted)	National sample in cities of population of 10,000 or more, men and women over 21 years of age
Fromm and Maccoby	by 1963	A village in Morelos	406	Men 16 years old and older, women 15 years old and older, 95% of total village population
Kahl	1963	Mexico City and several communities in Hidalgo with populations between 5000–10,000 all having commercialized economies	740	"Quota sample of convenience" — white collar workers and factory workers, males, aged 25–49; excluding illiterate casual laborers, peasants, and men with university degrees
Fagen and Tuohy	1966	Jalapa, Veracruz	399 1559 (weighted)	Sample stratified by economic level, men and women over 21
Segovia	1969	Jalisco, Nuevo León, Tabasco, Oaxaca, México, Distrito Federal	3584	Boys and girls, in rural and urban, private (religious and lay) and public schools, aged 10–15, in fifth and sixth grade and first through third of secondary school
Coleman	1969	Federal district and contiguous metropolitan area	408 (random sample) and 53 (upper class)	Men and women 18 and older

Author	Year of administration	Sampling sites(s)	Sample size	Sample composition
Cornelius	1970	Six predominantly lower-class communities on the periphery of Mexico City metropolitan area	747 1062 (weighted)	Communities selected purposively to be representative of variations in age of community, type of origin, and level of development; male heads of family, aged 18–65, stratified by length of residence in city, with subsample of eldest sons
Arterton	1971	Tzintzuntzan, Huiramba, Huaniqueo, and Erongarícuaro in Michoacán	440	Communities purposively selected to be representative of variations on an index of modernization; men and women, 18 and older
Coleman, and Davis	1973	Mexico City metropolitan area	346 (random sample) and 50 upper- and middle-class respondents	Men and women 18 and older
Landsberger	n.a.	*Ejidos* in La Laguna (Durango and Coahuila)	480	Male *ejido* credit-society members and *ejido* officials affiliated with three different peasant unions
Montaño	1973	Eight spontaneous settlements in Mexico City and Monterrey	n.a.	Settlements purposively selected to be representative of different patterns of relationships with government

| Cornelius | 1976 | Nine small, rural communities in Los Altos region, state of Jalisco | 1000 | Communities purposively selected to be representative of variations in land-tenure systems, rates of out-migration, and receipt of government services; male heads of families, aged 17–65, with subsample of eldest sons |

n.a. = not available.

Sources: Gabriel Almond and Sidney Verba, *The Civic Culture* (Princeton, N.J.: Princeton Univ. Press, 1963); F. Christopher Arterton, "Political Participation as Attempted Interpersonal Influence: Test of a Theoretical Model Using Data from Rural Mexican Villages," unpublished Ph.D. dissertation, Massachusetts Institute of Technology, Cambridge, Mass., 1974; Kenneth M. Coleman [1969]. *Public Opinion in Mexico City about the Electoral System* (Chapel Hill, N.C.: Univ. of North Carolina Press, 1972); Kenneth M. Coleman [1973], "The Capital City Electorate and Mexico's Acción Nacional: Some Survey Evidence on Conventional Hypotheses," *Social Science Quarterly* 56, no. 3 (December 1975); Kenneth M. Coleman [1973], *Diffuse Support in Mexico: The Potential for Crisis* (Beverly Hills, Calif.: Sage Publications, 1976); Charles L. Davis [1973]. "Toward an Explanation of Mass Support for Authoritarian Regimes: A Case Study of Political Attitudes in Mexico City," unpublished Ph.D. dissertation, University of Kentucky, Lexington, 1974; Charles L. Davis and Kenneth M. Coleman [1973], "Political Symbols, Political Efficacy, and Diffuse Support for the Mexican Political System," *Journal of Political and Military Sociology* 3, no. 1 (Spring 1975); Wayne A. Cornelius [1976], *Los Norteños: Mexican Migrants in the U.S. and Rural Mexico* (Berkeley: University Press, 1975); Wayne A. Cornelius [1970], *Politics and the Migrant Poor in Mexico City* (Stanford: Stanford Univ. Press, forthcoming); Richard R. Fagen and William S. Tuohy, *Politics and Privilege in a Mexican City* (Stanford: Stanford University Press, 1972); Erich Fromm and Michael Maccoby, *Social Character in a Mexican Village* (Englewood Cliffs, N.J.: Prentice-Hall, 1970); Joseph A. Kahl, *The Measurement of Modernism* (Austin: Univ. of Texas Press, 1968); Henry A. Landsberger, "The Limits and Conditions of Peasant Participation in Mexico: A Case Study," in *Críticas constructivas del sistema político mexicano*, William P. Glade and Stanley R. Ross, eds. (Austin: Institute of Latin American Studies, University of Texas, 1973); Jorge Montaño, *Los pobres de la ciudad en los asentamientos espontáneos* (México, D.F.: Siglo Veintiuno, 1976); and Rafael Segovia, *La politización del niño mexicano* (México, D.F.: El Colegio de México, 1975).

prising that they chose to compare their Mexican data with a model of democratic systems. Since 1963, however, students of Mexico have increasingly stressed the authoritarian features of Mexican politics and the formidable obstacles to genuine democratization of the system.[38] These scholars argue that although earlier optimistic assessments of political democracy in Mexico recognized the high concentration of political power, they tended to convey a basically pluralist image of competition and interest aggregation within the official party, and were therefore misdirected at best, fundamentally inaccurate at worst.[39]

Most studies of authoritarianism in politics have employed one of two approaches: (1) the study of individual attitudes or behaviors which are interpreted as "authoritarian"; and (2) the study of authoritarian patterns of decision making and political organization. In general, the first, "psychological," approach attributes more weight to personality and political culture (including nonrational and individual phenomena) as the basis of authoritarian politics. The second, "structural," approach relegates political culture to a relatively more derivative or supportive status, emphasizing instead authoritarian structures, the tactics of ruling elites, and rationality as the basis of political behavior.

Psychological Interpretations. In their seminal study, Adorno and his associates set forth a theory of the "authoritarian personality." [40] They conceptualized authoritarianism as a personality syndrome characterized by implicit antidemocratic (prefascist and ethnocentric) tendencies; that is, the authoritarian personality type has a predisposition to glorify, be subservient to and uncritical of authority figures in his "in-group," and to punish members of the "out-group." Adorno described nine dimensions of authoritarianism, and designed an "F-scale" composed of agree/disagree questionnaire items to tap these nine dimensions.[41] The Adorno "F-scale" and the concept of "the authoritarian personality" have been widely criticized in social science on both methodological and conceptual grounds. Except for Fromm and Maccoby,[42] students of Mexican politics do not refer to Adorno; yet some of the recent research clearly seeks to tap several of the dimensions of authoritarianism as defined by Adorno (albeit under different labels), in order to explain the bases of interpersonal and leader-follower relations and preferences for certain patterns of social organization in Mexico. This research deals with such topics as power relations (submissiveness and dominance), cynicism, intolerance of ambiguity or opposition viewpoints, and fatalism.

Fromm and Maccoby's *Social Character in a Mexican Village* represents one of the most detailed explorations of these topics in the Mexican context. Fromm and Maccoby found that the most frequent mode of sociopolitical relations in their village was "submissiveness" (49 percent of the residents), followed by "traditional authority" relations (20 percent) and "authoritarianism" (16 percent). Only 7 percent of the village's population exhibited predominantly democratic tendencies.[43] By "submissiveness," the authors refer to the "lack of hope, and fatalism about the future . . . the feeling of powerlessness to change events . . . submissiveness to nature and God's will . . . the submissiveness of young to old, women to men, and the poor to the rich." [44] "Authoritarian" individuals are characterized by a concern with obedience or disobedience in children, admiration for persons who have power and use force, and a tendency to justify inequality by attributing merit to strength. Fromm and Maccoby contrast this form of authoritarianism with traditionalism. The traditional peasant stresses custom and tradition in his desire for respect and obedience and in his acceptance of dominance relations. The extremely subtle distinctions drawn by Fromm and Maccoby among submissiveness, authoritarianism, and traditionalism are often problematic. On the basis of their guidelines it would be difficult to determine whether peasants' responses to "authoritarianism" items represent expressions of individual needs and preferences or simply reflections of traditional patterns of authority relations.

The Fromm and Maccoby study represents a significant effort to link social character to the evolution of political and economic structures in rural Mexico. They base their conclusions on historical data, participant observation, and data gathered with a standardized questionnaire. They conclude that the character orientation of the villagers is adaptive to the mode of production; the social character motivates to behavior which fulfills socioeconomic (and, we would add, political) functions. In general, they found that landless day laborers have a receptive, nonproductive orientation; free landowners tend to have a hoarding, productive orientation; and "new entrepreneurs" have a productive-exploitative orientation.[45]

Other studies examine only selected values or attitudes which might be considered dimensions of authoritarianism. For example, some authors have explained power relations in Mexico by focusing on *machismo,* a preoccupation with male power, expressed in displays of bravery, sexual prowess, and dominance.[46] Much of the early literature which discussed Mexican preoccupation with power, assertiveness, and strength interpreted these phenomena as a reflection of insecurity or inferiority feelings rooted in national historical experiences.[47] Such an interpretation, although not based on extensive empirical data, would be consistent with the concept of the authoritarian personality.

There are few hard data on the incidence of *machismo* within the Mexican population. Lola Romanucci-Ross, writing about the same village studied by Fromm and Maccoby, found that *machismo* was generally less prevalent than gossip and folk myth would suggest, and that it is found less frequently among young generations.[48] By contrast, Fromm and Maccoby found no relationship (correlation of .08) between *machismo* and age.[49]

There is also little empirical evidence linking *machismo* with political behavior. The presumption has been that *machismo* probably affects political leadership style, participation in politics (limiting participation by women), and family socialization to authority relations.[50] Octavio Paz, in his reflections on Mexican character, relates *machismo* to perceptions of men in power: ". . . in a world of *chingones* [literally, sexual violators], of difficult relationships, ruled by violence and suspicion . . . [the] only thing of value is manliness, personal strength, a capacity for imposing oneself on others. . . . This is the model — more mythical than real — that determines the images the Mexican people form of men in power. . . . They are all *machos, chingones.*" [51]

In survey research in Mexico, authoritarianism has more often been treated as a set of opinions on a range of "democratic" practices and preferences for particular styles of political leadership. Fagen and Tuohy, for example, report the responses to a series of items measuring support for free expression, universal suffrage, and minority rights. They found that members of all social classes in the city of Jalapa agreed (90 percent or more on all items) that "democracy is the best form of government; public officials should be chosen by majority vote; [and that] every citizen should have an equal chance to influence government policy." However, the responses of Jalapeños to eight items about the rights of minorities to free expression and the franchise revealed marked "anti-democratic tendencies," especially among the middle and lower classes. Jalapeños placed very little value upon the rights to free expression of such groups as Communists, speakers against the PRI or the Catholic Church, and critics of "life in Mexico." Fagen and Tuohy interpret these results (in which specific democratic practices do not receive the same support as general "platitudinous formulations") as a reflection of a status-quo orientation, a desire to restrict elements perceived as "disruptive," particularly among the less educated and socio-politically marginal members of the population for whom costs of disruption have generally been highest in the past.[52]

Evidence from surveys on authoritarian tendencies among the Mexican lower classes is contradictory, depending on which dimensions of authoritarianism are being tapped. For example, Coleman constructed a civil libertarianism index and found that in simple correlational analysis there was no relationship between civil libertarianism and income or education that could support the thesis of "working-class authoritarianism"[53] in Mexico. However, in multiplicative analysis, the combination of high income and more education was positively associated with civil libertarianism.[54]

The same study demonstrates some interesting class differences in replies to specific items, evidence which could support the Fagen and Tuohy thesis that responses to such questions may reflect group interests. Coleman's respondents were asked whether they agreed that "democracy demands that illiterates have the right to vote." Seventy-three percent of his random sample agreed or agreed strongly with the statement, whereas only 52.8 percent of the upper-class sample expressed similar sentiments. By contrast, when asked for their reaction to the statement that "Even though he may be an agitator, everyone has a right to say publicly what he thinks about political matters," 67.2 percent of the random sample agreed or agreed strongly, whereas 78.9 percent of the upper-class sample expressed such agreement.[55]

Among a predominantly low-income sample of Mexico City residents, Cornelius found that those who had been born and raised in a rural area showed significantly more authoritarian tendencies (defined as a preference for strong, autocratic leadership and a low level of tolerance for minority opinions) than city-born respondents, a difference which was independent of educational level. He also found that authoritarian tendencies were strongest among the most politically active stratum of lower-class migrants to the city. This finding may reflect the particular pattern of authoritarian leadership — *caciquismo* — which had prevailed in several of the settlement zones included in the study: "A *cacique* may devote considerable attention to political mobilization within the community under his control. . . . Authoritarian-minded residents may be more receptive than others to his inducements, and may thus be drawn more readily into political activity." [56] The same pattern of local community leadership is widely encountered in rural areas of Mexico. [57]

Theories of working-class authoritarianism in Mexico receive some support in Rafael Segovia's book on politicization of Mexican schoolchildren. Summarizing authoritarianism among the children he surveyed, Segovia describes them as characterized by *"desconfianza,"* — a general lack of trust, associated with decisions not to participate and with patterns of direct, personal dependence; a strong (not benevolent) leader image of the president; a lack of confidence in political parties, such that a majority believe that the government should have jurisdiction over parties; intolerance of Communists; rejection of the rights of political dissidents; and the belief that laws should be taken as givens, without citizen participation in their formulation. Segovia's data indicate that most of these orientations are more prevalent among children from lower-status families. [58] We are inclined to agree with Segovia that a substantial proportion of these differences may be due to variations in exposure and information, as well as to class-related differences in political efficacy (subjective political competence) to be discussed below.

Structural Interpretations. Many recent treatments of Mexican politics have stressed the authoritarian character of political decision-making processes and structures for political organization. Authoritarianism in this structural sense may be considered in conjunction with, or independently of, authoritarian tendencies among the general population. Discussions of structural authoritarianism generally rely upon Juan Linz's model of authoritarian regimes, which stresses the following characteristics: limited (not responsible) pluralism, low popular mobilization, weak ideological constraints on elite decision making, and the frequently arbitrary exercise of power by a single leader or small group.[59] Among Mexicanists there is now wide agreement that these features describe the Mexican political system, and that previous scholarship which focused on the possibilities for interest articulation, government accountability, and increasing mass participation in politics within the one-party-dominant system misinterpreted the way Mexican political institutions operate. This reconceptualization of political life in Mexico becomes important in explaining various aspects of Mexican political culture. In structural interpretations of authoritarianism, centralization of authority and decision making is epitomized by the key institution of Mexico's political structure: the presidency. Some students of Mexico prefer to describe the Mexican regime as "presidentialist," stressing the relatively unlimited powers of the president,[60] as well as the "cult of the glorification of the President." [61] In this view, government decisions can be influenced to some extent by certain powerful interest groups (national and foreign entrepreneurs, landowners, organized labor, the military) and regional or state-level power brokers, either through direct influence attempts or, more frequently, "preemptive" concessions by the government. But the president himself is the key initiator and shaper of all major public policies:

> In Mexico, the decision-making process is formally initiated by the executive. In the first stage, the president commits himself to a particular idea that he may or may not have originated. The actual origin of the idea is not important, however. What matters is the president's commitment to it. . . . [This] commitment to a particular course of action rarely is the result of direct pressure by concerned groups. The co-optation of group leaders (which reduces the autonomy of interest groups) and the low level of mobilization of the rank-and-file membership makes it difficult for groups to pressure the executive. . . . The main device the authoritarian elite uses to demobilize its critics is the incorporation of the malcon-

tents into the decision-making process. Incorporation occurs, however, *after* the initial vague version of the legislation has been approved by Congress or, if no legislation is involved, after the vague version of the decision has been publicly announced. . . . Participation is . . . confined to the elaboration of technical details and implies the acceptance by the groups of the President's political commitment.[62]

Congressional ratification (legitimation) of the president's will has been virtually automatic in most of the period since 1930.[63]

Stevens points out that until 1968, when President Gustavo Díaz Ordaz ordered the violent repression of student demonstrators in Mexico City, resulting in the loss of hundreds of lives, Mexican presidents were virtually immune to public criticism. In fact, Stevens's analysis shows that glorification of the president was one of the three dominant themes in newspaper reportage between January 1965 and March 1966, the period she selected for content analysis.[64] Since the president is regarded as personally responsible for all government policy, the media exhibit remarkable self-censorship in withholding critical news and problems in the execution of announced policies or programs, unless publication of such material has received prior authorization.[65] Press coverage tends to emphasize cultural and material progress and benefits to come. As a consequence, to the extent that critical opinions of government are based on facts and figures, the information must come from personal experiences, contacts within the regime, or other privileged sources.

Today the president remains the embodiment of paternalistic, authoritarian rule in Mexico. The regime continues to cultivate an image of presidential accessibility to citizen influence attempts, and, responding to this image, a large proportion of petitions for governmental action originating in low-income groups is routinely directed to the president himself.[66] This reliance on the president reflects two factors in addition to his "accessible" image: extreme centralization of authority not only in the executive but also in the federal government, and the saliency of the presidency as a political institution. Thus the common practice of directing petitions for government benefits as close to "the top" as possible reflects popular awareness of the fact that "the resources, opportunities, and decisional latitude available at the local level are everywhere in Mexico sharply diminished through the mechanisms of executive centralism." [67]

The saliency of the presidency over and above all other Mexican political institutions is reflected in the results from various surveys. Summarizing data on political information levels, Coleman concludes that "the office of the chief executive is much more salient to the average urban Mexican than are other political phenomena." In contrast to the relatively low levels of political information Coleman found among his respondents, he found that 100 percent of the upper-class sample, and 89 percent of the random sample could identify the preceding president by name and that (respectively) 93 percent and 90 percent of his samples knew the length of the presidential term of office.[68] Cornelius found that 99 percent of his low-income respondents in Mexico City could evaluate the overall performance of the incumbent president (Díaz Ordaz) and his immediate predecessor (López Mateos), while 88 percent could evaluate the performance of President Miguel Alemán, who held office from 1946 to 1952.[69] Segovia also found that the highest levels of political information among the Mexican children he studied were associated with the office of the president. Ninety percent of his respondents could identify the incumbent president by name; ex-presidents were the next category of officials most readily identified. Eighty-six percent knew that the President had been the PRI nominee five years before. Seventy-nine percent knew that he serves a six-year term.[70]

Each incumbent fosters the popular sense of dependence upon his office. One of the purposes of the highly elaborate, nine- to ten-month "electoral" campaigns conducted every six years by the presidential candidate of the official party, involving visits to hundreds of localities throughout the nation, is to enable citizens to make direct appeals to the president-to-be for various kinds of government assistance.[71] While only a small portion of these petitions is ever acted upon by the government bureaucracy, the symbolic impact of the extensive petition-gathering effort should not be underestimated. When government aid is not forthcoming, the citizen is likely to absolve the president of blame, attributing these failures of performance to corrupt, incompetent subordinate officials who thwart his will. This kind of rationalization is clearly reflected in the sharp contrast between highly positive mass orientations toward national political institutions (especially the presidency) and strongly negative citizen evaluations of government output performance, revealed by *The Civic Culture* and every subsequent survey study which has explored these aspects of Mexican political culture. We shall return to this point in our discussion of political cynicism in Mexico.

The image of the president as an authority figure, essential not only in policy making, but also in maintaining public order and containing the divisive forces (latent or overt) within the nation, seems deeply embedded in the Mexican political culture, and serves to reinforce and legitimize the authoritarian features of the regime. This vision of the president is already fixed in childhood:

> . . . this capacity to govern, to retain all of the power in his hands is what most attracts the young minds. . . . He is not the benevolent leader; he is above all the authoritarian leader, capable not only of governing but of creating a material world — subways, dams, highways, athletic stadia — by his own will. For the Mexican child, authority rests in a single person, and is confined to him.[72]

Segovia's research demonstrates convincingly that this presidential image is internalized at a relatively early point in the life cycle. Fifty-one percent of his sample of Mexican children in the fifth year of primary school expressed the belief that the president's principal function is to "maintain order in the country," while 30 percent felt that "the President fulfills the will of the people," and 17 percent believed that "the President makes the laws." [73] This widely held view of the president as the chief authority figure charged with guaranteeing "law and order" helps to explain the high degree of popular approval — especially among the poor — accorded President Díaz Ordaz's massacre of hundreds of unarmed student demonstrators and bystanders in Mexico City in 1968. By a margin of 59 percent to 15 percent (with 26 percent expressing no opinion), the low-income adults in Mexico City interviewed by Cornelius in 1970 approved the government's actions against the students, the majority feeling that these actions were necessary to restore order, or because the students had been openly "defying" the president.[74]

The imprint of authoritarian politics on mass orientations toward political participation is also clearly visible. Mexicans seem to have assessed the utility of participation in such limited "democratic" institutions as are available to them, and to have concluded that their interests are best served by abstention or participation through brokers. This pattern of mediated participation, or interest articulation through patron-client networks, is extremely important in Mexico. The widespread view of governmental authority (except that exercised by the president) as arbitrary and capricious, combined with awareness of the inefficiency, graft, and personalistic interpretation of rules which pervade Mexican public administration, leads to the extensive use of politically connected intermediaries (persons with *palanca,* or leverage) to facilitate dealings with government agencies. In some instances the brokerage function is performed by lower-level Partido Revolucionario Institucional officials,[75] in others by local community leaders who are themselves the "clients" of government bureaucrats or politicians.[76] While providing important channels for demand making by the poor, therefore increasing the responsiveness of the system, the brokers also assist the incumbent regime by helping to limit demands for excessively costly services or benefits and by fragmenting the political action of the lower classes into requests for highly particularistic, short-term benefits. The potential for large-scale demand making aimed at influencing overall government priorities or the broad outlines of public policy is thereby reduced.

POLITICAL EFFICACY (SUBJECTIVE POLITICAL COMPETENCE)

Almond and Verba accord great importance to the general concept of subjective competence; indeed, one might regard it as the single most important attitudinal orientation in their model of democratic participation and the stability of democratic systems. Much of their analysis is devoted to distinguishing several types of competence and to relating subjective competence to patterns of political socialization, political awareness, civic cooperation, and other politically relevant attitudes. Other scholars have preferred the label "political efficacy," and have generally accorded it less centrality in their analyses.

In their indexes of competence, Almond and Verba distinguish between political or citizen competence (the individual's perception of his or her ability to influence the formation of laws and policies), and administrative or subject competence (the individual's perception of his or her ability to affect the application of general policy in specific, personally relevant situations). Questions used to measure the various forms of political competence tap the individual's anticipated response to situations of stress in which rules or regulations harmful to the person's interests are being considered by local or national government. Administrative competence is measured by items which ask the individual to consider his or her relations with the bureaucracy and police in the case of personal problems or minor offenses.[77]

Throughout their analysis, Almond and Verba contend that the main distinguishing characteristic of Mexican political culture is that it is "aspirational" (and alienated). In part this characterization rests on their finding of a substantial difference between levels of political and administrative competence in Mexico. Fifty-two percent of their respondents were "locally" competent; that is, they felt able to affect a regulation being considered by the local government. Thirty-eight percent were "nationally" competent, believing themselves able to affect regulations under consideration by the national legislature. Thirty-three percent were both locally and nationally competent.[78] By contrast, on the dimension of administrative competence, only 14 percent of the sample expected their point of view to receive serious consideration from the bureaucracy and 12 percent expected similar attention from the police. The gap between political competence and administrative competence was greater in Mexico than in the other four countries surveyed, both in the total sample and among those with only primary education. When sex and secondary education are controlled, however, the gap in Mexico between the two kinds of competence begins to approximate the differences in competence levels encountered in the other countries.

Almond and Verba attach great significance to the relationship between the two kinds of competence in the five nations, because they regard it as a reflection of the process of the spread of competence and, by implication, of democratization. They attribute the relatively higher levels of political competence in

Mexico to the Revolutionary experience, which focused attention on national politics and political leaders, initiating membership in a political system which rejected traditional authority and promoted a democratic ideology. Lower levels of administrative competence are attributed to contacts with a bureaucracy which has remained essentially arbitrary and subject to political forces.[79]

We take issue with these assessments of the significance of the patterns of subjective competence in Mexico revealed by the *Civic Culture* survey. We suspect that Almond and Verba have not tapped two kinds of competence, but rather, that the items measuring administrative competence (questions about the expected treatment and attention from the police and bureaucracy) really measure more concrete cases of the same estimates of political system responsiveness tapped by their Guttman scale questions on local and national political competence.[80] Viewed in this context, it would be logical for responsiveness expectations to be reduced, as the hypothetical cases referred to in the questions become ever more concrete and proximate to the individual's experience. Although Almond and Verba refer to the effect on administrative competence of government responsiveness and the existence of channels of influence, these variables are not mentioned as important determinants of other forms of competence.[81] This omission of government responsiveness as an important contributor to the patterns of subjective competence found in Mexico is a serious oversight. We agree with Carole Pateman's criticism that the assumption in Almond and Verba (and most other studies of efficacy) is that "efficacious" replies accurately reflect system responsiveness, and that all other replies (including nonefficacious replies) must be indicative of individual or group psychology. Pateman contends that the subjective competence scale used in *The Civic Culture* reflects, instead, a cognitive element of efficacy, that is, that all replies to these questions reflect the respondent's estimates of system responsiveness and opportunities.[82]

Coleman and Davis, also convinced of the importance of distinguishing among various dimensions of political efficacy in Mexico, have argued that efficacy should be studied in terms of internal and external dimensions, depending on whether the individual is assessing his own skills or resources for taking advantage of influence opportunities ("internal efficacy"), or the instrumental payoff of influence attempts ("external efficacy").[83] This may be a useful theoretical distinction, but the practical consequences for the political involvement of Mexicans (in the absence of substantial system changes) are not significantly affected by the distinction.

With these assessments of the concept of political efficacy (or competence) in mind, we turn to the relevant research findings from Mexico. After reviewing the available data on levels and determinants of efficacy, we shall examine the relationships between efficacy and participation in the Mexican political system.

Political Efficacy in Mexico. Almond and Verba, Fagen and Tuohy, and Landsberger have all used roughly similar questions to tap the dimension of local political efficacy. In answer to the question "Suppose a regulation were being considered by the most local governmental unit which you considered very unjust or harmful . . . , what do you think you could do?" 52 percent of Almond and Verba's Mexican respondents believed they could do something about the unjust law. Using a similar question, but with a graduated scale of responses, Landsberger found that 80 percent of the rural credit-society members he studied in the Laguna region believed that it was quite likely or very likely that they would be able to stop the local authorities from taking steps injurious to themselves.[84] Fagen and Tuohy asked their respondents to consider a similar hypothetical situation, and then asked, "Do you think you could do anything about it?" Only 22 percent of their respondents replied in the affirmative. Probing further, Almond and Verba asked their respondents about the likelihood of their success, should they attempt to change the regulation. Forty-one percent considered it likely or very likely that they would succeed. Of their Jalapa respondents who thought they might really do something to try to change the regulation, Fagen and Tuohy asked about the anticipated probability of success; only 11 percent thought it probable or very probable that they might succeed.[85]

There are substantial differences in the responses obtained in each of these surveys which require explanation. In part, wording differences have created essentially distinct questions: Almond and Verba ask for hypothetically useful strategies, while

Fagen and Tuohy ask more bluntly about the possibility of influence. Landsberger's report is quite unclear about the precise content of his question. We suspect, however, that the much higher sense of efficacy among rural credit-society members might be attributed to the specific nature of the local (*ejidal*) government to which Landsberger's question presumably refers. All of the *ejidatarios* (land-holding residents of communities created through the government's agrarian reform program) together constitute the local government. Although one may expect that influence is unevenly distributed among the membership, the feasibility of an influence attempt is nevertheless greater in such a situation than in an urban area such as Jalapa, where the question referred to the *municipio* (county) government.

Other efforts to probe for manifestations of political efficacy in Mexico have more directly addressed the issue of government responsiveness to popular participation. Table IX.3 reports responses to identically worded items administered in Mexico City by Cornelius and in rural Michoacán by Arterton, along with data from the Almond and Verba survey. In general, we are inclined to accord reduced importance to the absolute values of the Almond and Verba replies because of the severe response-set bias problems often encountered (especially among poorly educated respondents) with these and other questions in the "agree/disagree" format.

Both rural and urban samples are in general agreement about the effect of the vote on government actions. The respondents' assessments are probably reasonably accurate, considering that the responsiveness of government functionaries and the ease or difficulty of acquiring government benefits may be influenced, at least in some localities, by voter turnout and rates of voting for opposition parties. A very different view, however, results from questions asking about the effect of the vote on election outcomes. Fagen and Tuohy asked their respondents whether they considered it useless to vote in municipal elections, since leaders are preselected by the official party. Eighty-two percent of their respondents agreed that municipal voting is useless in this respect.[86] Cornelius, asking a similar question, found that 50 percent of his sample believed that it is true or partially true that elections do not offer the voter a meaningful choice because the winners have already been selected by the PRI.[87] The dis-

TABLE IX.3. *Selected Political Efficacy Items* a *(in percentages)*

Item	Mexico City Lower class	Rural Michoacán
1. Popular influence on government:		
"We are responsible for bad government."	47.4	63.2
"People like me have no influence on what government does."	52.6	36.8
2. Effect of popular vote on what government does:		
"Much effect."	36.0	33.3
"A little effect."	47.8	51.9
"No effect."	16.1	14.9
3. Understanding public issues:		
"Politics is too complicated for the average man to understand."	29.7	44.2
"If people pay attention (or want to) they can understand politics."	70.3	55.8
4. Ability to influence government programs:		
"Can only wait and accept government programs."	55.6	69.4
"Can influence and make government help."	44.4	30.6

a Almond and Verba's survey included similar items in an agree/disagree format. The results for their national sample (which in no case differed by more than one percentage point from the response of a male, lower-class subsample of the *Civic Culture* data from Mexico which we analyzed separately) are:

78.9% agreed that people like themselves have no influence on what government does (cf. item 1 above).

69.5% agreed that the way people vote is the main thing determining how the government is run (cf. item 2 above).

73.4% agreed that politics is too complicated for the average man to understand (cf. item 3 above).

Sources: [Mexico City lower class] Wayne A. Cornelius, *Politics and the Migrant Poor in Mexico City* (Stanford: Stanford Univ. Press, 1975); [Rural Michoacán] F. Christopher Arterton, "Political Participation as Attempted Interpersonal Influence: Test of a Theoretical Model Using Data from Rural Mexican Villages," unpublished Ph.D. dissertation, Massachusetts Institute of Technology, Cambridge, Mass., 1974.

parity between the Mexico City and Jalapa results may be due to the greater visibility and importance of opposition party candidates in the capital, as well as to the importance in Mexico City of voter mobilization by local community leaders.[88]

The differences between the Mexico City and rural Michoacán

samples on questions dealing with the ability to understand politics and to influence government programs can probably be attributed to differences in participation opportunities, government resources, and information sources — all of which leave the rural dwellers at a relative disadvantage. By comparison, the Mexico City poor are a relatively efficacious group. For example, half of Cornelius's respondents believed that the "really powerful public officials and politicians" pay a great deal of attention, or at least some attention, to the opinions of men like themselves. This response probably reflects an expectation of attention to the opinions of a general social category (the poor, squatter settlement dwellers, etc.) rather than expectations of attention to the particular respondent.

With approximately a third of the rural and urban Mexicans included in these surveys believing that they have no influence on what government does and that politics is too difficult for them to understand, as well as one-half or more believing that their vote has little or no effect on government actions and that they can only wait and accept government programs, the dilemma of the average citizen becomes particularly acute, considering his or her dependence on the government for satisfaction of basic needs. Fagen and Tuohy found that 91 percent of the Jalapeños considered themselves helpless to do anything about the most serious problems facing Jalapa; 87 percent of them felt that the government had primary responsibility for solving their problems.[89] Similarly, in Mexico City, Cornelius found that 66 percent of his low-income respondents believed that the government was principally to blame for most of their neighborhood's problems. Yet when asked who outside their community could help to solve its problems, more than 97 percent of the respondents mentioned some government agency or official. When Arterton and Cornelius asked their respondents whether they considered good luck, government help, God's help, or the hard work of the residents as the most important factor for improving local conditions, 58 percent of the rural Michoacán residents and 41 percent of the Mexico City residents replied that government help was most important.[90] These data showing relatively low estimations of personal efficacy combined with a heavy sense of dependence on government assistance and programs to improve local conditions serve as a useful backdrop as we turn our attention to the relationship between efficacy and political participation in Mexico.

Efficacy and Political Participation. Earlier in this chapter, reference was made to the relative absence of behavioral data in *The Civic Culture,* and to the narrow range of participatory behaviors which are examined by Almond and Verba. Recent research on political participation in a variety of countries, including Mexico, has clearly demonstrated the need for more differentiated analysis of participation and the determinants of participant behavior. Verba and his associates, for example, in a comparative study of political participation in Austria, India, Japan, Nigeria, and the United States, isolated four basic modes of participation, and found that (1) people who tend to "specialize" in a given mode of participation often have different personal characteristics and attitudinal orientations toward politics than people who participate mostly in other modes of participation; (2) that participation in one mode does not necessarily lead the individual to participate in other modes; and (3) that the causal paths or processes which lead people to participate may differ substantially from one mode of participation to another.[91] In their research, the standard socioeconomic model of participation — in which higher income, education, or occupational status are the principal characteristics that lead some people to participate more than others — proved less adequate to explain some modes of participation (voting and particularistic contacting of public officials) than others (campaign activity and community involvement).

The Verba and Niĕ research, and studies which have partially replicated it in Mexico, Costa Rica, Peru, and Japan,[92] suggest that at least some forms of political participation among the rural and urban poor may be better explained by variables which are not as relevant for explanations of participation in general populations or among the middle and upper classes. Specifically, these studies find that the resources or characteristics of the individual (including personal sense of political efficacy) are often far less important as determinants of participation than certain aspects of the national or local political structure, or more generally, the group context in which the poor citizen finds himself.[93]

Similarly, Mathiason and Powell's research in Venezuela and Colombia has demonstrated that among peasants, personal efficacy — the perceived ability to influence government decisions individually and directly — is not a prerequisite for political activity. They found that much participation could be explained by "mediated political efficacy," wherein the peasant feels able to influence the government because of his relationship with a network of mediators or brokers who are, in turn, influential in government circles:

> The syndicate is something concretely visible and understandable to peasants. No ability to imagine oneself individually trying to influence national government is required for a sense of efficacy. A peasant need only learn that the syndicate exists as broker between himself and the government — and this lesson is learned by observing and especially by participating in the brokerage activities of the union. . . . Consequently, if the union is adept at brokerage . . . there is a greater likelihood that its members will be taught that they are, in fact, efficacious.[94]

Thus the sense of efficacy is tied more to the mediating structure, and the successful outcomes of its influence attempts, than to the individual. The authors also demonstrate that mediated political efficacy is not a product of childhood socialization but, rather, of direct political learning experiences during adulthood.

A variety of other factors have been found to be important in explaining political participation among the rural and urban poor: stressful experiences of a collective nature (e.g., land invasions), concrete experiences in dealing with political and governmental agencies, intensive mobilization by local-level leaders or government representatives, patron-client linkages, specific concrete needs or problems particular to a community, and awareness of the repressive capacity of the government and of the overall political opportunity structure at the national level — that is, perceptions of the kinds of political activity which are likely to be rewarded or punished by elites.[95]

These kinds of perceptions are also quite important in explaining the generalized preference among the poor for informal manipulation of the political system, as opposed to direct confrontation or protest tactics. Informal manipulation through mediating structures such as clientage networks may simply be a more efficient and less risky strategy for extracting benefits from the political system. For similar reasons, participation among the poor is most often focused on policy outputs rather than inputs, on efforts to influence low-level allocative decisions and local policy implementations, rather than on efforts to affect the content of public policy or the ordering of basic government priorities. In many third world countries, public officials are much more likely to regard efforts to influence the broad outlines of policy as illegitimate incursions which threaten the stability of the political system, and as a result are more likely to apply negative sanctions.

This fear of negative sanctions, such as physical or economic reprisals, or denial of future benefits to family or community, whether by local or more distant authorities, is often a key factor limiting lower-class political participation.[96] But sometimes a fear of negative sanctions may *increase* participation by the poor, if local leaders insist on frequent participation by their followers in certain forms of political activity. Whether directly or through the clientage networks of which they are a part, local leaders may be able to punish those who fail to participate by denying them land, housing, jobs, or other benefits whose allocation they control.[97]

Before turning to a brief summary of evidence on some of these patterns of political participation in Mexico, we would cite one additional piece of recent research which was not conducted in Mexico but which will doubtless prove influential in new research on political efficacy and participation. After considerable professional investment in psychological explanations of political behavior and efficacy, Kenneth Langton, in research conducted on university students, has found that individual psychological dispositions (general and situational efficacy) are poor direct predictors of participation, and that they have relatively minor importance even in complex interactive relationships with other variables. Langton was concerned with explaining the decision to participate based on general political efficacy, past situational learning, situational beliefs (situational efficacy), and context. Related to the latter two variables are the additional variables of strategies available and the level of government addressed. He found that situational variables were more important direct predictors of the decision to participate, especially among those respondents who had greater political interest, issue concern, and a history of past situational participation. Those who had used a particular strategy of influence before and found it helpful were much more confident than those who felt their action had had no influence. He concludes: "Assumptions about underlying psychological dispositions [general political efficacy] are not good guides to behavior in any of the situations examined. Past personal experience in similar situations remains the strongest direct explanation of the decision to participate." [98]

Traditionally, the chief preoccupation of participation studies has been voting. In Mexico, however, voting, campaign involvement, and partisanship assume special meanings. Attention to political campaigns must be interpreted in a context where the outcome is known before the campaign even begins, where candidate preferences do not depend heavily on being an informed voter, and where campaigns are not referenda on public issues. Despite that fact, only 8.7 percent of Cornelius's Mexico City respondents paid no attention to electoral campaigns. Moreover, in spite of frequent opposition party charges of electoral fraud and the lack of suspense surrounding election outcomes, there are indications of a relatively high degree of support for the electoral system. Fagen and Tuohy found that 74 percent of the residents of Jalapa consider the electoral system just and honest.[99] Coleman found that only 24 percent of his respondents could suggest any reforms in the current electoral process.[100]

The elections serve primarily to legitimize existing policies and to demonstrate mass support for the regime. As José López Portillo, the unopposed official party candidate for president in 1976, told a gathering of PRI candidates in Mexico City during his campaign: "What is at stake, my friends, is not each of our personal futures, but rather the future of the Mexican Revolution and the prestige of its institutions." [101] Voting is obligatory under federal law, with penalties for abstention including a 10 to 300 peso fine, and/or three to six months in jail, and the suspension of political rights for up to one year. In practice, however, the voting law is seldom enforced.

A very high proportion of Mexicans do claim to have voted. Landsberger found that 86 percent of the *ejido* credit-society members in his sample had voted at least once in state and federal elections.[102] Carlos reports comparably high voter turnout in local elections in the *ejidos* he studied: in twenty out of thirty-one *ejidos* more than 81 percent of the *ejidatarios* voted in the most recent election; in only three *ejidos* did voter turnout fall below 60 percent.[103] Fagen and Tuohy strongly question the validity of self-reported voting rates, but note that 78 percent of their respondents claimed to have voted in the 1964 presidential election and 64 percent claimed participation in the municipal election the same year.[104] In Almond and Verba's national sample, 63 percent of the eligible respondents voted in the 1958 election.[105] Our secondary analysis of a male, low-income subsample of their respondents shows that 73.8 percent of the low-income respondents voted in the same election. Ninety-five percent of Cornelius's Mexico City respondents reported voting in the 1964 general election, and 96 percent expressed an intention to vote in the 1970 election.[106] Ugalde and his associates found that 87 percent of the residents of a low-income neighborhood in the border city of Ciudad Juárez had voted in the 1964 election,[107] and the turnout for the 1973 congressional elections exceeded 89 percent in five of the six low-income settlements studied by Montaño in Mexico City.[108] It is clear that the rural and urban poor vote in higher proportions than the general population. Partly this is due to mobilization by local leaders and mediating networks such as the Confederación Nacional Campesina — the main PRI-affiliated organization for peasants — which are utilized by the regime to turn out the vote in low-income communities.[109] Segovia has observed that electoral participation in Mexico is nearly in inverse proportion to the economic development of the locality.[110]

In spite of the high voter-turnout rate, the vast majority of voters are not motivated by intense partisanship or by a belief that their action will somehow affect what the regime does, and much less who will rule. Surveys have yielded roughly similar figures on party membership: relatively few people (about 15 to 25 percent) belong to any party, and to the extent that they express a preference for any party at all, they are inclined to favor the PRI. Coleman's panel study of Mexico City residents showed a 6 percent decline in the percentage of people reporting a party identification between 1971 and 1973.[111] Partisanship receded even further into the background of the Mexican electoral process in 1976, when the principal opposition party, Acción

Nacional (PAN), failed even to nominate a candidate for president, owing to internal factionalism. Nevertheless, according to official statistics, 68 percent of the registered voters went to the polls, all but 5.6 percent casting their ballots for the PRI candidate, López Portillo (the non–López Portillo vote went to various nonregistered candidates). Although the officially claimed turn-out rate can be seriously questioned (50 percent is probably a closer approximation to reality), the government's fears of a sharply elevated rate of abstention proved largely unfounded.

When voting, the average citizen appears to respond to official exhortations to participate, viewing his activities on behalf of the official party as an opportunity to express gratitude for assistance received from previous or incumbent administrations as well as his solidarity with the goals of the Mexican Revolution and its heirs within the PRI. Others reason that by supporting the PRI, one (or one's local community) stands a better chance of receiving additional benefits from the government or preserving the gains already realized. Government coercion, real or feared, appears to be a relatively insignificant factor in voter turnout.[112]

The average citizen's reasons for undertaking forms of political activity not directly related to the electoral process tend to be more pragmatic and particularistic: he is usually bent on obtaining specific benefits from the government or the local community power structure. Because the amount of resources to be distributed, the variety of services that might be solicited, and the institutional opportunities for doing so are greater in the cities, participation of this type is more widespread in urban than rural areas. Participation is also restricted to a small minority of the population. As part of the sequence of questions measuring competence, Almond and Verba asked their respondents whether they had ever made an attempt to influence a local regulation which they regarded as unjust or harmful to their interests. Only 6 percent indicated that they had done so. In response to a similar question, 4 percent of the Jalapa residents reported that they had attempted to influence a decision about a government regulation.[113] As noted earlier, however, these items inquire about influence attempts at the policy input stage, whereas most contacting of public officials in Mexico seeks to influence low-level allocative decisions. Cornelius, asking generally about contacts with government or PRI functionaries, found that 26 percent of his Mexico City sample had attempted such influence.[114]

Membership in interest groups is one way of working, through collective action or brokerage networks, to obtain favorable decisions on government allocations. In rural areas there are relatively few organizational alternatives to choose from. Manuel Carlos has demonstrated that in the agriculturally productive region of the Fuerte Valley in Sinaloa, the number of formal organizations and interest groups in *ejidos* increases with the prosperity and resources available in the community. He also found that although in all *ejidos* the members are interested and involved in local governance problems, a higher proportion of *ejidatarios* in the economically complex and prosperous *ejidos* are politically involved.[115] In his study of *ejidos* in the Laguna region, Landsberger found that participation in economic units (such as credit societies) which must deal with government agencies is greater than in the strictly "community governance" meetings.[116] It seems clear that to the extent that participation is voluntary, it is probably more widespread in organizations which directly affect the material interests of the individual. The same has been found to be true in urban areas, where neighborhood organizations established to negotiate with the government for land titles, water systems, electricity, and other urban improvements have usually succeeded in involving a much higher proportion of residents in low-income areas than other types of organizations.[117]

Despite the limited number and nature of participation questions in the *Civic Culture* survey, Almond and Verba demonstrate that there is a consistently positive relationship between political involvement and subjective political competence (efficacy). Those with high scores on their competence scale are more likely than low-scoring respondents to expose themselves to political communications, to discuss politics, to be party activists or to have a party affiliation, and to be members of voluntary organizations which they perceive as having some political involvement. They also found that participation in the family, school, and workplace is associated with higher subjective competence scores.[118] They suggest that although levels of subjective political competence are partly determined by social status factors,[119] the fundamental explanation should be sought in psychological dynamics: "Rather, family or school participation and political self-confidence may both be affected by the extent to which the child has a strong ego."[120]

Subsequent research in Mexico has tended to support the social-status explanations of political efficacy. Segovia demonstrates that the sense of political efficacy is stronger among private-school students (most of whom come from middle- or upper-class families) than among their public-school counterparts. Moreover, while feelings of inefficacy remain essentially constant throughout the grade levels he studied in the public schools, they decrease appreciably over time among the private-school pupils.[121] Pointing out that the politically and socially advantaged residents of Jalapa also have a disproportionately higher sense of political efficacy, Fagen and Tuohy conclude that "a sense of efficacy cannot really be disentangled from the other strands in the web of advantage and disadvantage previously discussed. Those who feel unable to affect local politics are those who are least well situated and equipped to do so. The converse is also the case."[122]

Low socioeconomic status is not always an insurmountable obstacle to the development of a sense of political efficacy, however, particularly among those who become involved in voluntary associations. In research on the migrant poor in Mexico City, Cornelius found that

> community-improvement organizations provide important psychological support for the low-income migrant who wants something from the government. Participation in collective demand-making efforts requires much less individual initiative, and it provides the potential demand-maker with a clear strategy for influencing government decisions. Moreover, to the extent that community-based organizations are successful in securing benefits through collective demand-making efforts, they strengthen the migrant's perception of the political system as being subject to manipulation and thus his sense of political efficacy.[123]

Petitioning for government benefits through community organizations, however, does not significantly increase the petitioner's confidence in being able to deal with the government as an *individual.*

Other data from the same study demonstrate that personal

contact with public officials — most of which is obtained through influence attempts by community improvement groups — is positively related to a sense of political efficacy:

> A low-income migrant who has personal contact with government in the context of demand-making attempts often emerges with an enhanced sense of political efficacy, especially if the outcomes of the attempts are evaluated positively. Those who have experienced the satisfaction that comes when some action in which they have voluntarily participated brings them closer to their goals have a greater faith both in the feasibility of obtaining government assistance and in the means employed to obtain it.[124]

Conversely, persistent bureaucratic obstructionism or overt repression in response to influence attempts may reinforce feelings of powerlessness and significantly reduce the propensity of the low-income citizen to participate in the future. Thus the importance of the experiential and situational basis of political efficacy should not be underestimated, particularly among lower-income Mexicans.

We have devoted considerable attention to political efficacy as an element in Mexican political culture, not only because it occupied a central position in Almond and Verba's analysis, but because we regard the forms and distribution of political efficacy in Mexico as very important in understanding the functioning and maintenance of the Mexican system. The pattern of limited, mediated efficacy among the urban and rural poor in Mexico — what Stevens calls "the myth of the right connection" [125] — ensures that those among them who do attempt to influence government will do so through officially sanctioned organizations and patron-client networks which are vertically integrated into the political apparatus. The demands that are articulated through these structures remain largely unaggregated and can be dealt with by the government on a piecemeal and usually quite protracted basis. This pattern of highly fragmented, nonthreatening petitioning by the bulk of the population enables the regime to devote more time and resources to the satisfaction of demands by higher-status groups, which are seen as potentially more threatening to the political fortunes of incumbents and to the stability of the system itself.

As Segovia points out, a sense of *personal* inefficacy can be functional to, and even fostered by, authoritarian regimes seeking to minimize "spontaneous" political activity that might glut the system with demands that cannot be satisfied.[126] Almond and Verba recognized the important positive relationship between subjective competence and participation and the possibilities this holds for democratization of political systems. They failed to recognize, however, that this "democratization" can be manipulated and, more importantly, that *low* levels of subjective political competence can also be instrumental to system stability and legitimacy. We agree with Evelyn Stevens's assessment, based on detailed historical case studies, that "the [Mexican] regime's success in limiting, discouraging and manipulating [citizen] input is the system's most distinguishing characteristic." [127]

POLITICAL CYNICISM AND SUPPORT FOR THE SYSTEM

In this section we examine "cynicism" as an element of Mexican political culture, relating it to such variables as interpersonal trust, trust in the government and its functionaries, predispositions toward cooperative or collective action, and general political system support. As mentioned in our earlier discussion of authoritarianism, Adorno included cynicism, or the measure of trust in people and expectations for their behavior, as one dimension of the authoritarian personality. As Adorno expressed it, authoritarian personalities tend to attribute to others the negative and untrustworthy qualities which they could not accept in, and would not attribute to, themselves.[128] Political analysts have not employed the same interpretation of the basis of cynicism, nor have they necessarily treated it as a dimension of authoritarianism; but in general the implication of the analysis has been the same: that cynicism is more a reflection of the personality of the respondent or a character trait in a social group than a reasoned assessment of one's neighbors and government. This is clearly the perspective from which interpersonal trust and government support are examined in *The Civic Culture*. More recent studies of politics and values in Mexico remark on the high levels of negativism about politics, politicians, and the functioning of political institutions, as well as the very limited willingness to join with one's neighbors in cooperative efforts. These studies, however, generally seek explanations of such traits in past experiences and in political system performance.

Almond and Verba studied a variety of social attitudes (e.g., the proclivity to choose outgoing social activities, valuation of generosity as a character trait, faith in people) which they regarded as the roots of "civic cooperation" — the propensity to work with others in attempting to influence the government.[129] They argued that civic cooperation is important in the functioning of democratic systems because it helps to determine the amount of pressure an individual or group can exert, and the probability of success. Moreover, cooperation is required for the aggregation of interests in order to prevent the system from becoming overloaded with individual demands.

Almond and Verba found that education, occupation, and sex are less important than the "political styles" (national political culture) of a country in determining differences in the attitudes which are the basis of civic cooperation. This is particularly true for "cooperative competence," the preference for using informal groups to affect local and national regulations.[130] Examining a series of items measuring social trust and distrust, they found that among Mexicans at all educational levels, like Germans and Italians, "a feeling of suspicion about human relations tends to prevail. Interaction with others, outside the narrow circles of family and friends, is viewed as risky and dangerous." [131]

Mistrust and individualism have long been regarded by students of Mexico as important elements of Mexican culture. The national character literature has sought the origin of these traits in certain historical experiences which allegedly molded the Mexican character: repeated invasions by foreign powers, subjugations to foreign cultural patterns, internal betrayals of the national interest, racial mixing (*mestizaje*), and the spread of Catholic Church influence.[132] Other characterological analyses have relied on explanations focusing on socioeconomic structures[133] and the dynamics of family socialization.[134]

Whatever its origins, survey studies have consistently encountered low levels of interpersonal trust in Mexico. Eighty-two percent of Kahl's respondents agreed that people help others not so much because it is right, but because it is good business.[135]

Four out of five in Almond and Verba's Mexican sample believed that people are more inclined to look out for themselves than to help others.[136] Sixty percent of Cornelius's sample of low-income urban dwellers chose the mistrustful alternative when presented with the same choices.[137]

It seems clear that, as a general rule, Mexicans do not place great trust in each other. This does not, however, eliminate the possibility of collective political action should a cooperative strategy be regarded as the most effective means for achieving specific collective benefits. In general, the problems or needs which stimulate cooperative political action are those which are not viewed as being susceptible to "individual" solution. For example, individual title to illegally occupied land in urban squatter settlements can be obtained only through a government decision to recognize the land-tenure rights of all residents of the settlement. Similarly, residents of rural *ejido* communities may obtain credit from the government bank only by organizing "credit societies" and petitioning collectively for such assistance.

Apart from needs for these kinds of collective goods, the only situation which seems to provoke sustained cooperative action is one in which people must band together to confront an external threat to some highly salient group interest — for example, when the economic or even physical survival of a community is threatened by government eviction, encroachment by large landowners, or intrusions by some other common enemy.[138] Survey results indicate that most low-income Mexicans endorse the ideal of cooperative action, but that fear of the potential costs (in personal terms) of such actions, suspicions about the profit-seeking motivations of those who organize them, and concern about the potentially unequal distribution of benefits resulting from such actions are usually sufficient to dissuade them from participating.[139]

As mentioned earlier, the traditional assumption in political psychology has been that personal and political cynicism constitute facets of a single character trait. Evidence on the determinants of political cynicism in Mexico tends to dispute such an argument, however. Several different indicators of political cynicism in Mexico have been studied: expectations of treatment by the bureaucracy and the police, government performance evaluations (including feelings about politicians), and allegiance to and evaluations of national institutions and symbols. We shall summarize the research findings on each of these indicators in turn.

Several scholars have posed essentially similar questions inquiring about the treatment that Mexicans would expect to receive from the bureaucracy and the police. Fagen and Tuohy and Almond and Verba found that between 42 and 48 percent of their respondents expected that, if they took up some matter with a government office, they would receive equal treatment.[140] When Cornelius asked the same question, specifying that it might deal with a credential or a legal matter, he found that 74 percent of the low-income residents he interviewed in Mexico City would expect to receive satisfactory treatment.[141] But only 43 percent of the *ejido* credit-society members surveyed by Landsberger in La Laguna expected fair treatment.[142] When asked about the treatment they would expect to receive from the police in the case of a minor infraction, only about one-third of Almond and Verba's and Fagen and Tuohy's respondents expected to receive equal treatment. More than 78 percent of the low-income Mexico City residents interviewed by Cornelius anticipated only bad treatment in any encounter with the police.[143]

One must be cautious, however, in interpreting even the relatively optimistic expectations for "equal" treatment by government bureaucrats. As Fagen and Tuohy point out, the questions cited above ask only whether the individual would expect to receive a fair hearing for his problems, not that he would win.[144] Many respondents may have interpreted "equal treatment" to mean, "as badly as others are treated." In fact, less than one-fifth of the respondents in the Almond and Verba, Fagen and Tuohy, and Cornelius samples thought that their point of view would be given serious attention by either the bureaucracy or the police, and a third or more expected that they would be completely ignored. Interestingly, when Cornelius asked what would happen if they went to the government office with a representative of their community, only 8 percent expected that they would be ignored, and more than 40 percent believed they would receive a great deal of attention.[145]

This finding of higher expectations of good treatment when accompanied by a community representative underscores the importance of contacts with officials that are made through a clientage network or in collective demand-making efforts. By the same token, the importance of one's resources and status in the society is reflected in both the Jalapa and *Civic Culture* survey results, which demonstrate that individuals of higher socioeconomic status uniformly expect to receive better treatment from public officials.[146]

Mexicans are generally aware of the extreme concentration of power in their society and doubt that it is exercised for the general welfare. Approximately 89 percent of the respondents in the Jalapa and *Civic Culture* samples believed that a few people have a great deal of influence and that they ignore the interests of the majority.[147] When Segovia's schoolchildren were asked to rank various groups in terms of their political influence, they placed average citizens second from the bottom (above the church).[148]

Most Mexicans have an intense distrust or dislike of politicians and politics. Surveys have found that a majority believe that politicians sound good in their speeches, but consider their behavior unpredictable ("one can never tell what they will do once they are elected"). More than two-fifths, and as many as two-thirds, of those surveyed believe that public officials are more interested in advancing their own interests or careers than in helping people. They agree nearly unanimously that corruption is as (or more) prevalent in government service as in other careers.[149] Fagen and Tuohy also report that negativism toward politics and politicians is relatively equally distributed across sex, class, and educational lines, although lower-status individuals have a slight tendency toward greater negativism.[150]

One of the most fascinating questions about Mexican political culture becomes apparent when one juxtaposes the data on political cynicism cited above with evidence of overall support for the political system. Mexicans do believe in the "Mexican miracle" of national economic growth, and most feel that they have shared at least a little in that progress. They are also willing to accord the government substantial responsibility (probably more than its actual share) for the country's economic development. Yet they are generally quite cynical about politics, incumbents, and their own ability to influence the political decision-making process. Almond and Verba and every subsequent student of Mexican political culture have called attention to this contrast in attitudes. Kahl refers to "the ambivalent Mexican"; Cockcroft, Cornelius, and Davis discuss the discrepancy between "normative" and "descriptive" models of the political system held by most Mexicans; Almond and Verba refer to the allegiant and aspiring but alienated Mexican.[151]

Most scholars seem to agree that the Mexican regime's symbolic outputs, which stress its commitment to the pursuit of social justice and other goals of the "continuing Revolution," have strongly influenced mass support for the system. Indeed, Almond and Verba attribute much of the high system affect and (limited) pride in government and political institutions which they find in Mexico to symbolic identification with the revolution.[152] Seventy-eight percent of Kahl's respondents felt that Mexico is much better off because of the Revolution.[153] Segovia found that even when he controlled for father's occupation, about three-quarters of the schoolchildren he interviewed agreed that the Revolution had benefited mainly workers and peasants; between half and three-quarters agreed that all Mexicans had benefited from the Revolution. The most skeptical children were those whose fathers have occupations at the status extremes (professionals or peasants).[154] When asked whether the ideals and goals of the Mexican Revolution have been realized, forgotten, or are still being pursued, well over half of the respondents in three different surveys selected the last statement (about 10 to 25 percent believed that the goals had already been achieved).[155]

Segovia has examined four "nationalist myths" (liberty, national unity, democracy, and racial prejudice) and attitudes toward national heroes, and the distribution of these by region and demographic categories. He found that although there are differences in intensity, the myths are widely shared. As a general rule, the frequency of belief in the myths declines with age and tends to vary depending on whether group interests and myths coincide. He attributes the widespread internalization of national myths and symbols primarily to the efficient efforts of the schools.[156] We would also point out that the symbolic outputs of the regime are channeled incessantly through the press, radio and television, labor unions, and virtually every Mexican politician from the President of the Republic on down to local community leaders. All make frequent reference in their public statements to the accomplishments and unfinished tasks of the ongoing, "institutionalized" Revolution.

Coleman and Davis's research has addressed the interrelationships among symbolism, efficacy, and diffuse support for the political system. They find that the best predictors of diffuse support, particularly among lower- and upper-class Mexicans, are those variables which measure "cognitive symbol association," that is, the intensity with which the government and the PRI are cognitively associated with key symbols: social justice, democracy, and the ideals of the Mexican Revolution. They also found a strong positive relationship between cognitive symbol association and political efficacy.[157]

Although mass consumption of the symbolic outputs of the Mexican political system helps to explain the apparent contradiction between strongly supportive attitudes toward the system and highly negative evaluations of actual government performance in many problem areas, it is by no means a complete explanation. As the authors of *The Civic Culture* recognized, the Mexican case brings out "a general pattern of [citizen] experience with corruption, discrimination, and unresponsiveness." [158] Yet there is a persistent and widespread tendency for citizens to attribute failures of performance to the personal inadequacies of incumbent officials — especially lower- or middle-echelon functionaries. (There is also a tendency to believe that the president or other high-level central government officials would halt corruption and abuses of authority on the periphery — if only they knew!) Blame is rarely attributed to the political structure itself, or to the economic structures it supports. Instead, the average Mexican seems to believe, as did nearly 80 percent of the Mexico City residents interviewed by Cornelius, that the present system of government and politics is "good for the country." [159]

The system seems to derive its basic legitimacy in the eyes of the governed from three sources: (1) its origins in large-scale civil strife and turmoil; (2) its role in promoting economic and social development since the 1930s; and (3) its performance as a distributive apparatus which has dispensed concrete, material benefits (however limited or short-term) to a large proportion of the Mexican population since the 1930s. The massive human costs and the prolonged disruption of national economic life which attended the birth of the present regime from 1910 until the late 1930s are still remembered by an older generation of Mexicans; and even among younger generations there seems to be a residue of fear that the divisive, destructive forces within the country might be unleashed once again if the established regime were to be seriously challenged. The legitimating influence of the regime's role in Mexico's "economic miracle" of recent decades has also been important, though the severe economic reverses suffered by the country since 1970 (sharply increased rates of inflation and unemployment, a de facto currency devaluation) may have caused an erosion of support for the regime. Finally, the distribution of particularistic material rewards through the PRI and a multiplicity of government agencies has helped to maintain the credibility of Revolutionary ideology while providing millions of Mexicans with at least a minor stake in the preservation of the sociopolitical status quo. The agrarian reform program, agricultural credit, land titles for urban squatters, free or low-cost medical care provided through PRI-sponsored neighborhood clinics or periodic visits by brigades of public health workers, free lunches for schoolchildren, and low-cost foodstuffs and other basic commodities distributed through government retail outlets (the CONASUPO system) are only a few of the regime's social welfare programs which have affected the lives of Mexicans in recent decades. These programs have done little to redistribute wealth or to increase rates of socioeconomic mobility among disadvantaged Mexicans. They have, however, led many Mexicans to view the government as the most likely source of concrete benefits for the poor, especially in situations of acute, short-term need.

Clearly, there are limits to symbolic gratification. Recent research suggests that much support for the Mexican political system is rooted in specific, personalized instances of governmental distributive performance.[160] The proportion of people who support the regime simply because of its continuing identification with national heroes, symbols, and myths is probably small. Far more important is the fact that symbolic rewards have been effectively supplemented with particularistic material rewards, at least among some sectors of the population.

CONCLUSION

Why study political culture in Mexico? The answer, of course, depends on one's research task. A strong case could be made that those interested in public policy formation in Mexico would do well to concentrate upon decision-making processes within the PRI-government apparatus and/or the political culture of the political-administrative elite itself.[161] Given the extremely limited involvement of the general population in political input structures, careful studies of the values and personal alliances of PRI and government functionaries at the national, state, and local levels would undoubtedly shed more light on public policy making than any investigation of mass political culture. Our reading of the available literature suggests that mass attitudes and behavior enter into the policy-formation process primarily as parameters or constraints perceived by government decision makers, which may help to define the boundaries of politically feasible and legitimate action in a given problem area. Thus for prediction and explanation of policy *outputs,* it seems more important to understand how political decision makers *perceive* mass attitudes and behavior patterns than to know the actual distribution of attitudes and behaviors in the general population.

If policy *outcomes* — that is, the effectiveness or consequences of policy outputs — are of primary concern, however, general studies of political culture can be important and illuminating. As noted at several points in this chapter, most Mexicans attempt to influence public policy during the implementation stage, particularly at the local level, seeking preferential application of specific policies or programs to themselves or their community. But even those who do not seek actively to influence policy implementation to further their interests often possess (and utilize) the capacity to resist policy initiatives emanating from Mexico City. An excellent recent example of this is the frustration of the government's efforts to "collectivize" agricultural production and marketing in *ejido* communities throughout the nation. This campaign, promoted vigorously over a three-year period by President Echeverría, all of his cabinet members, and countless brigades of technicians dispatched by the Ministry of Agrarian Reform to visit and persuade each *ejido* to adopt collective practices, met with nearly uniform rejection. The peasants' distrust of government agencies and, more importantly, of their fellow *ejidatarios* led them to rebuff what the government continues to regard as one of its most important policy initiatives in the rural sector.[162]

The impact of public policies — and more generally, the political system itself — on individual attitudes and behavior is also an important and underresearched topic which should concern future students of Mexican political culture. In this chapter we have repeatedly stressed the importance of the citizen's actual experiences in dealing with the political system for explaining diffuse support, sense of political efficacy, and propensity to engage in various forms of political activity. But the study of political-system effects and individual adaptations to such effects should not be limited to self-initiated influence attempts or other types of personal contacts with public officials. It should encompass all government policies and programs which may have benefited or even proved detrimental to the interests of the average citizen. Almond and Verba included orientations toward "particular public policies, decisions, or enforcements" in their conception of political culture;[163] but neither in their survey nor in their analysis of the data did they devote more than passing attention to this class of "components of the political system." We believe that much could be gained in future research on Mexican political culture by the development of imaginative, contextually sensitive measures of the ways in which government outputs have affected the life chances and quality of life among the Mexican people, and how these outputs are perceived and evaluated by the target populations.

More generally, we believe that the impact of political, economic, and social structures upon individual attitudes and behavior is an appropriate concern for the student of political culture in Mexico. Fromm and Maccoby's pioneering research has shown how social character in rural Mexico is firmly rooted in socioeconomic structures. They observe that the Mexican child starts out with all the potential modes of relating himself to society and experiments with several of them. "Eventually those become dominant which are most suited for adaptation to his particular environment." [164] The possibilities for identifying such structural influences on the political learning process in Mexico remain virtually unexplored.

To what extent is change in Mexican political culture contingent upon thoroughgoing changes in political and economic structures and vice versa? We do not subscribe to the notion shared by some neo-Marxist or radical critics of research on political culture, to the effect that all significant, politically relevant patterns of attitudes and behaviors among the masses are structurally determined and that, therefore, empirical study of individual attitudes and behavior is meaningless (once the structures are changed, for example, via social revolution, attitudinal and behavioral change at the individual level will follow, almost automatically). As Dennis Kavanagh notes elsewhere in this volume, "Even if values are shown to be derivative [of social and economic structures] at one point in time, they may, once established, independently affect behavior." We would argue that there are certain highly stable attitudes, values, and beliefs held by the average Mexican peasant or low-income city dweller, which *are* important to an accurate assessment of his tolerance for socioeconomic inequality as well as his propensity to engage in certain kinds of political action — even under very different structural conditions.[165] This does not necessarily preclude substantial attitudinal or behavioral change in the wake of radical structural change, as the Cuban and Peruvian cases have demonstrated.[166] It does suggest, however, that the relationship between sociopolitical structures and individual attitudes and behaviors is far more complex and interactive than indicated either by most students of political culture or by their radical critics.

In the absence of fundamental regime change at the national level, research on this question in the Mexican context might usefully focus on states, regions, or local communities which have experienced significant structural changes — especially an "opening up" of the political opportunity structure, perhaps through a shift from PRI domination to multiparty electoral competition. Specifically, what barriers to expanded political participation were reduced or removed? How did the local population respond to such changes in constraints or opportunities? What new strategies of political influence were employed? What changes in the individual calculus of potential costs, risks, and benefits attending political action could be observed in response to the new situation? Panel studies of communities in political flux would be particularly valuable for exploring such questions.

Our recommendation of more political culture research focused on subnational political units stems in part from our pessimism about the feasibility (both technical and financial) in Mexico of national surveys that would include the rural population. Our own experience in sampling a small number of relatively accessible rural communities in Mexico leads us to believe that the task of developing an adequate nationwide sampling frame for the rural population, not to mention the formidable logistical problems involved in survey research in many parts of rural Mexico, would necessitate a huge investment of time and financial resources — well beyond the capabilities of most researchers.

Of course, the sample survey is not the only data-gathering technique available to the student of political culture. Indeed, it could be argued that some of the most subtle, subjective, latent elements of political culture can be tapped effectively only by some less reactive, less structured research method: depth-interviewing, participant observation, projective tests, and so forth. The fact that these techniques lend themselves primarily to microlevel research units further increases the attractiveness and importance of political culture studies confined to subnational units. Such studies, by virtue of their reduced scope, enable the investigator to gather detailed contextual data, often over a considerable period of time, which helps to ensure more accurate interpretation of sample survey data. Such research need not take the form of a narrow case study; it can be designed, through purposive selection of contrasting research sites, to test important hypotheses and explore causal chains more exhaustively than is usually possible in national-level studies based on "representative" samples.

If survey studies of Mexico at the national level are to be attempted in the future, we would advocate a stratified or modified "quota" sampling strategy which would provide enough respondents in each of several major sociocultural groups to permit detailed examination of the political subcultures which may be associated with these groups. Key stratification variables might include sex, religiosity, ethnicity, region, social class, and work experience in the United States.[167]

Finally, future cross-national researchers pondering the inclusion of Mexico in their studies might take greater cognizance of the authoritarian aspects of the Mexican political system. It could be argued that the Mexican system can be compared more fruitfully with other authoritarian or "authoritarian-corporatist" regimes in Latin America, southern Europe, or the Afro-Asian region than with stable democratic systems.[168] Full recognition of the authoritarian features of the Mexican regime would also lead the researcher to consider such questions as the incidence and determinants of participation in various regime-supportive political activities encouraged by the ruling elite — activities which may be quite important in explaining the stability over time of the Mexican regime; the obstacles (both cultural and structural) to genuine democratization; and the quality and societal consequences of the political participation which does occur in such a system. Who controls participatory behavior? Toward what ends? Does increased participation through vertically integrated clientage networks really help to improve the material condition of the poor as a class, or even on a communitywide basis? Or does it simply preserve or further the self-interests of the political leaders who control such networks, from the local to the national level? Who really gains from expanded participation in the Mexican system? What are the long-term human costs of a pattern of "mediated" political efficacy?

To the extent that systematic research on political culture and participation enables us to increase our understanding of how the Mexican system and others like it function, with what costs and what benefits to which groups, we believe it to be a worthy enterprise for political scientists.

NOTES

1. All chapter and page references are to the original edition of Gabriel A. Almond and Sidney Verba, *The Civic Culture* (Princeton, N.J.: Princeton Univ. Press, 1963).

2. The sampling sites and the proportion of respondents residing in each are as follows: Aguascalientes, Ags., 5.9%; Ameca, Jal., 1.8%; Culiacán, Son., 3.0%; Ciudad Victoria, Tams., 3.2%; Córdoba, Ver., 2.8%; Guadalajara, Jal., 5.8%; Iguala, Gro., 2.0%; La Barca, Jal., 1.6%; Lerdo, Dgo., 2.1%; Linares, N.L., 1.8%; Mérida, Yuc., 5.1%; México, D.F., 18.6%; Monterey, N.L., 5.9%; Morelia, Mich., 3.7%; Moroleón, Gto., 1.8%; Nogales, Son., 3.3%; Oaxaca, Oax., 3.1%; Parrás, Coah., 1.6%; Puebla, Pue., 5.2%; Querétaro, Qro., 3.1%; Salvatierra, Gto., 1.8%; San Andrés Tuxtla, Ver., 1.5%; San Luis Potosí, S.L.P., 5.7%; San Miguel Allende, Gto., 1.9%; Tehuacán, Pue., 2.2%;

Tijuana, B.C., 5.2%; Tlalnepantla, Mex., 2.0%. These percentages were calculated from a listing of places of residence of Mexican respondents for the
Civic Culture survey provided by Gabriel Almond.

3. Almond and Verba, *Civic Culture,* p. 90.

4. See Fernando Cámara Barbachano, "Láś subculturas mexicanas como
partes integrantes de los municipios: estructuras tradicionales y modernas
de su organización y gobierno," *Revista Mexicana de Ciencia Política* 18,
no. 67 (January–March 1972): 101–19; and Pablo González Casanova, *Democracy in Mexico* (London and New York: Oxford Univ. Press, 1970 [origi-
nally published in Spanish in 1965]).

5. González Casanova, *Democracy in Mexico,* pp. 73–74.

6. Almond and Verba, *Civic Culture,* pp. 514–15.

7. See, for example, Wayne A. Cornelius, *Politics and the Migrant Poor
in Mexico City* (Stanford: Stanford Univ. Press, 1975), pp. 27–32, 275.

8. See, for example, Cornelius, *Politics and the Migrant Poor,* p. 277.

9. Almond and Verba, *Civic Culture,* p. 104.

10. Ibid., p. 185.

11. See Cornelius, *Politics and the Migrant Poor,* p. 197, and Susan
Kaufman Purcell, *The Mexican Profit-Sharing Decision: Politics in an
Authoritarian Regime* (Berkeley: Univ. of California Press, 1975), pp. 131–42.

12. Almond and Verba, *Civic Culture,* p. 99 and passim.

13. See Thomas V. Greer, "An Analysis of Mexican Literacy," *Journal of
Inter-American Studies* 11 (July 1969): 466–76.

14. Almond and Verba, *Civic Culture,* pp. 80–81. A secondary analysis of
the Almond and Verba data revealed that 71.5 percent of their male, low-
income respondents perceived no impact of federal government "rules and
regulations" on their lives (Cornelius, *Politics and the Migrant Poor,* p. 82,
Table 4.1). The only comparable data come from Cornelius's 1970 survey of
male, low-income Mexico City residents. When questioned about the impact
of local and federal government *activities* on their daily lives, 43.4 percent
and 32.6 percent of his respondents perceived no effect of (respectively)
federal and local governments, compared with 14.6 percent and 19.1 percent
who perceived "much" effect of these governments on their lives. It is not
possible to determine whether the perception of relatively greater government impact in Mexico City is due to differences in question wording, to
increases in government activities between 1959 and 1970, to the relatively
higher concentration of government-provided goods and services in the capital
(compared with other urban areas included in the Almond and Verba survey),
or to the greater visibility of government activities in the capital city.

15. Almond and Verba, *Civic Culture,* p. 81 and passim.

16. See, for example, Joseph A. Kahl, *The Measurement of Modernism*
(Austin: Univ. of Texas Press, 1968), pp. 153–71; and Richard R. Fagen and
William S. Tuohy, *Politics and Privilege in a Mexican City* (Stanford:
Stanford Univ. Press, 1972), pp. 35–36, 85–96.

17. Fagen and Tuohy, *Politics and Privilege,* p. 117.

18. Kenneth M. Coleman, *Public Opinion in Mexico City About the Electoral System,* James Sprunt Series in History and Political Science, no. 53
(Chapel Hill, Univ. of North Carolina Press, 1972), p. 30.

19. Fagen and Tuohy, *Politics and Privilege,* pp. 193, 85.

20. Erich Fromm and Michael Maccoby, *Social Character in a Mexican
Village* (Englewood Cliffs, N.J.: Prentice-Hall, 1970), p. 63.

21. Evelyn P. Stevens, *Protest and Response in Mexico* (Cambridge, Mass.:
M.I.T. Press, 1974), pp. 63–64.

22. Coleman, *Public Opinion in Mexico City*, pp. 30–31.

23. Rafael Segovia, *La politización del niño mexicano* (México, D.F.: El Colegio de México, 1975), pp. 16–19, 39–40.

24. Ibid., pp. 19, 43.

25. For example, regional differences and some of the variables which perpetuate them are described by K. A. Appendini, D. Murayama, and R. M. Domínguez, "Desarrollo desigual en México, 1900 y 1960," *Demografía y Economía* 7, no. 1 (1972): 1–39; Fernando Cámara Barbachano, "Las subculturas mexicanas como partes integrantes de los municipios"; Roderic Ai Camp, "A Reexamination of Political Leadership and Allocation of Federal Revenues in Mexico, 1934–1973," paper presented at the Fifth National Meeting of the Latin American Studies Association, San Francisco, November 1974; Howard Cline, *The United States and Mexico*, rev. ed. (New York: Atheneum, [1953], 1968), pp. 88–111; González Casanova, *Democracy in Mexico*, p. 44 and passim; Paul W. Drake, "Mexican Regionalism Reconsidered," *Journal of Inter-American Studies* 12, no. 3 (1970); Marta Tienda, "Diferencias socioeconómicas regionales y tasas de participación de la fuerza de trabajo femenina: el caso de México," *Revista Mexicana de Sociología* 37, no. 4 (October–December 1975): 911–29; James W. Wilkie, *The Mexican Revolution: Federal Expenditure and Social Change Since 1910*, 2nd ed. (Berkeley: Univ. of California Press, 1970).

26. See, for example, Manuel L. Carlos, *Politics and Development in Rural Mexico* (New York: Praeger Special Studies, 1974), and Wayne A. Cornelius, *Los Norteños: Mexican Migrants in the U.S. and Rural Mexico* (Berkeley: Univ. of California Press, forthcoming).

27. Segovia, *La politización*, pp. 36–38.

28. Almond and Verba, *Civic Culture*, p. 234.

29. Cornelius, *Politics and the Migrant Poor*, and Jorge Montaño, *Los pobres de la ciudad en los asentamientos espontáneos* (México, D.F.: Siglo Veintiuno, 1976), pp. 105–98.

30. Cornelius, *Politics and the Migrant Poor*, chap. 8; Fagen and Tuohy, *Politics and Privilege*, p. 114; Kenneth M. Coleman and Charles L. Davis, "The Structural Context of Politics and Dimensions of Regime Performance: Their Importance for the Comparative Study of Political Efficacy," *Comparative Political Studies* 9, no. 2 (July 1976).

31. F. Christopher Arterton, "Political Participation as Attempted Interpersonal Influence: A Test of a Theoretical Model Using Data from Rural Mexican Villages," unpublished Ph.D. dissertation, Massachusetts Institute of Technology, 1974; Cornelius, *Politics and the Migrant Poor*, chaps. 4, 6, 7; Merilee S. Grindle, *Bureaucrats, Politicians and Peasants in Mexico: A Case Study in Public Policy* (Berkeley: Univ. of California Press, 1977).

32. Almond and Verba, *Civic Culture*, pp. 88–95.

33. For an exception to this generalization see Evelyn P. Stevens, *Protest and Response in Mexico;* and Evelyn P. Stevens, "Protest Movement in an Authoritarian Regime: The Mexican Case," *Comparative Politics* 7 (April 1975): 361–82.

34. Segovia, *La politización*.

35. For example, see Michael Maccoby, "On Mexican National Character," *The Annals of the American Academy of Political and Social Sciences* 370 (1967): 63–73. Representatives of this tradition, still among the most frequently cited authorities on Mexican political culture, include Victor Alba, *The Mexicans: The Making of a Nation* (New York: Praeger Publishers, 1967); Jorge Carrión, *Mito y magia del mexicano* (México, D.F.: Porrúa y

Obregón, 1952); Rogelio Díaz Guerrero, *Psychology of the Mexican: Culture and Personality* (Austin: Univ. of Texas Press, [1967], 1975); José Gómez Robleda, *Psicología del mexicano: motivos de perturbación de la conducta psico-social del mexicano de la clase media* (México, D.F.: Biblioteca de Ensayos Sociológicos, Instituto de Investigaciones Sociales, Universidad Nacional Autónoma de México, 1965); Francisco González Pineda, *El mexicano: su dinámica psicosocial,* 3rd ed. (México, D.F.: Editorial Pax-México, 1966) ; Octavio Paz, *The Labyrinth of Solitude.* Translated by Lysander Kemp. (New York: Grove Press, [1950], 1961); Octavio Paz, *The Other Mexico: Critique of the Pyramid.* Translated by Lysander Kemp. (New York: Grove Press, 1972); Santiago Ramírez, *El Mexicano: psicología de sus motivaciones,* 4th ed. (México, D.F.: Editorial Pax-México, 1966); Samuel Ramos, *Profile of Man and Culture in Mexico* (Austin: Univ. of Texas Press, [1938], 1964). Among the social scientists who built upon their work we include Martin Needler, "Politics and National Character: The Case of Mexico," *American Anthropologist* 73, no. 3 (June 1971): 757–61; Martin Needler, *Politics and Society in Mexico* (Albuquerque: Univ. of New Mexico Press, 1971), chap. 7; Robert Scott, "Mexico: The Established Revolution," in *Political Culture and Political Development,* Lucian W. Pye and Sidney Verba, eds. (Princeton, N.J.: Princeton Univ. Press, 1965); and, in part, Roger D. Hansen, *The Politics of Mexican Development* (Baltimore: Johns Hopkins Univ. Press, 1971).

There is a perceptive critical review of this literature, particularly of Hansen's book, in William S. Tuohy, "Psychology and Political Analysis: The Case of Mexico," *Western Political Quarterly* 27 (June 1974): 289–307. The work of Octavio Paz, Samuel Ramos, Jorge Carrión, and other Mexican contributors to the psychohistorical literature on Mexican identity is analyzed in Ann L. Craig, "History and Origins: An Element in Mexico's Group Identity," *Revista Interamericana* 3, no. 4 (Winter 1974): 377–95.

36. For example, John G. Corbett, "The Context of Politics in a Mexican Community: A Study in Constraints on System Capacity," unpublished Ph.D. dissertation, Stanford University, 1974; Fagen and Tuohy, *Politics and Privilege;* Lawrence S. Graham, *Politics in a Mexican Community,* Latin American Monographs, Series 1, No. 35 (Gainesville: Univ. of Florida Press, 1968); Charles I. Mundale, "Local Politics, Integration, and National Stability in Mexico," unpublished Ph.D. dissertation, University of Minnesota, 1971; and Antonio Ugalde, *Power and Conflict in a Mexican Community* (Albuquerque: Univ. of New Mexico Press, 1970).

37. Almond and Verba, *Civic Culture,* p. 40.

38. See especially Bo Anderson and James Cockcroft, "Control and Cooptation in Mexican Politics," *International Journal of Comparative Sociology* 7 (March 1966): 11–28; Frank Brandenburg, *The Making of Modern Mexico* (Englewood Cliffs, N.J.: Prentice-Hall, 1964); James Cockcroft, "Coercion and Ideology in Mexican Politics," in *Dependence and Underdevelopment: Latin America's Political Economy,* J. D. Cockcroft et al., ed. (Garden City, N.Y.: Doubleday–Anchor, 1972); James Cockcroft, "Misdeveloped Mexico," in *Latin America: The Struggle with Dependence and Beyond,* Ronald Chilcote and Joel Edelstein, eds. (Cambridge, Mass.: Schenkman, 1974); Kenneth M. Coleman, *Diffuse Support in Mexico: The Potential for Crisis,* Professional Papers in Comparative Politics, no. 01–057 (Beverly Hills, Calif.: Sage Publications, 1976); Coleman and Davis, "The Structural Context of Politics and Dimensions of Regime Performance"; Arnaldo Córdova, *La ideología de la revolución mexicana* (México, D.F.: Ediciones Era, 1972); Cornelius, *Politics*

and the Migrant Poor; Charles L. Davis, "Toward an Explanation of Mass Support for Authoritarian Regimes: A Case Study of Political Attitudes in Mexico City," unpublished Ph.D. dissertation, University of Kentucky, 1974); Susan Eckstein, *The Poverty of Revolution: The State and the Urban Poor in Mexico* (Princeton, N.J.: Princeton Univ. Press, 1976); Fagen and Tuohy, *Politics and Privilege;* González Casanova, *Democracy in Mexico;* Hansen, *The Politics of Mexican Development;* Kenneth Johnson, *Mexican Democracy: A Critical View* (Boston: Houghton Mifflin, 1971); Susan Kaufman Purcell, *The Mexican Profit-Sharing Decision;* José Luis Reyna, *An Empirical Analysis of Political Mobilization: The Case of Mexico,* Latin American Studies Program Dissertation Series, no. 26 (Ithaca, N.Y.: Cornell Univ., 1971); José Luis Reyna, "Control político, estabilidad y desarrollo en México," *Cuadernos del Centro de Estudios Sociológicos,* no. 3 (México, D.F.: El Colegio de México, 1974); David Ronfeldt, *Atencingo: The Politics of Agrarian Struggle in a Mexican Ejido* (Stanford: Stanford Univ. Press, 1973); Peter H. Smith, *Labyrinths of Power: Political Recruitment in Twentieth-Century Mexico* (Princeton: Princeton Univ. Press, 1979); Stevens, *Protest and Response;* and Stevens, "Mexico's One-Party State: Revolutionary Myth and Authoritarian Reality," in *Latin American Politics and Development,* Howard J. Wiarda and Harvey F. Kline, eds. (Boston: Houghton Mifflin, 1979).

39. For examples of such earlier relatively optimistic assessments, see Cline, *The United States and Mexico;* Martin Needler, "The Political Development of Mexico," *American Political Science Review* 55, no. 2 (June 1961); L. Vincent Padgett, "Mexico's One-Party System: A Reevaluation," *American Political Science Review* 51, no. 4 (December 1957); L. Vincent Padgett, *The Mexican Political System* (Boston: Houghton Mifflin, 1966); and Robert E. Scott, *Mexican Government in Transition* (Urbana: Univ. of Illinois Press, 1959). In his essay on "Daniel Cosío Villegas and the Interpretation of Mexico's Political System" *(Journal of Inter-American Studies and World Affairs* 18 [1976]: 242–52), Martin Needler has summarized the perspective of these earlier, more optimistic observers of Mexican politics as follows: "Mexico is on the whole a democracy in which the weaknesses of competition between the parties are made up for by competition among the sectors of the 'official' party, and whose other imperfections can be understood as the heritage of a predemocratic past that is gradually disappearing as the country develops toward a modern and fully democratic future." Needler himself has substantially revised his view of the Mexican system over the years (compare Needler, "The Political Development of Mexico," with Needler, *Politics and Society in Mexico* [Albuquerque: Univ. of New Mexico Press, 1971]).

40. T. W. Adorno, Else Frenkel-Brunswik, Daniel J. Levinson, and R. Nevitt Sanford, *The Authoritarian Personality* (New York: Norton [1950], 1969).

41. These dimensions include conventionalism ("rigid adherence to conventional, middle-class values"); authoritarian submission ("submissive, uncritical attitudes toward moral authorities of the in group"); authoritarian aggression (a "tendency to . . . condemn, reject, and punish people who violate conventional values"); antiintraception ("opposition to the subjective, the imaginative, the tenderminded"); power and toughness (a "preoccupation with the dominance-submission, strong-weak, leader-follower dimension; identification with power figures; . . . exaggerated assertion of strength and toughness"); destructiveness and cynicism ("generalized hostility, vilification

of the human [*sic*]"); projectivity ("the disposition to believe that wild and dangerous things go on in the world; the projection outwards of unconscious emotional impulses"); and "exaggerated concern with sexual 'goings-on' " (Adorno et al., *The Authoritarian Personality*, p. 228).

42. Fromm and Maccoby, *Social Character in a Mexican Village*.

43. Ibid., pp. 89–90.

44. Ibid., pp. 262–63.

45. Ibid., pp. 230, 110–11.

46. Evelyn Stevens has suggested that *marianismo* is a feminine counterpart to *machismo*. She defines *marianismo* as "the cult of feminine spiritual superiority, which teaches that women are semi-divine, morally superior to and spiritually stronger than men" (Evelyn P. Stevens, "*Marianismo*: The Other Side of *Machismo* in Latin America," in *Female and Male in Latin America*, Ann Pescatello, ed. [Pittsburgh: Univ. of Pittsburgh Press, 1973]). Stevens's concept of *marianismo* is supported by Romanucci-Ross's data on conflictive male-female relations and mother-son ties (see Lola Romanucci-Ross, *Conflict, Violence, and Morality in a Mexican Village* (Palo Alto, Calif.: National Press Books, 1973).

47. For example, Alba, *The Mexicans: The Making of a Nation;* Carrión, *Mito y magia del mexicano*; Fromm and Maccoby, *Social Character in a Mexican Village*, pp. 114–16; Paz, *The Labyrinth of Solitude;* Samuel Ramos, *Profile of Man and Culture in Mexico*.

48. Romanucci-Ross, *Conflict, Violence, and Morality*, pp. 145–54.

49. Fromm and Maccoby, *Social Character in a Mexican Village*, pp. 165–67.

50. See, e.g., Needler, "Politics and National Character," p. 80.

51. Paz, *The Labyrinth of Solitude*, pp. 79–82.

52. Fagen and Tuohy, *Politics and Privilege*, pp. 122–23, 125–26.

53. See Lewis Lipsitz, "Working Class Authoritarianism: A Re-evaluation," *American Sociological Review* 30, no. 1 (February 1965): 105–12.

54. Coleman, *Public Opinion in Mexico City*, pp. 42–44.

55. Ibid., p. 37.

56. Cornelius, *Politics and the Migrant Poor*, p. 96.

57. See Roger Bartra et al., *Caciquismo y poder político en el México rural* (México, D.F.: Siglo Veintiuno, 1975); Paul Friedrich, "The Legitimacy of a Cacique," in *Local-Level Politics: Social and Cultural Perspectives*, Marc J. Swartz, ed. (Chicago: Aldine, 1968); and González Casanova, *Democracy in Mexico*, p. 33.

58. Segovia, *La politización*, pp. 52–54, 105, 121–30.

59. Juan J. Linz, "An Authoritarian Regime: Spain," in *Cleavages, Ideologies and Party Systems*, E. Allardt and Y. Litunnen, eds. (Helsinki: Transactions of the Westermarck Society, 1964).

60. González Casanova, *Democracy in Mexico*, chap. 2. Cf. Segovia, *La politización*, pp. 112–20.

61. Stevens, *Protest and Response in Mexico*, pp. 32–33.

62. Purcell, *The Mexican Profit-Sharing Decision*, pp. 131–32, 139.

63. Statistics compiled by González Casanova show that between 1935 and 1964, the federal Chamber of Deputies approved all bills submitted by the president, and with the exception of the 1947–55 period, over 82 percent of the bills were unanimously approved. Opposing votes reached a high of 12 percent on all bills in 1964 (González Casanova, *Democracy in Mexico*, p. 210).

64. Stevens, *Protest and Response in Mexico*, p. 32.

65. See Fagen and Tuohy, *Politics and Privilege*, pp. 53–55; and Stevens, *Protest and Response in Mexico*, p. 47.

66. See Cornelius, *Politics and the Migrant Poor,* p. 189.

67. Fagen and Tuohy, *Politics and Privilege,* p. 21.

68. Coleman, *Public Opinion in Mexico City,* p. 26.

69. Cornelius, 1970 Mexico City survey, marginal frequencies.

70. Segovia, *La politización,* p. 26.

71. This practice was initiated during the presidential campaign of Lázaro Cárdenas in 1934 (see Wayne A. Cornelius, "Nation-building, Participation, and Distribution: The Politics of Social Reform Under Cárdenas," in *Crisis, Choice, and Change: Historical Studies in Political Development,* Gabriel Almond et al., eds. [Boston: Little, Brown, 1973], p. 434), and has been maintained by all subsequent PRI nominees. The campaign of the most recent PRI presidential candidate, José López Portillo, encompassed 221 campaign days (from October 9, 1975 to June 5, 1976), during which he traveled 78,000 kms., gave over 1550 speeches, visited 924 communities (and was reportedly received by demonstrations of support in about half of these), visited 310 families in their homes, attended 148 technical information meetings and 43 national affairs meetings, and listened to over 1650 presentations by local, state, and national leaders (*Excélsior,* Mexico City, June 6, 1976). The number of written petitions for government assistance received by López Portillo during the campaign was not reported, but they undoubtedly total several thousand. In rural areas, peasants often travel long distances to communities included in the candidate's itinerary to present personally their petitions to him.

72. Ibid., p. 58.

73. Calculated from data in Segovia, *La politización,* p. 51, Table 1.

74. Cornelius, *Politics and the Migrant Poor,* p. 184.

75. See, e.g., Fagen and Tuohy, *Politics and Privilege,* p. 31; and Antonio Ugalde et al., *The Urbanization Process of a Poor Mexican Neighborhood: The Case of San Felipe del Real Adicional, Juárez* (Austin: Institute of Latin American Studies, Univ. of Texas, 1974), pp. 139–49.

76. Cornelius, *Politics and the Migrant Poor,* chap. 6; and Graham, *Politics in a Mexican Community.*

77. For criticisms of the wording of these items, in the Mexican context, see our earlier discussion of validity and equivalence problems in the *Civic Culture* survey.

78. Almond and Verba, *Civic Culture,* pp. 185–86.

79. Ibid., pp. 217–29.

80. Ibid., p. 231.

81. Ibid., pp. 214–15.

82. Carole Pateman, "Political Culture, Political Structure, and Political Change," *British Journal of Political Science* 1, no. 3 (1971): 291–305; Cf. Davis, "Toward an Explanation of Mass Support for Authoritarian Regimes," pp. 54–56; Charles L. Davis and Kenneth M. Coleman, "Political Symbols, Political Efficacy, and Diffuse Support for the Mexican Political System," *Journal of Political and Military Sociology* 3, no. 1 (Spring 1975): 29; Kenneth P. Langton, "Situations, Psychological Dispositions, and Learning in Understanding the Decision to Participate Politically," paper presented at the Annual Meeting of the American Political Science Association, San Francisco, September 1975.

83. Davis and Coleman, "Political Symbols, Political Efficacy, and Diffuse Support"; Coleman and Davis, *Diffuse Support in Mexico;* Davis, "Toward an Explanation of Mass Support for Authoritarian Regimes."

84. Henry A. Landsberger, "The Limits and Conditions of Peasant Par-

ticipation in Mexico: A Case Study," in *Críticas constructivas del sistema político mexicano,* William P. Glade and Stanley R. Ross, eds. (Austin: Institute of Latin American Studies, Univ. of Texas, 1973), pp. 88–89.

85. Fagen and Tuohy, *Politics and Privilege,* p. 116, including the comparative data from Almond and Verba, *Civic Culture.*

86. Fagen and Tuohy, *Politics and Privilege,* p. 110.

87. Cornelius, *Politics and the Migrant Poor,* p. 79.

88. Ibid., pp. 159–60.

89. Fagen and Tuohy, *Politics and Privilege,* p. 73.

90. Cornelius, *Politics and the Migrant Poor,* p. 175.

91. See Sidney Verba, Bashir Ahmed, and Anil Bhatt, *Caste, Race, and Politics: A Comparative Study of India and the United States* (Beverly Hills, Calif.: Sage Publications, 1971); Sidney Verba, Norman H. Nie, and Jae-On Kim, *The Modes of Democratic Participation: A Cross-National Comparison,* Professional Papers in Comparative Politics, no. 01–013 (Beverly Hills, Calif.: Sage Publications, 1971); and Sidney Verba, Norman H. Nie et al., "The Modes of Participation: Continuities in Research," *Comparative Political Studies* 6 (1973).

92. See John A. Booth, "Are Latin Americans Politically Rational?—Citizen Participation and Democracy in Costa Rica," in *Political Participation in Latin America, Volume I: Citizen and State,* John A. Booth and Mitchell A. Seligson, eds. (New York: Holmes & Meier, 1978), pp. 98–113; Mitchell A. Seligson, "Development and Participation in Costa Rica: The Impact of Context," in Booth and Seligson, *Political Participation in Latin America,* pp. 145–153; Cornelius, *Politics and the Migrant Poor,* pp. 90–108; Henry A. Dietz, "Political Participation by the Urban Poor in an Authoritarian Context: The Case of Lima, Peru," *Journal of Political and Military Sociology* 5, no. 1 (Spring, 1977): 63–77; and James W. White, "Urbanization and Political Participation in Japan," Department of Political Science, University of North Carolina at Chapel Hill, in progress. Other studies which do not replicate the Verba et al. analytic approach but which share many of the same theoretical assumptions about the multidimensional nature of political participation include Arterton, "Political Participation as Attempted Interpersonal Influence," and Cynthia McClintock, "Structural Change and Political Culture in Rural Peru: The Impact of Self-Managed Cooperatives on Peasant Clientelism, 1969–1975," unpublished Ph.D. dissertation, Massachusetts Institute of Technology, 1976.

93. Cf. Samuel P. Huntington and Joan M. Nelson, *No Easy Choice: Political Participation in Developing Countries* (Cambridge, Mass.: Harvard Univ. Press, 1976).

94. John R. Mathiason and John D. Powell, "Participation and Efficacy: Aspects of Peasant Involvement in Political Mobilization," *Comparative Politics* 4, no. 3 (1972): 327.

95. Cornelius, *Politics and the Migrant Poor,* pp. 103–8; Huntington and Nelson, *No Easy Choice;* Anthony Leeds and Elizabeth Leeds, "Accounting for Behavioral Differences in Lower-Class Political Organization: Comparative Cases from Brazil, Peru, and Chile," in *The City in Comparative Perspective,* John Walton and Louis H. Masotti, eds. (Beverly Hills, Calif.: Sage Publications–Halsted Press, 1976); Alejandro Portes and John Walton, *Urban Latin America: The Political Condition from Above and Below* (Austin: Univ. of Texas Press, 1975), chap. 3.

96. The amount of physical repression actually employed by the regime against dissidents or protest movements has varied considerably from one

presidential administration to another and regionally within the country. But as Stevens points out, "the variation [in coercion levels] seems to correlate quite accurately with the size of the movements" (Stevens, *Protest and Response*, p. 259). In general, the regime attempts to limit the application of physical force to situations which clearly threaten to get out of control. Fagen and Tuohy's observation regarding the city of Jalapa seems equally applicable to the rural and urban communities with which we are personally familiar: "What is impressive about the politics of Jalapa is the manner in which both the behavior of ordinary citizens and the behavior of elites are shaped so as to *obviate* the formal and public exercise of political controls. . . . political failure is in part defined as the necessity of actually using the impressive state apparatus of public control and repression" (Fagen and Tuohy, *Politics and Privilege*, pp. 18–19).

97. Cornelius, *Politics and the Migrant Poor*, pp. 146–47. Cf. McClintock, "Structural Change and Political Culture in Rural Peru," chap. 5.

98. Langton, "Situations, Psychological Dispositions, and Learning," pp. 46–47.

99. Fagen and Tuohy, *Politics and Privilege*, p. 112.

100. Coleman, *Diffuse Support in Mexico*.

101. *Excélsior*, June 10, 1976, p. 1.

102. Landsberger, "The Limits and Conditions of Peasant Participation in Mexico," pp. 87–88.

103. Manuel L. Carlos, *Politics and Development in Rural Mexico* (New York: Praeger Special Studies, 1974), p. 82.

104. Fagen and Tuohy, *Politics and Privilege*, p. 88.

105. Almond and Verba, the Mexico civic culture survey, 1958, marginal frequencies.

106. Cornelius, *Politics and the Migrant Poor*, p. 82.

107. Ugalde et al., *The Urbanization Process of a Poor Mexican Neighborhood*, p. 45.

108. Montaño, *Los pobres de la ciudad*, p. 125.

109. See, e.g., Graham, *Politics in a Mexican Community*, p. 14 and passim.

110. Rafael Segovia, "La reforma política: el ejecutivo federal, el PRI y las elecciones de 1973," *Foro Internacional* 14, no. 3 (1974): 51–67; Segovia, *La politización*, p. 81.

111. Coleman, *Diffuse Support in Mexico*.

112. Cornelius, *Politics and the Migrant Poor*, pp. 79–80; George Foster, *Tzintzuntzan: Mexican Peasants in a Changing World* (Boston: Little, Brown, 1967), p. 177. Cf. Coleman, *Diffuse Support in Mexico*.

113. Fagen and Tuohy, *Politics and Privilege*, p. 116.

114. Cornelius, *Politics and the Migrant Poor*, p. 82.

115. Carlos, *Politics and Development in Rural Mexico*.

116. Landsberger, "The Limits and Conditions of Peasant Participation in Mexico," p. 92.

117. See Cornelius, *Politics and the Migrant Poor*, pp. 177–78; Montaño, *Los pobres de la ciudad;* and Eckstein, *The Poverty of Revolution*.

118. Almond and Verba, *Civic Culture*, pp. 236–53, 369.

119. Ibid., pp. 212–13.

120. Ibid., pp. 360–61.

121. Segovia, *La politización*, pp. 117, 127–30.

122. Fagen and Tuohy, *Politics and Privilege*, p. 118.

123. Cornelius, *Politics and the Migrant Poor*, p. 178.

124. Ibid., pp. 218–19.

125. Stevens, *Protest and Response in Mexico*, p. 94.

126. Segovia, *La politización*, pp. 126–27.

127. Stevens, *Protest and Response in Mexico*, p. 277.

128. Adorno et al., *The Authoritarian Personality*.

129. Almond and Verba, *Civic Culture*, p. 273.

130. Ibid., pp. 213.

131. Ibid., pp. 269.

132. Cf. Carrión, *Mito y magia del mexicano*; Needler, "Politics and National Character"; Paz, *The Labyrinth of Solitude*; Ramos, *Profile of Man and Culture*.

133. Fromm and Maccoby, *Social Character in a Mexican Village*.

134. Romanucci-Ross, *Conflict, Violence, and Morality in a Mexican Village*.

135. Joseph A. Kahl, *The Measurement of Modernism* (Austin: Univ. of Texas Press, 1968), p. 82.

136. Almond and Verba, *Civic Culture*, p. 267.

137. Cornelius, 1970 Mexico City survey, marginal frequencies.

138. Cornelius, *Politics and the Migrant Poor*, pp. 127–28, 131–32; Fromm and Maccoby, *Social Character in a Mexican Village*, pp. 206–7.

139. Cornelius, *Politics and the Migrant Poor*; Cornelius, *Los Norteños: Mexican Migrants in the U.S. and Rural Mexico*; Foster, *Tzintzuntzan*; Fromm and Maccoby, *Social Character in a Mexican Village*, pp. 62–65; 206-25.

140. Fagen and Tuohy, *Politics and Privilege*, pp. 118–22; Almond and Verba, *Civic Culture*, pp. 106–14.

141. Cornelius, 1970 Mexico City survey, marginal frequencies.

142. Landsberger, "The Limits and Conditions of Peasant Participation in Mexico," p. 90.

143. Cornelius, *Politics and the Migrant Poor*, p. 213.

144. Fagen and Tuohy, *Politics and Privilege*, pp. 119–21.

145. Cornelius, 1970 Mexico City survey, marginal frequencies.

146. Fagen and Tuohy, *Politics and Privilege*, p. 122; Almond and Verba, *Civic Culture*, p. 112.

147. Fagen and Tuohy, *Politics and Privilege*, p. 112; Almond and Verba, the Mexico civic culture survey, 1958, marginal frequencies.

148. Segovia, *La politización*, pp. 112–14.

149. Almond and Verba, the Mexico civic culture survey, 1958, marginal frequencies: Arterton, "Political Participation as Attempted Interpersonal Influence"; Cornelius, 1970 Mexico City survey, marginal frequencies; Fagen and Tuohy, *Politics and Privilege*, pp. 112, 110.

150. Fagen and Tuohy, *Politics and Privilege*, pp. 111–14.

151. Kahl, *The Measurement of Modernism*; Cockcroft, "Coercion and Ideology in Mexican Politics"; Cornelius, *Politics and the Migrant Poor*; and Davis, "Toward an Explanation of Mass Support for Authoritarian Regimes."

152. Almond and Verba, *Civic Culture*, pp. 102–3 and passim.

153. Kahl, *The Measurement of Modernism*.

154. Segovia, *La politización*, pp. 85–110.

155. Arterton, "Political Participation as Attempted Interpersonal Influence"; Cornelius, *Politics and the Migrant Poor*; Landsberger, "The Limits and Conditions of Peasant Participation in Mexico."

156. Segovia, "Nacionalismo e imagen del mundo exterior en los niños mexicanos," *Foro Internacional* 13, no. 3 (1972): 51–67; and Segovia, *La politización*.

157. Coleman and Davis, "The Structural Context of Politics and Dimensions of Regime Performance"; Davis, "Toward an Explanation of Mass Support for Authoritarian Regimes"; and Davis and Coleman, "Political Symbols, Political Efficacy and Diffuse Support."

158. Almond and Verba, *Civic Culture,* p. 113.

159. Only 7.6 percent of the Mexico City sample considered the system "bad for the country"; the remaining 13.6 percent felt that the system is good in some ways, bad in others (Cornelius, *Politics and the Migrant Poor,* p. 56).

160. Cornelius, *Politics and the Migrant Poor,* pp. 54–61, 202–8.

161. Systematic data on the political attitudes and behavior of elite groups in Mexico are extremely fragmentary, which explains our concentration in this chapter on lower-status groups. For a rare study of attitudes and behavior within the Mexican political elite, see Grindle, *Bureaucrats, Politicians, and Peasants in Mexico.*

162. Cornelius, *Los Norteños: Mexican Migrants in the U.S. and Rural Mexico.*

163. Almond and Verba, *Civic Culture,* p. 15.

164. Fromm and Maccoby, *Social Character in a Mexican Village,* p. 19.

165. Cf. Albert O. Hirschman, "The Changing Tolerance for Income Inequality in the Course of Economic Development," *Quarterly Journal of Economics* 87, no. 4 (1973): 544–66; Leeds and Leeds, "Accounting for Behavioral Differences in Lower Class Political Organization"; Portes and Walton, *Urban Latin America,* chap. 3.

166. See Richard R. Fagen, *The Transformation of Political Culture in Cuba* (Stanford: Stanford Univ. Press, 1969); and McClintock, "Structural Change and Political Culture in Rural Peru."

167. It is all too infrequently recognized by students of Mexico that there has been a steady flow of temporary migrant workers from many parts of Mexico to the United States for at least a quarter century (since the 1880s in some regions). In many rural communities, at least 50 percent of the economically active male population has had one or more work experiences in the United States, entering legally or illegally (the majority). Oral history interviews conducted in one *municipio* in the Los Altos region of the state of Jalisco (Ann L. Craig, *The First Agraristas: An Oral History of Agrarian Reform in Mexico* [Berkeley: Univ. of California Press, forthcoming]) have demonstrated that peasants with experience in the United States were particularly active in the struggle for agrarian reform in the 1930s. Survey interviews with a large sample of rural residents in the same region also revealed important differences in political participation and attitudinal modernity between those who have migrated to the United States and those who have not (Cornelius, *Los Norteños: Mexican Migrants in the U.S. and Rural Mexico*). These findings lead us to believe that the United States experience is a potentially significant variable for political culture research, at least in rural areas of Mexico.

168. See James M. Malloy, ed., *Authoritarianism and Corporatism in Latin America* (Pittsburgh, Penn.: Univ. of Pittsburgh Press, 1976); Purcell, *The Mexican Profit-Sharing Decision;* Alfred Stepan, *The State and Society: Peru in Comparative Perspective* (Princeton, N.J.: Princeton Univ. Press, 1978); Stevens, "Mexico's One-Party State: Revolutionary Myth and Authoritarian Reality."

CHAPTER X

On Revisiting The Civic Culture:
A Personal Postscript

Sidney Verba
Harvard University

THE CIVIC CULTURE was a bold and incautious book. Whether one uses the one adjective or the other will depend on one's evaluation of the work. Either adjective will do to describe a work that attempted one of the first systematic cross-national studies; that used as its research tool the sample survey, a technique that was still in the process of development and that had not been used extensively in several of the nations studied; and that dealt with the complex macropolitical problem of democratic stability, a problem for which the research tool had not been used even in a single nation. To have conducted a cross-national survey on a simpler and more traditional topic would have been a fairly bold venture; to have tried to use survey techniques to deal with the issue of democratic stability within a single nation such as the United States where, at least, these techniques were well developed would have been a bold venture; to have tried to explain democratic stability by comparing several nations using more traditional techniques would hardly have been a timid enterprise either. But to apply a new method on an unprecedented cross-national scope to a problem never studied by that method suggests that neither *bold* nor *incautious* is the proper word. *Foolhardy* might be more appropriate.

The fact that Almond and Verba rushed in where other social scientists had not even considered treading resulted in a book that had a large impact on comparative political studies, an impact larger than would have been attained by a more circumspect book. It also resulted in a book that has received a good deal of criticism in terms of method, scope, and theory. The essays in this volume are examples — among the best examples, I believe — of a long series of works that have attempted to assess the impact of *The Civic Culture* and to indicate where it was adequate or inadequate. Some of the praise is warranted. Much of the criticism, it is painful for an author to admit, is justified as well. But one gratifying aspect of much of the comment on the book is that it has been constructive. Critics have rarely been content to dismiss the work as wrong or irrelevant; they have used it as a basis for going several steps further. For some, *The Civic Culture* represented a correct approach to problems of democratic politics. These have responded with the most important kind of praise: they have modified and replicated parts of the work in other settings or in the same settings at a later time; extending the scope of the data on the subjects studied in *The Civic Culture* and/or giving them some depth over time.[1] Others have found the data gathered for the purposes of the book to be useful, but incompletely analyzed. They have carried out secondary analysis, applying other statistical techniques or dealing with other problems than those that concerned the authors of the original work.[2] Still others have found the method attractive as an approach to comparative political studies and the subject matter of political values important, but they have gone beyond the original work to improve the conceptualization and measurement of such values.[3] Some have found the method attractive, but have applied it to a somewhat different set of problems — to voting behavior, political participation, socialization, or other topics. Even those who have found both the method and the theoretical approach lacking have, it appears, been motivated to "take another step" — to show what should have been studied and how it should have been done.

This is not to claim for *The Civic Culture* the motivation for all comparative social science work since then. The spurt of comparative work that came after it would have come anyway. Nevertheless, *The Civic Culture* served, I believe, as an example of what to do for some, and what not to do for others. In either case it added to progress and to cumulation in the study of comparative politics. If being fruitful in a scholarly enterprise is more important than being correct, *The Civic Culture* probably deserves high marks. Nor was the fruitfulness accidental. As I shall suggest, it was the particular nature of the approach of *The Civic Culture* that made it an inspiration to some to do the same elsewhere, to others to do something similar but better, and yet others to do something different.

Albert Hirschman has written of the "hiding hand" in development projects. If one knew, at the moment of inception, how difficult a task one was beginning, one would never start. The fact that one does not know gives one the courage to begin. The difficulties, as well as the unforeseen consequences of what one is starting, appear only gradually — and only after one is already too committed to turn back. The metaphor is apt for development projects. It applies to other long-term human commitments too, be they the conception of children or the writing of books. For the junior author of *The Civic Culture,* the hiding hand worked. Luckily I lacked the imagination and vision to know that we were working on a book that would be as innovative, as widely read, or as controversial as it turned out to be. If I had had enough imagination to see its importance and consequent controversy, I might have lacked the courage to continue.

It may be useful to consider some of the characteristics of *The Civic Culture* that led to its wide impact as well as to much of the criticism of it. In each of the characteristics I shall cite, *The Civic Culture* was, I believe, innovative. In each of them, the discipline has moved beyond the stage of *The Civic Culture.* That there has been such movement does not suggest that one ought to apologize for *The Civic Culture.* It was a work meant to be superseded. Nor does the fact that the discipline moved beyond *The Civic Culture* suggest that it triggered off the ensuing flurry of comparative studies. The growth in systematic comparative studies derived from the same intellectual sources that led to *The Civic Culture*. But the fact that the five-nation study had been done provided a starting point and a stimulus for other work.

The origins of *The Civic Culture* help one to understand why it took the shape it did and had the impact it had. As Gabriel Almond describes it in the opening essay of this volume, the work emerged from the confluence of several streams of thought: public-opinion studies, macrosociological theorizing, psychocultural anthropology, and the technique of the sample survey. It was an unbeatable combination. The macrosociological theories of Weber and Parsons focused attention on general issues of the functioning of political systems. Psychocultural anthropology added a concern with the way in which basic cultural beliefs and values affected such functioning, as well as a concern with the origins of such beliefs and values. The psychocultural approach, furthermore, did not concentrate on individual beliefs or values, but on cultural patterns characterizing whole populations. This approach, however, was just coming out of a discredited "national character" era. Oversimple generalizations about complex populations were no longer acceptable. It was here that the tradition of public opinion research and the sample survey joined. Surveys offered a technique for dealing with belief systems in large populations that was more precise and better attuned to internal variations than the rather loose research procedures of the national character school.

The Civic Culture used *survey techniques* to study citizen *attitudes and values* within a set of quite *varied nations* to deal with the *macropolitical problem* of *democratic stability*. Each of the italicized terms in the previous sentence highlights a characteristic of the work that increased its importance to comparative politics at the same time as it increased its vulnerability to criticism. I would like to look at three of the problems posed by the task of *The Civic Culture* as outlined in that sentence: (1) the problem of the scope of the study: What are the gains and losses of the breadth of coverage of the study? (2) the problem of the use of survey data (microdata on the attitudes of individuals) to deal with a problem on the level of the political system (the macropolitical issue of democratic stability); (3) the problem of the choice of democratic stability rather than other aspects of politics as that which one wants to explain.

THE SCOPE OF THE STUDY

One incautious aspect of *The Civic Culture* was its scope. Five nations was five times as many as in previous studies of political behavior using national samples. There are a number of problems with such a broad scope.

One problem is that a cross-national study can never give to each individual nation the full attention and understanding that it deserves on its own. The cross-national scholar is rarely as familiar with the nations he or she studies as is the country specialist. The rich contextual knowledge possessed by a specialist in a particular nation — in his or her own native land or an adopted place of specialization — takes a long time to come by. It involves immersion in a culture, knowledge of a language, and understanding of history. One can only acquire such knowledge slowly; too slowly for one to be a specialist in more than a few nations. The social scientist who attempts to deal with a "sample" of nations, chosen not for their familiarity, but because they represent types of nation useful for a particular theoretical problem, must deal with nations less familiar than they should be.

Furthermore, the attempt to deal with a general theoretical problem, as was attempted in *The Civic Culture*, means that one may not deal with problems most immediately relevant to some of the nations studied. Internal complexities or particular historical patterns and experiences may receive short shrift. The authors of the various country chapters in this volume quite appropriately make this point in relation to each of their nations. *The Civic Culture*, by focusing on a broad problem of cross-national relevance, ignores significant aspects of the political situation in each of the nations studied.

In part, there are ways around this problem. Comparisons can be conducted by collaborative teams made up of specialists from each of the nations. Recent research has taken this format, usually involving scholars from each of the nations studied. Such a format is both intellectually more justified than the approach in *The Civic Culture* and more in tune with an approach to scientific research as an international cooperative venture.

But this way of dealing with the problem does not eliminate the main intellectual issue: the extent to which national polities represent an appropriate set of units about which to generalize. Are there functionally equivalent problems or processes in national polities that can be identified and about which we can usefully generalize? And, if so, are the problems or processes of enough significance that it is worth the effort to attempt to generalize about them?

The Civic Culture focused on those political attitudes that would be supportive of a democratic political system. The assumption was that a number of forces led to the development of such attitudes — education; the democratization of nongovernmental authority systems in the family, the school, and the workplace; general trust in one's fellow citizens. As a number of the authors in the present volume have pointed out, the implicit prediction in *The Civic Culture* of a tendency toward more widely held "civic" attitudes has not been borne out. In the United States and Britain, the nations in which we found such attitudes to be widespread, there has been a steady erosion of confidence in the government. We had assumed that other nations might move in the "civic" direction of the United States and Britain; in fact, the latter two nations moved away from that position. Each followed its own trajectory. Basic citizen attitudes have been affected by the particular set of political issues which the nation faced. In the United States, the erosion of supportive political beliefs probably derives from the political events of the 1960s — Vietnam and racial tension — capped by Watergate in the 1970s. In Britain, much can be traced to governmental incapacity to deal with severe economic strain. In the other nations as well, as the various essays in this volume point out, the specific configuration of political problems and political cleavages affected the evolution of political attitudes.

In general, the variations from nation to nation make clear that general sociological processes can easily be modified by political events. Our general approach was to seek the roots of political beliefs in long-term social processes. Basic political attitudes, we believed, were transmitted from generation to generation, through the family and the school. They were formed early in life and had a good deal of stability. If they were to change, the change would come gradually in response to changes in their basic social and psychological origins. This approach was consistent with much of the literature at the time. Note how similar it is to the analysis of the basic origins and stability of party identification in the voting literature.[4] What was not clear was the degree to which such political attitudes were labile and could be affected by political events.

Insofar as basic political attitudes respond to specific political events, the attempt to generalize about such attitudes across nations is made more difficult. The specific crises and problems that individual nations face undercut any broad sociological generalizations. Such a criticism of attempts at broad-scale cross-national generalizations is well taken. Any such generalizations must be seen as highly contingent on political events. But this does not imply that all one has left is description of the political events in a nation coupled with description of the way in which the public responds to such events. For one thing, the cross-national sociological generalizations — such as the one about the relationship between education and political involvement — may still hold if all else is equal. The evidence from *The Civic Culture* has been confirmed by other studies. The linkage between education and political attitudes and behavior does hold up, though the impact of the former on the latter is modified by macropolitical processes and events.[5] The recognition that political attitudes and behavior cannot be reduced to psychological and sociological forces does not mean that the latter are not important determinants of long-term political beliefs. Current studies of the origins of "postindustrial" values in young high-educated citizens illustrate that there may be cross-national tendencies in political beliefs that transcend the specific experiences within any particular nation.[6] Having recognized that individual political behavior and attitudes are in large part responses to specific political stimuli, we must now try to integrate those contingent factors into our analyses.

The existence of generational effect — that is, when a particular age cohort responds to a set of stimuli in a way different from others exposed to the stimuli and then carries the impact of that response through the life cycle — surely indicates that political attitudes are not solely the result of the political events of the period. Generational effects involve an interaction between the particular set of events taking place in a nation and longer-term formation of political beliefs, as when a postindustrial generation raised in an era of affluence takes on particular values that it then carries through life (or may carry through life, the evidence is not yet in), whereas older cohorts who are also exposed to contemporary affluence but had in addition experienced an era of greater economic want do not adopt new values.

Attempts to sort out the stable from the labile in political and social attitudes must be placed high on the research agenda. The general expectation has been that attitudes on specific issues or about specific people will change easily, but that basic beliefs about the rules of the political game, or authority patterns, or equality will remain more stable, as will fundamental attachments to groups or to political parties. There is some evidence that this is the case. In the United States, attitudes toward the incumbent president are quite variable, as are views as to performance of political institutions, but fundamental views as to the desirable nature of the political system have remained steadier. In this sense, *The Civic Culture*'s description of American political culture has held up despite the turmoil of the 1960s. Even in relation to party affiliation, which researchers have found to be less stable than was once assumed, there is evidence for basic stability compared with attitudes to particular candidates. At least for those who formed a partisan attachment before the late 1960s, party identification has remained fairly stable, and at the same time split-ticket voting has risen.[7]

It is, however, difficult to sort out the stable from the labile. For one thing, we cannot measure very well attitudes toward basic institutions in isolation from attitudes about specific events and people. The average citizen — and the average survey instrument — confounds attitudes to the office and attitudes toward the incumbent. Furthermore, we do not have adequate time series to estimate the effects of events on different types of belief.

The systematic study of the way in which such belief patterns change will require more time-series data with replicated questions. In the United States, where there are extended time series on specific items such as presidential popularity or party identification, beginnings are being made in tracing the impact of events on such beliefs.[8] The data in this book bring *The Civic Culture* up to date and are a step in that direction, though there are few extended time series on *Civic Culture* items. The *Civic Culture* items nevertheless form a base-line for comparison.

This brings me to the next characteristic of *The Civic Culture:*

its attempt to use sample surveys to deal with macropolitical problems.

SURVEY RESEARCH AND MACROPOLITICS

The data gathered for *The Civic Culture* were used within that book to raise a number of micropolitical questions. Most of the analyses relate demographic characteristics to political attitudes, or reports of early experiences to such attitudes, or relate one attitude to another. It is interesting, furthermore, that such microanalyses have received more attention in the literature, particularly among those who have used the *Civic Culture* data for further analyses.[9] Such microanalyses are easier to replicate than are more discursive macropolitical analyses of the source of democratic stability. The micropolitical use of *The Civic Culture* represents one of two types of impact that the authors did not fully anticipate — the other being the straightforward descriptive material that was presented. We were much more concerned with the macropolitical question of democratic stability and the uses of systematic surveys to deal with that question.

The key to the use of our survey data to deal with macropolitical issues was the fact that the data were comparative. If our study had been limited to a single political system, as most survey studies were, it would have been impossible to relate patterns of attitude to the functioning of the political system. There would have been no variation in the latter. By having a variety of polities representing different types of democracies, the potential existed for connecting survey findings to macropolitical processes. But the connection is a most complex one and far from fully realized in *The Civic Culture* (or since then).

One approach used in *The Civic Culture* was to relate average or modal attitude patterns to the functioning of the political system. This required a rather large inferential leap from that on which we had data to that about which we wanted to generalize. Our assumption was that we were not moving from the individual level to the level of the macropolitical system, but from the level of cultural patterns to the macrolevel. Erwin Scheuch is probably wrong in accusing us of committing an individualistic fallacy. We were moving from a macrocharacteristic (the set of attitudes found within the public) to another macrocharacteristic (the functioning of the political system).[10] But he is right in that the leap from citizen values to democratic functioning was very great. Our data were on individual beliefs. They could be aggregated to the beliefs of the citizenry, but the connection between these belief patterns and what we were trying to explain — why some nations had relatively successful and stable democracies and other polities did not — was tenuous. Furthermore, there was no way in which we could manipulate the data we had gathered — the data on the attitudes and beliefs of a sample of citizens in each nation — to see how variations in our data affected the dependent variable of system stability. The latter was not precisely measured and not directly linked to our own data.

The problem is not one confined to our cross-national work on democratic attitudes. A work carried out somewhat earlier than ours — Stouffer's study of attitudes toward civil liberties — triggered off a debate about democratic functioning within the United States. How could freedom of speech (a macropolitical characteristic of the American political system) survive if popular attitudes were by no means fully supportive of such civil liberties? The answer lay in the attitudes of local leaders, attitudes that were more in accord with democratic norms.[11] The data on local leaders added one additional bit of information to the Stouffer study that helped explain the connection — or rather, the lack of connection — between the public attitudes and the way institutions in fact worked in the United States. But the connection was by no means clear and involved several inferential leaps from citizen values to system functioning. It depended upon assumptions as to how citizen values affect system functioning that were neither tested nor testable with the data available. Recent studies show a major change in the level of commitment to free speech;[12] Americans express much more support for free speech for deviants than they did a couple of decades ago. The change in public attitudes toward free speech is unambiguous. The impact on the polity of the change is less clear. As with the *Civic Culture* data, which showed an increase in attitudes supportive of democracy as one moved from nations that appeared (on the basis of unsystematic criteria) to be less stable democracies to those that were more, we find an increase in citizen support for free speech that coincides with a more liberal interpretation of laws on matters of speech (though that judgment is based as well on unsystematic observation). But whether or not the change in attitudes and the change in the system actually move in tandem and, if they do, which causes which remain obscure.

There are several problems in connecting survey data and macropolitical outcomes. One has to do with the composition rules by which one sums up the results of a survey; another has to do with the process that connects citizen attitudes and behavior to the operation of the polity; and yet another with the macropolitical unit one chooses.

One can describe the marginal distribution of democratic beliefs in a population, but it is clear — as Stouffer's focus on the local leaders or our focus in *The Civic Culture* on the educated portion of our samples implied — that the beliefs of some are more important than those of others. The extent to which there are democratic values among those closest to the working of the polity — those who are more active, those who are likely to take political office, etc. — is more crucial in terms of democratic stability than the beliefs of those further from the political action. But in the study of basic political values, there are no precise rules as to how much weight one gives to the views of various groups.

Second, there is no clear understanding of the process by which basic political values affect the operation of a political system. It is usually simply asserted that there are such connections. Such an assertion is surely reasonable, but how exactly the beliefs within a populace affect political decisions or the way institutions operate remains inexplicit.

The micropolitical level and the macropolitical level have been most successfully linked in the area of voting studies. Earlier voting studies were analyses of individual political behavior rather than of elections. But as election studies have accumulated, they have thus provided a series of elections to compare, in the same way that comparative surveys provide a set of national polities to compare. This allows one to turn to the way in which the macrocharacteristics of an election affect voting choice and how that in turn affects the electoral outcome. Macropolitical characteristics are used to help explain micropolitical choices by voters, which, in turn, have macropolitical consequences in terms of election results. For example, Nie, Verba, and Petrocik use spatial analysis to show how the location of a pair of candidates on a left/right issue continuum affects voter decisions and, in turn, affects which candidate is likely to win the election.[13]

The linkage between microstudies of individual voting choice and electoral outcome is made possible by the fact that we know the composition rules to be applied. They are the laws for counting votes: each person's vote counts equally in presidential elections with modifications due to the winner-take-all rule in relation to electoral college votes. In addition, we know the process by which votes affect the macropolitical outcome. The winner of the election takes office. The link between election result and the outcome within the government is in fact not that simple. We do not know the impact of the size of the victory on the mandate that an office holder perceives, nor do we know in any precise way how the composition of the vote for the winner affects the behavior of the elected official. (What exactly is the impact on President Carter of the fact that black voters voted almost unanimously for him?) Such connections depend upon contingencies we cannot measure in any precise way. But the major election outcome — the victory of candidate A over B — is clearly linked to the sum of citizen votes.

Making such connections between individual behavior and system outcome is harder in other areas. In the study of political participation, we have been able to link individual behavior — the choice whether to be active or not and how to be active — back to some macropolitical antecedents (to the institutional structures that provide channels for political activity) as well as forward to the composition of the participant population in a society.[14] But we have had less success in taking the linkage a step further. We know how individual decisions to be active or not affect the degree to which the participant population in a nation is biased in favor of one social group rather than another, but the forward linkage of this to policies on the part of the government is less amenable to systematic study.

Third, an issue associated with a focus on macropolitical outcomes is the choice of the appropriate unit. As we have indicated, the assumption in *The Civic Culture* — as in most comparative politics — was that the nation-state was the most useful unit. For systematic attempts to link individual attitudes and behavior to characteristics of political units, however, comparisons across communities or other subnational units may be more fruitful. The essays in this volume also point to the importance of subcultural differentiation in political values, a subject to which *The Civic Culture* paid insufficient attention. *The Civic Culture* did not assume homogeneity within nations and heterogeneity across them. Indeed, one of its main themes was the internal differentiation in political attitudes across social groups and the extent to which similarly placed groups in different societies were closer to each other in attitude than were differently placed social groups within a single society. But the book raised this question in relation to educational groups, not in relation to regional or ethnic subgroups. The extension of analyses to subcultural groups represents an important body of work following up *The Civic Culture*.

As interesting an issue (and one that has received less systematic attention) is the extent to which the proper unit for cultural analysis transcends the nation-state. The nations and the world are, as the cliché tells us, in closer and closer contact and are subjected to the same international social and economic forces. Thus the study of cultural stability and change may involve a consideration of transnational forces. These take several forms. Nations can undergo parallel changes, which then have similar effects on cultural patterns across nations, though the effects take place independently within the nations. Examples would be similar consequences of the spread of higher education or television. Or nations can be exposed to similar international conditions with, perhaps, similar internal effects. An example might be inflation, which most nations experience at the same time because of international economic forces, such as the rise in energy costs, and which may have similar effects in each of the nations experiencing it. Last, there is the direct transmission of cultural values from nation to nation. The spread of the youth movement of the late 1960s or the current spread of consumerism often involves such direct communication and imitation of new ideas. Studies of political culture will have to take these transnational phenomena into account.

DEMOCRATIC SURVIVAL

One feature of *The Civic Culture* was its focus on democratic stability. We were concerned with the question of why some democracies survive while others collapse more than with the question of how well democracies perform. The focus was not inappropriate at the time. The survival of the democracies in the developed world was problematic and the potential for viable democracy in the developing world was even more problematic. Social science at that time was still trying to solve the puzzle of the pre-World War II replacement of democratic regimes by totalitarian ones. The democratic regimes in Germany and Italy were viewed by many as insecure. In addition, the French Fourth Republic had recently collapsed, and the extent to which the Fifth Republic would be democratic was uncertain. (Indeed, the original research design for *The Civic Culture* included France, but the fall of the Fourth Republic and the uncertainty of the political situation led us to shift to Italy.)

The focus on survival had an impact on the research, an impact that did somewhat reduce the fruitfulness of the work. Survival is an all-or-nothing phenomenon. It is not that we expected the imminent collapse of one of the nations we were studying as a test of our theory. Rather, our dependent variable was the likelihood of survival. This, unfortunately, is not a measureable phenomenon — unless one studies a large number of polities over an extended period of time. Thus we were not forced to face the problem of a more precise measurement of democratic functioning; our semiexplicit assumption was that the clustering of nations in terms of likelihood of democratic survival was fairly obvious. It would have been useful to have provided more explicit criteria of performance and to have, at least hypothetically, linked aspects of our data to various kinds of performance. It is uncertain how successful we would have been. The current concern with "governability" (a concept that seems to combine performance with viability) has not led to precise conceptualization or measurement.[15] But a more explicit concern with performance levels would have been useful.

Our concern with survival also led to a rather one-sided approach to stratification. We were concerned with those attitudes that were likely to be supportive of a democratic regime. We found these to be most frequently and fully held by the more educated members of the polity. In this, our data paralleled other studies of the time. Nor, despite extended debate about the implications of this finding, has the finding itself been contradicted by other data: the upper-educated remain the more active and involved as the more civic-minded citizens. From the perspective of democratic survival this implied that democracies would be more secure if less well-educated citizens were less active than the more well educated. From the point of view of democratic performance, the matter looks somewhat different. Even if upper-status citizens participate out of a sense of civic-mindedness and bring to that participation a set of attitudes more supportive of democracy, they also represent particular policy interests that are likely to skew governmental responsiveness in their favor and away from the needs of the less active members of society.[16]

The concerns expressed in *The Civic Culture* were products of their times. This, as I have pointed out, was reflected in the use of survey techniques and the focus on democratic stability. The book was, at the time, in the mainstream of the political science concern with mass politics, a concern that had grown with the "behavioral revolution" in political science and the turning of the discipline away from legal and historical studies. These studies of the political behavior of the citizenry focused on inputs into the policymaking process, but paid little or no attention to the process itself. The government became a "black box" that processed inputs into outputs.

Just as political beliefs change, so do the concerns of political scientists. Recent years have seen the revival of concern with the policy process: with government decision making and with bureaucratic behavior. Nevertheless, the mass political phenomenon studied in works like *The Civic Culture* remains relevant. Studies of electoral behavior — especially when linked to election outcomes — remain important to understand policymaking in nations controlled by democratic regimes. And for democratic and nondemocratic regimes, studies of nonelectoral political attitudes and behavior of the sort *The Civic Culture* dealt with may be even more important in understanding the policy process. The mass political movements directly involved in environmental policy or nuclear energy policies have had a major effect on public policy in a number of countries. A study of mass political behavior would certainly be relevant to policymaking in relation to these issues. And such a study would build on the type of work initiated in *The Civic Culture*.

In sum, how does one judge *The Civic Culture* many years after its appearance? Not by whether it obtained the right answers; that is too much to expect. Did it ask the right questions? That is a more relevant and fairer criterion. The answer is not completely clear. Many of the questions it raised remain important ones for comparative politics: What shapes individual political beliefs? Which beliefs are politically significant? How do political beliefs affect political systems? How do historical experiences affect what people think about politics? Studies that deal with general value change across nations or across generations continue to ask such questions. In many cases, *The Civic Culture* asked the right questions. It did not always ask them as precisely as they might have been asked, nor did it ask all the relevant questions about democratic stability. But it opened important areas of study.

The essays in this volume have called attention in a most appropriate fashion to some of the shortcomings in *The Civic Culture:* weaknesses of method and weaknesses of theory. Many of these, I have suggested, derive from the boldness (foolhardiness?) of the work. Would the work have been better if it had been more cautious: more limited in scope, less innovative in method, less grandiose in theory? It certainly would have been less open to criticism. But more cautious work is also more easily ignored or forgotten. If *The Civic Culture* had been more cautious, there would be little occasion for a volume of this sort. There would be less to criticize, but also less to remember that was worth criticizing.

NOTES

1. The *Civic Culture* questionnaire has been replicated, in whole or in part, in Japan, Ireland, Croatia, Turkey, and the Netherlands as well as among Mexican Americans.

2. Examples are Norman H. Nie, G. Bingham Powell, Jr., and Kenneth Prewitt, "Social Structure and Political Participation: Developmental Relationships," *American Political Science Review* 63 (June and September 1969): 361–78, 808–32; Glen H. Elder, Jr., "Family Structure and Educational Attain-

ment," *American Sociological Review* 30 (February 1965): 81–96; as well as Robert E. Lane, "Political Maturation in Germany and America," in Mattei Dogan and Richard Rose, eds., *European Politics* (Boston: Little, Brown, 1971), pp. 101–13; Philip E. Converse, "Of Time and Partisan Stability," *Comparative Political Studies* 2 (July 1969): 139–71; Ada W. Finifter, "Dimensions of Political Alienation," *American Political Science Review* 64 (June 1970): 389–410; Giuseppe di Palma, *Apathy and Participation* (New York: The Free Press, 1970); Sidney Verba, "Organizational Membership and Democratic Consensus," *Journal of Politics* 27 (August 1965): 467–97; Wayne A. Cornelius, Jr., "Urbanization as an Agent in Latin American Political Instability," *American Political Science Review* 63 (September 1969): 833–57; Dwaine Marvick, "The Political Socialization of the American Negro," *Annals* 361 (September 1965): 112–27; and Samuel H. Barnes, "Italy: Religion and Class in Electoral Behavior," in Richard Rose, ed., *Electoral Behavior* (New York: The Free Press, 1974), p. 200.

3. For example, Eric Nordlinger, *The Working Class Tories* (Princeton, N.J.: Princeton Univ. Press, 1967).

4. See Norman H. Nie, Sidney Verba, and John R. Petrocik, *The Changing American Voter* (Cambridge, Mass.: Harvard Univ. Press, 1976), chap. 2, for a discussion.

5. Alex Inkeles and David H. Smith, *Becoming Modern* (Cambridge, Mass.: Harvard Univ. Press, 1974); and Sidney Verba, Norman H. Nie, and Jae-On Kim, *Participation and Political Equality: A Seven Nation Comparison* (New York: Cambridge Univ. Press, 1978).

6. Ronald Inglehart, "The Silent Revolution in Europe: Intergenerational in Post-Industrial Societies," *American Political Science Review* 65 (1971).

7. Nie, Verba, and Petrocik, *Changing American Voter,* pp. 62–64.

8. On presidential popularity over time, see John E. Mueller, *War, Presidents and Public Opinion* (New York: John Wiley & Sons, 1973); James A. Stimson, "Public Support for American Presidents: A Cyclical Model," *Public Opinion Quarterly* 40 (Spring 1972): 1–21; and Friedrich Schneider, "Presidential Popularity Functions of Different Classes," unpublished manuscript, University of Zurich, no date.

9. In a survey of references to *The Civic Culture* in scholarly journals and books between 1964 and 1974, Eric Davis found 112 references to macrolevel aspects of the study and 259 references to microlevel aspects. (Eric Davis, "The Impact of *The Civic Culture,*" unpublished paper, Stanford University, February 1976.)

10. Erwin K. Scheuch, "The Cross-Cultural Use of Sample Surveys: Problems of Comparability," in Stein Rokkan, ed., *Comparative Research Across Nations and Cultures* (The Hague: Mouton, 1968), pp. 176–209.

11. Samuel Stouffer, *Communism, Conformity and Civil Liberties* (New York: John Wiley & Sons, 1955).

12. See James A. Davis, "Communism, Conformity, Cohorts and Categories," *American Journal of Sociology* 81 (November 1975): 491–513.

13. Nie, Verba, and Petrocik, *Changing American Voter,* pp. 307–44.

14. Verba, Nie, and Kim, *Participation and Political Equality.*

15. See Richard Rose, "Governing and Ungovernability: A Skeptical Inquiry," Center for the Study of Public Policy, University of Strathclyde, 1977.

16. See Verba, Nie, and Kim, *Participation and Political Equality,* chap. 14, for a discussion.

INDEX

competence and membership in, 74
in Germany, 218–219, 255
in Mexico, 368, 369
Voter turnout
in Mexico, 365–366
in the United States, 197
Voting, 13. *See also* Electoral participation
in Germany, 215
in Mexico, 359–360, 365–367

Wallas, Graham, 8, 13
Watergate scandal, 194–196
Weber, Max, 11–12, 24
West Germany. *See* Germany
Wildenmann, Rudolf, 215, 216
Wilson, Harold, 144, 157
Wilson, Woodrow, 7–10
Wolin, S., 93
Women, 77–79
in Germany, 237, 260–261
in Great Britain, 78
in the United States, 78

Workers' self-management in Yugoslavia, 89–94
Working class. *See also* Class; Labor unions; Socioeconomic status
in Great Britain, 128, 129, 167
Workplace participation, 77, 96
competence and, 72–74
democratization of the civic culture and, 88–94
in Yugoslavia, 89–94

Young people. *See also* Generational differences
in Germany, support for the system and, 234
in the United States, 200
Young, R., 142
Yugoslavia, 104, 106
workplace participation (workers' self-management) in, 89–94

Zukin, S., 92